Promoting Sustainable Consumption in Fashion With AI

Luzia Arantes
https://orcid.org/0000-0003-1179-9113

Águeda School of Technology and Management, University of Aveiro, Portugal & Polytechnic University of Cávado and Ave, Portugal

IGI Global
Scientific Publishing
Publishing Tomorrow's Research Today

Vice President of Editorial	Melissa Wagner
Director of Acquisitions	Mikaela Felty
Director of Book Development	Jocelynn Hessler
Production Manager	Mike Brehm
Cover Design	Jose Rosado

Published in the United States of America by
IGI Global Scientific Publishing
701 East Chocolate Avenue
Hershey, PA, 17033, USA
Tel: 717-533-8845 | Fax: 717-533-7115
Website: https://www.igi-global.com E-mail: cust@igi-global.com

Library of Congress Cataloging-in-Publication Data

LCCN: 2025034556 (CIP Data Pending)
ISBN13: 9798337355252
Isbn13Softcover: 9798337355269
EISBN13: 9798337355276

British Cataloguing in Publication Data
A Cataloguing in Publication record for this book is available from the British Library.

Table of Contents

Detailed Table of Contents

options, fairness screens, and human oversight. A measurement and experimentation program specifies primary, perceptual, and composite KPIs, including Carbon per Conversion, Impact@K, FairExposure, and the Autonomy Cost Index, along with A/B tests, uplift targeting, contextual bandits, and off-policy evaluation. Practical thresholds and reporting cadences support safe operation. The chapter closes with sectoral guidance, limitations, and implications for policymakers and practitioners.

This chapter explores the ethical implications of AI-driven personalization in fashion e-commerce and proposes an "Ethical Personalization Framework" that balances commercial success with societal and environmental responsibility. It critiques conventional personalization systems for promoting impulsive buying and unsustainable consumption. Drawing from ethical theories—Virtue Ethics, Utilitarianism, and Deontology—and case studies like Patagonia and Zalando, the chapter outlines principles of fairness, transparency, user autonomy, privacy, and sustainability. It recommends operational strategies and policy interventions for retailers, developers, and regulators to embed ethical design in AI systems, thereby supporting responsible consumption and aligning fashion retail with the UN Sustainable Development Goals.

In this chapter, the author discusses how to mediate sustainable consumption, referring to ethical personalization and e-commerce in the realm of fashion. Incorporating 390 study participants, we resorted to qualitative methods of quantitative investigation in showing interaction between these variables. The paper will commence with justifying the significance of sustainable consumption as a growing dimension of the modern fashion industry, in which the ethical individualization of style is in demand among consumers. We found that ethical personalization has a noteworthy impact on the behavior of sustainable consumption in fashion e-commerce environments. Moreover, the approach reveals that the relationship is mediated by consumer trust and perceived value, and this aspect emphasizes the importance of a differentiated approach to

Artificial intelligence-powered virtual digital wardrobes encourage sustainability by enabling customers to make better decisions about their wardrobe management and fashion consumption. These platforms encourage less waste, longer product usage, and responsible purchasing by combining AI with personalized suggestions, lifecycle evaluation, gamification, and integration with circular models like resale and leasing. The chapter describes system architectures that facilitate industry-wide data sharing, platform-level analytics, and consumer-level nudges for supply chain efficiency and transparency. Scalability, data protection, and the requirement to democratize these technologies globally are major obstacles.

The integration of artificial intelligence into the fashion industry is reshaping the way consumers engage with sustainability. This chapter explores the role of smart labels and AI-enabled eco-tracking tools in promoting sustainable fashion consumption. By using smart labelling and eco-tracking technologies such as RFID, QR codes, NFC tags and provenance tracking into fashion products, brands can provide real-time access to product lifecycle data. Additionally, they can give information on ethical sourcing, and environmental impact metrics of their products. AI enhances these tools by providing personalized sustainability suggestions, usage analytics, and predictive maintenance or reuse suggestions. This approach helps in motivating consumers towards more conscious choices. Through a mix of theoretical exploration and real-world case studies, this chapter demonstrates how AI-powered intelligent systems not only increase transparency, but also drive behavior change. It helps bridge the gap between intention and action, and moves the fashion industry towards a more sustainable future.

Preface

INTRODUCTION

The global fashion industry stands at a defining moment. Long characterized by rapid production cycles, trend acceleration, and resource-intensive supply chains, the sector now faces mounting scrutiny over its environmental and social impact. Issues such as overconsumption, textile waste, carbon emissions, and labor inequities demand not incremental adjustments but systemic transformation. At the same time, artificial intelligence (AI) has emerged as a powerful force reshaping retail, logistics, consumer engagement, and product design. This volume brings these two trajectories together, asking a central question: *Can AI become a catalyst for genuinely sustainable fashion consumption?*

AI's influence in fashion is already visible — through personalized recommendations, demand forecasting, dynamic pricing, virtual try-ons, and predictive supply chains. Yet these capabilities are often deployed to maximize sales and engagement rather than to reduce waste or encourage mindful purchasing. The chapters in this book challenge that paradigm. They investigate how AI can be intentionally designed to promote environmental responsibility, foster transparency, and empower consumers to make conscious decisions. Rather than treating sustainability as an afterthought, this volume positions it as a foundational design principle in AI-enabled fashion systems.

Equally important is the ethical dimension. The application of AI in consumer contexts raises pressing concerns about algorithmic bias, greenwashing, privacy, manipulation, and autonomy. Sustainable consumption cannot be achieved by substituting one form of excess with another form of opaque digital influence. Therefore, this book adopts an interdisciplinary lens — integrating insights from marketing, behavioral economics, data ethics, psychology, information systems, and sustainability science — to explore how trust, transparency, fairness, and governance shape the effectiveness of AI-driven interventions. Across its chapters, the book argues that technological sophistication must be matched by ethical intentionality.

CHAPTER OVERVIEW

Chapter 1: Green by Design – AI in Fashion Retail and the Rise of the Conscious Consumer

This opening chapter establishes the conceptual foundation of the volume by examining how AI-driven personalization and recommendation systems influence sustainable decision-making. Emphasizing social trust as a mediating factor, the authors demonstrate that transparency and perceived ethical intent are critical in shaping consumer receptivity to AI-guided sustainability initiatives. The chapter situates AI not merely as a technical tool but as a relational system embedded within brand–consumer trust dynamics.

Chapter 2: AI, Fashion, and Climate Conscious Consumers – Promoting Sustainable Consumption Through Intelligent Systems

Chapter 2 expands the discussion to the broader environmental footprint of fast fashion, highlighting water consumption, carbon emissions, and microplastic pollution. It explores how AI, combined with blockchain, digital wardrobes, and smart labeling technologies, enhances traceability and empowers climate-conscious consumers. The chapter balances technological optimism with ethical caution, underscoring risks related to privacy, bias, and greenwashing.

Chapter 3: Algorithmic Nudging for Eco-Friendly Fashion – A Framework for Ethical AI Interventions

Drawing from behavioral economics and consumer psychology, this chapter proposes a structured framework for ethical algorithmic nudging. It examines mechanisms such as defaults, social proof, and visual cues while carefully considering autonomy and fairness. The authors argue that reflective and transparent nudging can influence sustainable fashion choices without compromising user liberty.

Chapter 4: From Click to Conscious Choice – Algorithmic Nudging Architectures for Eco-Friendly Fashion Consumption

Building on the prior chapter, Chapter 4 provides a socio-technical blueprint for implementing nudging architectures within digital fashion platforms. It introduces measurable KPIs such as Carbon per Conversion and FairExposure, along with governance mechanisms including explainability and opt-out options. This chapter is particularly valuable for practitioners seeking operational pathways toward responsible AI deployment.

Chapter 5: Ethical Personalisation in Fashion E-commerce – Leveraging AI for Sustainable Consumption

This chapter critiques conventional personalization systems that often incentivize impulse buying. Through an Ethical Personalization Framework grounded in virtue ethics, utilitarianism, and deontology, the authors propose actionable strategies for retailers and policymakers. Case illustrations from brands such as Patagonia and Zalando demonstrate how ethical principles can align commercial objectives with sustainability goals.

Chapter 6: Mediation of Sustainable Consumption Between Ethical Personalization and Fashion E-commerce

Offering empirical insight based on data from 390 participants, Chapter 6 analyzes how ethical personalization influences sustainable consumption behaviors. The findings reveal that consumer trust and perceived value mediate this relationship, reinforcing the volume's broader emphasis on trust as a cornerstone of effective AI-enabled sustainability.

Chapter 7: Digitally Mediated Wardrobes – Advancing Sustainable Consumption in the Fashion Ecosystem

This chapter explores AI-powered wardrobe management systems, virtual platforms, and AR/VR fitting technologies. By promoting rewearing, mindful purchasing, and circular practices, digitally mediated wardrobes redefine consumer engagement with apparel. Ethical issues of inclusivity, privacy, and digital access are examined alongside systemic implications for the fashion ecosystem.

Chapter 8: Behavioural AI for Sustainable Wardrobes – Insights and Innovations in Fashion Tech

Integrating behavioral science with AI applications, Chapter 8 analyzes interventions that reduce overconsumption and product returns. Drawing from industry cases and survey data, the authors provide strategic guidance for brands seeking to balance profitability with measurable sustainability outcomes.

Chapter 9: Empowering Sustainable Fashion Through Virtual Digital Wardrobe Technologies

Focusing on AI-powered virtual wardrobe systems, this chapter highlights lifecycle evaluation, gamification, and integration with resale and leasing models. It addresses scalability challenges and the democratization of sustainable technologies, emphasizing the need for global accessibility.

Chapter 10: Smart Labels and Eco-Tracking Tools for Sustainable Fashion Consumption

The concluding chapter explores RFID, QR codes, NFC tags, and AI-enhanced eco-tracking systems that provide real-time lifecycle transparency. By bridging the gap between consumer intention and action, smart labels and predictive analytics emerge as powerful instruments for behavior change and supply chain accountability.

CONCLUSION

Taken together, the chapters in this volume illustrate that AI is neither inherently sustainable nor inherently exploitative. Its impact depends on how it is designed, governed, and embedded within institutional and cultural frameworks. Sustainable fashion consumption requires more than technological innovation; it demands alignment between data systems, ethical principles, regulatory oversight, and consumer trust.

One of the most consistent insights across this collection is the centrality of trust — trust in algorithms, in brands, in data governance, and in the authenticity of sustainability claims. Without transparency, fairness, and accountability, AI-driven sustainability efforts risk being dismissed as greenwashing or manipulative influence. Conversely, when designed responsibly, AI can amplify positive behaviors, reduce waste, optimize supply chains, and empower consumers to act in accordance with their environmental values.

This volume aligns particularly with SDG 12 (Responsible Consumption and Production), SDG 9 (Industry, Innovation and Infrastructure), and SDG 13 (Climate Action), positioning AI-driven fashion innovation within a broader global agenda for sustainable and accountable development.

As editors, we hope this volume serves scholars, practitioners, policymakers, and technology developers alike. It offers conceptual frameworks, empirical findings, practical architectures, and ethical guidelines that collectively chart a pathway toward responsible innovation. The future of fashion will be shaped not only by aesthetics and algorithms but by our collective commitment to sustainability and integrity. By reimagining AI as a partner in conscious consumption, we move closer to a fashion ecosystem that is not only intelligent — but truly sustainable.

Chapter 1
Green by Design AI in Fashion Retail and the Rise of the Conscious Consumer

Ashok Malhi
http://orcid.org/0000-0001-9756-5865
Mittal School of Business, Lovely Professional University, India

Abhishek Sharma
http://orcid.org/0000-0001-9190-3341
Mittal School of Business, Lovely Professional University, India

Pinnika Syam Yadav
http://orcid.org/0000-0003-4954-1273
Christ University, India

Ankitha Sharma
http://orcid.org/0009-0007-9222-3736
Mittal School of Business, Lovely Professional University, India

Deepak Bisht
Mittal School of Business, Lovely Professional University, India

B. H. Rashmi
http://orcid.org/0000-0003-4793-4196
Christ University, India

ABSTRACT

The fashion industry stands at a transformative crossroads, where artificial intelligence (AI) and sustainable values reshape consumer behavior and retail strategies. Green by Design: AI in Fashion Retail and the Rise of the Conscious Consumer investigates how AI-driven personalization, product recommendations, and algorithmic nudging can foster environmentally responsible choices while navigating the ethical limits of automated influence. This volume presents theoretical and empirical contributions that examine social trust as a critical mediating factor in the relationship between AI technologies and sustainable consumer decisions. Trust—both in technology and in the ethical intent of fashion brands emerges as a determinant of consumer

DOI: 10.4018/979-8-3373-5525-2.ch001

receptivity to AI-guided sustainable behavior. Through interdisciplinary analysis that spans marketing, data ethics, psychology, and digital retail, the book explores how perceived transparency, fairness, and inclusivity in AI systems influence the formation of social trust and, in turn, amplify or constrain sustainable consumption.

1. INTRODUCTION

The advent of Large Language Models (LLMs) has heralded a profound transformation within Artificial Intelligence, particularly since the public release of models such as ChatGPT in November 2022 (Petro anu et al., 2023). These sophisticated systems have rapidly captured considerable attention due to their exceptional performance across various natural language tasks. Their remarkable ability to comprehend and generate human-like text at an unprecedented scale has positioned them as pivotal components in the ongoing development of general-purpose AI systems(Triguero et al., 2023). The field itself is characterized by an extraordinary pace of evolution, with novel models, groundbreaking findings, and innovative techniques emerging within mere months or weeks (Sridhar et al., 2025; Corea, 2017). This rapid velocity underscores the critical need for timely and comprehensive surveys, which serve as invaluable resources for researchers and practitioners navigating this dynamic landscape. The sheer volume of new information makes it challenging for AI researchers and practitioners to discern the most effective approaches for building LLM-powered AI systems for their specific tasks (Yang et al., 2024; D'Souza et al., 2025). This review aims to consolidate the current body of knowledge, offering a structured and accessible overview to mitigate this confusion and accelerate practical application in a highly dynamic environment.

1.1 Defining LLMs and FMs, Distinguishing Them From Earlier Language Models

To fully appreciate the current state of AI, it is essential to delineate the concepts of Large Language Models and Foundation Models, distinguishing them from their predecessors (Gallotta et al., 2024).

Large Language Models (LLMs): Primarily, LLMs are characterized as transformer-based neural language models with many parameters, typically ranging from tens to hundreds of billions. These models are pre-trained on immense quantities of text data. Prominent examples that have defined this category include the GPT, LLaMA, and PaLM families (Raiaan et al., 2024). The distinction between LLMs and earlier pre-trained language models (PLMs) is not merely quantitative regarding model size. Crucially, LLMs exhibit superior language understanding and generation abilities, and, more significantly, demonstrate "emergent abilities" that are not observed in their smaller-scale counterparts(Min et al., 2023; Hu et al., 2023). These emergent abilities represent a qualitative leap, allowing LLMs to perform tasks they were not explicitly trained for, such as complex reasoning or advanced problem-solving.

Foundation Models (FMs): Foundation Models represent a broader and more encompassing paradigm. An FM is formally defined as "any model trained on broad data that can be adapted to a wide range of downstream tasks" (Mai et al., 2023). While technically rooted in long-established deep neural networks and standard transfer learning techniques, the unprecedented scale of their size and training data leads to newly emergent capabilities (Huang et al., 2025). These capabilities can be transferred across diverse applications without requiring extensive training or fine-tuning for each new task (Jung, 2023; Guo et al., 2019). Thus, LLMs can be considered a prominent class of Foundation Models, specifically those focused on language. Beyond text, FMs can model not only natural language tokens but also elements from arbitrary sequences, encompassing modalities such as images, video, and even biological sequences like DNA. This multimodal capability allows FMs to combine sensory input (sound, images, video) with symbolic interpretation of text, moving towards a more holistic understanding of the environment (Vrbančič & Podgorelec, 2020).

The perceived "new paradigm" in AI, often attributed to LLMs and FMs, is not primarily driven by the invention of entirely novel algorithms from first principles (Mao et al., 2024). Instead, it stems from a qualitative leap in capability that arises from applying existing architectural principles, such as the Transformer architecture, at unprecedented scales of parameters and data. This suggests that future advancements may continue to be propelled by scaling efforts (Lianos, 2024). Consequently, understanding and effectively controlling these emergent properties becomes a critical frontier for ongoing research. This shift also signals a broader evolution in AI development, moving from creating highly specialized, task-specific models towards developing highly adaptable, general-purpose models (Kumar et al., 2024). This convergence within the AI industry means a growing number of AI applications are adjustments of only a few foundational models, often owned by a limited number of well-resourced organizations.

1.2 Motivation for a Comprehensive Review

The rapid advancements and increasing complexity inherent in LLMs and FMs necessitate a comprehensive review to consolidate the current body of knowledge. Such a review is vital for highlighting key architectural innovations, surveying the diverse applications, and critically examining the inherent challenges and ethical considerations associated with these technologies. The extraordinary pace at which the field of LLMs is progressing, with new findings and techniques emerging in weeks or months, creates a significant challenge for AI researchers and practitioners(Petro anu et al., 2023). They often find it difficult to discern the most effective approaches for building LLM-powered AI systems for their specific tasks (Shethiya, 2024). This comprehensive review aims to serve as a structured resource, offering a timely and accessible overview that helps to mitigate this confusion and accelerate practical application in a highly dynamic environment(Allioui & Mourdi, 2023). The inherent velocity of the field, while driving innovation, simultaneously limits the long-term currency of any single survey (Kant, et al., 2025; Kant, Adula, & Badi, 2025; Pandey & Yadav, 2023), implying a continuous need for updated academic contributions to keep pace with the ongoing evolution(National Academies of Sciences, Engineering, and Medicine, 2019).

2. HISTORICAL CONTEXT AND ARCHITECTURAL EVOLUTION

The journey to contemporary Large Language Models represents the culmination of decades of dedicated research and development in language modeling. This progression can be broadly categorized into distinct "waves," each building upon the limitations and innovations of its predecessors (Musiol, 2024).

2.1 Tracing the Lineage From Statistical to Neural to Pre-Trained Language Models

The earliest wave of language models involved Statistical Language Models, exemplified by N-gram models. These were widely adopted in many early Natural Language Processing (NLP) systems. Originating in the 1950s with rule-based systems, the 1990s saw a pivotal shift towards statistical approaches, leveraging vast text datasets to uncover intricate patterns (Kulkarni, 2023). In the 1990s and early 2000s, N-gram models gauged the probability of a word's appearance by considering preceding words, introducing a mechanism for understanding context (Fink, 2014). However, their utility was inherently constrained by their inability to fully capture the diversity and variability of natural language due to data sparsity issues. They were incomplete in their representation of linguistic patterns. The subsequent emergence of Neural Language Models marked a significant improvement. The late 2000s witnessed a resurgence of interest in neural networks, intense learning techniques (Sejnowski, 2018). Recurrent Neural Networks (RNNs) and Long Short-Term Memory (LSTM) networks were employed to process sequential data, leading to improved language understanding and generation (Sundermeyer et al., 2015). These models moved beyond simple statistical counts, leveraging neural networks to learn distributed representations of words and their contexts, offering a more nuanced understanding of language (Bengio et al., 2003). A breakthrough application was machine translation. Google transitioned its translation service to neural machine translation (NMT) in 2016, replacing statistical phrase-based models with deep recurrent neural networks (Mohamed et al., 2024). The third primary wave introduced Pre-trained Language Models (PLMs), characterized by the "pre-training and fine-tuning paradigm". In this approach, language models, frequently based on recurrent neural networks but more significantly on the nascent Transformer architecture, were pre-trained on vast, unlabeled web-scale text corpora (Matarazzo & Torlone, 2025). This pre-training phase focused on general tasks such as word prediction. Following this, the models could be fine-tuned on smaller, labeled datasets to adapt their learned general knowledge to specific downstream tasks. A pivotal advancement in this era was the introduction of Bidirectional Encoder Representations from Transformers (BERT) by Google in 2018, which showcased this transformative approach. This paradigm shifts significantly advanced the application of transfer learning in NLP (Yang et al., 2025).

2.2 Deep Dive Into Transformer Architecture as the Backbone of Modern LLMs

The Transformer architecture, introduced in 2017, is the foundational deep learning architecture underpinning the most potent modern AI language models, including contemporary LLMs. Its core innovation lies in its sophisticated "attention mechanisms" (Chen et al., 2024). These mechanisms enable the model to dynamically weigh the importance of different words within a sentence, thereby allowing for a comprehensive understanding of context previously (Kant, et al., 2025; Kant, Adula, & Badi, 2025; Pandey & Yadav, 2023) challenging for sequential models like RNNs. Unlike RNNs, Transformers can simultaneously process all words in a sequence, significantly reducing training time and effectively capturing long-range dependencies (Bhattacharya et al., 2024; Sun et al., 2023).

The response generation process within Transformer-based LLMs typically unfolds through a series of interconnected steps:

- Tokenization: Initially, the input text is segmented into discrete units called tokens. These tokens can vary in length, ranging from single characters to complete words (e.g., "a" or "apple"). These tokens are then converted into numerical representations via lookup from a word embedding table (Spathis & Kawsar, 2024; Raschka, 2024).

- Context Understanding: The LLM then analyzes these tokens and their sequential order to grasp the context. It employs its attention mechanisms to assign varying levels of importance to each token compared to others within the input. This allows the model to focus on specific parts of the input sequence when producing each element of the output sequence (Guan et al., 2025; Tang & Yang, 2024).
- Prediction: Drawing upon the established context and the intricate patterns learned during its extensive training (Singh et al., 2025), the LLM statistically predicts the most probable next token in the sequence. This prediction is based on the probabilities assigned during training (Mirchandani et al., 2023; Ji et al., 2025).
- Generation: The newly predicted token is appended to the existing input string. This augmented string (original input plus the new token) is then fed back into the model, and the prediction process iteratively repeats. This cycle continues until a predefined stop signal, such as a period at the end of a sentence, is generated, or a specified maximum length is reached (Wang et al., 2024; Chen et al., 2024).
- Decoding: Finally, the stream of generated output tokens is converted back into human-readable text (Liao et al., 2021).

The Transformer architecture utilizes several types of attention mechanisms to achieve its robust contextual understanding:

- Scaled Dot-Product Attention: This is the fundamental building block. It computes attention scores based on the dot product of query (Q) and key (K) vectors, scales it by the square root of the dimension of the key vectors, and applies a softmax function to calculate attention weights. These weights are then used to compute a weighted sum of value (V) vectors (Qin & Rusu, 2017; Ramasubramanian & Paliwal, 1992).
- Multi-Head Attention: This mechanism enhances the model's ability to simultaneously focus on different parts of the input sequence. It involves multiple attention heads, each with its own set of query, key, and value matrices. The outputs of these heads are concatenated and linearly transformed to produce the final output, allowing the model to capture diverse relationships (Jin et al., 2024; Pecoraro et al., 2022; Lu et al., 2020).
- Self-Attention (Intra-Attention): Applied in both the encoder and decoder layers, self-attention allows the model to consider different positions of the same sequence when computing the representation of a word (Singh et al., 2025; Dahiya et al., 2024). This is crucial for capturing long-range dependen-

cies and relationships within the input sequence (Wang & Li, 2018; Shao et al., 2019).

- Encoder-Decoder Attention (Cross-Attention): Used in the decoder layers, the decoder can focus on relevant parts of the input sequence (encoded by the encoder) when generating each word of the output sequence (Singh et al., 2025; Dahiya et al., 2024). This ensures the decoder accesses the entire input context, leading to more accurate and contextually appropriate outputs (Luo et al., 2022; Ates et al., 2023).

Other key components of the Transformer architecture include positional encoding, which adds information about the position of tokens in the sequence, and feedforward networks (FFNs), which are 2-layered multilayer perceptrons applied to each position independently (Bebis & Georgiopoulos, 1994; Mangan & Alon, 2003). When scaled with billions of parameters, the sophisticated contextual understanding facilitated by the Transformer's attention mechanisms is the fundamental mechanism that gives rise to the complex, non-linear "emergent abilities" observed in LLMs (Mangan & Alon, 2003). These capabilities, such as intricate reasoning, accurate code generation, or nuanced dialogue, are not explicitly programmed but manifest from the vast training data (Han et al., 2024). This suggests that further advancements in LLM capabilities may depend less on the invention of entirely new architectures and more on refining attention mechanisms, expanding context windows, or developing more efficient methods for scaling these attention-based models, thereby pushing the boundaries of what "context understanding" signifies for an artificial intelligence (Kant, et al., 2025; Kant, Adula, & Badi, 2025; Pandey & Yadav, 2023).

2.4 Discussion of Key LLM Families (e.g., GPT, LLaMA, PaLM) and Their Distinguishing Characteristics

Several prominent LLM families have significantly shaped the current landscape of the field. These include the GPT series (e.g., GPT-3, GPT-4), LLaMA, and PaLM (Raiaan et al., 2024). These models, distinguished by their immense parameter counts—ranging from tens to hundreds of billions—represent the pinnacle of current language model development. While all leverage the underlying Transformer architecture, their specific training datasets, architectural nuances, and fine-tuning strategies contribute to their unique performance profiles and their particular emergent capabilities (Minaee et al., 2024).

- GPT (Generative Pre-trained Transformer) Series: Developed by OpenAI, the GPT series, starting with GPT-1 in 2018 and notably GPT-3 (175 billion parameters) in 2020, has focused on creating models that learn from vast amounts of text data to excel in general language understanding and generation (Kublik & Saboo, 2022). GPT models are known for their high accuracy and fluency in generating text, making them excellent for tasks requiring deep context understanding and coherent responses. They are proprietary, owned, and controlled by OpenAI and are typically accessed via subscription or special permission, which ensures responsible use but can limit customization. Typical applications include customer service chatbots for complex interactions, content creation (drafting emails, articles, poetry), and creative industries (brainstorming, scriptwriting, music lyrics) (Zong & Krishnamachari, 2022).

- LLaMA (Large Language Model Meta AI) Series: Developed by Meta AI, LLaMA models are designed to be flexible and adaptable, with a focus on being lightweight enough for broader access. LLaMA 2, for instance, incorporates technologies similar to GPT-4 (Zong & Krishnamachari, 2022). Its open-source nature allows users to adjust and scale the model to fit their needs, making it ideal for smaller organizations, individual developers, and academic research (Roumeliotis et al., 2023). While it may not always match the sheer scale of GPT models, LLaMA aims to offer competitive performance by leveraging community input and diverse applications, excelling in scenarios where customization to a particular tone or style is necessary. LLaMA 2 also offers API support for Google GPT-4, facilitating integration into existing business applications (Raiaan et al., 2024).
- PaLM (Pathways Language Model) Series: Developed by Google, PaLM models, such as PaLM 2, are cutting-edge language models with notably improved capabilities in multilingualism, logical reasoning, and programming. PaLM 2 focuses on API technology to process text more effectively and can process and analyze business code, providing deeper insights into underlying business logic (Veeramachaneni, 2025). It demonstrates high accuracy and speed in analyzing large amounts of data, supporting efficient business decisions. Its multilingual capabilities make it suitable for diverse language environments, and it is used for data processing, text comparison, and plagiarism checks. While LLaMA 2 might offer faster processing times for large amounts of text, PaLM 2 has shown an advantage in precision, responding more accurately to what has been written (Hadi et al., 2023).

The architectural evolution of language models, from statistical to neural to pretrained and finally to large language models, reflects a continuous drive towards greater generalization and efficiency. Each successive wave has addressed fundamental limitations of its predecessors. N-gram models were constrained by data sparsity and their inability to capture the full diversity of language (Minaee et al., 2024). Neural models offered improvements, and PLMs introduced the concept of transfer learning, enabling adaptation to specific tasks. LLMs, with their unprecedented scale and emergent abilities, further propel the field towards developing general-purpose AI agents, capable of "performing tasks they were not explicitly trained for". This clear, continuous trend points towards models that are increasingly versatile, adaptable, and proficient at generalizing across diverse tasks and domains, thereby reducing the need to develop task-specific models (Matarazzo & Torlone, 2025). This progression suggests a future where a limited number of powerful foundation models could serve as the bedrock for many AI applications, potentially leading to a convergence within the AI industry. However, this also raises important considerations regarding the concentration of power in the hands of a few organizations (Yadav et al., 2025; Pandey, Yadav & Pothireddy, 2024).

Table 1.

Model Type	Key Characteristics/Innovations	Advantages	Limitations	Representative Models/Concepts
Statistical Language Models	N-grams, Markov assumption, rule-based systems	Simplicity, early NLP utility, pattern discovery from text datasets	Data sparsity, inability to capture long-range dependencies, or semantic diversity	N-gram models, ELIZA
Neural Language Models	Recurrent Neural Networks (RNNs), Long Short-Term Memory (LSTM), distributed representations	Improved contextual understanding, learned word embeddings, and a breakthrough in machine translation.	Vanishing/exploding gradients, difficulty with long sequences	Word2Vec, early RNNs, LSTM-based NMT
Pre-trained Language Models (PLMs)	Pre-training & fine-tuning paradigm, early Transformers	Transfer learning improves performance on specific tasks with less labeled data	Limited scalability, fewer emergent abilities compared to LLMs	BERT, ELMo
Large Language Models (LLMs)	Transformer architecture, billions of parameters, massive datasets, attention mechanisms, emergent abilities	General-purpose understanding/generation, few-shot/zero-shot learning, complex reasoning	High computational cost, bias, hallucinations, and ethical concerns	GPT, LLaMA, PaLM

3. TRAINING METHODOLOGIES AND SCALING LAWS

The development of Large Language Models and Foundation Models relies on sophisticated and resource-intensive training methodologies designed to imbue them with remarkable capabilities.

3.1 Pre-Training on Massive Datasets

The foundational step in LLM development is pre-training on "massive amounts of text data" or "Web-scale text corpora" (Minaee et al., 2024). This extensive collection of documents, often comprising billions of words from diverse sources, enables the model to learn the statistical distribution of words, the intricacies of syntactic structures, and the complex semantic relationships inherent in correct and fluent language (Liu & Croft, 2005). This data's sheer volume and diversity are critical for the models to acquire their general-purpose language understanding and generation capabilities. The models learn to predict the next word in a sequence, fill in missing words, or understand the relationships between words, forming a robust internal representation of language. Recent dataset projects like RefinedWeb, Dolma, and Yi provide insights into the essential steps in creating large-scale pretraining datasets, emphasizing the importance of dataset curation for LLM performance.

3.2 Fine-Tuning and Instruction-Tuning Paradigms

While pre-training establishes a broad and general understanding of language, LLMs frequently undergo further adaptation to enhance their performance on specific tasks or to align their behavior with human preferences.

Fine-tuning: This is a traditional paradigm where a pre-trained model is further trained on smaller, task-specific, labeled datasets. The objective is to adapt the model's general knowledge to a particular application, such as sentiment analysis, question answering, or machine translation (Too et al., 2019). This process allows the model to specialize while leveraging pre-training knowledge. Fine-tuning is crucial for customizing AI to meet specific business needs (Yadav et al., 2025).

Instruction-tuning: A more recent and increasingly powerful paradigm, instruction-tuning involves training LLMs to follow natural language instructions, often called prompts, without requiring extensive task-specific fine-tuning for every new task (Too et al., 2019). This approach significantly enhances the model's versatility and adaptability, allowing it to be "instructed by prompts" to solve a wide range of novel functions through zero-shot or few-shot learning. This represents a shift towards more intuitive and flexible interaction with the models, enhancing a model's ability to follow complex commands (Parthasarathy et al., 2024).

3.3 The Role of Scaling Laws in Performance Gains

A fundamental observation and guiding principle in LLM research is "scaling laws" (Ruan et al., 2024). These laws indicate that "by increasing the number of parameters, the size of the training data and the computing effort, the performance of the models can always be increased" (Xiong et al., 2024). This empirical relationship predicts how model performance improves with increased computational resources, model size, and dataset size. These scaling laws have directly informed and driven the development of increasingly larger and more capable models, leading to the pursuit of models with billions of parameters (Kaplan et al., 2020). The consistent performance gains observed through scaling have solidified its position as a primary pathway for advancing LLM capabilities.

A notable example of research into scaling laws is the Chinchilla language model, developed by Google DeepMind. Chinchilla was explicitly created to investigate these scaling laws (Lohn, 2023). DeepMind's research determined that the number of training tokens must also be doubled for every doubling of the model size (Kaplan et al., 2020). This finding suggests that larger, higher-quality training datasets can improve downstream task results (Yadav et al., 2025). With 70 billion parameters, Chinchilla notably outperformed GPT-3 and achieved an average accuracy of 67.5% on the Measuring Massive Multitask Language Understanding (MMLU) benchmark, a 7% increase over its predecessor, Gopher. A significant advantage of Chinchilla is that it requires considerably less computational power for inference and fine-tuning than larger models like Gopher 280B, simplifying its downstream utilization. This development contributes to an effective training paradigm for large autoregressive language models, especially when computational resources are limited (Hoffmann et al., 2022).

The necessity of immense computational resources and vast datasets, dictated by these scaling laws, directly contributes to a concentration of power and development within the AI industry (Hwang, 2018). This leads to a growing number of AI applications being adjusted from only a few foundational models, which are often owned by a limited number of well-resourced organizations and trained on a few massive datasets. This concentration can create a potential for "economic monopolies" and poses significant challenges to existing AI governance frameworks. This is not merely a business trend but a direct consequence of the technical requirements for achieving the current levels of AI capability, establishing a high barrier to entry for developing truly competitive foundational models (Safadi & Watson, 2023).

3.4 Augmentation Techniques (e.g., External Knowledge, Tools, RLHF)

Beyond core training, LLMs can be significantly enhanced through various augmentation techniques, expanding their utility and robustness.

External Knowledge and Tools: LLMs can be augmented by integrating external knowledge bases or granting access to specialized tools (Xi et al., 2024). This enables them to retrieve up-to-date information, perform specific calculations, or interact with external systems. Such augmentation allows LLMs to interact more effectively and dynamically with users and their environment, overcoming their static training data limitations. For instance, an LLM could be given access to a search engine to retrieve real-time information or a calculator to perform complex mathematical operations (Mansurova et al., 2024).

Reinforcement Learning with Human Feedback (RLHF): RLHF is a crucial technique for aligning LLM outputs with human preferences and safety guidelines. In this process, models continually improve by learning from feedback data collected through interactions, often provided by human evaluators (Bai et al., 2022). This iterative refinement helps to reduce undesirable behaviors, such as factual inaccuracies (hallucinations) or the perpetuation of biases, by rewarding preferred responses and penalizing undesirable ones. RLHF is a form of alignment tuning, ensuring outputs align with human values (Casper et al., 2023).

The evolution from traditional fine-tuning to instruction-tuning and the increasing emphasis on augmentation techniques signify a profound shift in the role of LLMs. The goal is no longer merely language generation or understanding in a static setting. Instead, these advancements aim to transform LLMs into dynamic, interactive "AI agents" that can "sense their environment, make decisions, and take actions" (Minaee et al., 2024). This progression moves LLMs from being sophisticated text processors to potentially becoming the cognitive core of advanced AI systems capable of complex reasoning and interaction in real-world environments, blurring the lines between language models and broader artificial intelligence.

Table 2.

Category	Specific Challenge/Risk	Description	Key Implications	Relevant Mitigation Strategies (if mentioned)
Technical Limitations	Hallucinations	Generation of factually incorrect or nonsensical information with high confidence	Erosion of trust, spread of misinformation	Hallucination correction
	Domain Mismatch	Performance degradation on out-of-distribution data	Limited generalizability in diverse real-world applications	Improved generalization techniques
	Real-time Efficiency	Computational demands are hindering real-time applications	Constraints on deployment in latency-sensitive systems	Optimization of model architecture and inference
Ethical Concerns	Bias	Perpetuation/amplification of societal biases from training data	Discriminatory outputs, unfair treatment	Bias detection, evaluation, and debiasing strategies
	Disinformation	Generation of convincing fake text, images, or videos	Spread of misinformation, erosion of public trust	Fake media detection
	Misuse & Deception	Intentional use for harmful purposes (e.g., propaganda, fraud)	Threat to social stability.	Countermeasures, ethical guidelines

4. CAPABILITIES AND DIVERSE APPLICATIONS

Large Language Models and Foundation Models have demonstrated remarkable capabilities, leading to widespread application across numerous domains.

4.1 General-Purpose Language Understanding and Generation

At their core, LLMs excel in their "ability of general-purpose language understanding and generation" (Yao et al., 2021). They can process and produce human-like text across various contexts, from engaging in fluid conversations and answering complex factual queries to generating creative content such as stories, poems, or code. This inherent versatility is a defining characteristic of their advanced capabilities, allowing them to adapt to varied linguistic tasks with minimal or no specific fine-tuning (Kosar et al., 2012). Their extensive training on diverse data sources enables them to predict and produce text based on input, allowing them to engage in conversations, answer queries, or write code.

4.2 Emergent Abilities Not Present in Smaller Models

A pivotal characteristic distinguishing LLMs from their smaller pre-trained counterparts is the manifestation of "emergent abilities". These capabilities are not explicitly programmed or evident in smaller models but spontaneously appear as models scale in size and are trained on increasingly vast datasets (Yuan et al., 2024). Examples include complex reasoning, advanced problem-solving, and the capacity to perform tasks for which they were not explicitly taught. The nature of these emergent abilities has sparked considerable debate, notably encapsulated by the "stochastic parrot" metaphor, coined by Emily M. Bender and colleagues in 2021. This metaphor frames LLMs as systems that statistically mimic text without genuine understanding.

However, leading AI researchers dispute this notion. Geoffrey Hinton, for instance, argues that "to predict the next word accurately, you have to understand the sentence". He also uses logical puzzles to demonstrate that LLMs understand language. A 2024 Scientific American investigation described a closed Berkeley workshop where state-of-the-art models solved novel tier-4 mathematics problems and produced coherent proofs, indicating reasoning abilities beyond mere memorization. These instances suggest that the models are not simply parroting their training data but are capable of understanding and reasoning. This ongoing discussion highlights the profound nature of these emergent capabilities and their implications for our understanding of artificial intelligence.

The "stochastic parrot" debate, which posits that LLMs merely mimic without proper comprehension, is not solely a philosophical discussion; it carries profound practical implications (Boussen et al., 2023). Suppose LLMs are indeed only mimicking their training data. In that case, inherent risks such as "hallucinations and bias", the generation of "disinformation", and the potential for "deception" become more challenging to mitigate, necessitating constant "human oversight and refinement"

(Schneider, 2025). The inscrutability of these models, as highlighted by Bender and colleagues, makes detecting and effectively mitigating deeply embedded biases particularly challenging given their black-box nature(Salzano et al., 2024). Conversely, suppose LLMs possess genuine reasoning abilities, as suggested by their capacity to solve novel logical puzzles or advanced mathematical problems. The path towards Artificial General Intelligence (AGI) becomes more plausible in that case (Hassija et al., 2024). However, this also significantly elevates the ethical stakes, raising critical questions about accountability, control, and the responsible deployment of increasingly autonomous systems. The resolution, or continued existence, of this debate will undoubtedly shape public perception, influence regulatory frameworks, and directly impact the trajectory of AI safety research, particularly concerning the level of trust that can be placed in LLM-generated content and decisions.

4.3 Applications Across Various Domains

The broad capabilities of LLMs have led to their integration and transformative impact across a multitude of domains:

Natural Language Processing (NLP):

- Text Summarization: LLMs can efficiently condense lengthy texts into concise, coherent summaries, extracting key information (El-Kassas et al., 2021).
- Code Generation and Debugging: They are adept at generating code snippets, functions, or even entire modules from natural language descriptions, significantly reducing development time (Sakib et al., 2024). For example, an LLM can generate a Python function to filter even numbers from a list based on a simple prompt. Furthermore, they can identify and suggest fixes for common programming errors, potentially integrating with Integrated Development Environments (IDEs) to provide real-time assistance.
- Language Translation: LLMs facilitate translation between different languages, often achieving high accuracy depending on the languages involved and the model's training data (Brown et al., 1988).
- Dialogue Systems: Powering sophisticated chatbots, LLMs enable adaptive and context-aware responses for applications ranging from customer service and interactive storytelling to educational platforms. They can provide insightful, helpful responses that adapt to user input (Chen et al., 2017).
- Paraphrasing and Rewriting: They can rephrase text while preserving its original meaning, which is proper for content creation and stylistic adjustments. This includes restoring or repairing incomplete or corrupted text (Fitria, 2021).

- Document Retrieval: LLMs can accept natural language queries and return ordered lists of relevant text documents from extensive collections, often by evaluating the similarity of embeddings to retrieve precise passages(Blair & Maron, 1985).

AI Agents and Interaction with Dynamic Environments: LLMs increasingly serve as the foundational building blocks for general-purpose AI agents. These agents are designed to sense their environment, make informed decisions, and execute actions, moving beyond static response generation to dynamic interaction within complex environments. This capability is further enhanced by their augmentation with external knowledge sources and tools. For example, conversational AI frameworks based on LLMs, like Talk2Drive, can interpret human voice commands to guide autonomous vehicles.

Scientific Research:

- Epidemiological Surveillance: LLMs have demonstrated the capacity to assess the likelihood of real-world disease outbreaks from social media content and to classify epidemiological features such as outbreak type, size, severity, etiology, and community setting from diverse data sources, including Twitter/X /X/X/X/X, forums, and YouTube posts (Moncayo & Silveira, 2017). They have shown reliable capacity for nuanced epidemiological analysis, even compared to human experts.
- Neuroscience and Psychology: LLMs are utilized to unravel complexities in these fields, evaluating LLM transformers using human cognition and psychology principles. For instance, they have shed light on the biological brain by using models like BERT to determine the timing of pediatric linguistic productivity milestones(Ke et al., 2024). They are also employed to identify patterns from vast amounts of complex biological data captured by technologies like fMRI, MEG, and EEG. Notably, LLMs have even outperformed human neuroscience experts in predicting specific neuroscience outcomes. The observed convergence between LLM processing and human brain activity recordings suggests that a deeper understanding of human language processing mechanisms can significantly accelerate advancements in AI (Hu et al., 2024).
- General Research Tool: Scientists increasingly use LLMs throughout the entire research study lifecycle. This includes information gathering, editing, formatting, grammar checks, synonym searches, background data collection, and even assisting with producing published research (Sontake, 2025; Khalifa & Albadawy, 2024).

Initially, LLMs were subjects of research or tools utilized *by* researchers for specific tasks, such as generating text for a paper. However, their emergent abilities, particularly in recognizing complex patterns from vast datasets and even surpassing human experts in specific predictive tasks, transform them into active partners or agents of the research process (Liang et al., 2024). They are becoming integral to the methodology of scientific inquiry, not merely contributing to the output. This progression is driven by their capacity to process and synthesize enormous amounts of information and to identify non-obvious correlations, thereby accelerating scientific discovery (Lukin & Gülseren, 2024). This shift necessitates the development of new ethical guidelines and calls for greater "transparency and disclosure when LLMs are used and how they are used to produce research studies", reflecting a broader demand for responsible AI development within academia.

Multimodal Applications: Foundation Models can model natural language and elements from other sensory modalities, leading to a new class of Multimodal Large Language Models (MLLMs) (Chen et al., 2024).

- Text-to-Image Generation: These models can generate images from textual descriptions, demonstrating a cross-modal understanding (Qiao et al., 2019).
- Video Analysis: Comprehensive evaluation benchmarks, such as Video-MME, have been developed specifically for MLLMs in video analysis (Fu et al., 2025). These benchmarks cover various video lengths (short, medium, and long-term) and feature newly collected and human-annotated data to ensure robust and unbiased evaluation.
- Speech and Control: FMs can integrate various sensory inputs, including sound and video, and potentially incorporate action and DNA sequences, moving towards a more holistic understanding and interaction with the environment (Akbar & Tohar, 2021). This ability to combine sensory input with symbolic text interpretation is a key property of Foundation Models.

Table 3.

Application Area	Specific Use Cases	Key Benefits/Impact
Natural Language Processing (NLP)	Text Summarization , Code Generation/Debugging , Language Translation , Dialogue Systems , Paraphrasing , Document Retrieval	Automates and enhances text-based tasks; improves efficiency and accuracy in content creation and information access.
AI Agents & Dynamic Environments	General-purpose AI agents, interactive systems, and autonomous vehicle guidance	Enables AI to sense, decide, and act in dynamic settings; moves beyond static responses to proactive interaction
Scientific Research	Epidemiological surveillance, Neuroscience/Psychology research (pattern identification, prediction), general research tool (information gathering, editing)	Accelerates scientific discovery; aids in data analysis, hypothesis generation, and research workflow automation
Multimodal Applications	Text-to-Image Generation, Video Analysis, Speech processing, integration of DNA sequences	Bridges understanding across different data modalities; enables more comprehensive perception and generation capabilities.

5. EVALUATION BENCHMARKS AND METRICS

Evaluating the performance and capabilities of Large Language Models is a complex and multifaceted endeavor. It requires a comprehensive suite of metrics and benchmarks to assess their proficiency across various dimensions, including linguistic understanding, generation quality, factual accuracy, and task-specific performance (Chang et al., 2024).

5.1 Review of Widely Used LLM Evaluation Metrics

While specific metrics are not exhaustively detailed in the provided information, the general necessity for "widely used LLM evaluation metrics" is explicitly highlighted. In practice, these metrics typically encompass quantitative measures such as:

- Accuracy: This is a fundamental metric for tasks involving classification or factual recall, measuring the proportion of correct predictions (Hu & Zhou, 2024).
- Fluency and Coherence: These aspects are often assessed through human evaluation, which provides subjective judgments on the naturalness, readability, and logical flow of generated text. Proxy metrics, such as perplexity, can also be used to estimate how well a language model predicts a text sample, with lower perplexity indicating better fluency (Barbosa, 2024).
- Task-specific Performance: Specific metrics are employed for specialized NLP tasks (Murugadoss et al., 2025). Examples include:
    - F1-score: Commonly used for information extraction, named entity recognition, or text classification, it is the harmonic mean of precision and recall (Banerjee et al., 2024).
    - BLEU (Bilingual Evaluation Understudy): A widely used metric for machine translation, it measures the similarity between a machine-generated translation and a set of high-quality human translations (Alkaoud, 2024).
    - ROUGE (Recall-Oriented Understudy for Gisting Evaluation): Primarily used for text summarization, it measures the overlap of n-grams, word sequences, and word pairs between the generated summary and reference summaries (Joshi, 2025).
- Robustness: This measures how well models perform under various perturbations or adversarial inputs, assessing their resilience to slight changes in input that should not alter the intended output (Banerjee et al., 2024).
- Bias and Fairness Metrics: Given the concerns about bias, specialized metrics are developed to detect and quantify various forms of bias (e.g., gender, racial, occupational) in model outputs (Li et al., 2024).
- Hallucination Rate: Quantifying the frequency and severity of factually incorrect or fabricated information generated by the model is crucial for trustworthiness (Joshi, 2025).

5.2 Discussion of Comprehensive Benchmarks (e.g., MME, Video-MME)

As LLMs continue to evolve, particularly with the emergence of multimodal capabilities, developing comprehensive and robust evaluation benchmarks has become paramount. These benchmarks provide standardized platforms for comparing different models and identifying areas for further improvement.

- General LLM Benchmarks: Before the rise of multimodal models, benchmarks like GLUE (General Language Understanding Evaluation), SuperGLUE, and MMLU (Measuring Massive Multitask Language Understanding) were crucial for assessing general language understanding and reasoning across diverse NLP tasks and factual recall. For instance, the Chinchilla model achieved 67.5% accuracy on MMLU, demonstrating its strong performance (Ivanov & Penchev, 2024; Hamernik & Qiu, 2001).
- MME (A Comprehensive Evaluation Benchmark for Multimodal Large Language Models): This benchmark is designed explicitly for Multimodal Large Language Models (MLLMs), offering a representative framework for their evaluation. It aims to assess how well these models integrate and process information from various modalities, moving beyond text-only understanding (Li et al., 2024).
- Video-MME: This benchmark is tailored explicitly for video analysis and is described as the "first-ever comprehensive evaluation benchmark of MLLMs in Video Analysis". It incorporates a diverse range of video lengths, including short (less than 2 minutes), medium (4-15 minutes), and long-term (30-60 minutes) videos, ranging from 11 seconds to 1 hour. Crucially, all data within Video-MME is newly collected and human-annotated, ensuring a robust and unbiased evaluation of MLLMs' capabilities in understanding and processing video content. This benchmark also includes efforts to correct hallucinations in multimodal LLMs (Qi et al., 2025).

The existence and continuous development of such benchmarks underscore the collective effort within the research community to standardize evaluation practices, facilitate fair comparisons between models, and pinpoint specific areas requiring further research and development. This is particularly vital as models are increasingly expected to handle complex, real-world, and multimodal data.

The development of specific multimodal benchmarks like MME and Video-MME, particularly those featuring human-annotated data, signifies a fundamental expansion in the scope of LLMs. This progression indicates a significant trend where "language" models are no longer confined to processing linguistic data alone. Instead, they actively integrate "sensory input (sound, images, video) with symbolic interpretation of text". The necessity for specialized benchmarks arises because traditional text-based metrics are insufficient to evaluate these new cross-modal understanding and generation abilities adequately (Li et al., 2024). This trend points towards a future where AI systems are truly "multimodal" and "general-purpose," capable of perceiving and interacting with the world through diverse sensory channels, moving closer to human-like cognition. This also implies an increasing complexity in the methodologies required for comprehensive evaluation, often necessitating interdisciplinary expertise.

Table 4.

Benchmark Name	Primary Focus	Key Features	Significance
General LLM Benchmarks (e.g., GLUE, SuperGLUE, MMLU)	General language understanding and reasoning	Diverse NLP tasks, multiple-choice questions, and factual recall	Standardized comparison of LLM performance across broad linguistic capabilities
MME (Multimodal Evaluation)	Multimodal Large Language Models (MLLMs)	Representative evaluation framework for MLLMs, which assesses cross-modal understanding.	Provides a holistic view of MLLM capabilities beyond text
Video-MME	MLLMs in Video Analysis	Includes short, medium, and long-term videos; newly collected and human-annotated data	First comprehensive benchmark for video analysis in MLLMs; ensures robust, unbiased evaluation; includes hallucination correction efforts

6. CHALLENGES, RISKS, AND ETHICAL CONSIDERATIONS

Despite their unprecedented capabilities and transformative potential, Large Language Models and Foundation Models present various technical limitations, inherent risks, and profound ethical considerations that demand rigorous attention.

6.1 Technical Limitations

LLMs, while powerful, are not without their technical shortcomings. These include:

- Domain Mismatch: Models may exhibit degraded performance when applied to data that significantly differs from their pre-training distribution, a phenomenon known as "domain mismatch". This limits their generalizability in diverse real-world applications where data characteristics vary widely (Wang et al., 2024).

- Word Prediction Challenges: While generally proficient, LLMs can still face challenges with precise "word prediction" in highly nuanced or ambiguous contexts, leading to less accurate or contextually inappropriate outputs. This can manifest as subtle errors that are difficult to detect without careful human review (Kumar, 2024).
- Real-time Translation Efficiency: For specific applications, particularly real-time translation, LLMs may struggle with "real-time translation efficiency," impacting their practical deployment in time-sensitive scenarios. The computational demands for generating responses quickly can be a bottleneck (Wang et al., 2024).
- Hallucinations: A significant and widely recognized concern is "hallucinations," where LLMs generate factually incorrect, nonsensical, or fabricated information with high confidence. This is a critical area of ongoing research, with dedicated efforts focused on "hallucination correction". Hallucinations erode trust in LLM outputs and can contribute to the spread of misinformation (Huang et al., 2025).

6.2 Bias Detection, Evaluation, and Debiasing Strategies

LLMs learn from vast datasets that inevitably reflect societal biases present in the real world. This can perpetuate and amplify "unknown dangerous biases" in model outputs, leading to unfair or discriminatory outcomes. Addressing this pervasive issue requires systematic approaches, including "bias detection and evaluation" methods to identify prejudiced outputs and "debiasing" strategies to mitigate their impact (Lin et al., 2024). The "stochastic parrot" argument, which questions the proper understanding of LLMs, also highlights the inherent inscrutability of these models, making detecting and effectively mitigating deeply embedded biases particularly challenging given their black-box nature (Lin et al., 2024). These biases can manifest in various forms, such as gender stereotypes, racial discrimination, or unfair treatment in critical applications like hiring or loan approvals.

6.3 Disinformation (Fake Media Generation and Detection)

The advanced generative capabilities of LLMs pose a substantial risk of facilitating "disinformation" by creating "fake media generation". This includes producing highly realistic yet fabricated text, images, or videos (Sun et al., 2024). The ease with which LLMs can generate convincing fake content makes it difficult for the public to discern truth from falsehood, threatening public trust and potentially influencing public opinion or political processes (Coeckelbergh, 2025). In response to this threat, a parallel area of research is dedicated to "fake media detection" to develop countermeasures against the malicious use of these generative technologies.

6.4 Ethical Concerns and Misuse

Beyond technical biases, LLMs raise broader ethical concerns. The potential for "deception" is considerable, given their ability to generate human-like text indistinguishable from human-written content, making it difficult for users to discern authenticity. This can be exploited for malicious purposes such as phishing, fraud, or propaganda (Tomalin et al., 2021). The very "stochastic parrot" debate embodies an ethical concern, questioning the fundamental nature of LLM intelligence and the societal implications of deploying systems that may not genuinely "understand" but can cause significant harm (Roberts et al., 2024). As highlighted in security surveys, the potential for the deliberate "misuse" of LLMs is a substantial concern. This includes using LLMs for cyberattacks, generating harmful content, or automating social engineering tactics.

The technical limitations of LLMs, such as hallucinations and inherent biases, are not isolated engineering problems; they are deeply intertwined with profound ethical and societal risks. Hallucinations, a technical flaw, directly contribute to the generation of disinformation and deception, which are significant ethical and societal harms (Shi et al., 2024). Similarly, biases learned from imperfect training data, a technical consequence, directly lead to unfair or discriminatory outputs, posing severe ethical risks. The inherent "inscrutability" of LLMs, a technical characteristic, exacerbates the difficulty in detecting and mitigating these biases and hallucinations, making the associated ethical risks harder to control (Sewell & Hiller, 2025). This means that addressing these technical challenges, for instance, by improving factual accuracy or developing more effective debiasing algorithms, is not merely an engineering pursuit but a fundamental prerequisite for responsibly addressing the widespread societal and ethical implications of LLM deployment (Ferdaus et al., 2024). This interconnectedness necessitates integrating ethical considerations into every stage of the AI lifecycle, from data curation and model architecture design to deployment and ongoing monitoring, compelling interdisciplinary collaboration among AI researchers, ethicists, policymakers, and social scientists (De Silva & Alahakoon, 2022).

6.5 Attacks and Privacy Violations

LLMs are susceptible to various "attacks," including adversarial attacks designed to manipulate their outputs or extract sensitive information from their training data.

These attacks can compromise the reliability and security of LLM-powered systems (Thuraisingham, 2020). "Privacy violation" is another critical issue, as models trained on vast and diverse datasets might inadvertently memorize and subsequently reproduce private or sensitive information, posing significant risks to individual privacy (Khosravy et al., 2022). This could include personal identifiable information (PII), confidential business data, or copyrighted material. Data privacy during training and deployment is paramount (Albustanji et al., 2025).

6.6 Computational Demands and Resource Intensiveness

The training of state-of-the-art LLMs is an immensely resource-intensive and computationally demanding undertaking, requiring substantial energy consumption and specialized hardware infrastructure (Vankayalapati, 2022). This contributes to significant "environmental and financial costs", raising concerns about sustainability and accessibility. The high computational barrier also directly contributes to the concentration of LLM development and ownership among a limited number of large organizations (Chkirbene et al., 2024). This creates a high barrier to entry for smaller entities and can limit diversity in AI development.

6.7 Socio-Economic Implications

The rapid rise of Foundation Models, particularly their concentration among a few dominant developers, creates a tangible risk of "economic monopolies" within the AI industry. This could lead to a few powerful entities controlling critical AI infrastructure and capabilities (De Manuel et al., 2023). Furthermore, the increasing automation capabilities of LLMs across various language-based tasks raise legitimate concerns about potential "unemployment" and shifts in labor markets in sectors where such tasks are prevalent (Fazil et al., 2023). This necessitates proactive policy adjustments and workforce retraining initiatives to mitigate negative societal impacts.

6.8 The Urgent Need for Legal and Ethical Regulation

Given LLMs' profound and widespread implications, there is an "urgent need for a legal regulation of the construction and deployment of these models". Future efforts must focus on developing comprehensive frameworks for AI governance that effectively address critical issues such as accountability, safety, fairness, transparency, and the broader societal implications of AI (Agrawal, 2024). There is also a growing call for "transparency and disclosure when LLMs are used and how they are used to produce research studies", reflecting a broader societal demand for responsible AI development (Liao & Vaughan, 2023). The shift to a foundational approach to

AI development inherently “challenges existing approaches of AI governance”, necessitating a proactive and adaptive regulatory response that can keep pace with technological advancements.

The concentration of power in LLM development, where a few organizations own and control the most advanced foundational models, creates a significant governance challenge. The immense resources required to train competitive Foundation Models, as dictated by scaling laws, inherently lead to their ownership by a limited number of powerful entities. This concentration then creates a disproportionate influence over the capabilities and deployment of foundational AI, potentially leading to “economic monopolies” and shaping societal norms (Subramanian et al., 2023). The “urgent need for legal regulation” and the fact that this shift “challenges existing approaches of AI governance” are direct consequences of this power dynamic. These challenges aim to ensure equitable access, prevent misuse, and mitigate systemic risks that could arise from such centralized control (Taeihagh, 2021). This implies that LLMs' future success and societal acceptance will depend as much on robust governance and ethical considerations as on continued technological breakthroughs (Nithish et al., 2023). Effective governance mechanisms are crucial to harness the benefits of LLMs while mitigating the risks associated with concentrated power and potential misuse, necessitating interdisciplinary collaboration between technologists, legal experts, ethicists, and policymakers (Ferdaus et al., 2024).

Table 5.

Methodology	Purpose	Key Characteristics	Examples/Benefits
Pre-training	Acquire general language understanding.	Training on massive, diverse, unlabeled text data; learns syntax, semantics, and world knowledge	Foundation for general-purpose language abilities; enables transfer learning.
Fine-tuning	Adapt to specific downstream tasks.	Further training on smaller, labeled task-specific datasets; adjusts model weights	Improves performance on narrow tasks; traditional adaptation paradigm; customizes AI for business needs.
Instruction-tuning	Enable zero-shot/few-shot task performance.	Training on diverse tasks described via natural language instructions (prompts)	Enhanced versatility; allows models to follow instructions for unseen tasks without specific training; improves the ability to follow complex commands
Augmentation (External Knowledge/Tools)	Expand capabilities beyond training data	Integrating external databases, APIs, or computational tools	Access to real-time information, complex calculations, and interaction with external systems
Reinforcement Learning with Human Feedback (RLHF)	Align model behavior with human preferences	Iterative learning from human feedback on model outputs; rewards desired behavior	Reduces undesirable outputs (e.g., hallucinations, bias); improves safety and helpfulness; alignment tuning

7. FUTURE RESEARCH DIRECTIONS AND OPEN CHALLENGES

Large Language Models and Foundation Models are characterized by their dynamic nature, continuous innovation, and evolving challenges. Future research will build upon current advancements while striving to address existing limitations and explore new frontiers.

7.1 Addressing Current Limitations and Improving Model Robustness

A primary focus for future research will be on mitigating identified technical limitations. This includes intensified efforts to reduce "hallucinations", enhance performance in "domain mismatch" scenarios, and improve "real-time translation efficiency" (Bai et al., 2022; Casper et al., 2023). Researchers will explore novel architectural designs, training objectives, and data curation techniques to improve factual consistency and reduce the generation of nonsensical outputs (Maity, 2019; Thirumuruganathan et al., 2020; Chang et al., 2021; Zhang et al., 2023). Furthermore, significant research will be directed towards making models more robust to various adversarial attacks and bolstering their privacy-preserving capabilities. This involves developing more secure training methods and inference procedures to prevent data leakage and malicious manipulation. These technical refinements are crucial for ensuring the reliability and trustworthiness of LLMs in real-world deployments, particularly in sensitive applications.

7.2 Further Exploration of Emergent Abilities and AGI Potential

The "emergent abilities" phenomenon remains a fertile ground for scientific inquiry. It is paramount to understand precisely how these capabilities arise from scale and how they can be reliably elicited, controlled, and steered towards beneficial outcomes. This involves delving into the internal mechanisms of LLMs to understand the representations they learn and how these representations give rise to complex behaviors like reasoning and problem-solving. The compelling potential for LLMs to serve as "the basic building block for the development of general-purpose AI agents or artificial general intelligence (AGI)" continues to drive ambitious research (Fahad et al., 2024). The goal is to bridge the existing "gap to a truly general AI" by progressively enhancing LLMs' reasoning, learning, and adaptive capacities, moving beyond mere statistical mimicry towards genuine understanding and cognitive flexibility (Clune, 2019). This includes exploring how LLMs can learn continuously and adapt to novel situations without catastrophic forgetting.

The pursuit of Artificial General Intelligence (AGI), particularly envisioned through developing LLMs and Foundation Models, is intrinsically linked to understanding and controlling these emergent properties (Mumuni & Mumuni, 2025). The path to a truly general AI is unlikely to be paved solely by incremental improvements on existing tasks. Instead, it will likely involve discovering and harnessing new, sometimes unpredictable, capabilities that arise from increased scale and complexity (Daugherty & Wilson, 2024). This implies that future research must shift from purely performance-driven metrics to more nuanced evaluations of reasoning, understanding, and adaptability, especially when models encounter novel or out-of-distribution situations. This also raises profound questions about the nature of intelligence itself and the critical safety implications of creating increasingly autonomous and capable AI systems. Developing robust alignment techniques, beyond current RLHF methods, will ensure that AGI systems are beneficial and safe for humanity (Hari & Abdulla, 2023).wit

7.3 Integration With Human Cognition and Neuroscience

A particularly promising interdisciplinary direction involves evaluating LLM transformers using human cognition and psychology principles (Xu et al., 2021). Research is actively exploring how LLMs can provide insights into the biological brain's functioning and how they can identify complex patterns within neural data obtained from techniques like fMRI, MEG, and EEG(Ke et al., 2024).The observed convergence between LLM processing and human brain activity recordings suggests that a deeper understanding of human language processing mechanisms can significantly accelerate advancements in AI (Abd Ali, 2024; Sharma et al., 2024). For example, studies have used LLMs like BERT to determine the timing of pediatric linguistic productivity milestones, offering potential benefits for child development and speech therapy. This bidirectional relationship provides exciting avenues for both neuroscience and artificial intelligence, potentially leading to bio-inspired AI architectures and more accurate models of human language (Wang et al., 2024; Dehghani & Levin, 2024).

7.4 The Growing Role of LLMs as Research Tools

As LLMs continue to mature in their capabilities, their role expands beyond mere research subjects to becoming integral research tools. This includes assisting scientists throughout the entire research study lifecycle, performing tasks such as information gathering, editing, formatting, grammar checks, synonym searches, and background data collection(Rane et al., 2023). They can even assist with the production of published research. This transformative shift necessitates the development of new methodologies for effectively integrating AI into scientific workflows, potentially accelerating the pace of discovery across various disciplines (Xu et al., 2021). This also raises questions about authorship and accountability in scientific publications, requiring clear guidelines for LLM usage.

7.5 The Urgent Need for Legal and Ethical Regulation

LLMs' rapid deployment and pervasive societal impact underscore the "urgent need for a legal regulation of the construction and deployment of these models"(Sinha & Lee, 2024; Akpobome, 2024). Future efforts will be critically focused on developing comprehensive and adaptive frameworks for AI governance. These frameworks must effectively address the multifaceted challenges of bias, disinformation, privacy, accountability, and the broader socio-economic implications of advanced AI(Agapiou, 2024). The growing call for "transparency and disclosure when LLMs are used" will become increasingly important, reflecting a broader societal demand for responsible and ethically sound AI development and deployment. This includes clearly labeling AI-generated content and auditing mechanisms for model behavior(Wittenberg et al., 2024). The fact that Foundation Models "challenge existing approaches of AI governance" further highlights the necessity for proactive and adaptive regulatory responses that can keep pace with the rapid evolution of the technology.

The future success and societal acceptance of LLMs will depend as much on robust governance and ethical considerations as on continued technological breakthroughs(Roco, 2008). The repeated emphasis on regulation and governance across multiple sources indicates that the challenges posed by LLMs—such as bias, disinformation, and the potential for economic monopolies—are not merely technical bugs that can be fixed with algorithmic patches(Course, 2021). Instead, they represent systemic issues that require a comprehensive societal response through policy, law, and ethical guidelines. The fact that Foundation Models "challenge existing approaches of AI governance" further highlights that current legal and ethical frameworks are insufficient, necessitating a proactive and adaptive approach to regulation rather than a reactive one that waits for harms to materialize(O'Sullivan et al., 2019). This implies that responsible AI development will require sustained, interdisciplinary collaboration among technologists, legal experts, ethicists, and policymakers to ensure that AI serves the broader public good(De Almeida et al., 2021).

8. CONCLUSION

Large Language Models and Foundation Models represent a pivotal paradigm shift in Artificial Intelligence, driven by unprecedented scale and the emergence of novel capabilities. Rooted in the Transformer architecture, these models have evolved from basic statistical models to sophisticated general-purpose AI systems capable of understanding and generating human-like language with remarkable fluency. Their development is guided by scaling laws, which predict performance gains with increased parameters, data, and computational effort. Advanced training techniques like instruction-tuning and augmentation techniques like Reinforcement Learning with Human Feedback enhance them.

The transformative potential of LLMs and FMs is evident in their diverse applications, spanning from core Natural Language Processing tasks like code generation and translation to their emerging roles as general-purpose AI agents interacting with dynamic environments. Furthermore, their utility extends into scientific research, becoming indispensable tools for epidemiological surveillance, neuroscience, and broader data analysis. The rise of multimodal LLMs signifies a further expansion of their scope, enabling them to process and integrate information across various sensory modalities, moving closer to human-like perception.

However, this rapid advancement is accompanied by significant challenges and risks. Technical limitations such as hallucinations, domain mismatch, and efficiency concerns persist. More profoundly, the models inherit and can amplify societal biases from their training data, posing ethical dilemmas related to fairness, disinformation, and potential misuse. The immense computational demands raise environmental and economic sustainability questions, contributing to a concentration of power within the AI industry that necessitates careful governance.

The path forward for LLMs and FMs involves a dual imperative: continued technological refinement and robust ethical and regulatory development. Future research will improve model robustness, mitigate biases, and enhance factual accuracy. A deeper understanding of emergent abilities is crucial for realizing Artificial General Intelligence's potential, while integrating human cognition and neuroscience insights to build more capable and aligned AI systems. Crucially, these powerful technologies' responsible development and deployment hinge upon establishing proactive legal and ethical frameworks. These frameworks must address accountability, transparency, and societal impact to ensure that LLMs and Foundation Models serve humanity beneficially and equitably. The continued success and societal acceptance of these transformative AI systems will ultimately depend on a concerted, interdisciplinary effort to navigate their complexities and harness their capabilities responsibly.

REFERENCES

Abd Ali, H. N. (2024). Advancements in Natural Language Processing: Towards Human-Like Understanding and Generation of Text by AI. *BIOS: Jurnal Informatika dan Sains, 2*(02), 129-139.

Agapiou, A. (2024). A systematic review of the socio-legal dimensions of responsible AI and its role in improving health and safety in construction. *Buildings (Basel, Switzerland), 14*(5), 1469. DOI: 10.3390/buildings14051469

Agrawal, G. (2024). Accountability, trust, and transparency in AI systems from the public policy perspective: Elevating ethical standards. In *AI healthcare applications and security, ethical, and legal considerations* (pp. 148–162). IGI Global. DOI: 10.4018/979-8-3693-7452-8.ch009

Akbar, Z., & Tohar, K. (2021). Fundamental movement skills and sensory movement strategies to support online learning in early childhood. *Journal of Physical Education and Sport, 21*, 2364–2371.

Akpobome, O. (2024). The impact of emerging technologies on legal frameworks: A model for adaptive regulation. *International Journal of Research Publication and Reviews, 5*(10), 5046–5060. DOI: 10.55248/gengpi.5.1024.3012

Albustanji, R. N., Alkhatib, A., & Shaheen, A. (2025, May). Technical and Ethical Strategies to Prevent Machine Learning Models from Exploiting Personally Identifiable Information (PII). In *2025, the 12th International Conference on Information Technology (ICIT)* (pp. 253-257). IEEE.

Alkaoud, M. (2024). A bilingual benchmark for evaluating large language models. *PeerJ. Computer Science, 10*, e1893. DOI: 10.7717/peerj-cs.1893

Allioui, H., & Mourdi, Y. (2023). Exploring the full potential of IoT for better financial growth and stability: A comprehensive survey. *Sensors (Basel), 23*(19), 8015. DOI: 10.3390/s23198015

Ates, G. C., Mohan, P., & Celik, E. (2023). Dual cross-attention for medical image segmentation. *Engineering Applications of Artificial Intelligence, 126*, 107139. DOI: 10.1016/j.engappai.2023.107139

Bai, Y., Jones, A., Ndousse, K., Askell, A., Chen, A., DasSarma, N., . . . Kaplan, J. (2022). Training a helpful and harmless assistant with reinforcement learning from human feedback. *arXiv preprint arXiv:2204.05862*.

Banerjee, S., Agarwal, A., & Singh, E. (2024). The Vulnerability of Language Model Benchmarks: Do They Accurately Reflect True LLM Performance? *arXiv preprint arXiv:2412.03597.*

BARBOSA, B. K. D. S. (2024). LLMs as tools for evaluating textual coherence: a comparative analysis.

Bebis, G., & Georgiopoulos, M. (1994). Feed-forward neural networks. *IEEE Potentials, 13*(4), 27–31. DOI: 10.1109/45.329294

Bengio, Y., Ducharme, R., Vincent, P., & Jauvin, C. (2003). A neural probabilistic language model. *Journal of Machine Learning Research, 3*(Feb), 1137–1155.

Bhattacharya, P., Prasad, V. K., Verma, A., Gupta, D., Sapsomboon, A., Viriyasitavat, W., & Dhiman, G. (2024). Demystifying ChatGPT: An in-depth survey of OpenAI's robust large language models. *Archives of Computational Methods in Engineering, 31*(8), 4557–4600. DOI: 10.1007/s11831-024-10115-5

Blair, D. C., & Maron, M. E. (1985). An evaluation of retrieval effectiveness for a full-text document-retrieval system. *Communications of the ACM, 28*(3), 289–299. DOI: 10.1145/3166.3197

Boussen, S., Denis, J. B., Simeone, P., Lagier, D., Bruder, N., & Velly, L. (2023). ChatGPT and the stochastic parrot: Artificial intelligence in medical research. *British Journal of Anaesthesia, 131*(4), e120–e121. DOI: 10.1016/j.bja.2023.06.065

Brown, P. F., Cocke, J., Della Pietra, S. A., Della Pietra, V. J., Jelinek, F., Mercer, R. L., & Roossin, P. (1988). A statistical approach to language translation. In *Coling Budapest 1988* Volume 1*: International Conference on Computational Linguistics.*

Casper, S., Davies, X., Shi, C., Gilbert, T. K., Scheurer, J., Rando, J., . . . Hadfield-Menell, D. (2023). Open problems and fundamental limitations of reinforcement learning from human feedback. *arXiv preprint arXiv:2307.15217.*

Chang, K., Gidwani, M., Patel, J. B., Li, M. D., & Kalpathy-Cramer, J. (2021). Data Curation Challenges for Artificial Intelligence. In *Auto-Segmentation for Radiation Oncology* (pp. 201–216). CRC Press. DOI: 10.1201/9780429323782-17

Chang, Y., Wang, X., Wang, J., Wu, Y., Yang, L., Zhu, K., Chen, H., Yi, X., Wang, C., Wang, Y., Ye, W., Zhang, Y., Chang, Y., Yu, P. S., Yang, Q., & Xie, X. (2024). A survey on evaluation of large language models. *ACM Transactions on Intelligent Systems and Technology, 15*(3), 1–45. DOI: 10.1145/3641289

Chen, H., Liu, X., Yin, D., & Tang, J. (2017). A survey on dialogue systems: Recent advances and new frontiers. *SIGKDD Explorations*, *19*(2), 25–35. DOI: 10.1145/3166054.3166058

Chen, L., Wang, Z., Ren, S., Li, L., Zhao, H., Li, Y., . . . Chang, B. (2024). Next token prediction towards multimodal intelligence: A comprehensive survey. *arXiv preprint arXiv:2412.18619.*

Chen, Z., Xu, L., Zheng, H., Chen, L., Tolba, A., Zhao, L., Yu, K., & Feng, H. (2024). Evolution and Prospects of Foundation Models: From Large Language Models to Large Multimodal Models. *Computers, Materials & Continua*, *80*(2), 1753–1808. DOI: 10.32604/cmc.2024.052618

Chkirbene, Z., Hamila, R., Gouissem, A., & Devrim, U. (2024, December). Large language models (llm) in industry: A survey of applications, challenges, and trends. In *2024 IEEE 21st International Conference on Smart Communities: Improving Quality of Life using AI, Robotics and IoT (HONET)* (pp. 229-234). IEEE.

Clune, J. (2019). AI-GAs: AI-generating algorithms, an alternate paradigm for producing general artificial intelligence. *arXiv preprint arXiv:1905.10985.*

Coeckelbergh, M. (2025). LLMs, truth, and democracy: An overview of risks. *Science and Engineering Ethics*, *31*(1), 4. DOI: 10.1007/s11948-025-00529-0

Corea, F. (2017). *Artificial intelligence and exponential technologies: Business models evolution and new investment opportunities*. Springer.

Course, L. L. M. (2021). Algorithms and Legal Challenges: An Analysis of Specific Issues from the Viewpoint of Law and Economics.

D'Souza, J., Al Mustafa, T., Auer, D. F., Bachinger, S. T., Brinner, M., Daniel, C., ... & Heger, T. (2025). Reflections from the 2025 EcoHack: AI & LLM Hackathon for Applications in Evidence-based Ecological Research & Practice.

Dahiya, V. K., Dahiya, R., Dev, R., Sharma, A., Sharma, A., Kiran, P. B. N., Yadav, P. S., & Yadav, S. (2024). Exploring the Role of Artificial Intelligence in Predictive Analytics for Financial Markets. In 2024 International Conference on Computing, Sciences and Communications (ICCSC) (pp. 1–5). 2024 International Conference on Computing, Sciences and Communications (ICCSC). IEEE. https://doi.org/DOI: 10.1109/ICCSC62048.2024.10830442

Daugherty, P. R., & Wilson, H. J. (2024). *Human+ Machine, Updated and Expanded: Reimagining Work in the Age of AI.* Harvard Business Press.

De Almeida, P. G. R., Dos Santos, C. D., & Farias, J. S. (2021). Artificial intelligence regulation: A framework for governance. *Ethics and Information Technology*, *23*(3), 505–525. DOI: 10.1007/s10676-021-09593-z

De Manuel, A., Delgado, J., Parra Jounou, I., Ausín, T., Casacuberta, D., Cruz, M., Guersenzvaig, A., Moyano, C., Rodríguez-Arias, D., Rueda, J., & Puyol, A. (2023). Ethical assessments and mitigation strategies for biases in AI-systems used during the COVID-19 pandemic. *Big Data & Society*, *10*(1), 20539517231179199. DOI: 10.1177/20539517231179199

De Silva, D., & Alahakoon, D. (2022). An artificial intelligence life cycle: From conception to production. *Patterns (New York, N.Y.)*, *3*(6), 100489. DOI: 10.1016/j.patter.2022.100489

Dehghani, N., & Levin, M. (2024). Bio-inspired ai: Integrating biological complexity into artificial intelligence. *arXiv preprint arXiv:2411.15243.*

El-Kassas, W. S., Salama, C. R., Rafea, A. A., & Mohamed, H. K. (2021). Automatic text summarization: A comprehensive survey. *Expert Systems with Applications*, *165*, 113679. DOI: 10.1016/j.eswa.2020.113679

Fahad, M., Basri, T., Hamza, M. A., Faisal, S., Akbar, A., Haider, U., & Hajjami, S. E. (2024). The benefits and risks of artificial general intelligence (AGI). In *Artificial general intelligence (AGI) security: Smart applications and sustainable technologies* (pp. 27–52). Springer Nature Singapore.

Fazil, A. W., Hakimi, M., & Shahidzay, A. K. (2023). A comprehensive review of bias in AI algorithms. *Nusantara Hasana Journal*, *3*(8), 1–11. DOI: 10.59003/nhj.v3i8.1052

Ferdaus, M. M., Abdelguerfi, M., Ioup, E., Niles, K. N., Pathak, K., & Sloan, S. (2024). Towards trustworthy ai: A review of ethical and robust large language models. *arXiv preprint arXiv:2407.13934.*

Fink, G. A. (2014). N-gram models. In *Markov Models for Pattern Recognition: From Theory to Applications* (pp. 107–127). Springer London. DOI: 10.1007/978-1-4471-6308-4_6

Fitria, T. N. (2021). QuillBot as an online tool: Students' alternative in paraphrasing and rewriting of English writing. *Englisia: Journal of Language, Education, and Humanities*, *9*(1), 183–196. DOI: 10.22373/ej.v9i1.10233

Fu, C., Dai, Y., Luo, Y., Li, L., Ren, S., Zhang, R., & Sun, X. (2025). Video-mme: The first-ever comprehensive evaluation benchmark of multi-modal llms in video analysis. In *Proceedings of the Computer Vision and Pattern Recognition Conference* (pp. 24108-24118). DOI: 10.1109/CVPR52734.2025.02245

Gallotta, R., Todd, G., Zammit, M., Earle, S., Liapis, A., Togelius, J., & Yannakakis, G. N. (2024). Large language models and games: A survey and roadmap. *IEEE Transactions on Games*, 1–18. DOI: 10.1109/TG.2024.3461510

Guan, Z., Wu, L., Zhao, H., He, M., & Fan, J. (2025). Attention Mechanisms Perspective: Exploring LLM Processing of Graph-Structured Data. *arXiv preprint arXiv:2505.02130.*

Guo, Y., Shi, H., Kumar, A., Grauman, K., Rosing, T., & Feris, R. (2019). Spottune: transfer learning through adaptive fine-tuning. In *Proceedings of the IEEE/CVF conference on computer vision and pattern recognition* (pp. 4805-4814).

Hadi, M. U., Qureshi, R., Shah, A., Irfan, M., Zafar, A., Shaikh, M. B., & Mirjalili, S. (2023). Large language models: a comprehensive survey of its applications, challenges, limitations, and future prospects. *Authorea preprints, 1*(3), 1-26.

Hamernik, R. P., & Qiu, W. (2001). Energy-independent factors influencing noise-induced hearing loss in the chinchilla model. *The Journal of the Acoustical Society of America, 110*(6), 3163–3168. DOI: 10.1121/1.1414707

Han, S., Wang, M., Zhang, J., Li, D., & Duan, J. (2024). A review of large language models: Fundamental architectures, key technological evolutions, interdisciplinary technologies integration, optimization and compression techniques, applications, and challenges. *Electronics (Basel), 13*(24), 5040. DOI: 10.3390/electronics13245040

Hari, A., & Abdulla, M. S. (2023). *Ai safety: where do we stand presently* (No. 584).

Hassija, V., Chamola, V., Mahapatra, A., Singal, A., Goel, D., Huang, K., Scardapane, S., Spinelli, I., Mahmud, M., & Hussain, A. (2024). Interpreting black-box models: A review on explainable artificial intelligence. *Cognitive Computation, 16*(1), 45–74. DOI: 10.1007/s12559-023-10179-8

Hoffmann, J., Borgeaud, S., Mensch, A., Buchatskaya, E., Cai, T., Rutherford, E., . . . Sifre, L. (2022). Training compute-optimal large language models. *arXiv preprint arXiv:2203.15556.*

Hu, J., Dong, T., Gang, L., Ma, H., Zou, P., Sun, X., & Wang, M. (2024). Psychology: Enhancing LLM for psychological understanding and evaluation. *IEEE Transactions on Computational Social Systems.*

Hu, L., Liu, Z., Zhao, Z., Hou, L., Nie, L., & Li, J. (2023). A survey of knowledge-enhanced pre-trained language models. *IEEE Transactions on Knowledge and Data Engineering*, *36*(4), 1413–1430. DOI: 10.1109/TKDE.2023.3310002

Hu, T., & Zhou, X. H. (2024). Unveiling LLM evaluation focused on metrics: Challenges and solutions. *arXiv preprint arXiv:2404.09135.*

Huang, J., Xu, Y., Wang, Q., Wang, Q. C., Liang, X., Wang, F., Zhang, Z., Wei, W., Zhang, B., Huang, L., Chang, J., Ma, L., Ma, T., Liang, Y., Zhang, J., Guo, J., Jiang, X., Fan, X., An, Z., & Fei, A. (2025). Foundation models and intelligent decision-making: Progress, challenges, and perspectives. *Innovation (Cambridge (Mass.))*, *6*(6), 100948. DOI: 10.1016/j.xinn.2025.100948

Huang, L., Yu, W., Ma, W., Zhong, W., Feng, Z., Wang, H., Chen, Q., Peng, W., Feng, X., Qin, B., & Liu, T. (2025). A survey on hallucination in large language models: Principles, taxonomy, challenges, and open questions. *ACM Transactions on Information Systems*, *43*(2), 1–55. DOI: 10.1145/3703155

Hwang, T. (2018). Computational power and the social impact of artificial intelligence. *arXiv preprint arXiv:1803.08971.*

Ivanov, T., & Penchev, V. (2024). AI Benchmarks and Datasets for LLM Evaluation. *arXiv preprint arXiv:2412.01020.*

Ji, W., Yuan, W., Getzen, E., Cho, K., Jordan, M. I., Mei, S., . . . Zhang, L. (2025). An overview of large language models for statisticians. *arXiv preprint arXiv:2502.17814.*

Jin, P., Zhu, B., Yuan, L., & Yan, S. (2024). Moh: Multi-head attention as mixture-of-head attention. *arXiv preprint arXiv:2410.11842.*

Joshi, S. (2025). Evaluation of Large Language Models: Review of Metrics, Applications, and Methodologies.

Jung, K. H. (2023). Uncover this tech term: Foundation model—Korean. *Journal de Radiologie*, *24*(10), 1038.

Kant, S., Adula, M., & Badi, S. (2025). Digital Transition Effect on Green Jobs by Mediation of Knowledge Management in Circular Economy. In Insights Into Digital Business, Human Resource Management, and Competitiveness (pp. 171-190). IGI Global Scientific Publishing. DOI: 10.4018/979-8-3693-9440-3.ch007

Kant, S., Adula, M., Nimbrain, N., & Kumari, M. (2025). Optimizing Resource Allocation for Green IT Future by Mediation of AI in the Horn of Africa. In Sustainable Information Security in the Age of AI and Green Computing (pp. 503-522). IGI Global Scientific Publishing. DOI: 10.4018/979-8-3693-8034-5.ch025

Kaplan, J., McCandlish, S., Henighan, T., Brown, T. B., Chess, B., Child, R., . . . Amodei, D. (2020). Scaling laws for neural language models. *arXiv preprint arXiv:2001.08361.*

Ke, L., Tong, S., Cheng, P., & Peng, K. (2024). Exploring the frontiers of LMS in psychological applications: A comprehensive review. *arXiv preprint arXiv:2401.01519.*

Khalifa, M., & Albadawy, M. (2024). Using artificial intelligence in academic writing and research: An essential productivity tool. *Computer Methods and Programs in Biomedicine Update, 5*, 100145. DOI: 10.1016/j.cmpbup.2024.100145

Khosravy, M., Nakamura, K., Pasquali, A., Witkowski, O., Nitta, N., & Babaguchi, N. (2022, December). When AI facilitates trust violation: an ethical report on deep model inversion privacy attack. In the *2022 International Conference on Computational Science and Computational Intelligence (CSCI)* (pp. 929–935). IEEE. DOI: 10.1109/CSCI58124.2022.00166

Kosar, T., Mernik, M., & Carver, J. C. (2012). Program comprehension of domain-specific and general-purpose languages: Comparison using a family of experiments. *Empirical Software Engineering, 17*(3), 276–304. DOI: 10.1007/s10664-011-9172-x

Kublik, S., & Saboo, S. (2022). *GPT-3* (pp. 1-150). Sebastopol, CA, USA: O'Reilly Media, Incorporated.

Kulkarni, C. (2023). The evolution of large language models in natural language understanding. *J. Artif. Intell. Mach. Learn. Data Sci, 1*(4), 49–53. DOI: 10.51219/JAIMLD/chinmay-shripad-kulkarni/28

Kumar, A., Lu, C., Kirsch, L., Tang, Y., Stanley, K. O., Isola, P., & Ha, D. (2024). Automating the search for artificial life with foundation models. *arXiv preprint arXiv:2412.17799.*

Kumar, P. (2024). Large language models (LLMs): Survey, technical frameworks, and future challenges. *Artificial Intelligence Review, 57*(10), 260. DOI: 10.1007/s10462-024-10888-y

Li, B., Ge, Y., Ge, Y., Wang, G., Wang, R., Zhang, R., & Shan, Y. (2024). Seed-bench: Benchmarking multimodal large language models. In *Proceedings of the IEEE/CVF Conference on Computer Vision and Pattern Recognition* (pp. 13299-13308).

Li, H., Dong, Q., Chen, J., Su, H., Zhou, Y., Ai, Q., . . . Liu, Y. (2024). Llms-as-judges: a comprehensive survey on llm-based evaluation methods. *arXiv preprint arXiv:2412.05579.*

Li, L., Chen, G., Shi, H., Xiao, J., & Chen, L. (2024). A survey on multimodal benchmarks: In the era of large AI models. *arXiv preprint arXiv:2409.18142.*

Liang, W., Zhang, Y., Wu, Z., Lepp, H., Ji, W., Zhao, X., . . . Zou, J. Y. (2024). Mapping the increasing use of LLMs in scientific papers. *arXiv preprint arXiv:2404.01268.*

Lianos, I. (2024). *Synthetic Futures and Competition Law: Towards the Emergence of Precautionary Principle-Minded Approaches.* Forthcoming Theoretical Inquiries in Law.

Liao, J., Shi, Y., Gong, M., Shou, L., Eskimez, S., Lu, L., . . . Zeng, M. (2021, June). Generating a human-readable transcript for automatic speech recognition with a pre-trained language model. In *ICASSP 2021-2021 IEEE International Conference on Acoustics, Speech and Signal Processing (ICASSP)* (pp. 7578–7582). IEEE. DOI: 10.1109/ICASSP39728.2021.9414626

Liao, Q. V., & Vaughan, J. W. (2023). Ai transparency in the age of llms: A human-centered research roadmap. *arXiv preprint arXiv:2306.01941, 10.*

Lin, L., Wang, L., Guo, J., & Wong, K. F. (2024). Investigating bias in LLM-based bias detection: Disparities between LLMs and human perception. *arXiv preprint arXiv:2403.14896.*

Lin, Z., Guan, S., Zhang, W., Zhang, H., Li, Y., & Zhang, H. (2024). Towards trustworthy LLMs: A review on debiasing and dehallucinating in large language models. *Artificial Intelligence Review, 57*(9), 243. DOI: 10.1007/s10462-024-10896-y

Liu, X., & Croft, W. B. (2005). Statistical language modeling for information retrieval. *Annual Review of Information Science & Technology, 39*(1), 1–31. DOI: 10.1002/aris.1440390108

Lohn, A. (2023). *Scaling AI.* Technical report, Center for Security and Emerging Technology.

Lu, S., Wang, M., Liang, S., Lin, J., & Wang, Z. (2020, September). Hardware accelerator for multi-head attention and position-wise feed-forward in the transformer. In *2020, IEEE 33rd International System-on-Chip Conference (SOCC)* (pp. 84–89). IEEE. DOI: 10.1109/SOCC49529.2020.9524802

Lukin, A., & Gülseren, O. (2024). *Unlocking the Hidden Potential of the Data-Driven Nanocarbon Genome: Unleashing Novel Neural Pathways.* Elucidating Growth-Property Relationships, and Enabling Inverse Design.

Luo, Q., Su, J., Yang, C., Gui, W., Silven, O., & Liu, L. (2022). CAT-EDNet: Cross-attention transformer-based encoder–decoder network for salient defect detection of strip steel surface. *IEEE Transactions on Instrumentation and Measurement, 71*, 1–13. DOI: 10.1109/TIM.2022.3165270

Mai, G., Huang, W., Sun, J., Song, S., Mishra, D., Liu, N., . . . Lao, N. (2023). On the opportunities and challenges of foundation models for geospatial artificial intelligence. *arXiv preprint arXiv:2304.06798.*

Maity, S. (2019). Identifying opportunities for artificial intelligence in the evolution of training and development practices. *Journal of Management Development, 38*(8), 651–663. DOI: 10.1108/JMD-03-2019-0069

Mangan, S., & Alon, U. (2003). Structure and function of the feed-forward loop network motif. *Proceedings of the National Academy of Sciences of the United States of America, 100*(21), 11980–11985. DOI: 10.1073/pnas.2133841100

Mansurova, A., Mansurova, A., & Nugumanova, A. (2024). QA-RAG: Exploring LLM reliance on external knowledge. *Big Data and Cognitive Computing, 8*(9), 115. DOI: 10.3390/bdcc8090115

Mao, Y., Yu, X., Huang, K., Zhang, Y. J. A., & Zhang, J. (2024). Green edge AI: A contemporary survey. *Proceedings of the IEEE.*

Matarazzo, A., & Torlone, R. (2025). A survey on large language models with insights into their capabilities and limitations. *arXiv preprint arXiv:2501.04040.*

Matarazzo, A., & Torlone, R. (2025). A survey on large language models with insights into their capabilities and limitations. *arXiv preprint arXiv:2501.04040.*

Min, B., Ross, H., Sulem, E., Veyseh, A. P. B., Nguyen, T. H., Sainz, O., Agirre, E., Heintz, I., & Roth, D. (2023). Recent advances in natural language processing via large pre-trained language models: A survey. *ACM Computing Surveys, 56*(2), 1–40. DOI: 10.1145/3605943

Minaee, S., Mikolov, T., Nikzad, N., Chenaghlu, M., Socher, R., Amatriain, X., & Gao, J. (2024). Large language models: A survey. *arXiv preprint arXiv:2402.06196.*

Mirchandani, S., Xia, F., Florence, P., Ichter, B., Driess, D., Arenas, M. G., . . . Zeng, A. (2023). Large language models as general pattern machines. *arXiv preprint arXiv:2307.04721.*

Mohamed, Y. A., Khanan, A., Bashir, M., Mohamed, A. H. H., Adiel, M. A., & Elsadig, M. A. (2024). The impact of artificial intelligence on language translation: A review. *IEEE Access : Practical Innovations, Open Solutions*, *12*, 25553–25579. DOI: 10.1109/ACCESS.2024.3366802

Moncayo, Á., & Silveira, A. C. (2017). Current epidemiological trends of Chagas disease in Latin America and future challenges: Epidemiology, surveillance, and health policies. *American Trypanosomiasis Chagas Disease*, 59-88.

Mumuni, A., & Mumuni, F. (2025). Large language models for artificial general intelligence (AGI): A survey of foundational principles and approaches. *arXiv preprint arXiv:2501.03151.*

Murugadoss, B., Poelitz, C., Drosos, I., Le, V., McKenna, N., Negreanu, C. S., Parnin, C., & Sarkar, A. (2025, April). Evaluating the evaluator: Measuring LLMs' adherence to task evaluation instructions. *Proceedings of the AAAI Conference on Artificial Intelligence*, *39*(18), 19589–19597. DOI: 10.1609/aaai.v39i18.34157

Musiol, M. (2024). *Generative AI: Navigating the course to the artificial general intelligence future*. John Wiley & Sons.

National Academies of Sciences. Medicine, Division on Engineering, Physical Sciences, Space Studies Board, Committee on the Decadal Survey for Earth Science, & Applications from Space. (2019). *Thriving on our changing planet: A decadal strategy for Earth observation from space*. National Academies Press.

Nithish, K. K., Karthikeyan, P., Dharmesh Nithil, K., Reshma, P., Vaishnavi, V., & Prakash, N. (2023, December). The Study of Ethical Aspects of Implementing Large Language Models in Business and Society. In *International Conference on Soft Computing and Pattern Recognition* (pp. 156–166). Cham: Springer Nature Switzerland.

O'Sullivan, S., Nevejans, N., Allen, C., Blyth, A., Leonard, S., Pagallo, U., Holzinger, K., Holzinger, A., Sajid, M. I., & Ashrafian, H. (2019). Legal, regulatory, and ethical frameworks for the developing standards in artificial intelligence (AI) and autonomous robotic surgery. *International Journal of Medical Robotics and Computer Assisted Surgery*, *15*(1), e1968. DOI: 10.1002/rcs.1968

Pandey, M., & Yadav, P. S. (2023). Understanding the role of individual concerns, attitude, and perceived value in green apparel purchase intention; the mediating effect of consumer involvement and moderating role of generation Z&Y. *Cleaner and Responsible Consumption*, *9*, 100120. DOI: 10.1016/j.clrc.2023.100120

Pandey, M., Yadav, P. S., & Pothireddy, R. R. (2024). Role of Gamification in Influencer Marketing. In *Marketing and Gamification* (pp. 157–169). Routledge., DOI: 10.4324/9781032694238-13

Parthasarathy, V. B., Zafar, A., Khan, A., & Shahid, A. (2024). The ultimate guide to fine-tuning LMS from basics to breakthroughs: An exhaustive review of technologies, research, best practices, applied research challenges, and opportunities. *arXiv preprint arXiv:2408.13296.*

Pecoraro, R., Basile, V., & Bono, V. (2022). Local multi-head channel self-attention for facial expression recognition. *Information (Basel), 13*(9), 419. DOI: 10.3390/info13090419

Petro anu, D. M., Pîrjan, A., & Tăbu că, A. (2023). Tracing the influence of large language models across the most impactful scientific works. *Electronics (Basel), 12*(24), 4957. DOI: 10.3390/electronics12244957

Qi, J., Yao, Y., Bai, Y., Xu, B., Li, J., Liu, Z., & Chua, T. S. (2025). An LMM for Efficient Video Understanding via Reinforced Compression of Video Cubes. *arXiv preprint arXiv:2504.15270.*

Qiao, T., Zhang, J., Xu, D., & Tao, D. (2019). Mirrorgan: Learning text-to-image generation by redescription. In *Proceedings of the IEEE/CVF conference on computer vision and pattern recognition* (pp. 1505-1514).

Qin, C., & Rusu, F. (2017, June). Dot-product join: Scalable in-database linear algebra for big model analytics, in *Proceedings of the 29th International Conference on Scientific and Statistical Database Management* (pp. 1–12). DOI: 10.1145/3085504.3085512

Raiaan, M. A. K., Mukta, M. S. H., Fatema, K., Fahad, N. M., Sakib, S., Mim, M. M. J., Ahmad, J., Ali, M. E., & Azam, S. (2024). A review on large language models: Architectures, applications, taxonomies, open issues, and challenges. *IEEE Access : Practical Innovations, Open Solutions, 12*, 26839–26874. DOI: 10.1109/ACCESS.2024.3365742

Raiaan, M. A. K., Mukta, M. S. H., Fatema, K., Fahad, N. M., Sakib, S., Mim, M. M. J., Ahmad, J., Ali, M. E., & Azam, S. (2024). A review on large language models: Architectures, applications, taxonomies, open issues, and challenges. *IEEE Access : Practical Innovations, Open Solutions, 12*, 26839–26874. DOI: 10.1109/ACCESS.2024.3365742

Ramasubramanian, V., & Paliwal, K. K. (1992). Fast k-dimensional tree algorithms for nearest neighbor search with application to vector quantization encoding. *IEEE Transactions on Signal Processing*, *40*(3), 518–531. DOI: 10.1109/78.120795

Rane, N. L., Tawde, A., Choudhary, S. P., & Rane, J. (2023). Contribution and performance of ChatGPT and other Large Language Models (LLM) for scientific and research advancements: A double-edged sword. *International Research Journal of Modernization in Engineering Technology and Science*, *5*(10), 875–899.

Raschka, S. (2024). *Build a large language model (from scratch)*. Simon and Schuster.

Roberts, J., Baker, M., & Andrew, J. (2024). Artificial intelligence and qualitative research: The promise and perils of large language model (LLM) 'assistance'. *Critical Perspectives on Accounting*, *99*, 102722. DOI: 10.1016/j.cpa.2024.102722

Roco, M. C. (2008). Possibilities for global governance of converging technologies. *Journal of Nanoparticle Research*, *10*(1), 11–29. DOI: 10.1007/s11051-007-9269-8

Roumeliotis, K. I., Tselikas, N. D., & Nasiopoulos, D. K. (2023). Llama 2: Early Adopters' Utilization of Meta's New Open-Source Pretrained Model.

Ruan, Y., Maddison, C. J., & Hashimoto, T. B. (2024). Observational scaling laws and the predictability of language model performance. *Advances in Neural Information Processing Systems*, *37*, 15841–15892.

Safadi, H., & Watson, R. T. (2023). Knowledge monopolies and the innovation divide: A governance perspective. *Information and Organization*, *33*(2), 100466. DOI: 10.1016/j.infoandorg.2023.100466

Sakib, F. A., Khan, S. H., & Karim, A. R. (2024, July). Extending the frontier of ChatGPT: Code generation and debugging. In *2024 International Conference on Electrical, Computer and Energy Technologies (ICECET* (pp. 1–6). IEEE. DOI: 10.1109/ICECET61485.2024.10698405

Salzano, M., Fung, N., Lin, A., Marchetta, S., Colombo, F., Davis, K., & Zhuang, W. (2024). *AI and Advocacy: Maximizing Potential*. Minimizing Risk.

Schneider, S. (2025). Chatbot Epistemology. *Social Epistemology*, •••, 1–20.

Sejnowski, T. J. (2018). *The deep learning revolution*. MIT Press. DOI: 10.7551/mitpress/11474.001.0001

Sewell, D., & Hiller, J. S. (2025). Presumptions Of AI Malfunction. *Available at SSRN* 5143853.

Shao, H., Xu, Y., Ji, Y., Yang, J., & Liu, C. (2019, December). Intra-modality feature interaction using self-attention for visual question answering. In *International Conference on Neural Information Processing* (pp. 215-222). Cham: Springer International Publishing. DOI: 10.1007/978-3-030-36802-9_24

Sharma, D., Sundravadivelu, K., Khengar, J., Thaker, D. J., Patel, S. N., & Shah, P. (2024). Advancements in Natural Language Processing: Enhancing Machine Understanding of Human Language in Conversational AI Systems. *Journal of Computational Analysis and Applications, 33*(6).

Shethiya, A. S. (2024). Architecting Intelligent Systems: Opportunities and Challenges of Generative AI and LLM Integration. *Academia Nexus Journal, 3*(2).

Shi, D., Shen, T., Huang, Y., Li, Z., Leng, Y., Jin, R., . . . Xiong, D. (2024). Large language model safety: A holistic survey. *arXiv preprint arXiv:2412.17686.*

Singh, M., Michael, R. A., Saheb, S. S., Yadav, P. S., Kiran, P. B. N., & Malhi, A. (2025). A Study on Digital Intelligence and Influencer Marketing for Sustainable Diversification of India's Retail Economy. In Advances in Logistics, Operations, and Management Science (pp. 1–22). IGI Global. https://doi.org/DOI: 10.4018/979-8-3693-8492-3.ch001

Singh, M., Syed, S. M., Saheb, S. S., Yadav, P. S., & Kiran, P. B. N. (2025). Role of Influencer Marketing in the Indian Retail Business Sector. In Advances in Marketing, Customer Relationship Management, and E-Services (pp. 105–130). IGI Global. https://doi.org/DOI: 10.4018/979-8-3693-8542-5.ch005

Sinha, S., & Lee, Y. M. (2024). Challenges with developing and deploying AI models and applications in industrial systems. *Discover Artificial Intelligence*, *4*(1), 55. DOI: 10.1007/s44163-024-00151-2

Sontake, P. (2025). A Review of Artificial Intelligence (AI) Tools in Research Writing. *International Journal of Scientific Research and Technology*.

Spathis, D., & Kawsar, F. (2024). The first step is the hardest: Pitfalls of representing and tokenizing temporal data for large language models. *Journal of the American Medical Informatics Association : JAMIA*, *31*(9), 2151–2158. DOI: 10.1093/jamia/ocae090

Sridhar, A., Pesala, B., Radhakrishnan, G., Niezgoda, J., & Gopalakrishnan, S. (2025). Evolution of Artificial Intelligence. In *Artificial Intelligence and Biological Sciences* (pp. 26–37). CRC Press. DOI: 10.1201/9781003492726-2

Subramanian, S., Harrington, P., Keutzer, K., Bhimji, W., Morozov, D., Mahoney, M. W., & Gholami, A. (2023). Towards foundation models for scientific machine learning: Characterizing scaling and transfer behavior. *Advances in Neural Information Processing Systems*, *36*, 71242–71262.

Sun, J., Zheng, C., Xie, E., Liu, Z., Chu, R., Qiu, J., & Li, Z. (2023). A survey of reasoning with foundation models: Concepts, methodologies, and outlook. *ACM Computing Surveys.*

Sun, Y., He, J., Cui, L., Lei, S., & Lu, C. T. (2024). Exploring the deceptive power of LLM-generated fake news: A study of real-world detection challenges. *arXiv preprint arXiv:2403.18249.*

Sundermeyer, M., Ney, H., & Schlüter, R. (2015). From feedforward to recurrent LSTM neural networks for language modeling. *IEEE/ACM Transactions on Audio, Speech, and Language Processing*, *23*(3), 517–529. DOI: 10.1109/TASLP.2015.2400218

Taeihagh, A. (2021). Governance of artificial intelligence. *Policy and Society*, *40*(2), 137–157. DOI: 10.1080/14494035.2021.1928377

Tang, Y., & Yang, Y. (2024). Pooling and attention: What are effective designs for LLM-based embedding models? *arXiv preprint arXiv:2409.02727.*

Thirumuruganathan, S., Tang, N., Ouzzani, M., & Doan, A. (2020). Data Curation with Deep Learning. In *EDBT* (pp. 277–286).

Thuraisingham, B. M. (2020, March). Can AI be for good amid cyber attacks and privacy violations? A position paper. In *Proceedings of the Tenth ACM Conference on Data and Application Security and Privacy* (pp. 1–4).

Tomalin, M., Byrne, B., Concannon, S., Saunders, D., & Ullmann, S. (2021). The practical ethics of bias reduction in machine translation: Why domain adaptation is better than data debiasing. *Ethics and Information Technology*, *23*(3), 419–433. DOI: 10.1007/s10676-021-09583-1

Too, E. C., Yujian, L., Njuki, S., & Yingchun, L. (2019). A comparative study of fine-tuning deep learning models for plant disease identification. *Computers and Electronics in Agriculture*, *161*, 272–279. DOI: 10.1016/j.compag.2018.03.032

Triguero, I., Molina, D., Poyatos, J., Del Ser, J., & Herrera, F. (2023, January). *General-purpose artificial intelligence systems (GPIS): Properties, definition, taxonomy, open challenges, and implications*. arXiv preprint arXiv:2307.14283.

Vankayalapati, R. K. (2022). AI Clusters and Elastic Capacity Management: Designing Systems for Diverse Computational Demands. *Available at SSRN* 5115889.

Veeramachaneni, V. (2025). Large language models: A comprehensive survey on architectures, applications, and challenges. *Advanced Innovations in Computer Programming Languages*, *7*(1), 20–39.

Vrbančič, G., & Podgorelec, V. (2020). Transfer learning with adaptive fine-tuning. *IEEE Access : Practical Innovations, Open Solutions*, *8*, 196197–196211. DOI: 10.1109/ACCESS.2020.3034343

Wang, G., Bao, H., Liu, Q., Zhou, T., Wu, S., Huang, T., Yu, Z. F., Lu, C. W., Gong, Y. H., Zhang, Z. X., & He, S. (2024). Brain-inspired artificial intelligence research: A review. *Science China. Technological Sciences*, *67*(8), 2282–2296. DOI: 10.1007/s11431-024-2732-9

Wang, J., & Li, S. (2018). Self-attention mechanism-based system for DCASE2018 Challenge Task 1 and Task 4. *Proc. DCASE Challenge*, 1-5.

Wang, W., Li, Z., Lian, D., Ma, C., Song, L., & Wei, Y. (2024). Mitigating the language mismatch and repetition issues in LLM-based machine translation via model editing. *arXiv preprint arXiv:2410.07054*. DOI: 10.18653/v1/2024.emnlp-main.879

Wang, X., Zhang, X., Luo, Z., Sun, Q., Cui, Y., Wang, J., . . . Wang, Z. (2024). Emu3: Next-token prediction is all you need. *arXiv preprint arXiv:2409.18869.*

Wang, Y., Zhang, J., Shi, T., Deng, D., Tian, Y., & Matsumoto, T. (2024). Recent advances in interactive machine translation with large language models. *IEEE Access : Practical Innovations, Open Solutions*, *12*, 179353–179382. DOI: 10.1109/ACCESS.2024.3487352

Wittenberg, C., Epstein, Z., Berinsky, A. J., & Rand, D. G. (2024). Labeling AI-generated content: promises, perils, and future directions.

Xi, Y., Liu, W., Lin, J., Cai, X., Zhu, H., Zhu, J., & Yu, Y. (2024, October). Towards open-world recommendation with knowledge augmentation from large language models. In *Proceedings of the 18th ACM Conference on Recommender Systems* (pp. 12–22). DOI: 10.1145/3640457.3688104

Xiong, Y., Chen, X., Ye, X., Chen, H., Lin, Z., Lian, H., . . . Ding, G. (2024). Temporal scaling law for large language models. *arXiv preprint arXiv:2404.17785.*

Xu, Y., Liu, X., Cao, X., Huang, C., Liu, E., Qian, S., Liu, X., Wu, Y., Dong, F., Qiu, C.-W., Qiu, J., Hua, K., Su, W., Wu, J., Xu, H., Han, Y., Fu, C., Yin, Z., Liu, M., & Zhang, J. (2021). Artificial intelligence: A powerful paradigm for scientific research. *Innovation (Cambridge (Mass.))*, *2*(4), 100179. DOI: 10.1016/j.xinn.2021.100179

Yadav, P. S., Kiran, P. B. N., Sharma, A., Vemula, R., & Shrama, A. (2025). Customer Acceptance of Sustainable Fintech Innovation. In Financial Innovation for Global Sustainability (pp. 337–357). Wiley. https://doi.org/DOI: 10.1002/9781394311682.ch14

Yadav, P. S., Kiran, P. B. N., Vemula, R., Kumar, V., Kumari, P., & Michael, R. A. (2025). Leveraging AI and Digital Solutions to Enhance Sustainability in Green and Blue Economies. In Advances in Computational Intelligence and Robotics (pp. 53–84). IGI Global Scientific Publishing. https://doi.org/DOI: 10.4018/979-8-3373-0159-4.ch002

Yang, J., Jin, H., Tang, R., Han, X., Feng, Q., Jiang, H., & Hu, X. (2024). Harnessing the power of LMS in practice: A survey on ChatGPT and beyond. *ACM Transactions on Knowledge Discovery from Data, 18*(6), 1–32.

Yang, L., Wang, H., Zou, M., Chai, H., & Xia, Z. (2025). Artificial intelligence-driven plant bio-genomics research: a new era. *Tropical Plants, 4*(1).

Yao, Y., Dong, Q., Guan, J., Cao, B., Zhang, Z., Xiao, C., . . . Sun, M. (2021). Cuge: A Chinese language understanding and generation evaluation benchmark. *arXiv preprint arXiv:2112.13610.*

Yuan, X., Yuan, S., Cui, Y., Lin, T., Wang, X., Xu, R., . . . Yang, D. (2024). Evaluating character understanding of large language models via character profiling from fictional works. *arXiv preprint arXiv:2404.12726.* DOI: 10.18653/v1/2024.emnlp-main.456

Zhang, Z., Fort, J. M., & Mateu, L. G. (2023). Exploring the potential of artificial intelligence as a tool for architectural design: A perception study using Gaudí's gaudí'sworks. *Buildings (Basel, Switzerland), 13*(7), 1863. DOI: 10.3390/buildings13071863

Zong, M., & Krishnamachari, B. (2022). A survey on GPT-3. *arXiv preprint*

Chapter 2
AI, Fashion, and Climate Conscious Consumers Promoting Sustainable Consumption Through Intelligent System

Muhammad Ramdani
http://orcid.org/0009-0004-2516-3399
Universitas Esa Unggul, Indonesia

Ahmad Maulana Ulumuddin
http://orcid.org/0009-0000-3623-6128
Universitas Esa Unggul, Indonesia

Binastya Anggara Sekti
http://orcid.org/0000-0001-5489-4888
Universitas Esa Unggul, Indonesia

ABSTRACT

This chapter explores the transformative role of Artificial Intelligence (AI) in addressing the environmental and social challenges of the global fashion industry. It outlines the significant ecological footprint of fast fashion, including excessive water use, carbon emissions, and microplastic pollution. By integrating AI with digital tools such as blockchain, digital wardrobes, and smart labels, fashion brands can enhance transparency, traceability, and sustainability. The chapter further discusses how AI-driven personalization, recommendation systems, and sentiment analysis empower climate-conscious consumers to make informed ethical choices. While

DOI: 10.4018/979-8-3373-5525-2.ch002

AI presents opportunities for circular fashion and real-time behavioral insights, it also introduces risks related to privacy, algorithmic bias, and greenwashing. Through an ethical lens, this chapter emphasizes the need for inclusive governance, data transparency, and responsible design in deploying AI for sustainable fashion transformation.

INTRODUCTION

The fashion industry is widely recognized as one of the most resource-intensive and environmentally damaging global industries. High water consumption, greenhouse gas emissions, chemical pollution, and escalating textile waste have positioned fashion consumption as a significant contributor to climate change and ecological degradation. The rise of fast fashion has further intensified these challenges by promoting high-volume, low-cost production cycles that encourage overconsumption and shorten garment lifespans. Beyond environmental impacts, the fashion industry is also associated with persistent social issues, including labor exploitation, unsafe working conditions, and systemic inequality across global supply chains.

In recent years, growing public awareness of climate change and social responsibility has led to the emergence of climate-conscious consumers—individuals who actively consider environmental and ethical implications in their purchasing decisions. These consumers increasingly demand transparency, accountability, and sustainability from fashion brands. However, despite heightened awareness, significant information asymmetries remain. Sustainability claims are often difficult to verify, supply chains lack visibility, and greenwashing practices undermine consumer trust. As a result, consumers face structural barriers that limit their ability to translate ethical intentions into informed and consistent consumption behavior. AI's role in fostering sustainable fashion through innovation in production, retail, and consumer engagement (Vladimirova et al., 2024)

Digital technologies have begun to reshape this landscape by mediating the relationship between fashion brands and consumers. Among these technologies, artificial intelligence (AI) has gained particular attention for its capacity to process large-scale data, personalize consumer experiences, and enhance operational efficiency. Within the context of sustainable fashion, AI-powered systems can support demand forecasting, inventory optimization, transparency tools, and personalized recommendations that align consumption with environmental and ethical values. Rather than functioning solely as efficiency-driven tools, intelligent systems increasingly operate as socio-technical infrastructures that influence consumer awareness, decision-making, and behavioral change. AI tools like image recognition and natural language processing help identify sustainable materials, evaluate transparency, and counter greenwashing (Ray & Nayak, 2023;Adamkiewicz et al., 2022).

Despite growing interest in AI-enabled sustainability solutions, existing research often treats technological innovation, consumer behavior, and ethical governance as separate domains. Limited attention has been given to how intelligent systems mediate climate-conscious consumption in an integrated manner, or to the ethical risks associated with personalization, data governance, and algorithmic bias. This chapter addresses this gap by examining how intelligent systems, particularly AI-driven tools, interact with climate-conscious consumers to promote sustainable fashion consumption, while critically assessing the ethical and governance challenges that accompany these technologies.

THE ENVIRONMENTAL IMPACT OF FASHION CONSUMPTION

The fast fashion industry drives high-volume, low-cost clothing production, encouraging overconsumption and short garment lifespans. This accelerates textile waste and depletes natural resources, degrading water quality and harming aquatic ecosystems (Bailey et al., 2022). Operating under a linear "take-make-dispose" model, most discarded clothes are landfilled or incinerated, releasing greenhouse gases. The Ellen MacArthur Foundation reports that a truckload of textiles is discarded every second—many made from polyester, which takes centuries to decompose. Yet, many consumers remain unaware of these environmental costs (Long & Nasiry, 2022).

From 2000 to 2015, global clothing production doubled, while garment use dropped by 36%, highlighting an unsustainable consumption pattern (Gomes de Oliveira et al., 2022), In addition, fast fashion often depends on exploitative labor and resource-intensive practices. Ting and Stagner (2023) argue that embracing slow fashion—focusing on durability and ethics—is vital to reducing environmental and social harm.

ENVIRONMENTAL FOOTPRINT OF FASHION PRODUCTION

Fashion production is resource-intensive, requiring vast water, energy, and materials. Producing one cotton T-shirt consumes around 2,700 liters of water—enough for over two years of drinking needs. Dyeing and finishing processes worsen this impact, contributing to 20% of global industrial water pollution through discharge of untreated dyes and heavy metals (Bailey et al., 2022) hese pollutants are persistent in the environment, threatening aquatic ecosystems and public health.

The industry emits 1.2 billion tonnes of CO_2-equivalent annually—more than international aviation and shipping combined—arising from farming, energy-heavy manufacturing, and fossil-fuel-based transport (Leal Filho et al., 2022). Garment data show that short-lived, resource-heavy items have the highest environmental impact. Table 1 shows the Environmental Footprint of Fashion Production.

Table 1. Environmental Footprint of Fashion Production

Types of Clothing	Water Consumption (Liters)	Carbon Footprint (kg CO_2e)	Average Useful Life (Times)
Cotton T Shirt	2.700	2,1	30
Celana Jeans	10.000	33,4	50
Gaun Poliester	6.000	17,5	25
Synthetic Sportswear	4.500	12,0	20

To reduce impact, strategies include extending product lifespans and adopting low-impact materials. Sustainable production and mindful consumption are essential for climate and water conservation.

MICROFIBER POLLUTION AND OCEAN CONTAMINATION

Modern fashion consumption contributes significantly to microfiber pollution. These microscopic plastic particles are shed from synthetic fabrics like polyester and nylon during machine washing. Each wash can release up to 700,000 microfibers, most of which bypass wastewater treatment and flow into rivers and oceans. The International Union for Conservation of Nature estimates over 500,000 tons of microfibers enter marine environments annually—comparable to billions of plastic bags. Microfibers have been found even in remote Arctic regions, indicating their wide dispersion through water and air currents (Kaliszewicz et al., 2023) Once in aquatic systems, microfibers pose two major risks: they absorb toxic chemicals such as heavy metals, and they are ingested by marine organisms—bioaccumulating along the food chain and reaching humans through seafood.

These microfibers carry two main dangers. First, they absorb other chemical pollutants such as heavy metals and pesticides, thus serving as a "toxic vehicle" in the water. Secondly, these particles can be ingested by plankton, small fish, shellfish, and other marine organisms. Because they cannot be digested, microfibers accumulate in the bodies of these animals and continue to move up the food chain until they are eventually consumed by humans through seafood such as fish and Microfiber pollution is a form of microplastic contamination that is invisible, difficult to handle, and highly widespread. Public awareness and technological interventions in both clothing design and wastewater filtration are key to mitigating this threat. Recent research also underscores the importance of initial treatments such as the use of chitosan coatings to reduce microfiber release during washing (Kang et al., 2021). Figure 1 shows the Microfiber Pollution Pathway from Clothing to the Ocean.

Figure 1. Microfiber Pollution Pathway from Clothing to the Ocean.

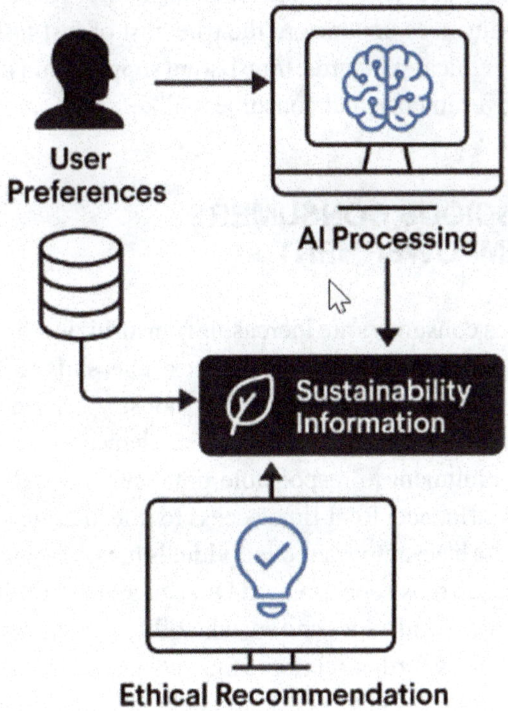

Exploitative Labor and Social Injustice

Behind the appeal of affordable fashion lies widespread labor exploitation and systemic injustice. Many brands outsource production to developing countries, taking advantage of weak labor regulations and low wages. Garment workers, mostly young women, often work long hours without contracts, healthcare, or fair wages. In some regions, reports of child labor and forced labor persist. A study in Bangladesh found violations across nine human rights indicators, including harassment and unjust salary deductions. (Basirulla & Tasnim, 2023)

This reflects a deep imbalance: while global brands profit, workers remain trapped in poverty. Programs like the ILO's Better Work Bangladesh emerged after the 2013 Rana Plaza collapse—an eight-story garment factory disaster that killed over 1,100 people—yet safety compliance remains inadequate (Mahmood et al., 2021) profit pressures often override worker welfare in countries like Bangladesh.

Exploitation also contributes to environmental harm. To cut costs, some factories dump untreated chemicals into rivers, affecting nearby communities. In India, textile waste containing harmful dyes has led to water pollution and health risks such as skin diseases and respiratory problems (Karadayi Usta, 2024). These intertwined social and environmental injustices underscore the true cost of fast fashion. Real change demands enforceable ethical standards, transparent supply chains, and responsibility shared by brands, governments, and consumers alike.

CLIMATE-CONSCIOUS CONSUMERS AND DIGITAL EMPOWERMENT

Climate-conscious consumers are increasingly prioritizing sustainability, ethics, and environmental impact in their fashion choices. This shift reflects growing concerns about climate change and the fast fashion industry's harm to ecosystems and labor conditions. Today, purchasing decisions are shaped not only by cost or style but by a brand's commitment to responsible practices. Digital technologies have amplified consumer influence. Real-time access to information and the use of platforms like social media have empowered individuals to voice opinions and advocate for sustainable fashion. Tools such as Good On You and the Fashion Transparency Index offer insights into brand ethics and sustainability (Mądra Sawicka et al., 2020)

E-commerce platforms further reinforce this movement by offering features that allow users to filter products based on eco-labels, recycled content, or fair trade certification. These tools enable consumers to make more deliberate choices aligned with their ethical values, fostering a deeper connection between consumption and climate responsibility (Li et al., 2022). E-commerce platforms also support conscious choices, enabling users to filter items based on eco-labels or ethical certifications (Li et al., 2022). A 2024 survey found that over 70% of Gen Z and Millennials are willing to pay more for ethical products—signaling a shift from passive consumption to active engagement. These consumers now act as change agents, pushing for greater transparency and sustainability in the fashion industry (Lingling & Ye, 2023)

Intelligent Systems for Sustainable Fashion

Artificial Intelligence (AI) is increasingly guiding consumers toward sustainable fashion choices. By analyzing spending patterns and preferences, AI systems can recommend products that align with users' environmental and ethical values. For instance, if a user often purchases organic or cruelty-free items, the AI will prioritize similar alternatives. This aligns with the concept of sustainable nudging—subtle, non-intrusive prompts that encourage ethical behavior. When users search for fast fashion items, the system may suggest garments made from recycled materials, locally sourced, or produced under fair labor conditions (Canhoto et al., 2024) These nudges foster behavioral change without restricting freedom.

AI also enhances transparency by providing real-time data on a product's carbon footprint, recyclability, material durability, and production ethics (Huang & Rust, 2021) This equips consumers with the insights needed to make informed, values-driven decisions. A 2024 global survey confirms this shift: consumers now prioritize sustainable materials (82%), fair labor practices (78%), and supply chain transparency (74%) (Rafieian & Yoganarasimhan, 2022) AI's influence extends beyond efficiency—it reshapes consumer behavior and values in the digital retail space. Table 2 shows the Factors Valued by Climate Conscious Consumers.

Table 2. Factors Valued by Climate Conscious Consumers

Factor	Percentage of Consumers
Sustainable Materials	82%
Fair Labor Practices	78%
Transparency in the Supply Chain	74%
Product Carbon Footprint	68%
Circular Business Model (rental, resale)	59%
Minimal Packaging / Waste Free	66%

From Passive Buyers to Active Change Agents

The role of consumers in the fashion industry has shifted dramatically. No longer passive buyers, modern consumers act as active change agents, pushing for more ethical and sustainable practices. Their influence extends beyond purchasing decisions to shaping narratives and demanding accountability through digital channels (Berestova et al., 2022). Social media has become a central arena for activism and collective pressure. Campaigns like #WhoMadeMyClothes and #PayUp exemplify how consumer voices can impact corporate behavior and influence global supply chains (Schweiger et al., 2020)

Artificial Intelligence (AI) further amplifies consumer influence. On the industry side, AI is used to monitor real-time demand for sustainable products, forcing brands to adapt swiftly (Bulchand Gidumal et al., 2024). On the consumer side, AI-powered tools such as browser extensions, ethical product filters, and informative chatbots help users make informed, sustainability-aligned decisions (Gao et al., 2023). These innovations empower consumers to act based on credible data rather than assumptions. In doing so, they bridge the gap between personal awareness and collective impact, promoting a shift from impulsive consumption to reflective, values-driven behavior (Rafieian & Yoganarasimhan, 2022).

Figure 2. AI Processes in Recognizing and Supporting Climate Conscious Consumers

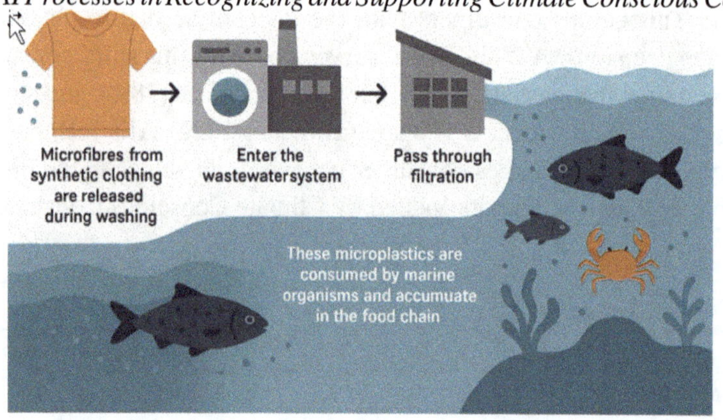

Figure 2 demonstrates how AI processes input from user behavior, sustainability preferences, and contextual data to provide tailored recommendations that support climate-conscious consumption. This evolution strengthens the consumer's role in reshaping the fashion ecosystem. As active participants, they not only demand transparency but also ensure that AI innovations serve ethical and environmental goals—not just commercial interests.

ETHICAL PERSONALIZATION AND ALGORITHMIC NUDGING

As digital innovation intersects with sustainability, Artificial Intelligence (AI) plays a crucial role in shaping more responsible consumer behavior. Two emerging approaches—ethical personalization and algorithmic nudging—aim to guide users toward sustainable choices without restricting freedom. (Gao et al., 2023)

Ethical personalization refers to AI systems that consider consumers' ethical preferences, not just click patterns or purchase history. When users consistently choose organic, cruelty-free, or fair-trade products, the algorithm adjusts and prioritizes results that align with those values, reinforcing sustainable consumption habits (Schmauder et al., 2023).

Algorithmic nudging, meanwhile, influences behavior through visual cues like "climate-friendly" badges, green icons, or carbon footprint labels, and by positioning sustainable products more prominently. These nudges adapt to user behavior; for example, when someone searches for fast fashion, AI may suggest recycled or ethically sourced alternatives. However, transparency remains essential. Consumers must understand why certain suggestions appear and retain control to adjust them. Without explainability and user autonomy, these tools risk manipulation. Therefore, ethical AI must balance promoting sustainability with respecting individual agency (Gao et al., 2023; Schmauder et al., 2023).

Ethical Personalization

Ethical personalization refines traditional recommendation systems by embedding sustainability values directly into algorithmic logic. In fashion, this means AI not only tracks behavioral cues—such as clicks and past purchases—but also learns user preferences related to organic, cruelty-free, or recycled products (Onitiu, 2022) Systems designed with ethical considerations can dynamically prioritize eco-friendly items while filtering out those that conflict with user values (Rydenfelt et al., 2024).

To support this alignment, platforms may offer filters like "locally produced" or "biodegradable packaging." These features improve search relevance and act as soft nudges toward sustainable choices (Ryan, 2023). Rather than prescribing behavior, such tools elevate ethical options, empowering users to make informed decisions. However, this approach carries challenges. Excessive personalization risks creating filter bubbles—exposing users only to a narrow range of ethically labeled products, potentially limiting diversity. To prevent this, AI systems must strike a balance by allowing users to control the degree of ethical filtering and explore a broader product spectrum (Mattis et al., 2024). Table 3 shows the Comparison of Traditional and Ethical Personalization.

Table 3. Comparison of Traditional and Ethical Personalization

Feature	Traditional	AI Based Ethics
Purpose	Maximize engagement & sales	Encourage sustainable consumption
Input Data	Click & Purchase History	Additional ethical preferences & values
Basis of Recommendation	Popularity & similarities	Carbon footprint, materials, ethical sources
Sample Output	Popular polyester t shirts	Organic cotton t shirt with green label
Risk	Encourage impulsive consumption	Reduce the variety of products in the eyes of consumers

Algorithmic Nudging

Algorithmic nudging refers to subtle design techniques that use AI to promote sustainable consumer choices without limiting freedom. Unlike manipulative strategies, nudging is transparent and preserves autonomy. It draws on behavioral psychology to influence decisions through visual prompts like "Climate Friendly," "Zero Waste," or "Locally Produced" tags (Gao et al., 2023)

In the fashion industry, nudging is operationalized through visual cues such as "Climate Friendly," In fashion e-commerce, these tags are often placed prominently—such as atop search results—to gently steer attention. While all products remain available, those aligned with environmental values are visually highlighted to increase engagement.(Onitiu, 2022). AI enhances this by analyzing behavioral patterns (e.g., browsing frequency, search history) to deliver nudges at optimal times. For instance, users frequently browsing fast fashion may be presented with alternatives emphasizing ethical materials or local production (Ryan, 2023).

Visual tools—such as carbon footprint scores, energy use indicators, or product comparison charts—further amplify nudges' impact. These visuals combine data transparency with emotional resonance, encouraging more thoughtful decision-making. (Mattis et al., 2024).

Figure 3. Interface Based Nudging Examples

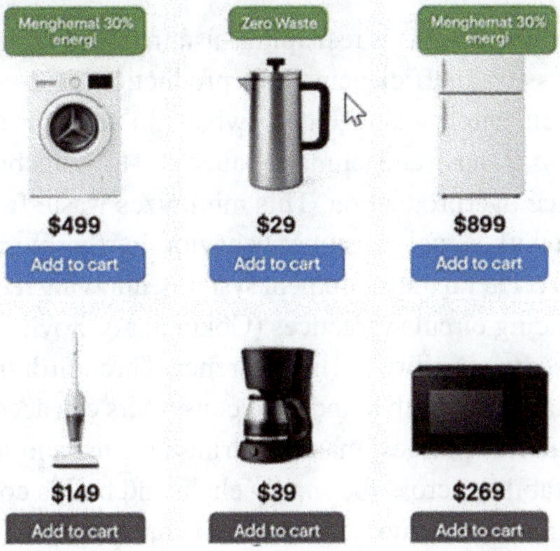

Figure 3 illustrates examples of interface-based nudging techniques, such as sustainability badges, low-impact filters, and eco-sorting options that subtly guide users toward more environmentally friendly fashion choices.

Transparency and Autonomy

Ensuring transparency and autonomy is essential in the ethical application of AI for sustainable fashion. Transparency means users must understand how algorithms function—what data are collected, how they are used, and why specific recommendations appear. For example, if an organic cotton jacket is suggested, users should be clearly informed whether this results from their past searches, material preferences, or sustainability ratings—without overwhelming them with technical jargon Wachner et al., 202; Wang et al., 2023).

Meanwhile, autonomy ensures that users retain control over their decisions. When systems hide non-sustainable options or impose filters by default without notice, users may feel manipulated. Respecting autonomy involves offering manual controls, such as customizable filters or visible "view all" options, allowing consumers to browse freely (Dogruel et al., 2022).

Ethically designed systems must guide without coercion, encouraging users to reflect on sustainable alternatives while preserving their freedom. The goal is not to force sustainable behavior, but to support informed, voluntary choices—enhancing user trust and engagement. By achieving this balance, AI systems can promote eco-consciousness without undermining the user experience (Methnani et al., 2021)

AI POWERED SUSTAINABLE FASHION TOOLS

Artificial Intelligence (AI) is reshaping sustainability efforts across the fashion industry by addressing inefficiencies, overproduction, and waste. One major application is smart inventory management, where AI analyzes real-time data—such as historical sales, trends, and climate patterns—to help brands better forecast demand and reduce overproduction. This minimizes waste from unsold items and aligns production with actual consumer behavior. Furthermore, AI integrated with blockchain supports lateral transshipment systems, allowing redistribution of unsold textiles and advancing circular practices (Gökbunar & Soylu, 2024)

AI also enhances traceability and transparency. Through digital product passports and blockchain platforms, both brands and consumers can access garment lifecycle data—such as material sources, manufacturing origins, and labor standards. This improves accountability across the supply chain and builds consumer trust (Mohiuddin Babu et al., 2024). In circular fashion, AI enables resale, rental, and recycling by using image recognition to assess garment condition, match products with users, and predict resale potential. It even evaluates wear frequency and market trends to suggest optimal repurposing times.

On the consumer side, tools like virtual try-ons and eco-impact calculators reduce returns and inform users of each product's environmental footprint. These innovations support conscious choices by visualizing fit and highlighting carbon emissions or water use. AI also contributes to the evolution of ethnic fashion by combining traditional aesthetics with modern sustainability through machine learning—preserving heritage while fostering eco-innovation (Deng et al., 2023).

Smart Labels and Eco Tracking

Smart labels have emerged as a vital consumer-facing innovation in sustainable fashion, utilizing technologies like QR codes, NFC, or RFID to embed digital identifiers in garments. These tools grant users access to real-time information about a product's environmental impact, such as water consumption, carbon footprint, factory certifications, and recycling guidelines—simply by scanning the label. Unlike static hang tags, smart labels dynamically present up-to-date data, especially when integrated with AI and blockchain. AI allows continuous tracking of environmental metrics, while blockchain ensures data integrity, reducing the risk of misleading sustainability claims. Retail innovations such as RFID-enabled fitting rooms further enhance both transparency and operational efficiency.

These labels also function as educational platforms, translating complex sustainability metrics into understandable insights through visualizations of sourcing paths, emissions, and impact scores. This fosters transparency, builds consumer trust, and promotes informed decision-making. Moreover, research shows that green certifications and eco-labels significantly influence sustainable purchasing intentions. When supported by verifiable data, smart labels not only inform but also persuade, aligning with broader environmental values (Rizkiatami et al., 2023)

As sustainability regulations become stricter and consumer awareness grows, smart labeling is poised to become a standard practice in ethical fashion retail. It serves both brands and consumers by making sustainability visible, credible, and actionable at the point of sale.

Digital Wardrobes

AI-powered digital wardrobes are reshaping consumer interactions with fashion by enabling users to visualize their clothing inventory, track usage frequency, and receive contextual outfit recommendations. These features promote thoughtful consumption and reduce unnecessary purchases by encouraging users to utilize existing garments more effectively. Table 4 shows the core features and their contributions to sustainability.

Table 4. Key Functions of AI Based Digital Wardrobes and Their Contribution to Sustainability

Feature	Contribution to Sustainability
Item Tracking	Reduce unnecessary repeat purchases
Outfit Recommendations	Encourage maximum utilization of the clothes owned
Upcycling/Donation Suggestions	Extend the life cycle of clothing, reduce textile waste
Usage Analytics	Uncovering consumption patterns to drive behavior change

Extending garment use is a critical strategy in reducing the environmental footprint of fashion. According to de Wagenaar, Galama, and Sijtsema, "Extending the use of garments is often seen as an important strategy to decrease the impact of the fashion industry. Additionally, this exploration provides insights into how to improve international monitoring and the value of reuse in consumers' clothing systems." (de Wagenaar et al., 2022)

Technically, such systems must be energy-efficient. "In a bottom-up fashion, which can lead to up to a 94% reduction in the overall system power with negligible loss in performance."(Hadizadeh Hafshejani et al., 2022).

Circular Fashion Platforms

Circular fashion promotes sustainable consumption by extending the lifecycle of garments through resale, rental, repair, and recycling. Artificial intelligence plays a critical role in enabling this model by powering digital platforms that support personalized, circular consumption. AI can analyze shopping history, style preferences, and body metrics to recommend second-hand or rental alternatives—minimizing the need for new purchases and reducing environmental impact. As (Akram et al., 2022) observed, this approach lowers textile waste while maintaining user satisfaction.

Predictive AI models also help estimate the lifespan of clothing based on use, material, and wearer behavior. Smart systems can issue timely prompts suggesting when to recycle or donate garments, encouraging users to make decisions with environmental consequences in mind. (Rathore, 2023) emphasized that machine learning advances allow platforms to refine these interventions through data-driven personalization, retargeting pre-owned items, and subscription-based rentals.

Moreover, platforms can map nearby inventories of used clothing, calculate carbon savings per transaction, and streamline logistics for circular services. These intelligent features enhance user experience while reinforcing sustainable habits (Das et al., 2023). stressed that such AI-enabled systems are key to achieving ecological goals through transparent, data-informed circular supply chains.

By integrating personalization, predictive analytics, and sustainability metrics, AI-driven platforms bridge fashion with environmental stewardship—supporting a shift from fast fashion to a circular, conscious model of consumption.

DATA DRIVEN CONSUMER BEHAVIOR ANALYSIS

Artificial Intelligence (AI) has significantly transformed how fashion brands interpret and anticipate consumer behavior, particularly in the context of sustainability. Traditional methods such as surveys and post-sale reports often yielded delayed and generalized insights. In contrast, AI enables the real-time processing of vast and diverse digital data, allowing for a more accurate and timely understanding of shifting consumer attitudes and preferences (Sharma et al., 2023)

For example, AI systems can detect when a consumer begins adopting minimalist fashion habits or shows a preference for second-hand goods. These insights enable brands to align product recommendations, marketing initiatives, and inventory decisions with individual sustainability values. Furthermore, AI-powered behavioral tracking supports ethical nudging, such as suggesting low-impact alternatives or showcasing the environmental benefits of specific product choices (Akram et al., 2022).

The integration of AI-driven behavioral insights into sustainability initiatives empowers fashion brands to be more agile, transparent, and accountable. It transforms raw behavioral data into actionable intelligence that influences product design, supply chain planning, and post-purchase engagement (Sharma et al., 2023)

The technical foundation of this transformation lies in the availability and quality of behavioral data. The next section explores these data sources and the systems through which AI derives its insights (Akram et al., 2022).

Behavioral Data Sources

Artificial intelligence has revolutionized how fashion brands capture and analyze consumer behavior, particularly in sustainability contexts. Traditional methods such as surveys are now complemented by real-time behavioral data sourced from social media, e-commerce activity, and user-generated content. These data enable brands to identify nuanced patterns within eco-conscious consumer segments and adapt strategies accordingly.

AI allows for micro-level segmentation for instance, detecting shifts toward minimalist preferences or secondhand engagement informing targeted marketing, ethical nudging, and sustainable inventory planning.(Mahmoud et al., 2021). demonstrated how natural language processing (NLP) can interpret emotional responses from fashion consumers across generational lines, revealing distinct sentiment patterns. Meanwhile,(Devakunchari & Valliyammai, 2016) emphasized the broader role of big data in capturing public sentiment and enabling timely, sustainability-driven engagement. Table 5 shows the summarizes findings from AI-based sentiment analysis using social media data.

Table 5. Summarizes findings from AI-based sentiment analysis using social media data

Generation Segment	Dominant Emotions	Hashtags / Common Expressions	AI Interpretation
Gen Z (Ages 18–24)	Enthusiastic, FOMO	#trendingfashion, #OOTD	Attracted to fast trends and self expression through fashion
Millennials (Ages 25–40)	Optimistic, Caring	#sustainablefashion, #brandwithvalues	Prioritize ethics and sustainability in fashion consumption
Gen X (Ages 41–55)	Skeptical, Cautious	#timelesslook, #qualityfirst	Focused on quality, longevity, and long term value
Loyal Customers	Positive, Supportive	“love this brand”, “best ever”	Likely to recommend and repurchase from the brand
Critical Consumers	Negative, Disappointed	“bad quality”, “not as shown”	Require brand intervention to improve reputation and product experience

By relying on AI- and NLP-based analytics technologies, fashion brands can not only interpret user sentiment with greater accuracy but also craft more ethical and sustainability-oriented responses to consumer feedback.

Strategic Benefits for Brands

Artificial intelligence enables fashion brands to derive actionable insights from behavioral data, supporting strategic decision-making for sustainable consumption. By facilitating real-time demand forecasting based on consumer preferences, AI helps reduce overproduction and minimize environmental and financial waste. In addition, AI-driven micro-segmentation allows brands to tailor sustainability messaging to distinct consumer groups, enhancing engagement and differentiation. Continuous analysis of social media sentiment, reviews, and digital interactions further enables brands to refine product design, marketing strategies, and sourcing practices, ensuring alignment with evolving sustainability expectations.

Research (Farzin et al., 2023) affirms the strategic importance of behavioral segmentation. The study found that purchase intentions and willingness to pay a premium for eco-fashion were significantly influenced by environmental concern, social norms, and altruistic motivations. These insights validate AI's role in identifying and activating value-based consumer clusters.

Ultimately, by integrating AI into segmentation and communication strategies, fashion brands can cultivate authentic consumer relationships, foster long-term loyalty, and reinforce their sustainability positioning in a competitive market.

Ethical Considerations

The integration of AI in sustainable fashion brings ethical concerns regarding data privacy, algorithmic bias, and user autonomy. As brands harness personal data for sustainability-driven personalization, transparency is essential. Consumers must be clearly informed about data collection practices and retain full agency over their information

(Rodrigues Schon & Colombi, 2023) argue that ethical frameworks must be embedded from the design stage of AI systems—not added retrospectively. This includes addressing risks like digital exclusion and discriminatory outcomes. If, for instance, algorithms favor affluent consumers in recommending eco-products, they may unintentionally marginalize lower-income but sustainability-minded users. Ethical AI must ensure equitable access to green fashion options.

Algorithmic accountability is also vital. Routine audits should detect and mitigate unintended biases that reinforce social inequalities. AI systems should promote fairness, inclusivity, and ethical consumption—not just operational efficiency.

(Marti, 2024) highlights the importance of value pluralism and intersectional ethics. AI must avoid reinforcing dominant beauty standards or cultural stereotypes. Instead, it should foster diversity of expression, respect cultural differences, and support social justice in consumption.

Furthermore, user agency must be preserved. Rather than manipulative nudging, AI systems should empower users with accurate data on environmental impacts and ethical alternatives. Aligning AI with climate literacy and personal values—not just profit—ensures its ethical alignment.

Ultimately, ethical AI in sustainable fashion demands that brands uphold digital dignity, fairness, and social responsibility, turning AI into a force for inclusive, sustainable transformation.

AI for Transparent and Trustworthy Fashion Ecosystemss

Transparency is essential for building trust in sustainable fashion. As consumers increasingly demand proof of ethical production, environmentally responsible sourcing, and low carbon footprints, traditional fashion systems face pressure to eliminate opacity (Thiebes et al., 2021).

By aggregating data from IoT sensors, satellite imagery, logistics systems, and audit records, AI enables the construction of traceable, fact-based product histories (L. Chen et al., 2020). These digital narratives offer verifiable insights into raw material origins, production processes, and environmental impacts, giving consumers the knowledge they need to make informed choices.

Beyond consumer engagement, AI also supports brands in meeting Environmental, Social, and Governance (ESG) benchmarks. Its ability to create auditable digital trails helps reduce the risk of greenwashing while promoting operational accountability. In doing so, AI strengthens corporate credibility and enhances resilience against reputational damage.

(Davenport et al., 2020) emphasize that trust is now a competitive asset in fashion. Integrating AI into transparency infrastructures is not optional—it is a strategic necessity. As global fashion moves toward circularity and responsibility, AI's role in creating a visible, verifiable ecosystem positions it as a linchpin in driving long-term industry transformation.

AI for Supply Chain Visibility

Supply chain visibility is a critical component in establishing a transparent and sustainable fashion system. Amid the complexities of globalized manufacturing, many stages of production remain obscured from consumers and regulators, creating opportunities for unethical or environmentally harmful practices. In this context, the holistic application of Artificial Intelligence (AI) emerges as a strategic solution to enable data-driven monitoring across the entire product lifecycle—from raw material sourcing to post-consumer logistics (Jöhnk et al., 2021).

AI integrates a range of advanced technologies such as computer vision for image and video analysis, IoT sensors for real-time data acquisition, and natural language processing (NLP) to extract insights from unstructured documents and reports. These capabilities enable automated audits and enhance oversight across various supply chain domains. Notable implementations include:

- **Automated factory monitoring** using CCTV video analysis to detect violations such as excessive working hours, unsafe worker density, or hazardous conditions.
- **NLP-powered document mining** to scrutinize contracts, procurement records, and invoices, thereby identifying potential breaches of ethical sourcing standards—such as the use of conflict-area materials or uncertified suppliers.
- **Carbon and water footprint tracking** across each stage of production, achieved through IoT integration and AI-based predictive modeling, allowing companies to create accurate and evidence-based environmental impact assessments.

Beyond improving adherence to Environmental, Social, and Governance (ESG) criteria, AI-driven visibility accelerates response times to supply chain disruptions, minimizes resource waste, and enhances overall logistical efficiency. As a result, AI contributes not only to enhanced accountability but also to operational optimization and sustainability advancement—demonstrating that ethical oversight and business performance can progress in tandem.

Blockchain for Immutable Verification

Blockchain technology has emerged as a pivotal enabler in achieving independently verifiable supply chain transparency. Within the sustainable fashion ecosystem, blockchain does not operate in isolation; rather, it complements Artificial Intelligence (AI) by adding a robust layer of data integrity. While AI aggregates, filters, and interprets information from sources such as sensors, surveillance systems, and digital documents, blockchain functions as a decentralized and tamper-proof digital ledger that permanently records verified data (Han et al., 2023)

Blockchain's core strength lies in its ability to ensure end-to-end data authenticity across the fashion supply chain, from raw material sourcing to retail distribution. By recording transactions in cryptographically linked and immutable blocks, blockchain enables transparent and auditable verification of sustainability claims, reducing the risk of greenwashing. Through mechanisms such as QR codes on garment labels, consumers can access reliable information on material origins, manufacturing processes, environmental impacts, and labor compliance, thereby enhancing trust and supporting more responsible consumption. (Vu et al., 2023). Table 6 shows the Comparison: Traditional vs. AI + Blockchain Supply Chain Transparency.

Table 6. Comparison: Traditional vs. AI + Blockchain Supply Chain Transparency

Aspect	Traditional Approach	AI + Blockchain Approach
Data Collection	Manual reports, often inconsistent	Real time via sensors, IoT devices, and AI driven analytics
Trust Level	Low (prone to data manipulation)	High (data is secured and immutable on the blockchain ledger)
Traceability	Partial	End to end (from raw materials to store shelves)
Consumer Access to Info	Very limited	Transparent access via QR codes or online blockchain explorers

The convergence of AI and blockchain technologies represents a transformative shift in fashion supply chains. Together, they create a transparent, accountable, and data-driven ecosystem that empowers consumers with verified information and compels brands to uphold higher standards of environmental and social responsibility. (Taherdoost, 2022)

Real World Application

The real implementation of AI and blockchain integration in the fashion industry is no longer just a concept, but has begun to be implemented by a number of global companies that want to build a strong transparency and accountability system. This step not only meets consumers' expectations of sustainability, but also creates a competitive advantage through trust and technological innovation (Iranmanesh et al., 2023).

Salah satu contoh paling menonjol adalah Everledger, sebuah platform berbasis AI dan blockchain yang awalnya dirancang untuk melacak berlian, namun kini telah diperluas ke industri kulit dan tekstil. Dengan AI yang mendeteksi anomali dalam data asal usul material dan blockchain yang mencatat data tersebut secara permanen, Everledger membantu memastikan bahwa bahan yang digunakan benar benar berasal dari sumber yang etis dan berkelanjutan (Xu et al., 2021).

Meanwhile, Provenance leverages AI algorithms to assess sustainability risks in the supply chain and combines them with blockchain systems to store verification results. The platform allows consumers to view product sustainability claims transparently through a digital interface that connects directly to audited supply chain data (Alabaddi et al., 2023)

Major fashion brands such as H&M have also started implementing similar systems. In a pilot project, H&M displayed the carbon footprint and sustainability information of the product directly on the clothing tag. The data is collected through AI and stored on the blockchain network so that it cannot be changed. Consumers only need to scan the QR code to see the complete history of the product's journey from the manufacturer to the store shelf (Alabaddi et al., 2023)

These steps mark a digital transformation towards a more transparent and responsible fashion ecosystem. In a world that increasingly demands openness, brands that adopt this approach not only meet regulations or market trends but also shape a more equitable and climate conscious industry future (Sunny et al., 2020)

Consumer Empowerment via Transparency

The integration of Artificial Intelligence (AI) and blockchain technologies in the fashion industry serves not only as a mechanism for internal governance but also as a powerful catalyst for consumer empowerment. In an era increasingly defined by climate awareness and ethical accountability, consumers are no longer passive recipients of marketing narratives; they are active participants with access to real-time, verifiable data regarding the lifecycle of the products they purchase (Yang et al., 2022).

Through technologies such as scannable QR codes embedded in clothing tags, consumers are granted detailed insights into the full provenance of a garment. This includes information about material origin, manufacturing locations, labor conditions, carbon emissions, packaging, and distribution. The availability of such data enables individuals to conduct independent validation of sustainability claims, reducing dependence on unverifiable brand messaging (Tajurahim et al., 2020).

Enhanced transparency enables consumers to verify labor standards, material sourcing, and environmental impacts, allowing purchasing decisions to align with ethical and sustainability values. At the same time, AI-driven analytics mediate feedback loops between consumers and brands by translating user interactions and preferences into insights that inform product innovation, ethical sourcing, and sustainable design. Together, transparency, AI, and blockchain support a participatory fashion ecosystem in which informed consumers and accountable brands share responsibility for advancing environmental and social sustainability (Itani et al., 2023).

ETHICAL AI CONSIDERATIONS

While the integration of Artificial Intelligence (AI) into fashion transparency systems provides significant benefits—such as improved accountability, operational efficiency, and consumer trust—it simultaneously introduces critical ethical challenges that must not be overlooked. The deployment of such technology should be governed by a robust ethical framework to safeguard the rights and dignity of all stakeholders, particularly the workers embedded within the global fashion supply chain (Bankins & Formosa, 2023).

A primary ethical concern pertains to worker privacy. As AI systems increasingly rely on data sourced from surveillance cameras, biometric attendance logs, and Internet of Things (IoT) sensors that track real-time factory activities, the collection and processing of such sensitive information must adhere to principles of informed consent, data minimization, and secure data storage. Workers must be fully aware of how their data is used and have the agency to opt out without retaliation or disadvantage.

Secondly, algorithmic bias in AI systems presents a systemic risk, especially in the context of automated sustainability audits or ethical compliance checks. There is a real danger that these systems may disproportionately scrutinize manufacturers in developing countries or small-scale suppliers due to biased training datasets or flawed assumptions. To mitigate this, AI models must be developed using diverse, representative datasets and undergo rigorous bias testing. The audit mechanisms must ensure procedural fairness across geographic, economic, and cultural boundaries (Chen et al., 2023).

A third and equally critical issue is algorithmic transparency and accountability. Questions arise as to who designs and controls these AI systems, what level of public oversight exists, and whether algorithmic decisions can be independently audited or contested. For AI-driven decisions to be ethically acceptable, they must be explainable, auditable by third parties, and open to correction. Moreover, human oversight must remain central to decision-making processes, particularly in contexts that impact livelihoods and social justice.

By embedding ethical considerations into the design and deployment of AI systems, fashion companies can avoid replicating exploitative practices under a technological guise. Instead, they can position AI as a force for positive transformation—one that reinforces transparency, upholds human rights, and supports equitable practices across the value chain (Eitel Porter, 2021).

Challenges and Ethical Considerations

Despite the transformative potential of Artificial Intelligence (AI) in steering the fashion industry toward sustainable development, its implementation is not devoid of multifaceted challenges—ranging from technical limitations to ethical and socio-economic concerns. Without the establishment of rigorous governance frameworks and clear accountability mechanisms, the application of AI risks exacerbating the very issues it aims to resolve.

One of the most pressing challenges is the emergence of technology-enabled greenwashing. In such cases, AI tools are employed to construct persuasive sustainability narratives through polished data visualizations, automated sustainability certificates, or algorithmic product recommendations that are not necessarily grounded in verifiable data. In the absence of robust oversight, this practice can mislead consumers and undermine genuine sustainability efforts.

Privacy and data ethics also present a critical area of concern. The deployment of AI systems that process data from factory surveillance cameras, biometric attendance systems, or consumer behavioral analytics must be conducted transparently and with explicit consent. Failure to do so risks violating individual privacy rights and contravening international data protection standards (Milano et al., 2020). . Furthermore, the extraction and use of such sensitive data must adhere to the principles of necessity, proportionality, and secure data management.

Another structural issue lies in the unequal access to AI technologies. While large multinational fashion brands often possess the financial and technical capabilities to implement advanced AI-driven sustainability systems, small- and medium-sized enterprises (SMEs), particularly those in developing countries, face significant barriers to adoption. This asymmetry not only widens the digital divide but also reinforces systemic inequities in regulatory compliance and consumer visibility (Kumar et al., 2020)

To address these issues, a comprehensive and inclusive approach is required—one that does not merely prioritize technological efficiency but actively integrates ethical accountability, stakeholder engagement, and social equity. Regulatory safeguards, third-party audits, and participatory governance mechanisms must be embedded within the AI ecosystem of the fashion industry to ensure that its sustainability trajectory is inclusive, credible, and ethically grounded (Mitchell et al., 2022).

Bias in Recommendations

AI-driven recommendation systems in fashion often reinforce unsustainable consumption patterns due to biased training data. Most algorithms are trained on historical sales, which heavily favor fast fashion products. As a result, AI tends to suggest previously popular items rather than ethical or sustainable alternatives (Edizel et al., 2020).

This creates a self-reinforcing loop: large brands gain more visibility and dominance, while small or ethical labels are excluded. Additionally, recommendation systems often promote trendy or discounted items, encouraging impulsive consumption over quality or durability. Table 7 shown the Bias in AI Recommendation Systems

Table 7. Bias in AI Recommendation Systems

Source of Bias	Potential Impact
Historical sales data	Reinforces fast fashion as the default consumer preference
Imbalanced brand visibility	Overlooks smaller or ethical brands with limited market reach
Consume behavior profiles	Sustains impulsive and unsustainable shopping habits

To address this, developers must adopt fairness-aware design: balance the datasets, include sustainability metadata, and conduct regular algorithm audits. Without these steps, AI could hinder—not help—the transition toward sustainable fashion (Simon et al., 2020).

Greenwashing Risks

Greenwashing, which is the practice of making misleading environmental claims or not supported by accurate data. In this context, AI can play a dual role as a tool that empowers transparency, or conversely, as a manipulative instrument that frames the sustainability narrative without substantial change (de Freitas Netto et al., 2020).

Generative AI can be used by companies to craft "green" sounding marketing narratives, such as eco friendly product descriptions or sustainability campaigns. However, without integration with sensor based data, independent audits, or objective supply chain tracking, such claims are prone to becoming mere cosmetics. Furthermore, machine learning trained with internal company data can also be biased in prioritizing success metrics based on public impressions, rather than actual sustainability.

Examples of Real Cases

A global fashion company promoted its "Conscious Choice" clothing line with the help of AI marketing tools. Although its look and narrative emphasize environmental commitment, third party audits show that the line is manufactured in manufacturing facilities that do not have environmental certifications or low emission production practices. In addition, no public information is available regarding the carbon footprint of products or supply chain transparency. Table 8 shows the Comparison between AI Based Greenwashing vs Real Transparency.

Table 8. Comparison between AI Based Greenwashing vs Real Transparency

Aspect	Greenwashing via AI	Genuine Transparency (AI + Audit)
Product Description	Generative narratives without verifiable data	Based on emission data, materials, and independent audits
Public Information Access	Limited, only through promotional campaigns	Open access via QR codes and online dashboards
Independent Audit	Absent or unpublished	Mandatory and publicly available
Primary Objective	Enhancing brand image	Ensuring systemic and accountable change

The practice of greenwashing not only harms consumers, but also hinders progress towards true sustainability. Therefore, strict regulation, data driven labeling, and collaboration with independent stakeholders are key to mitigating the potential for AI misuse in this area (Adamkiewicz et al., 2022).

Privacy Concerns in Personalization

Greenwashing refers to the act of making deceptive environmental claims without evidence or verifiable data. In this context, AI can serve either as a catalyst for transparency or as a manipulative tool that shapes sustainability narratives without real progress (Canhoto et al., 2024).

Companies may employ generative AI to produce marketing content that emphasizes eco-consciousness—such as "green" product descriptions or sustainability-themed campaigns. However, without integration with sensor data, third-party audits, or transparent supply chain monitoring, these claims risk becoming superficial. AI systems trained solely on internal performance data may prioritize public appeal over measurable sustainability outcomes. Table 9 shows the AI Personalization vs. Data Ethics.

Table 9. AI Personalization vs. Data Ethics

Aspect	Ideal (Ethical)	Risk (Unethical)
Data Collection	Based on informed consent, with full transparency	Hidden in Terms of Service (ToS) or implied without explicit agreement
Data Processing	Data is anonymized and encrypted	Vulnerable to leaks without proper security protocols
Third Party Access	Limited, audited, and transparently reported	Sold to advertisers or partners without user accountability
User Rights	Access, correction, and deletion of personal data	Not provided or buried in confusing interfaces

Therefore, it is important for companies to implement privacy practices that are aligned with data protection principles, such as the General Data Protection Regulation (GDPR) in Europe. Transparency, user control, and system security should be an integral part of the AI architecture in the fashion industry, to ensure that technological advances do not sacrifice an individual's right to privacy (Kozyreva et al., 2021).

Other Ethical Dilemmas

Beyond technical concerns, the integration of artificial intelligence (AI) into the fashion industry exposes deeper ethical and structural challenges. If left unaddressed, these gaps can worsen inequality and compromise the integrity of sustainable innovation.

One key issue is the Technology Access Gap. Smaller brands, independent designers, and ethical fashion producers often don't have the financial or technical means to adopt advanced AI tools. As a result, innovation in sustainability becomes concentrated in the hands of major global fashion players, sidelining efforts from the Global South or local ethical initiatives. This imbalance slows down inclusive progress toward sustainability goals (Morley et al., 2023).

Another major concern is Data Ownership. AI models for demand forecasting, marketing personalization, or supply chain efficiency rely on massive datasets—ranging from customer behavior to logistics. But who actually owns this data? The fashion brand? The e-commerce platform? The customer? The absence of clear guidelines opens the door to potential misuse, undermining consumer trust and raising legal and ethical red flags.

Then there's the issue of Opaque or "Black Box" Algorithms. Many AI systems are proprietary and lack transparency, making it nearly impossible to trace how decisions are made. This becomes especially problematic in critical contexts—such as monitoring labor practices, evaluating environmental impact, or verifying ethical compliance. Without explainable AI, there's no way to assess whether decisions are fair, unbiased, or aligned with sustainability values.

Addressing these dilemmas requires more than just technical fixes—it demands collaboration across sectors. Regulators, AI developers, fashion brands, and civil society must work together to build systems that are not only innovative, but also equitable, transparent, and ethically responsible (Heilinger, 2022).

Towards Ethical AI in Fashion

To address the ethical challenges posed by AI in the fashion industry, it is necessary to implement guiding principles that prioritize transparency, accountability, and sustainability.

First, AI transparency must be enforced. Algorithms used for recommendation systems, sustainability labeling, and supply chain decisions should be explainable and open to external scrutiny. This is essential to prevent algorithmic bias and ensure accountability when AI influences consumer decisions or supplier assessments (Peters et al., 2020).

Second, all AI-driven sustainability claims must be grounded in verifiable environmental data. If a product is labeled as "eco-friendly" by an AI system, it must be supported by metrics such as carbon footprint, water usage, renewable energy use, or third-party certifications. This minimizes the risk of greenwashing and ensures alignment with scientific standards (Peters et al., 2020).

Third, consumer rights must be protected in all AI interactions. Users should be able to access, control, and delete their data, with meaningful consent mechanisms that are not hidden behind complex terms of service. Personal data must be treated as a responsibility, not merely a resource for commercial exploitation (Mylrea & Robinson, 2023)

Finally, multi-stakeholder governance is critical. Ethical oversight should involve regulators, civil society, environmental experts, and labor representatives. AI systems must be monitored by independent institutions to ensure that they serve collective interests, rather than unilateral corporate agendas (Prikshat et al., 2022). Establishing these principles allows the fashion industry to adopt AI technologies without compromising ethical or environmental commitments.

FUTURE TRENDS AND INNOVATIONS

The role of artificial intelligence (AI) in the sustainable fashion industry continues to evolve from just a predictive analytics tool to a strategic partner in systemic transformation. In the future, AI is expected to play a more complex role, not only supporting supply chain efficiency or providing product recommendations, but also reshaping consumption, design, and production values within the framework of sustainability (Ruiz Real et al., 2020).

One of the main trends is the emergence of value centric AI, which is a system that not only understands numerical data, but is also able to interpret the user's ethical preferences, environmental values, and emotional state. This type of AI can suggest fashion choices that not only suit aesthetic tastes, but also align with the principles of sustainability and social responsibility of users. This creates the potential to encourage a more conscious and reflective lifestyle.

On the production side, generative AI will be increasingly used in creating fashion designs that reduce textile waste and minimize overproduction. Through digital simulations, prototypes can be tested virtually before entering the physical production stage, saving natural resources and energy. In addition, technologies such as AI powered life cycle assessment (LCA) will be more precise in mapping the environmental impact of each product in real time.

Last but not least, AI based personalization in the future will be increasingly integrated with user privacy rights, where the system is not only adaptive, but also transparent and controlled by individuals. Thus, AI innovation in the fashion field will not only create economic value, but also support the transformation towards a more equitable, inclusive, and environmentally friendly industry (Dwivedi et al., 2023).

Emotion Aware AI

One significant innovation in the integration of artificial intelligence within the sustainable fashion sector is the development of emotion-aware AI—systems designed to recognize and respond to users' emotional states. These systems utilize a combination of computer vision, natural language processing, and behavioral data analysis to detect emotional cues from facial expressions, voice intonation, and digital interaction patterns.

In fashion applications, emotion-aware AI can serve as a strategic tool to guide more responsible consumer behavior. For instance, when the system detects emotional states such as stress, sadness, or impulsivity, it can dynamically alter the digital content presented to users. Rather than promoting impulsive purchases through discount-driven campaigns, the system may instead present information on the environmental impact of overconsumption, tips for garment maintenance, or messages encouraging repair and reuse practices (Rohde et al., 2024)

This ethically driven approach reduces the likelihood of unsustainable consumption and fosters a more conscientious relationship between brands and consumers. It positions the consumer not merely as a transactional entity, but as an individual whose emotional and psychological contexts are acknowledged and respected. Over time, such interactions may reinforce long-term brand loyalty and contribute to broader sustainability goals..

Figure 4. The AI system analyzes the user's facial expressions through the device's camera and identifies the user's mood.

Figure 4 shows how the AI system utilizes facial expression analysis via the user's device camera to detect emotional states, enabling real-time content adjustments to encourage more mindful fashion consumption.

AI Sustainability Scores

To promote more responsible consumer behavior, one emerging innovation in sustainable fashion is the development of artificial intelligence-based sustainability assessment systems, known as AI Sustainability Scores. These systems aim to provide consumers with transparent, standardized, and easily interpretable information regarding the environmental and ethical impacts of fashion products—areas that are often opaque and inaccessible to the average buyer.

The system functions by aggregating data across the entire product lifecycle, including raw material sourcing, manufacturing processes, logistics, usage, and end-of-life recycling. AI algorithms then analyze this data using predefined quantitative indicators such as carbon emissions, water consumption, proportion of recycled content, and ethical labor conditions in factories. The output is a sustainability score, visually presented through digital labels in physical stores or within online shopping interfaces, enabling users to compare products not merely by price or aesthetics but also by their environmental impact (Rohde et al., 2024).

The implementation of such scoring mechanisms empowers consumers to align their purchasing decisions with personal ethical and ecological values. Simultaneously, it places pressure on manufacturers and brands to increase transparency and invest in sustainability improvements throughout their operations. Over time, AI Sustainability Scores have the potential to become a standardized metric across the fashion industry, reinforcing corporate accountability and driving systemic change. Table 10 shows the Examples of Product Sustainability Assessments.

Table 10. Examples of Product Sustainability Assessments

Product Name	Carbon Footprint	Water Usage	Recycled Materials	Sustainability Score
Jacket A (Brand X)	Low	Medium	80%	8.5 / 10
Jacket B (Brand Y)	High	High	10%	4.2 / 10

Explanation: Jacket A shows higher sustainability performance because it uses large amounts of recycled materials and has a low carbon footprint. In contrast, Jacket B although visually similar, has a much greater environmental impact, reflected in its low score.

Collaborative Filtering for Sustainability

One of the most common approaches in recommendation systems is the collaborative filtering technique, which essentially works by analyzing similar user behavior patterns. In the context of sustainable fashion, this technique can be evolved to consider not only the similarities in taste in style or shopping habits, but also the sustainability values embraced by the user.

The AI system will identify users who tend to choose products with a low ecological footprint, organic ingredients, or from producers who have ethical commitments. Through analysis of their purchase history and interactions, the system can provide recommendations to other users who show similar sustainability preferences. The result is a form of "peer powered sustainability recommendation", where users feel that the recommendations they receive are not only personally relevant, but also reflect the norms and values of a highly ecologically conscious community

This approach has several positive impacts. First, it reinforces a sense of community in the conscious consumption ecosystem, which is essential to collectively shaping behavior change. Second, by embedding a sustainability dimension into the algorithm, collaborative filtering no longer simply optimizes sales or instant gratification, but also directs users towards more responsible choices. Third, these systems can help reduce greenwashing, as recommended products are the result of real preferences from communities that prioritize sustainability, not just based on marketing claims.

Figure 5. AI recommends products based on the similar behavior and sustainability values of other users, forming collectively conscious consumption patterns

Figure 5 illustrates how the AI system recommends fashion products by analyzing user behavior patterns and shared sustainability values, thereby fostering a peer-driven, ecologically conscious consumption ecosystem.

Voice Activated Green Shopping Assistants

Advances in speech recognition and natural language processing (NLP) have enabled the emergence of voice-based shopping assistants tailored to sustainable consumption. These systems cater to the increasing need for convenience and accessibility in the digital shopping experience (P. Li et al., 2023).

Designed for continuous, hands-free interaction, these assistants allow users to vocalize their preferences—such as product type, budget, or sustainability value—and instantly receive filtered recommendations powered by integrated environmental data. This feature is especially beneficial for users with visual impairments, mobility challenges, or multitasking lifestyles.

Beyond basic functionality, these AI systems serve an educational role. They provide real-time explanations of product sustainability attributes, including carbon footprint, raw material status, or supply chain transparency. The assistants also offer personalized reminders and green recommendations, supporting environmentally conscious habits such as reducing frequency of purchases or prioritizing recycled goods.

For instance, a user may request: *"Find an eco-friendly shirt under 300 thousand rupiah."* The assistant could reply: *"I found three options from local brands with sustainability scores above 8. Would you like to hear their environmental impact?"*

By integrating sustainability into intuitive voice interfaces, these systems foster informed and ethical consumption patterns while maintaining ease of use (Mari et al., 2020).

CONCLUSION

Intelligent systems, particularly AI-enabled technologies, offer significant potential to support sustainable fashion consumption by empowering climate-conscious consumers and enhancing transparency across the fashion ecosystem. Digital tools that reduce information asymmetry, enable ethical personalization, and provide verifiable sustainability insights can encourage more reflective consumption patterns and strengthen trust between consumers and brands. When aligned with sustainability objectives, these systems help shift fashion consumption away from volume-driven models toward longer product lifecycles and more responsible purchasing behavior.

At the same time, the integration of AI into sustainable fashion raises critical ethical and governance challenges. Algorithmic bias, data privacy risks, greenwashing, and unequal access to advanced technologies may undermine sustainability goals if not properly addressed. Responsible adoption therefore requires transparent system design, human oversight, and inclusive governance frameworks that prioritize consumer autonomy and social accountability. Sustainable transformation in fashion depends not only on technological innovation, but on the balanced integration of intelligent systems, empowered consumers, and ethical responsibility.

REFERENCES

Adamkiewicz, J., Kochańska, E., Adamkiewicz, I., & Łukasik, R. M. (2022a). Greenwashing and sustainable fashion industry. *Current Opinion in Green and Sustainable Chemistry*, *38*, 100710. DOI: 10.1016/j.cogsc.2022.100710

Adamkiewicz, J., Kochańska, E., Adamkiewicz, I., & Łukasik, R. M. (2022b). Greenwashing and sustainable fashion industry. *Current Opinion in Green and Sustainable Chemistry*, *38*, 100710. DOI: 10.1016/j.cogsc.2022.100710

Akram, S. V., Malik, P. K., Singh, R., Gehlot, A., Juyal, A., Ghafoor, K. Z., & Shrestha, S. (2022). Implementation of Digitalized Technologies for Fashion Industry 4.0: Opportunities and Challenges. *Scientific Programming*, *2022*, 1–17. DOI: 10.1155/2022/7523246

Alabaddi, Z., Obidat, A., & Alziyadat, Z. (2023). Exploring the effect of blockchain technology on supply chain resilience and transparency: Evidence from the healthcare industry. *Uncertain Supply Chain Management*, *11*(2), 787–798. DOI: 10.5267/j.uscm.2023.1.001

Bailey, K., Basu, A., & Sharma, S. (2022a). The Environmental Impacts of Fast Fashion on Water Quality: A Systematic Review. *Water (Basel)*, *14*(7), 1073. DOI: 10.3390/w14071073

Bailey, K., Basu, A., & Sharma, S. (2022b). The Environmental Impacts of Fast Fashion on Water Quality: A Systematic Review. *Water (Basel)*, *14*(7), 1073. DOI: 10.3390/w14071073

Bankins, S., & Formosa, P. (2023). The Ethical Implications of Artificial Intelligence (AI) For Meaningful Work. *Journal of Business Ethics*, *185*(4), 725–740. DOI: 10.1007/s10551-023-05339-7

Basirulla, M. D., & Tasnim, F. (2023). Nature of Human Rights Violation on Female Garments Workers in Bangladesh. *Khazanah Hukum*, *5*(1), 1–17. DOI: 10.15575/kh.v5i1.22713

Berestova, A., Kim, D.-Y., & Kim, S.-Y. (2022). Consumers' Active Reaction to Brands Taking Stands on Public Issues on Twitter. *Sustainability (Basel)*, *14*(1), 567. DOI: 10.3390/su14010567

Bulchand-Gidumal, J., William Secin, E., O'Connor, P., & Buhalis, D. (2024). Artificial intelligence's impact on hospitality and tourism marketing: Exploring key themes and addressing challenges. *Current Issues in Tourism*, *27*(14), 2345–2362. DOI: 10.1080/13683500.2023.2229480

Canhoto, A. I., Keegan, B. J., & Ryzhikh, M. (2024a). Snakes and Ladders: Unpacking the Personalisation-Privacy Paradox in the Context of AI-Enabled Personalisation in the Physical Retail Environment. *Information Systems Frontiers*, *26*(3), 1005–1024. DOI: 10.1007/s10796-023-10369-7 PMID: 36684411

Canhoto, A. I., Keegan, B. J., & Ryzhikh, M. (2024b). Snakes and Ladders: Unpacking the Personalisation-Privacy Paradox in the Context of AI-Enabled Personalisation in the Physical Retail Environment. *Information Systems Frontiers*, *26*(3), 1005–1024. DOI: 10.1007/s10796-023-10369-7 PMID: 36684411

Chen, L., Chen, P., & Lin, Z. (2020). Artificial Intelligence in Education: A Review. *IEEE Access : Practical Innovations, Open Solutions*, *8*, 75264–75278. DOI: 10.1109/ACCESS.2020.2988510

Chen, X., Wang, X., & Qu, Y. (2023). Constructing Ethical AI Based on the "Human-in-the-Loop" System. *Systems*, *11*(11), 548. DOI: 10.3390/systems11110548

Das, S., Barve, A., Sahu, N. C., & Muduli, K. (2023). Enabling artificial intelligence for sustainable food grain supply chains: An agri 5.0 and circular economy perspective. *Operations Management Research : Advancing Practice Through Research*, *16*(4), 2104–2124. DOI: 10.1007/s12063-023-00390-z

Davenport, T., Guha, A., Grewal, D., & Bressgott, T. (2020). How artificial intelligence will change the future of marketing. *Journal of the Academy of Marketing Science*, *48*(1), 24–42. DOI: 10.1007/s11747-019-00696-0

de Freitas Netto, S. V., Sobral, M. F. F., Ribeiro, A. R. B., & Soares, G. R. (2020). Concepts and forms of greenwashing: A systematic review. *Environmental Sciences Europe*, *32*(1), 19. DOI: 10.1186/s12302-020-0300-3

de Wagenaar, D., Galama, J., & Sijtsema, S. J. (2022). Exploring Worldwide Wardrobes to Support Reuse in Consumers' Clothing Systems. *Sustainability (Basel)*, *14*(1), 487. DOI: 10.3390/su14010487

Deng, M., Liu, Y., & Chen, L. (2023). AI-driven innovation in ethnic clothing design: An intersection of machine learning and cultural heritage. *Electronic Research Archive*, *31*(9), 5793–5814. DOI: 10.3934/era.2023295

Devakunchari, R., & Valliyammai, C. (2016). Big Social Data Analytics: Opportunities, Challenges and Implications on Society. Online Journal of Communication and Media Technologies, 6(September 2016-Special Issue), 17–32. DOI: 10.30935/ojcmt/5659

Dogruel, L., Facciorusso, D., & Stark, B. (2022). 'I'm still the master of the machine.' Internet users' awareness of algorithmic decision-making and their perception of its effect on their autonomy. *Information Communication and Society*, *25*(9), 1311–1332. DOI: 10.1080/1369118X.2020.1863999

Dwivedi, Y. K., Sharma, A., Rana, N. P., Giannakis, M., Goel, P., & Dutot, V. (2023). Evolution of artificial intelligence research in Technological Forecasting and Social Change: Research topics, trends, and future directions. *Technological Forecasting and Social Change*, *192*, 122579. DOI: 10.1016/j.techfore.2023.122579

Edizel, B., Bonchi, F., Hajian, S., Panisson, A., & Tassa, T. (2020). FaiRecSys: Mitigating algorithmic bias in recommender systems. *International Journal of Data Science and Analytics*, *9*(2), 197–213. DOI: 10.1007/s41060-019-00181-5

Eitel-Porter, R. (2021). Beyond the promise: Implementing ethical AI. *AI and Ethics*, *1*(1), 73–80. DOI: 10.1007/s43681-020-00011-6

Farzin, M., Shababi, H., Shirchi Sasi, G., Sadeghi, M., & Makvandi, R. (2023). The determinants of eco-fashion purchase intention and willingness to pay. *Spanish Journal of Marketing - ESIC*, *27*(3), 348–366. DOI: 10.1108/SJME-07-2022-0158

Gao, B., Wang, Y., Xie, H., Hu, Y., & Hu, Y. (2023). Artificial Intelligence in Advertising: Advancements, Challenges, and Ethical Considerations in Targeting, Personalization, Content Creation, and Ad Optimization. *SAGE Open*, *13*(4), 21582440231210759. Advance online publication. DOI: 10.1177/21582440231210759

Gökbunar, H. B., & Soylu, B. (2024). *Blockchain Enabled Lateral Transshipment System for the Redistribution of Unsold Textile Products in a Circular Economy*., DOI: 10.1007/978-981-99-6062-0_58

Gomes de Oliveira, L., Miranda, F. G., & de Paula Dias, M. A. (2022). Sustainable practices in slow and fast fashion stores: What does the customer perceive? *Cleaner Engineering and Technology*, *6*, 100413. DOI: 10.1016/j.clet.2022.100413

Hadizadeh Hafshejani, E., TaheriNejad, N., Rabbani, R., Azizi, Z., Mohin, S., Fotowat-Ahmady, A., & Mirabbasi, S. (2022). Self-Aware Data Processing for Power Saving in Resource-Constrained IoT Cyber-Physical Systems. *IEEE Sensors Journal*, *22*(4), 3648–3659. DOI: 10.1109/JSEN.2021.3133405

Han, H., Shiwakoti, R. K., Jarvis, R., Mordi, C., & Botchie, D. (2023). Accounting and auditing with blockchain technology and artificial Intelligence: A literature review. *International Journal of Accounting Information Systems*, *48*, 100598. DOI: 10.1016/j.accinf.2022.100598

Heilinger, J.-C. (2022). The Ethics of AI Ethics. A Constructive Critique. *Philosophy & Technology*, *35*(3), 61. DOI: 10.1007/s13347-022-00557-9

Huang, M.-H., & Rust, R. T. (2021). A strategic framework for artificial intelligence in marketing. *Journal of the Academy of Marketing Science*, *49*(1), 30–50. DOI: 10.1007/s11747-020-00749-9

Iranmanesh, M., Maroufkhani, P., Asadi, S., Ghobakhloo, M., Dwivedi, Y. K., & Tseng, M.-L. (2023). Effects of supply chain transparency, alignment, adaptability, and agility on blockchain adoption in supply chain among SMEs. *Computers & Industrial Engineering*, *176*, 108931. DOI: 10.1016/j.cie.2022.108931

Itani, O. S., Loureiro, S. M. C., & Ramadan, Z. (2023). Engaging with omnichannel brands: The role of consumer empowerment. *International Journal of Retail & Distribution Management*, *51*(2), 238–261. DOI: 10.1108/IJRDM-02-2022-0044

Jöhnk, J., Weißert, M., & Wyrtki, K. (2021). Ready or Not, AI Comes— An Interview Study of Organizational AI Readiness Factors. *Business & Information Systems Engineering*, *63*(1), 5–20. DOI: 10.1007/s12599-020-00676-7

Kaliszewicz, A., Panteleeva, N., Karaban, K., Runka, T., Winczek, M., Beck, E., Poniatowska, A., Olejniczak, I., Boniecki, P., Golovanova, E. V., & Romanowski, J. (2023). First Evidence of Microplastic Occurrence in the Marine and Freshwater Environments in a Remote Polar Region of the Kola Peninsula and a Correlation with Human Presence. *Biology (Basel)*, *12*(2), 259. DOI: 10.3390/biology12020259 PMID: 36829537

Kang, H., Park, S., Lee, B., Ahn, J., & Kim, S. (2021). Impact of Chitosan Pretreatment to Reduce Microfibers Released from Synthetic Garments during Laundering. *Water (Basel)*, *13*(18), 2480. DOI: 10.3390/w13182480

Karadayi-Usta, S. (2024). Role of artificial intelligence and augmented reality in fashion industry from consumer perspective: Sustainability through waste and return mitigation. *Engineering Applications of Artificial Intelligence*, *133*, 108114. DOI: 10.1016/j.engappai.2024.108114

Kozyreva, A., Lorenz-Spreen, P., Hertwig, R., Lewandowsky, S., & Herzog, S. M. (2021). Public attitudes towards algorithmic personalization and use of personal data online: Evidence from Germany, Great Britain, and the United States. *Humanities & Social Sciences Communications*, *8*(1), 117. DOI: 10.1057/s41599-021-00787-w

Kumar, R., Singh, R., & Dwivedi, Y. K. (2020). Application of industry 4.0 technologies in SMEs for ethical and sustainable operations: Analysis of challenges. *Journal of Cleaner Production*, *275*, 124063. DOI: 10.1016/j.jclepro.2020.124063 PMID: 32921931

Leal Filho, W., Perry, P., Heim, H., Dinis, M. A. P., Moda, H., Ebhuoma, E., & Paço, A. (2022). An overview of the contribution of the textiles sector to climate change. *Frontiers in Environmental Science*, *10*, 973102. Advance online publication. DOI: 10.3389/fenvs.2022.973102

Li, P., Wu, C., & Spence, C. (2023). Comparing the influence of visual information and the perceived intelligence of voice assistants when shopping for sustainable clothing online. *Humanities & Social Sciences Communications*, *10*(1), 727. DOI: 10.1057/s41599-023-02244-2

Li, Z., Li, H., & Wang, S. (2022). How Multidimensional Digital Empowerment Affects Technology Innovation Performance: The Moderating Effect of Adaptability to Technology Embedding. *Sustainability (Basel)*, *14*(23), 15916. DOI: 10.3390/su142315916

Lingling, L., & Ye, L. (2023). The impact of digital empowerment on open innovation performance of enterprises from the perspective of SOR. *Frontiers in Psychology*, *14*, 1109149. Advance online publication. DOI: 10.3389/fpsyg.2023.1109149 PMID: 36844287

Long, X., & Nasiry, J. (2022). Sustainability in the Fast Fashion Industry. *Manufacturing & Service Operations Management*, *24*(3), 1276–1293. DOI: 10.1287/msom.2021.1054

Mądra-Sawicka, M., Nord, J. H., Paliszkiewicz, J., & Lee, T.-R. (2020). Digital Media: Empowerment and Equality. *Information (Basel)*, *11*(4), 225. DOI: 10.3390/info11040225

Mahmood, M. S., Ruma, N. H., Ahmed, T., & Nagai, Y. (2021). Exploring Suppliers' Approaches toward Workplace Safety Compliance in the Global Garment Sector: From Bangladesh Perspective. *Social Sciences (Basel, Switzerland)*, *10*(3), 90. DOI: 10.3390/socsci10030090

Mahmoud, A. B., Hack-Polay, D., Grigoriou, N., Mohr, I., & Fuxman, L. (2021). A generational investigation and sentiment and emotion analyses of female fashion brand users on Instagram in Sub-Saharan Africa. *Journal of Brand Management*, *28*(5), 526–544. DOI: 10.1057/s41262-021-00244-8

Mari, A., Mandelli, A., & Algesheimer, R. (2020). *The Evolution of Marketing in the Context of Voice Commerce: A Managerial Perspective.*, DOI: 10.1007/978-3-030-50341-3_32

Marti, P. (2024). WEAVING FASHION WITH A.I. *Fashion Highlight*, *2*(2), 52–58. DOI: 10.36253/fh-2500

Mattis, N., Masur, P., Möller, J., & van Atteveldt, W. (2024a). Nudging towards news diversity: A theoretical framework for facilitating diverse news consumption through recommender design. *New Media & Society*, *26*(7), 3681–3706. DOI: 10.1177/14614448221104413

Mattis, N., Masur, P., Möller, J., & van Atteveldt, W. (2024b). Nudging towards news diversity: A theoretical framework for facilitating diverse news consumption through recommender design. *New Media & Society*, *26*(7), 3681–3706. DOI: 10.1177/14614448221104413

Methnani, L., Aler Tubella, A., Dignum, V., & Theodorou, A. (2021). Let Me Take Over: Variable Autonomy for Meaningful Human Control. *Frontiers in Artificial Intelligence*, *4*, 737072. Advance online publication. DOI: 10.3389/frai.2021.737072 PMID: 34595471

Milano, S., Taddeo, M., & Floridi, L. (2020). Recommender systems and their ethical challenges. *AI & Society*, *35*(4), 957–967. DOI: 10.1007/s00146-020-00950-y

Mitchell, J. R., Mitchell, R. K., Hunt, R. A., Townsend, D. M., & Lee, J. H. (2022). Stakeholder Engagement, Knowledge Problems and Ethical Challenges. *Journal of Business Ethics*, *175*(1), 75–94. DOI: 10.1007/s10551-020-04550-0

Mohiuddin Babu, M., Akter, S., Rahman, M., Billah, M. M., & Hack-Polay, D. (2024). The role of artificial intelligence in shaping the future of Agile fashion industry. *Production Planning and Control*, *35*(15), 2084–2098. DOI: 10.1080/09537287.2022.2060858

Morley, J., Kinsey, L., Elhalal, A., Garcia, F., Ziosi, M., & Floridi, L. (2023). Operationalising AI ethics: Barriers, enablers and next steps. *AI & Society*, *38*(1), 411–423. DOI: 10.1007/s00146-021-01308-8

Mylrea, M., & Robinson, N. (2023). Artificial Intelligence (AI) Trust Framework and Maturity Model: Applying an Entropy Lens to Improve Security, Privacy, and Ethical AI. *Entropy (Basel, Switzerland)*, *25*(10), 1429. DOI: 10.3390/e25101429 PMID: 37895550

Onitiu, D. (2022). Algorithmic abstractions of 'fashion identity' and the role of privacy with regard to algorithmic personalisation systems in the fashion domain. *AI & Society*, *37*(4), 1749–1758. DOI: 10.1007/s00146-021-01235-8

Peters, D., Vold, K., Robinson, D., & Calvo, R. A. (2020). Responsible AI—Two Frameworks for Ethical Design Practice. *IEEE Transactions on Technology and Society*, *1*(1), 34–47. DOI: 10.1109/TTS.2020.2974991

Prikshat, V., Patel, P., Varma, A., & Ishizaka, A. (2022). A multi-stakeholder ethical framework for AI-augmented HRM. *International Journal of Manpower*, *43*(1), 226–250. DOI: 10.1108/IJM-03-2021-0118

Rafieian, O., & Yoganarasimhan, H. (2022a). AI and Personalization. SSRN Electronic Journal. DOI: 10.2139/ssrn.4123356

Rafieian, O., & Yoganarasimhan, H. (2022b). AI and Personalization. SSRN Electronic Journal. DOI: 10.2139/ssrn.4123356

Rathore, B. (2023). Beyond Trends: Shaping the Future of Fashion Marketing with AI, Sustainability and Machine Learning. Eduzone : International Peer Reviewed/ Refereed Academic Multidisciplinary Journal, 06(02), 16–24. DOI: 10.56614/ eiprmj.v6i2y17.341

Ray, S., & Nayak, L. (2023). Marketing Sustainable Fashion: Trends and Future Directions. *Sustainability (Basel)*, *15*(7), 6202. DOI: 10.3390/su15076202

Rizkiatami, A., Masnita, Y., & Kurniawati, K. (2023). Embracing Sustainability in Purchase Behavior Using the Theory of Planned Behavior. *MIX: JURNAL ILMIAH MANAJEMEN*, *13*(1), 15. DOI: 10.22441/jurnal_mix.2023.v13i1.002

Rodrigues Schon, V., & Colombi, C. (2023). Ethical Implications in AI-Powered Trend Research Platforms. *Fashion Highlight*, *1*(1), 50–59. DOI: 10.36253/fh-2261

Rohde, F., Wagner, J., Meyer, A., Reinhard, P., Voss, M., Petschow, U., & Mollen, A. (2024). Broadening the perspective for sustainable artificial intelligence: Sustainability criteria and indicators for Artificial Intelligence systems. *Current Opinion in Environmental Sustainability*, *66*, 101411. DOI: 10.1016/j.cosust.2023.101411

Ruiz-Real, J. L., Uribe-Toril, J., Torres, J. A., & De Pablo, J. (2020). ARTIFICIAL INTELLIGENCE IN BUSINESS AND ECONOMICS RESEARCH: TRENDS AND FUTURE. *Journal of Business Economics and Management*, *22*(1), 98–117. DOI: 10.3846/jbem.2020.13641

Ryan, M. (2023). The social and ethical impacts of artificial intelligence in agriculture: Mapping the agricultural AI literature. *AI & Society*, *38*(6), 2473–2485. DOI: 10.1007/s00146-021-01377-9

Rydenfelt, H., Haapanen, L., Haapoja, J., & Lehtiniemi, T. (2024). Personalisation in Journalism: Ethical insights and blindspots in Finnish legacy media. *Journalism*, *25*(2), 313–333. DOI: 10.1177/14648849221138424

Schmauder, C., Karpus, J., Moll, M., Bahrami, B., & Deroy, O. (2023). Algorithmic Nudging: The Need for an Interdisciplinary Oversight. *Topoi*, *42*(3), 799–807. DOI: 10.1007/s11245-023-09907-4

Schweiger, G., Eckerstorfer, L. V., Hafner, I., Fleischhacker, A., Radl, J., Glock, B., Wastian, M., Rößler, M., Lettner, G., Popper, N., & Corcoran, K. (2020). Active consumer participation in smart energy systems. *Energy and Building*, *227*, 110359. DOI: 10.1016/j.enbuild.2020.110359

Sharma, M., Shail, H., Painuly, P. K., & Kumar, A. V. S. (2023). *AI-Powered Technologies Used in Online Fashion Retail for Sustainable Business*., DOI: 10.4018/979-8-3693-0019-0.ch028

Simon, J., Wong, P.-H., & Rieder, G. (2020). Algorithmic bias and the Value Sensitive Design approach. *Internet Policy Review*, *9*(4). Advance online publication. DOI: 10.14763/2020.4.1534

Sunny, J., Undralla, N., & Madhusudanan Pillai, V. (2020). Supply chain transparency through blockchain-based traceability: An overview with demonstration. *Computers & Industrial Engineering*, *150*, 106895. DOI: 10.1016/j.cie.2020.106895

Taherdoost, H. (2022). A Critical Review of Blockchain Acceptance Models—Blockchain Technology Adoption Frameworks and Applications. *Computers*, *11*(2), 24. DOI: 10.3390/computers11020024

Tajurahim, N. N. S., Abu Bakar, E., Md Jusoh, Z., Ahmad, S., & Muhammad Arif, A. M. (2020). The effect of intensity of consumer education, self-efficacy, personality traits and social media on consumer empowerment. *International Journal of Consumer Studies*, *44*(6), 511–520. DOI: 10.1111/ijcs.12585

Thiebes, S., Lins, S., & Sunyaev, A. (2021). Trustworthy artificial intelligence. *Electronic Markets*, *31*(2), 447–464. DOI: 10.1007/s12525-020-00441-4

Vladimirova, K., Henninger, C. E., Alosaimi, S. I., Brydges, T., Choopani, H., Hanlon, M., Iran, S., McCormick, H., & Zhou, S. (2024). Exploring the influence of social media on sustainable fashion consumption: A systematic literature review and future research agenda. *Journal of Global Fashion Marketing*, *15*(2), 181–202. DOI: 10.1080/20932685.2023.2237978

Vu, N., Ghadge, A., & Bourlakis, M. (2023). Blockchain adoption in food supply chains: A review and implementation framework. *Production Planning and Control*, *34*(6), 506–523. DOI: 10.1080/09537287.2021.1939902

Wang, R., Bush-Evans, R., Arden-Close, E., Bolat, E., McAlaney, J., Hodge, S., Thomas, S., & Phalp, K. (2023). Transparency in persuasive technology, immersive technology, and online marketing: Facilitating users' informed decision making and practical implications. *Computers in Human Behavior*, *139*, 107545. DOI: 10.1016/j.chb.2022.107545

Xu, P., Lee, J., Barth, J. R., & Richey, R. G. (2021). Blockchain as supply chain technology: Considering transparency and security. *International Journal of Physical Distribution & Logistics Management*, *51*(3), 305–324. DOI: 10.1108/IJPDLM-08-2019-0234

Yang, X., Weber, A., & Grimm, A.-K. (2022). The effects of green consumer empowerment in advertising on corporate evaluations and purchase intention: The case of organic food. *Review of Managerial Science*, *16*(6), 1877–1909. DOI: 10.1007/s11846-021-00495-4

Chapter 3
Algorithmic Nudging for Eco-Friendly Fashion:
A Framework for Ethical AI Interventions

Muhammad Usman Tariq
http://orcid.org/0000-0002-7605-3040
Abu Dhabi University, UAE & University College Cork, Ireland

ABSTRACT

This chapter examines how algorithmic nudging may inspire environmentally friendly decisions within the fashion sector, particularly if it's conducted in ethical and sustainable manners. It applies concepts from behavioral economics, consumer psychology, and AI ethics to develop a comprehensive framework for designing, testing, and applying AI-driven nudges on internet shopping websites. The chapter outlines several nudges, including default options, social proof, visual cues, and immediate feedback, and discusses them theoretically as well as in real-world examples. It also explores issues like greenwashing, trust, and discriminatory AI bias and calls for strong rules, transparency, and fairness. The article suggests potential future steps such as the use of generative AI, emotion detection technology, and industry standardization to support ethical innovation. It argues that if used in a neutral and reflected way, algorithmic nudging could be a powerful tool for influencing green fashion choices without unconstraining user liberty or trust.

INTRODUCTION

Fashion has always been perceived as a place where creative forces, self-expression, and expressing oneself are an option. However, in recent decades, it has also begun

DOI: 10.4018/979-8-3373-5525-2.ch003

to be associated with aspects such as damaging the environment, unfair treatment of labor, and stimulating individuals to purchase and discard clothes too fast. The role of fast fashion is significant because it always requires new fashion and manages to create garments in a short time. This has created a culture where individuals tend to purchase garments and dispose of them in a very short period of time. Cheap costs, numerous offers, and fluctuating trends lure people into purchasing more than they require, generating excessive waste. In the last 20 years, the amount of clothing bought has doubled, but people are wearing it less frequently than before. The impact of these actions on the environment is massive: the industry not only generates a substantial amount of greenhouse gases but also causes water pollution and is a source of waste because of clothing that goes to waste. Workers, especially those in poor working conditions, have been exploited due to the demand to manufacture more apparel at a low cost. The way clothes are produced and the way people behave and feel when shopping are not the only causes of this phenomenon. Such behaviors are difficult to change; however, technological solutions, particularly artificial intelligence, can provide new solutions. Artificial intelligence is already being experienced across much of life, from how people shop, communicate, and make purchasing decisions. Brands and web-based retailers leverage AI to understand what individuals want, predict what can be done and what cannot be done in terms of fashion trends, improve how items are made and delivered, and enhance the overall purchasing experience.

Social influence, such as demonstrating the product's broad appeal among environmentally conscious people or using testimonials from sustainable influencers, can also be added. Such nudges may create a sense of community and shared values and make the sustainable choice not just easier but also more socially beneficial. Over time, these nudges may alter what people consider "normal" and can push fashion forward toward more intelligent and responsible consumption patterns. Of course, to the degree algorithmic nudging works at all, it will depend on how well it has been designed and how well it has been tracked over time. Adopting nudges and hoping for the best is not going to cut it; we need to pay attention to how well they work in real life and tweak them accordingly. You can observe what is effective and what is not by examining factors such as the frequency of service use, how often they purchase something, or their evolution. You should also listen to what people say about you. This prevents nudges from being intrusive or irritating. Being honest and transparent is very significant: people should realize that they are being nudged and have the freedom to change how they are presented with content or even refuse to see it in the first place. With most fashion choices made online, such tools have the potential to turn sustainable options into a default and not an exception. The key will be to use these tools well, with care, and for the sake of a better world. As the fashion world keeps changing, the blending of AI with a focus on sustainability could be the secret to achieving real and practical change that respects individuals' freedom of choice and the shared responsibility we have.

BACKGROUND AND THEORETICAL FOUNDATIONS

Human behavior is typically determined not by hard thinking but by the small factors around us; this is what lies at the heart of behavioral economics. In contrast to traditional economics, which assumes that people always act in their best interests with all the correct information, behavioral economics contends that individuals are generally influenced by factors such as emotions, mental heuristics, and the presentation of alternatives. This has led to something called choice architecture, which is the design of environments or settings to influence people to make good choices without being coercive (Alves et al., 2024). Choice architecture is even more powerful in digital environments. Online stores, especially fashion stores, are carefully designed settings where tiny details, from the positioning of items on the page to the color of buttons, can be used to influence what people purchase. These choices are made after a lot of data about what individuals do. They decide what gets shown first, how things are presented, and what gets set as defaults. Responsible ethical AI for nudging also requires responsible systems. Designers are already responsible for the safety of what they produce; therefore, people who create digital systems must be responsible for the cognitive and behavioral effects of their AI. There must be clear standards to ensure that nudges are equitable and transparent, and third-party organizations can ensure that these standards are applied. Users also need to be able to complain, and feedback should be used to improve things. Moreover, collaboration is required. Ethical AI nudging cannot be tackled by computer experts alone. People from other fields, such as psychology, ethics, and sociology, as well as affected communities, need to be part of the discussion. Thus, digital nudges can perform not only business functions, but also promote values such as fairness, sustainability, and consumer empowerment (Tariq, 2025; Suroto, 2025).

Understanding why and how individuals make green choices is crucial for effective nudging. Psychological studies show that environmental concern per se is not enough to change people's conduct. People claim to support sustainability but continue to make decisions that contradict their claims. This disparity between what people intend to do and what they actually do is influenced by several mental and social factors (Antil et al., 2022). For instance, as someone is about to complete a purchase, informing them about the environmental impact of their actions and providing more sustainable options may cause them to reconsider their choices. AI can assist in scheduling nudges based on consumer behavior. If a person tends to browse but does not make a purchase late at night, sending them a subtle reminder or providing an incentive related to sustainability in the morning may work better. Holidays, events, and personal occasions, such as birthdays, can be used to make sustainability messages appealing. Trust is necessary for this type of nudge to be effective. If users do not trust the platform or believe that the nudges are pushing something down their throats for the good of the company, they will react negatively. Honesty, consistency, and transparency are ways to build trust. Fashion companies that use an open definition of how they make products last and provide transparent information on the origin of their products are more likely to be trusted. AI can help make nudges more evidence-based and data-driven. For example, if something is billed as "sustainable," it should be supported by real certifications or clear impact reports, not false promises. At this time, a trusted website is more than a place to shop; it can be a community where people can make choices that are consistent with their values (Apriliani, 2025). By incorporating the principles of behavioral economics, ethical AI, and psychology, digital nudges can have a significant impact. They can Over influence behavior that is both effective and respectful of people's ability to make their own choices

TYPOLOGY OF ALGORITHMIC NUDGES IN FASHION RETAIL

As objects of online shopping, in which apps and websites assist one in picking clothes, how applications and sites persuade one to acquire them has become clever. These websites and applications subtly and intelligently change their form and behavior to direct users in each direction. These nudges are referred to as algorithmic nudges, and they utilize practices in human behavior and machine learning to redirect or force other individuals in specific directions. These nudges can be quite helpful for sustainable buying (Bicchieri & Dimant, 2022). They can easily nudge consumers toward more sustainable alternatives, making default fast fashion habits more considerate. Some of the most effective ways to apply these nudges involve defaulting to eco-friendly products, modeling others' behavior, employing visual cues, and providing timely cues, such as demonstrating how much carbon a product consumes. Figure 1 provides an overview of the four primary nudge types in fashion e-commerce, linking theory to application.

Figure 1. Typology of Algorithmic Nudges for Sustainable Fashion

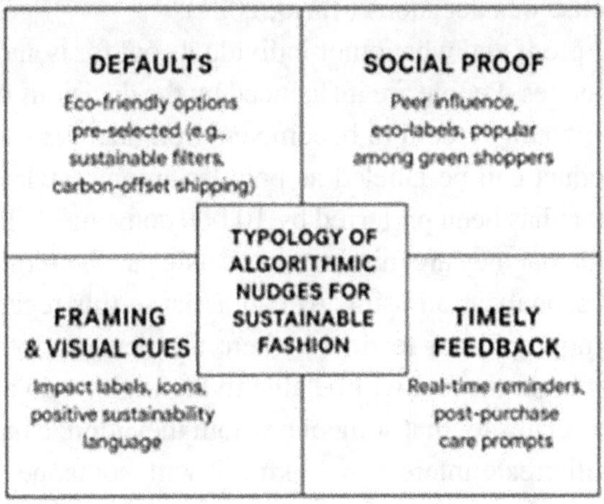

Using the default option is probably one of the most critical and powerful nudges. Most people tend to go along with the first option they come across without pausing to think about it. In fashion online shopping, highlighting environmentally friendly or fairly made goods as the initial choice when looking at a product or searching for an item can change the shopping experience. For example, if you visit a product page, the site can show sustainable items first instead of other options (Caraban et al., 2019). This does not eliminate the ability to choose less sustainable items but changes the first options that one sees. If this happens repeatedly, it causes individuals to start thinking of green shopping as the norm. Retailers can also make default options for products using recycled content, less harmful dyes, or products that support circular economies. Defaults' power is that they are not pushy, but they lead the way of least resistance to being the optimal choice, and therefore, more sustainable options are being chosen.

The fact that AI can make default options more personalized makes them even better. Machine learning considers what people like and do to decide on the optimal alternatives among others. For example, when an individual enjoys watching or purchasing environmentally friendly clothes, the system may offer solutions in the future (Carlson et al., 2024). Although the default nudges may be unnoticed by those who did not pay much attention to sustainability in the first place, these products will be continuously promoted and even become more attractive. This is just a question of ensuring that sustainability becomes the normal and ordinary aspect of everyday shopping, as opposed to an extension. There are other applications of defaults besides product selection. Customers can be given the option of carbon offsets or recyclable packaging at the checkout stage, or slower yet eco-friendlier delivery. All of this needs to be placed in the shopping flow so that people can make environmentally conscious decisions (Tariq, 2025).

Exposing social proof and what other individuals opt for is another effective alternative to using nudges. People are influenced by the decisions of others, and this can be utilized to encourage them to become environmentalists in their shopping. For example, a product can be labeled as popular among environmentally aware consumers or one that has been preferred by 10,000 consumers. The markings also make consumers feel that they are missing out on using such products, which makes them feel better. Personalization using AI can assist in this regard. In the case of creating a user demographic or territory where the demand for environmentally friendly products is high, the site will be able to highlight it. In addition, showing it to people the user relates to, that someone whom they idolize has bought or liked a green product, will create interest by linking it with someone the user admires. Customer reviews and user content also influence social media. When others share photos or write about their green purchases, this generates feedback that encourages good choices. Platforms can use AI to present reviews that flag their environmental sustainability or contain feedback from people who are well documented to be nature-friendly. These nudges introduce credibility and shareability, especially when people notice others like them endorsing specific products. In social shopping environments where buying and sharing are combined, peer influence is even more substantial. Diets that promote sustainable trends within a user's community or network can stimulate interest and alter individuals' perceptions of what is trendy and acceptable. Gradually, sustainability is becoming not just a smart option but also something that is perceived as fashionable and desirable.

Framing also includes the types of products that are framed (Hertwig & Grune-Yanoff, 2017). Instead of being general, sustainable products can be framed using words that describe their benefits to the environment or people. For example, putting "Made with 90% less water," "Supports fair wages," or "Uses ocean-bound plastics" on the product makes it appealing. Not only do these words tell people something about the product, but they also make them feel good about purchasing it. AI can help write these types of messages to different people. For instance, an individual who cares about the environment will look at messages about a product's environmental benefits. In contrast, an individual who is concerned about employees will consider factors such as equal pay and a pleasant work environment. Framing also means how a sustainable product is better than a regular one. For example, showing that a product uses less water than usual helps people understand the benefits and makes them more inclined to buy it. Messages received in real time, as well as messages received at the right time, are another way to influence people using AI (Tariq, 2025). AI can send messages at the appropriate time. For example, at the very moment when a person is about to buy a shirt, a message can pop up stating,

"This shirt contains half the carbon footprint." The message comes at the right time when the person is ready to make a decision. These messages can also appear earlier in the buying process, such as when someone adds something to their cart, inviting them to "Want to go greener? Try this eco-alternative." The messages work best when they help people without being annoyed or putting people on a guilt trip.

Carbon footprint messages are becoming increasingly common in sustainable fashion. AI can also utilize various methods of sending messages to create a lasting impact. Consumers who watch green products will then receive emails with personalized suggestions and information about the company's eco-friendly activities. If the customer has not made a purchase, then a reminder will appear saying, "Still on the fence? This dress supports clean water projects." All these reminders repeat the same message and send the customer back to green options without bombarding them (Weinmann et al., 2016). Messages can even be sent timely after a buy to promote people to take care of, repair, or sell their products, which is a part of a more cyclical system of fashion. The combination of these AI technologies is a collection of practices through which online fashion retailers can guide individuals to make more sustainable decisions. Every strategy, default options, and social proof, making the product images too attractive, and communicating at the appropriate moment, is achieved through deciding easier and more inviting. AI assists in making these even more accommodating and individual to the point they become even more robust. However, the real power of these tools can alter not only behaviors but also the thinking processes of people regarding fashion. If sustainable options are taken as the norm and are preferred by others, they should be attractive, and the manner of attaining their endorsement through timely feedback should become a matter of routine. Such transformation is important because it can introduce tremendous reforms in an industry that must rethink its relationship with the world (Johnsen et al., 2024). These interventions do not provide an all-in-one remedy to all the ills but are colossal towards the creation of more responsible fashion consumption behaviors. These methods can transform the practice of fashion retailing to the advantage of human beings and the planet through the convergence of technology, behavioral science, and design ethics. The second is to implement strategies in an open, transparent, and fair fashion and not to make a push towards sales. When applied in subtle amounts, these nudges offer a soft yet effective means of creating a more positive and sustainable future for fashion.

DESIGNING ETHICAL NUDGES FOR ECO-FRIENDLY FASHION

Designing ethical nudges for sustainable fashion must allow the nudge to balance the influence on people making sustainable decisions and their freedom and autonomy. As social media platforms with data and machine intelligence influence individuals to buy items and utilize consumables, ethical and practical issues arise. Nudges work because they have soft power over individuals, and that is their virtue, but this is also why they are morally problematic. Developers and designers must adhere to principles that help people make sustainable decisions so that their rights and values are respected. The principles revolve around being open, acknowledging people's autonomy, and treating everyone fairly. These principles guarantee that nudges are helpful, not misleading, and empowering, not dominating (Juneja and Mitra, 2022). Transparency is the most essential aspect of ethical nudging. People should know when they are being nudged and the reasons for it. Although it is not always feasible to present everything in detail, users require easy and simplified information regarding how their information is utilized. For instance, if a platform is displaying products that have reduced environmental effects, it should clearly indicate, "This product is displayed because it has less carbon footprint." Transparency does not merely mean having a message; rather, it is about ensuring that the message is comprehensible. The use of complex or vague language can deceive people. Clear language that shows respect for the intelligence of the user is a means of gaining trust, which is the foundation of any system that modifies behavior. Deceived users are likely to stop using a platform or resist its recommendations (Kalpokas, 2019).

The other imperative rule is adherence to people's freedom of choice. Ethical nudging should not remove decision-making ability from users. Nudges can inconspicuously encourage eco-friendly decisions, but they should not bury or make less eco-friendly alternatives difficult to find. The goal is to make eco-friendly decisions easier, more visible, and more appealing without forcing people to do so. People should also have control over their interactions with the platform. Settings should enable users to choose whether to accept specific suggestions or nudges (Matthew et al., 2019). For example, a pop-up can say, "This shirt uses organic cotton, which requires 90% less water compared to regular cotton." This allows users to make informed decisions rather than impulsive ones. Websites and apps should also avoid using fear, guilt, or shame as the primary means of persuasion. Although emotions can be potent, they must be handled responsibly. Nudges that evoke hope, pride, and a sense of cooperation are more respectful and typically more effective in the long run (Mattis et al., 2024).

Inclusion and accessibility in designing nudges are critical because they enable sustainable fashion for everyone, not just a privileged few. Online platforms should understand the different challenges people face in trying to behave in environmentally responsible ways. These challenges include financial matters, a lack of knowledge about sustainability, language differences, and physical or mental issues that make it impossible for some to use digital tools (Mills, 2022). Ethical nudge design begins with research that includes people from diverse backgrounds. This helps make nudges work for everyone from the very beginning. In the case of people with disabilities, the design should incorporate features that make it more accessible to them, such as including images along with the text so that the screen reader can read the text aloud, using easily distinguishable colors in the case of a person with color blindness, and ensuring that the buttons used are big and separated sufficiently to enable a person with disabilities to use them easily. Accessibility is not a luxury but an essential part of proper ethics.

Language and culture also succeed in pushing a larger number of people to travel. Sustainability communications on international platforms should be such that they are appealing to different communities regarding their values and concerns (Mills, 2022). An appeal to water shortage, for example, will be more helpful in areas where individuals realize the existence of a problem, whereas other people will respond better to appeals about labor rights. The messages must be decent and contextual and should not be based on assumptions that can create prejudice regarding the things that people are interested in. Presenting a variety of individuals through photos and users leads to sustainable fashion appearing as the daily practice of more people. Similar individuals who see other people engaging in green fashion are likely to consider the activity as something that can be done. The second important element of inclusive nudge design is the price. The general attitude of most people is that sustainable fashion is unaffordable. Ethical nudges are required to demonstrate that there are cheaper alternatives, such as second-hand stores, rental spaces, repair kits, and cheap brands that meet minimal sustainability requirements. Even durable commodities such as eternal fashion can be sold to people through nudging, since they will not only be given maintenance advice, but also advice on ways of utilizing what they are already being given (Onitui, 2021). This encourages rational buying that is acceptable to different budgets without undermining sustainability of the product. Data ethics are also crucial for designing nudges. These schemes depend on user data, so there is a need to guarantee that people are adequately informed about what data they gather and why. Consent is key; people must be clearly informed and choose whether their data are used in a certain way. AI systems must be checked for bias, especially when they are nudging based on criteria such as age, gender, or spending. If data are skewed, it can lead to skewed nudges; for example, nudging eco-friendly products to those with a bigger budget and ignoring the needs of others. Moral design involves regularly checking for fairness in algorithms and improving them. Designing sustainable fashion ethical nudges is an ongoing process involving inputs from different disciplines, such as behavioral science, design ethics, user experience, sustainability, and product users. Feedback counts: Sites should permit users to comment, rate nudges, and provide feedback. Such responses improve nudges over time, making them more thoughtful and respectful. Ethical nudges are not perfectionist; they are thoughtful, responsible, and respectful in their application of influence. In a world with so much information and so many choices, nudges can be subtle but potent forces for change. If designed ethically, they can help people make choices that are consistent with their values and good for the planet (Tariq, 2025).

CASE STUDIES AND INDUSTRY EXAMPLES

While the fashion world struggles with its environmental credentials, some of the globe's largest online shops are testing new ways to encourage people to make greener choices. These "green nudges" can vary from subtle hints to firm ones, such as exposing how much damage a product will cause or offering green choices by default (Mills, 2022). Some of the bigger fashion brands and newer entrants have been at the vanguard here, with explicit examples of how nudges can help people make more planet-friendly decisions. These efforts raise significant questions about the ethics of personalization and the extent to which persuasion technology should be used to direct what people buy.

An example of this is Zalando, an online clothing store that has attempted to be green. It engages algorithms to use nudges, such as labeling sustainable choices and allowing customers to filter their products based on environmental results, such as organic content or low emissions. Periodically, a search will only result in the generation of products that have passed specific tests on sustainability, and this is having a negative impact on the shopping habits. At Zalando, extensive product information, such as the place of origin and environmental impact of the product, is also available. Such initiatives push green solutions even closer to the top and make them more transparent but do not deprive people of the freedom of choice. ASOS and H&M are no exceptions and have directed their customers to green alternatives in specific sections such as "Conscious" or "Responsible Edit, ' among others. Smaller platforms, such as Good On You, are more specialized in their strategies. This app and website are a fashion guide and grading system for brands based on their sustainability (Bicchieri & Dimant, 2022). They used AI and external data to review brands based on ethics and eco-performance. Nudges are offered to consumers through custom suggestions, relative comparisons between several brands, and reminders when they use less sustainable alternatives. Good On You makes people more aware and encourages them to take action. Similarly, ThredUp, an online second-hand shop, leverages these nudges to promote reuse. When consumers shop, they are reminded of the carbon and water they conserve when they buy second-hand instead of new. They frame environmental gain in concrete and measurable terms, making it appealing to shop sustainably (Walsh et al., 2019).

This is true, yet there exists a moral issue with the use of algorithmic nudges, particularly with tailored messages of sustainability. Data are normally used on websites to tailor nudges by past behavior, preferences, and even mood and time of day for the user. While this can be more persuasive with messages of sustainability, it raises issues of manipulation and the agency of the user (Mills, 2022). For instance, an algorithm could encourage a sustainability project at midnight or when one is particularly vulnerable, perhaps taking the chance to urge a purchase in the name of saving the earth. Even with the altruistic goal of promoting eco-friendly actions, this would cross moral boundaries. There is also the question of whether these personalized nudges represent what matters to people or simply reinforce the habits they already have. If a person is in the habit of purchasing cheap clothing, should the program continue to recommend the same things, continuing this unsustainable behavior? Should it counteract these habits by presenting alternative options? Success in this case relies on a delicate balance of factors. Ethical personalization must not encourage destructive consumption and instead promote actual alternatives in a non-intrusive and respectful way (Caraban et al., 2019). Transparency and user agreement are key factors. Users need to be informed as to when and why they are being nudged and can change their preferences. Most websites fail to make this clear, which is a disconnect between ethical ideals and user experience.

An additional concern is that sustainability nudges can amount to a "green distraction," where the real motivation is to make more sales in the guise of being green. Marveling over a product's eco-worth can make it more attractive, but if the same site is forever leaking fresh stuff, urging people to purchase ever more, the green bonus might still be in the red. Nudges are only effective if they are incorporated into a broader sustainability strategy. This does not only mean selling more friendly products, but also avoiding the consumption of more than is needed, facilitating second-hand and rental economies, and making things last longer and be put back together (Hertwig & Gruneyanoff, 2017). Otherwise, nudging would become a mere marketing ploy and not always be in the interest of the environment. With more sites utilizing green nudges, there is some evidence surfacing on how effective they are. Several companies have reported increased sales of products certified as sustainable. Studies show that consumers are more likely to choose products with green stamps or social good certification, e.g., "10,000 customers chose this green alternative." A study by a giant online retailer found that sustainable products converted 22% more than non-labeled products (Kalpokas, 2019). This shows that nudges do work to shape short-term behavior. However, such successes are often more focused on revenues than on long-term environmental benefits. Additional "green" sales still create resource use, emissions, and waste if total buying continues to grow.

Quantifying the actual environmental benefits of nudging is a more subtle approach to this study. It is not just a case of what people choose to buy, but also how much, how often, and what happens to them in the long run. Some companies are starting to take metrics such as the amount of carbon saved, the amount of water saved, and the amount of trash avoided in landfills (Juneja & Mitra, 2022). They use customer dashboards or websites that uncover the complete life cycle of products. For example, Patagonia posts estimates of the environmental impact of a product on its website and promotes its Worn Wear program, which encourages consumers to have items repaired or buy second-hand items. Although it is difficult to measure these efforts in exact terms, they add to the awareness of what real influence means. They also showed that nudging does not need to occur at the point of purchase. Encouraging people to continue their behavior afterward, for example, taking good care of their clothes, not washing them too much, or engaging in recycling programs, can shape their behavior after the initial purchase. Few studies have focused on the impact of nudging on sustainability. However, the initial findings indicate that when individuals receive consistent messages about sustainability across various areas, they are more likely to adopt sustainable behaviors.

For instance, when one views environmentally friendly options first in search results, receives personalized reminders on sustainability, and then receives an email on how to look after their purchase later, they are likely to recall these values and be responsive to them the next time. However, there is a problem in ensuring that these messages are not repeated too often or come across as insincere. People are becoming better at knowing when companies are greenwashing or not being honest. When nudges do not back their commitments with real facts and behavior, it makes others question or even infuriate them. Another salient point is how green nudges affect different types of people. More affluent consumers might like nudges to present sustainability as luxury or aspirational, while others might like saving money or getting durable products (Shin & Ahmad, 2023; Shin et al., 2023). Companies must consider these factors when designing and pitching their nudges. Marketing used products as both eco-friendly and cheap, for example, might resonate with more consumers than marketing organic cotton as a luxury product would. The green impact is most significant when nudges lead to a choice and nudge people who otherwise would not have made a sustainable choice.

Finally, the effectiveness of green nudges in online shopping for clothes cannot be measured solely by the number of clicks or purchases (Sunstein, 2014). While these numbers represent some behavioral changes, they need to be interpreted against the backdrop of environmental goals. Are people using fewer products overall? Are people buying more durable clothing? Are industries creating less overproduction in line with changing needs These metrics are important. Green nudges only work as designed if they are part of a larger movement within a system. These include ethical production, treating workers with dignity, employing a clear and truthful supply chain, and designing sustainable fashion. The fact that attention is finally paid to the use of algorithm-oriented nudges is a good step in the right direction. Through trial and error, the fashion industry will be able to devise better, more just, and successful means of influencing consumer choices. The potential of applying behavioral science in web shopping is immense, and it has a heavy burden on the destiny to influence the appropriate way. Green nudges can help make fashion more sustainable; only in case they are transparent, do not meddle with the free will of people, and are really interested in minimizing harm. The true trial will be whether they lead to more sustainable purchasing and eventually more sustainable practices, cultures, systems, etc., and more companies and brands start to use them.

RISKS AND LIMITATIONS

With the growing momentum of online fashion, the role of algorithmic nudges has never been as important as it is now. Although nudges can be used to encourage the adoption of sustainable decisions, the covert nature of a nudge can equally create ethical issues and undesirable effects. The main issue is that companies employ nudges to appear sustainable while continuing to sell unsustainable products. This is referred to as greenwashing, and it may mislead consumers into assuming that a given brand is more sustainable than it is. In the case of the illusion of sustainability, no real action is taken to combat the environment using nudge practices. They can then control others, alter their attitude towards goods, and weaken the work in the sphere of sustainability in the fashion sphere (Johnsen et al., 2024). This type of greenwashing by digital nudges is a giant issue until controlled and regulated, and it can negatively affect trust and impede real sustainability gains. In other instances, the platforms selectively highlight certain product features at the expense of the rest of the features to present the features as sustainable. For example, businesses can call products ecologically oriented or conscious choices when they have made minimal or no decrease in their contribution or are simply meeting the minimum requirements. The language is deceptive and creates an illusion for consumers that they are buying a sustainable product when, in reality, the item is still causing excess harm to the environment. Even more difficult is that such performative sustainability under rhetorical design makes it much harder to be heard by already established ethical brands. For example, an algorithm trained on data from individuals whose main engagement with sustainable fashion is high might fail to send green nudges to the poor and areas where sustainability is not perceived as an essential factor or a luxury. This forms a circle, with people already inclined towards sustainable living getting even more signals towards that line, and leaving out others (Schmidt & Engelen, 2020). The availability of varied information, openness of the way things are conducted, and regular testing of the system are key to avoiding the exclusion that can arise because of algorithms. In addition, the media must provide individuals with increased agency over their online moments. Giving individuals the agency to adapt the way they are personalized, file abusive or discriminatory advice, and give feedback on the quality of a system's performance can be more interactive and respectful in the way that the system is set up (Shin and Zhou, 2024). This approach values people's choices and appreciates diversity.

FRAMEWORK FOR ETHICAL AI NUDGING IN FASHION

Creating an ethical AI nudging framework in fashion involves developing a strategic framework that integrates behavioral science, sustainability, and data ethics into a single system that can be used by experts. Nudging has the potential to change the way people decide on more sustainable options within the context of online fashion shopping, but only if undertaken knowingly, for a good reason, and clearly (Matthew et al., 2019). A good framework would lead individuals step-by-step through creating, utilizing, testing, and adding nudges that align with the firm's aims as well as ecological and ethical principles. This means designing behaviors that modify behavior, tracking the extent to which they do so from a range of different perspectives, and incorporating them into the larger framework of marketing and sustainability without reducing the way people feel about the site or their ability to make decisions. Figure 2 provides a practical step-by-step model for researchers, designers, and fashion retailers to follow when implementing ethical nudges.

Figure 2. Framework for Ethical AI Nudging in Fashion

The first thing for whoever does this is to define reasonable, ethical, and sustainable goals before creating any nudging tools. The second step is to observe users and discover where they struggle to make sustainable choices. It is not enough to take an informed guess at what customers want and need; moral impact demands a detailed understanding of how people engage with digital channels and where there are impediments, misunderstandings, or unconscious prejudice that hold them back from making sustainable choices. For example, research may show that customers miss sustainability filters because they are placed in the wrong position, or they stop buying sustainable products because they are too expensive, or they lack information (Alves et al., 2024). This includes coupling techniques such as interviewing and user testing with statistical analysis of the data, such as the application of heatmaps or studying how users move around the site. Insights into the real-world behavior of users allow designers to create nudges that help people make better decisions and do not coerce or push them toward specific choices.

The third step is to implement the nudge. At this point, participants should implement behavior-based design suggestions to develop interventions that are appropriate for their goals and informed by psychological results. These could vary from defaulting, for example, automatically enabling the sustainability filter upon searching, showing the number of people who have selected green products, using visual cues to indicate green products, or instant suggestions when adding a high-impact product to a cart. The trick is to choose the right kind of nudge based on past learning, so that it is both practical and unobtrusive (Titi & Victor, 2024). It is also essential to ensure that nudges never trap or manipulate users; every nudge should support free user choice, facilitate easy exit, and clearly relate to sustainability objectives. The fourth step is to test the nudge using A/B tests or small pilots. However, before releasing the nudge to the masses, the team must test its effectiveness. Reviewing changes in user behavior, such as more clicks on sustainability filters or more sales of less impactful products, but also looking for any adverse side effects, such as user irritation, more people leaving the site, or loss of trust. Ethical nudging is not only effective but also harmless. Testing also involves obtaining users' feedback to see how they feel about the nudges; do they feel they are being informed, respected, or manipulated? Repeated testing enables the team to hone nudges based on real results rather than abstract ideas.

Once the nudges are tested and perfected, the next step is to roll them out across the entire user experience. The team must ensure that nudges are delivered consistently and are accessible to everyone, regardless of device, location, or background. Accessibility and fairness are aspects of the process; nudges need to work for people with varying abilities, levels of tech-savviness, and cultures. Evaluating the structure is another significant aspect. The team should also create solid metrics that are not merely based on clicks and sales. Responsible AI nudging in fashion must be tracked in three main areas: behavior, ethics, and environment. Behavior metrics track how users interact with a website, such as increased usage of sustainability filters, increased time spent looking at eco-friendly products, or more frequent purchasing of sustainable products. This reveals whether nudges help users make good choices in the right way. Ethics metrics consider users' perceptions of nudges (Carlson et al., 2024). This includes ratings on whether they feel the nudges are fair and honest, how often they turn off personalized options, and whether they have any issues with data use or manipulation. Measuring ethics may also involve feedback from impartial experts or ethics panels. Measuring how users feel respected, whether they feel they were guided more than compelled, and how much choice they have over decisions is essential to ensure that nudges do not destroy user trust or freedom. Using feedback, such as interviews or surveys, helps to understand how users truly feel about nudges. Environmental interventions must record how real-world behavior changes because of nudges. This is the hardest but most important part of ascertaining how well the nudges work. Those using nudges need to ascertain the decrease in pollution, water use, or waste produced when people buy more eco-friendly products, return fewer, or choose products with longer lifespans instead of disposable alternatives. This could entail looking at the entire life cycle of a product, computer programs that calculate carbon footprints, and a company's sustainability reports. Even if exact numbers are difficult to obtain, knowing the general direction could still guide improved planning. For example, if a nudge lowers the carbon footprint per product sold by an average of 10%, it is a real result that should be quantified and improved.

The final step is to integrate ethical AI nudges into the brand's overall sustainability and marketing strategy. Nudges need not be stand-alone or small-scale tests. Nudges must conform to the fundamental ideas, messages, and ambitions of the company. Marketing units need to adopt the same ideas as nudges and implement them in their campaigns, promoting transparency, informed choice, and shared responsibility. A brand that encourages buying through advertising but encourages people to impulse purchase on its website sends mixed messages. Aligning everything increases the power of nudges by reinforcing the same principles across the different parts of a business. From a sustainability perspective, nudges can be implemented alongside other initiatives such as circular fashion, product take-back initiatives, or rental propositions (Apriliani, 2025). For example, a website might nudge people to rent for a one-off event rather than buying new items or suggest tools and tutorials for mending clothes post-purchase. These nudges not only help individuals change their behaviors but also enable broader system shifts. Nudge data can help create sustainability reports and invent new products. By observing which nudges work best, companies can discover what motivates their audience and change their collections or rules accordingly. Some companies might even allow people to review sections of their code or decision-making algorithms and encourage others to validate or improve them collectively. In short, successful ethical AI nudging for fashion requires clear goals, a good understanding of users' behavior, considered design, honest testing, fair implementation, thorough evaluation, and thoughtful planning.

FUTURE DIRECTIONS

As more advanced AI-based nudging in fashion comes into play, the focus has shifted to how we regulate, standardize, and supercharge these instruments for a sustainable future. Since it is merely a design modification of the tiniest nudge in design that becomes a part of the choice-making process on websites and applications that individuals are browsing, affecting what they see, what they pick, and what they purchase, this is not such a big deal anymore. On the one hand, it is an excellent idea to promote green decisions; however, it raises essential questions of openness, transparency, accountability, and long-term impacts (Onitiu, 2022). The next step is to establish firm AI regulations, unite the representatives of different fields, provide common ethical principles, and use new technological advances, such as generative AI, to nudge to be more adaptive, responsive, and human value-sensitive. In the case of fashion retailing, this will consist of ensuring that AI recommends a green product or places some products higher than others in search results without unfairness, invisibility, or any deception. Governance must include people checking in along the way through the AI algorithm, especially where decisions involve values, such as which sustainability elements to highlight or how to trade environmental goals off against commercial needs (Perra & Rocha, 2019).

No business or industry can be managed independently. As the need for sustainability increases, increasing numbers of people are coming to feel that coordination across disciplines is the only means of creating regulations and promoting the practice of nudging responsibly (Reviglio & Agosti, 2020). Brands, technology companies, researchers, non-profits, and government leaders must come together and agree on what ethical digital influence is in a climate-obsessed age. A possible result could be a certification seal for sustainable nudging, such as organic or fair trade. This could occur when a website or product suggestion follows the standards for how nudges are used that have been agreed upon. This accreditation can be for online stores, AI systems, or the collection of information to educate consumers and policymakers on whether nudges are helping sustainability initiatives.

Working together also enables groups to pool resources, data, and knowledge to help solve shared problems. For example, the construction of common sets of data regarding the way humans evolve and what matters to them in the context of sustainability serves to ensure that the data remains anonymous, and use is not abusive, which can enlighten AI systems throughout the entire industry. Moreover, nudges can be evaluated on the same basis everywhere because of the same environmental indicators, such as carbon footprint or water usage (Antil et al., 2022). They can also contribute to collaboration across the globe, which is necessary because fashion brands are in various nations that share diverse values, laws, and levels of technology adoption. The price of increased personalization is increased responsibility, not only to eliminate manipulation but also to ensure that such systems are sensitive to the boundaries of the individuals and do not infringe on them. Generative models will require training on balanced and non-biased information, and their results will have to be controlled regularly to eliminate discriminatory stereotypes or eco-anxiety. Because these tools are more informal and may be persuasive, transparency is even more important. People should never lose sight of the fact that they are communicating with AI, the reason why they are communicating with AI, and how their data are being utilized to generate such interactions.

Cross-sector partnerships enable various groups to pool information, resources, and knowledge and overcome common problems. By developing common pools of information about the way individuals purchase and what they prioritize in the backdrop of sustainability, well-managed data collected in a safe manner may grow the learning curve of nudging systems in the entire industry. In addition, having exact measurements of the damage each product causes to the environment, such as the amount of carbon or water it uses, makes the advice given by these nudges based on the same facts rather than just picking some numbers that seem a little better (Mattis et al., 2024). This collective action also helps when working with other countries to achieve the SDGs. This is more important as fashion companies operate in many places around the world, where people have different cultures and laws. A nudge that works well in a place like Europe, where sustainability is essential, will be less effective in other places with different ideas, limitations, or access to digital technologies. Co-creation guarantees that nudging is not only practical and fair but also inclusive and culturally relevant.

Looking ahead, one of the most interesting and exciting advancements in ethical nudging is harnessing new technologies, especially that of generative AI. The more tailored it is, the more the responsibility, not only to avoid trying to manipulate people but also to ensure that such systems respect personal boundaries and treat people with dignity (Zingales, 2018). They must be trained on data that reflect many individuals and exclude biased or unfair data. Their outputs should be regularly checked to prevent them from reinforcing stereotypes or causing undue worry about the environment. In addition, the closer these tools get to an actual conversation and persuasion, the more crucial it becomes that a user knows they are communicating with AI, the purpose of AI, and how their data are being used to fuel these conversations.

Another significant innovation is wearable technology, virtual reality (AR), and smart helpers to provide nudges in everyday life. A smart medical mirror in a dressing room could offer more sustainable options on the spot, via voice or gesture. An AR app could allow customers to scan clothes in the store to view their environmental impact immediately and propose more environmentally friendly alternatives (Yu et al., 2024). It can be employed to enhance the user experience because it can aid in cases where one is lost or under pressure. However, it can also create the problem of manipulative use when websites begin to customize sustainability messages according to the emotions of an individual to push them to a purchase or they will feel guilty about not purchasing. As AI is increasingly capable of reading human emotions, designers and policymakers must set clear limits. For instance, emotional signals should never be used to push people to buy anything, even sustainable products. Instead, such tools should help people reflect, learn, and empower themselves to make better decisions (Opitz et al., 2023).

Along with new technology, people's wants have also changed. The next generation of consumers is not only more tech-savvy but also more cynical about marketing. They want honesty, real impact, and transparency in their interactions. Future nudge strategies must go beyond environmental goals and align with the new norms of data honesty, digital identity, and social responsibility (Zingales, 2019). This includes using open-source tools, working with users in the co-design of experiences, and offering options that people choose rather than imposing them on them. A nudge is most effective when it is transparent and helpful, not hidden or automatic. In short, the future of AI nudging in fashion revolves around rules, cooperation, and innovation. Good rules should exist to make AI nudging just and promote planetary safety. Collaboration among various spheres will establish clear standards, confidence, and confusion because of what is right. Emerging technologies, such as artificial intelligence (AI) that produce things, bright clothes, and virtual reality, can become even more personal and effective, but they require clear and precise use (Wozniak et al., 2022). Innovative tools are not enough in the future; the future requires systems that are just, all-encompassing, and people-centered. Ethical nudging can also transform the way we buy clothes, whereby shopping becomes more than a bare buy and purchase of items but is more of a way of expressing what is important to us. The best thing is to ensure that the instruments that affect our decisions are credible and create a future that we are all convinced of.

CONCLUSION

The concept of algorithmic nudging is promising, as it is suggested as a way of nudging individuals to have more sustainable fashion consumption habits. However, its efficiency and fairness will depend on how open, fair, and responsible it is developed and implemented (Schmauder et al., 2023). To maintain ethics, organizations should initiate training their employees regarding nudging, wherein they will be shown the operation of behavioral science, sustainability ethics, and AI principles. As the knowledge of data is relevant to technology, it is necessary in the future of fashion in the digital economy to know how nudging works or what it is. Thus, institutions of learning and industry associations may provide ethical behavioral design training programs, which will prepare professionals with the appropriate knowledge to manage the complex nexus of technology, business, and sustainability.

REFERENCES

Alves, G., Jannach, D., de Souza, R. F., Damian, D., & Manzato, M. G. (2024). Digitally nudging users to explore off-profile recommendations: Here be dragons. *User Modeling and User-Adapted Interaction*, *34*(2), 441–481. DOI: 10.1007/s11257-023-09378-7

Antil, H., Löhner, R., & Price, R. (2022). *NINNs: Nudging induced neural networks* (arXiv:2203.07947). arXiv. https://arxiv.org/abs/2203.07947

Apriliani, L. (2025). Hypernudging in the digital era: Exploring the impact and ethical considerations of advanced behavioral interventions. *UPY Business and Management Journal*, *4*(2), 200–215. Advance online publication. DOI: 10.31316/ubmj.v4i2.7947

Bicchieri, C., & Dimant, E. (2022). Nudging with care: The risks and benefits of social information. *Public Choice*, *191*(3-4), 443–464. DOI: 10.1007/s11127-019-00684-6

Caraban, A., Karapanos, E., Gonçalves, D., & Campos, P. F. (2019). 23 ways to nudge: A review of technology-mediated nudging in human–computer interaction. In *Proceedings of the 2019 CHI Conference on Human Factors in Computing Systems* (Paper No. 373). Association for Computing Machinery. https://doi.org/DOI: 10.1145/3290605.3300733

Carlson, E., Farhat, A., Martinez, V. R., & Victor, C. (2024). *On the infinite-nudging limit of the nudging filter for continuous data assimilation* (arXiv preprint). https://arxiv.org/abs/2408.02646

Hertwig, R., & Grüne-Yanoff, T. (2017). Nudging and boosting: Steering or empowering good decisions. *Perspectives on Psychological Science*, *12*(6), 973–986. DOI: 10.1177/1745691617702496 PMID: 28792862

Johnsen, E. B., Kobialka, P., Pferscher, A., & Tapia Tarifa, S. L. (2024). Nudging strategies for user journeys: Take a path on the wild side. In *Lecture Notes in Computer Science* (Vol. 15230). Springer. https://doi.org/DOI: 10.1007/978-3-031-73751-0_6

Juneja, P., & Mitra, T. (2022). *Algorithmic nudge to make better choices: Evaluating effectiveness of XAI frameworks to reveal biases in algorithmic decision making to users* (arXiv:2202.02479). arXiv. https://arxiv.org/abs/2202.02479

Kalpokas, I. (2019). Personalisation, emotion, and nudging. In *Algorithmic governance: Politics and law in the post-human era* (pp. 49–65). Palgrave Pivot., DOI: 10.1007/978-3-030-31922-9_4

Mattis, N., Masur, P. K., Moeller, J., & van Atteveldt, W. (2024). Nudging towards news diversity: A theoretical framework for facilitating diverse news consumption through recommender design. *New Media & Society*, *26*(7), 3681–3706. DOI: 10.1177/14614448221104413

Mills, S. (2022). Personalised nudging. *Behavioural Public Policy*, *6*(1), 150–159. DOI: 10.1017/bpp.2020.7

Onitiu, D. (2022). Algorithmic abstractions of "fashion identity" and the role of privacy with regard to algorithmic personalisation systems in the fashion domain. *AI & Society*, *37*(4), 1749–1758. DOI: 10.1007/s00146-021-01235-8

Opitz, S., Sliwka, D., Vogelsang, T., & Zimmermann, T. (2023). *The algorithmic assignment of incentive schemes. SSRN.* https://doi.org/DOI: 10.2139/ssrn.4077778

Perra, N., & Rocha, L. E. C. (2019). Modelling opinion dynamics in the age of algorithmic personalisation. *Scientific Reports*, *9*(1), 7261. Advance online publication. DOI: 10.1038/s41598-019-43830-2 PMID: 31086228

Reviglio, U., & Agosti, C. (2020). Thinking outside the black box: The case for "algorithmic sovereignty" in social media. *Social Media + Society*, *6*(2), 2056305120915613. Advance online publication. DOI: 10.1177/2056305120915613

Schmauder, C., Karpus, J., Moll, M., Bahrami, B., & Deroy, O. (2023). Algorithmic nudging: The need for an interdisciplinary oversight. *Topoi*, *42*(3), 799–807. DOI: 10.1007/s11245-023-09907-4

Schmidt, A. T., & Engelen, B. (2020). The ethics of nudging: An overview. *Philosophy Compass*, *15*(4), e12658. DOI: 10.1111/phc3.12658

Shin, D., & Ahmad, N. B. (2023). Algorithmic nudge: An approach to designing human-centered generative artificial intelligence. *Computer*, *56*(8), 95–99. DOI: 10.1109/MC.2023.3278156

Shin, D., Kee, K. F., & Shin, E. Y. (2023). The nudging effect of accuracy alerts for combating the diffusion of misinformation. *Journal of Broadcasting & Electronic Media*, *67*(2), 141–160. DOI: 10.1080/08838151.2023.2175830

Shin, D., & Zhou, S. (2024). A value- and diversity-aware news recommendation system: Can algorithmic gatekeeping nudge readers to view diverse news? *Journalism & Mass Communication Quarterly*, 10776990241246680. Advance online publication. DOI: 10.1177/10776990241246680

Sunstein, C. R. (2014). Nudging: A very short guide. *Journal of Consumer Policy*, *37*(4), 583–588. DOI: 10.1007/s10603-014-9273-1

Suroto. (2025). Digital nudging strategies, applications, and ethical considerations: A systematic literature review. *International Journal of Innovation in Enterprise System, 9*(1). https://doi.org/DOI: 10.25124/ijies.v9i01.663

Tariq, M. U. (2025). Green FinTech–Driving sustainable finance and empowering underserved communities. In Masri, M., Sait, M., & Anshari, M. (Eds.), *Promoting inclusivity and accessibility with FinTech* (pp. 279–306). IGI Global Scientific Publishing., DOI: 10.4018/979-8-3373-1112-8.ch010

Tariq, M. U. (2025). AI tools and technologies for management education: Enhancing learning through innovation. In M. R. & S. R. (Eds.), *Integrating AI and machine learning into business and management education* (pp. 105–132). IGI Global Scientific Publishing. https://doi.org/DOI: 10.4018/979-8-3373-2150-9.ch005

Tariq, M. U. (2025). Live streams and community interaction in digital broadcasting. In Erdem, M., & Kuş, Ö. (Eds.), *Advancements in digital broadcasting and content platforms* (pp. 215–240). IGI Global Scientific Publishing., DOI: 10.4018/979-8-3373-1459-4.ch008

Tariq, M. U. (2025). AI-driven digital nomads: Transforming labor markets and industrial growth in the digital economy. In Ordóñez de Pablos, P., Zhang, X., Anshari, M., & Almunawar, M. (Eds.), *AI and digital nomads shaping global industrial technology transitions* (pp. 113–138). IGI Global Scientific Publishing., DOI: 10.4018/979-8-3373-0159-4.ch004

Tariq, M. U. (2025). Influence of leadership styles on passion-cultivating purpose-driven leadership. In Paradiso-Testa, M. (Ed.), *The purpose of passion in leadership* (pp. 237–262). IGI Global Scientific Publishing., DOI: 10.4018/979-8-3373-2404-3.ch009

Titi, E. S., & Victor, C. (2024). *On the inadequacy of nudging data assimilation algorithms for non-dissipative systems* (arXiv preprint). https://arxiv.org/abs/2411.08273

Walsh, T., Levy, N., Bell, G., Elliott, A., Maclaurin, J., Mareels, I. M. Y., & Wood, F. M. (2019). *The effective and ethical development of artificial intelligence: An opportunity to improve our wellbeing*. Australian Council of Learned Academies. https://www.acola.org

Weinmann, M., Schneider, C., & vom Brocke, J. (2016). Digital nudging. *Business & Information Systems Engineering, 58*(6), 433–436. DOI: 10.1007/s12599-016-0453-1

Wozniak, T., Stieger, M., Schaffner, D., Schu, M., & Lu, G. (2022). Algorithmic nudging for sustainability in e-commerce: Conceptual framework and research agenda. In *Digital Restructuring and Human (Re)action*. DOI: 10.18690/um.fov.4.2022.43

Yu, X., Haroon, M., Menchen-Trevino, E., & Wojcieszak, M. (2024). Nudging recommendation algorithms increases news consumption and diversity on YouTube. *PNAS Nexus*, *3*(12), pgae518. Advance online publication. DOI: 10.1093/pnasnexus/pgae518 PMID: 39618512

Zingales, N. (2018). Google Shopping: Beware of "self-favouring" in a world of algorithmic nudging. *Competition Policy International – Europe Column*. https://ssrn.com/abstract=3707797

Zingales, N. (2019). Antitrust intent in an age of algorithmic nudging. *Journal of Antitrust Enforcement*, *7*(3), 386–418. DOI: 10.1093/jaenfo/jnz010

KEY TERMS AND DEFINITIONS

Algorithmic Nudging: Subtle digital prompts guiding sustainable consumer behavior.

Choice Architecture: Design of environments prompting decision-making behavior.

Greenwashing: Confusing marketing claiming false environmental responsibility.

Chapter 4
From Click to Conscious Choice:
Algorithmic Nudging Architectures for Eco-Friendly Fashion Consumption

Munise Hayrun Sağlam
http://orcid.org/0000-0003-3847-1337
Yıldız Technical University, Turkey

ABSTRACT

This chapter offers a socio-technical blueprint for algorithmic nudging in fashion platforms. It defines nudging as the data-driven orchestration of choice architecture that steers customers toward lower-impact products, slower shipping, and fewer returns, while preserving autonomy and fairness. The chapter outlines a layered architecture that spans data, modeling, policy, and interface actions, linking interventions to psychological mediators such as salience, perceived consumer effectiveness, trust, and reactance. It formalizes governance through transparency, explainability, opt-out options, fairness screens, and human oversight. A measurement and experimentation program specifies primary, perceptual, and composite KPIs, including Carbon per Conversion, Impact@K, FairExposure, and the Autonomy Cost Index, along with A/B tests, uplift targeting, contextual bandits, and off-policy evaluation. Practical thresholds and reporting cadences support safe operation. The chapter closes with sectoral guidance, limitations, and implications for policymakers and practitioners.

DOI: 10.4018/979-8-3373-5525-2.ch004

1. INTRODUCTION

Global fashion continues to generate significant environmental pressures, including water use, energy demand, chemical inputs, waste, and reverse logistics, alongside persistent social externalities such as labour precarity and opaque supply chains (Hyun et al., 2021; Aydin, 2025). Over the last decade, brands have proliferated sustainability claims and labels; yet, conventional informational tools such as eco-labels (Lee et al., 2015; Lou & Xu, 2024), CSR pages (Dourado et al., 2024), and sustainability badges (Assaker & O'Connor, 2023) rarely translate declared concern into consistent behavior. At the moment of purchase, many consumers still fall back on habit, hedonic appeal, convenience, or price (Kapoor et al., 2025). In parallel, AI-driven recommendation systems, dynamic pricing, search ranking, and interface personalization have begun to reshape digital choice environments in fashion e-commerce and mobile applications. This socio-technical shift has a double edge. It can accelerate fast-fashion impulses through infinite scroll, urgency cues, and subtle frictions that privilege short-term rewards. It can also support more sustainable decisions if it is designed and governed as an ethical form of algorithmic nudging that protects user autonomy, transparency, and fairness.

In this chapter, algorithmic nudging refers to the systematic, data-driven, and continuously optimized orchestration of micro-decisions within digital choice architecture. The core question is what the user sees, in which order, and at which moment. The purpose is to gently steer choices toward predefined sustainability outcomes such as lower-carbon shipping, more durable or ethically produced items, and reduced return propensity, while preserving meaningful autonomy and explainability.

Algorithmic nudging differs from static interfaces (Mattis et al., 2024). A universal "green shipping" default is a one-size-fits-all intervention. An algorithmic approach utilizes machine-learning pipelines that determine in real-time what to show, to whom, and when. Contextual bandits identify which intervention is most promising for the present user state, then update beliefs through rapid learn-and-test cycles. Reinforcement learning optimizes a policy over time so that the system improves against explicit sustainability goals, such as emissions reduction or the probability of choosing a lower-impact option (Ayabe et al., 2025). Collaborative and content-based filtering personalise exposure by learning from adjacent preference profiles and item attributes. Causal uplift modelling adds a crucial safeguard by estimating whether an intervention is likely to change behaviour, rather than targeting consumers who would choose the sustainable option anyway. Through iteration, the system refines which sustainability-relevant interventions are displayed to which users and at what times, with the promise of closing the intention-action gap at a segment-of-one granularity.

The same machinery that can help can also harm. Four ethical risks are central. First, opacity undermines autonomy when users cannot grasp why a particular option or message appears. Second, manipulation and drift into dark patterns can emerge when engagement or conversion is rewarded without countervailing constraints. Third, fairness can drift if exposure and outcomes systematically disadvantage specific groups. Fourth, mission creep can shift the system from facilitating genuine sustainability to sales-optimising "green-sheen" personalisation. For these reasons, algorithmic nudging is legitimate only when it is subject to explicit governance safeguards. These include clear transparency and explainability layers, accessible opt-out pathways, routine impact and fairness audits, human-in-the-loop kill switches, and the publication of objective functions and constraints so that stakeholders understand what the system optimizes and what it refuses to optimize (see also Perra & Rocha, 2019).

Digital nudging is often presented as a static taxonomy of interface heuristics (Michels et al., 2024). AI personalisation is typically framed as a performance or engagement enhancer rather than a vehicle for social or environmental goals. Sustainable fashion research has been most substantial at the macro or supply-chain level, producing important insights into materials, labor, logistics, and reporting (Shin et al., 2023; Shen et al., 2025; von Zahn et al., 2024; Repenning, 2024). What is still missing is an integrated and normatively grounded account that connects the algorithmic stack (data inputs, model objectives, and policy-layer outputs) to the psychological mechanisms through which people interpret and act on interventions. Salience, perceived consumer effectiveness, moral elevation, and anticipated guilt or pride are likely mediators, yet they are rarely measured in situ. Empirical work seldom examines heterogeneity with the precision needed for responsible deployment. We know little about which nudge families work for which psychographic clusters, under what temporal or contextual conditions, and with what ethical boundary parameters, such as transparency level, autonomy-preserving design, and fairness across demographic or socioeconomic strata. Finally, there is limited operational guidance for multi-objective optimisation. Practitioners need methods to balance lifecycle-impact reduction with revenue, customer lifetime value, and user satisfaction, and to do so without covert coercion.

This chapter addresses these gaps with a socio-technical, psychologically informed, and governance-anchored framework for algorithmic nudging on fashion platforms. The contribution is fourfold. First, the chapter proposes a layered architecture that maps data, modelling families, policy constraints, and interface actions, and that can be implemented with standard MLOps practices. Second, it articulates a behavioural model that links interventions to psychological mediators and measurable endpoints, such as click-through rates on lower-impact products, basket share of low-impact SKUs, selection of slower or lower-carbon delivery options, and reduction in returns. The model is presented with testable hypotheses and observable metrics, allowing it to guide field experiments. Third, it outlines a multi-objective optimisation approach that makes trade-offs explicit and auditable. Revenue, impact, fairness, and autonomy are treated as competing but commensurable objectives through transparent weighting or constraint-based formulations, which allows teams to trace how design choices affect outcomes. Fourth, it offers a governance blueprint that specifies transparency duties, consent and opt-out mechanics, fairness diagnostics, audit cadence, and human oversight, together with practical thresholds and triggers for safe operation.

The scope is intentionally pragmatic. "Sustainability outcomes" are defined at the level of the consumer decision points that platforms control or strongly influence, including ranking and recommendation, option defaults, comparative feedback, and light frictions that help users slow down and reflect. The approach is non-coercive by design. It rejects deception, hidden scarcity mechanics, and non-reversible obstacles. It assumes compliance with privacy and data-protection laws and supports user agency through clear explanations and easy-to-find controls.

In short, the chapter argues that algorithmic nudging is a robust and scalable means to narrow the intention-action gap in fashion, provided it is built and run within a transparent and accountable framework that protects autonomy and fairness while delivering measurable environmental benefits.

2. CONCEPTUAL FOUNDATIONS AND BOUNDARIES

2.1. Personalization, Persuasion, and Nudging: Distinctions and Overlaps

In digital consumer experience, three concepts often overlap yet differ in purpose and means: personalization, persuasion, and nudging. Personalization is a matching and ranking problem that connects the "right content to the right user" based on prior preferences, behavior of similar users, or item attributes; its function is to reduce information load and increase relevance (Felfernig et al., 2013). Persuasion encompasses communicative strategies that aim to alter beliefs and attitudes, ultimately targeting the intention itself. Nudging adjusts elements of the choice architecture to shift behavior in predictable ways without narrowing the option set or materially changing monetary incentives. It is grounded in the principle of libertarian paternalism, which retains freedom of choice (Thaler & Sunstein, 2008; Hansen & Jespersen, 2013). In digital contexts, digital nudging refers to the systematic use of interface design elements in online decision environments to guide choices by shaping what users see, in what order, and with which contextual cues (Janson & Barev, 2024).

These distinctions matter even more once AI adaptivity is introduced. The dynamism of personalization algorithms and continuous experimentation raises the risk that the lines between persuasion and manipulation blur. Manipulation can be understood as practices that erode a person's decision-making power through hidden influence; digital technologies can make such practices scalable and hard to detect (Feng et al., 2025). Without explicit commitments to explainability, autonomy, and fair exposure, digital nudges can overstep from legitimate "framing" into coercion. Research on dark patterns reveals that deceptive interface patterns in e-commerce can lead users toward unwanted outcomes, underscoring the importance of maintaining a clear distinction between nudging and manipulative design, and ensuring that this boundary is visible and enforceable in management and ethics (Cao et al., 2025).

Personalization increases relevance, persuasion changes attitudes, and nudging adjusts behavioral frictions and cues without closing the option set. In algorithmic settings, legitimacy depends on declaring objectives and constraints in transparent terms. These distinctions anchor the measurement and governance framework developed later in the chapter.

2.2. Static Versus Algorithmic Nudging: Decision Cycles, Context, and Timing

Static nudging applies a one-size-fits-all intervention, such as showing the same sustainability badge everywhere or setting the same default for everyone. Algorithmic nudging answers "who should see what and when" in real time, updating a decision policy through continuous learn-and-test cycles. Three components are central: contextual bandits, reinforcement learning, and causal targeting.

Contextual bandits select the most promising intervention for a given user and moment, balancing exploration and exploitation. In high-volume settings such as news recommendation, contextual bandits have demonstrated low regret and rapid adaptation (Mattis et al., 2024). Reinforcement learning optimizes a policy over time to maximize cumulative rewards, thereby improving system behavior through experience. Canonical treatments formalize policy learning around the state–action–reward triad (Sutton & Barto, 2018). To update policies safely and data-efficiently, off-policy evaluation and doubly robust estimators help infer the expected performance of new policies from logged data while limiting bias (Dudík et al., 2014).

The third component, causal targeting, focuses on uplift modeling. Traditional personalization learns relevance without distinguishing who is actually influenceable. Uplift models estimate whether an intervention will truly change behavior for an individual, reducing over-targeting of users who would have chosen the sustainable option anyway and reallocating effort to segments with higher marginal impact (Gutiérrez & Gérardy, 2017).

Operationalizing these learning loops in production requires brakes calibrated to ethics as well as an appetite for experimentation. Exploration strategies should be constrained so that no group is systematically shown fewer "better options." Fair-exposure constraints for bandits and RL are increasingly discussed in the literature. Intervention intensity should be monitored using indicators of user fatigue and reactance, with automatic throttling when needed. The KPI set, detailed in the measurement section, is designed to track environmental impact, fairness, and autonomy simultaneously.

The difference between static and algorithmic approaches is not merely technical. Static nudges are normatively predictable but may be limited in effectiveness. Algorithmic nudges can capture temporal and contextual heterogeneity and therefore hold greater promise for narrowing the intention–action gap. However, this potential comes with a risk of sliding toward manipulation unless supported by transparent objective functions, explicit constraints, routine fairness audits, and user-facing explanations. The governance section, therefore, specifies policy cards, explanation layers, and opt-out mechanics.

2.3. Sustainable Fashion Metrics: SKU-Level Measurement Aligned With Policy Goals

For algorithmic nudging to be legitimate and effective in sustainability contexts, measurement must reach the SKU level and align directly with policy goals. Three key metric families are essential: life-cycle assessment (LCA)– based impacts, return probability and reverse logistics impacts, and durability and use-phase longevity indicators.

A systematic assessment of a product's environmental footprint, from raw materials to end-of-life, is framed by ISO 14040/14044 (ISO, 2006). These standards specify goal and scope definition, inventory analysis, impact assessment, and interpretation. In fashion, SKU-level tracking should cover carbon footprint, water use and scarcity, chemical releases, and waste, with clear documentation of data quality and system boundaries (ISO, 2006; Niinimäki et al., 2020). Sector-wide evidence indicates substantial climate impacts for the apparel and footwear sectors, highlighting where water and waste hotspots concentrate across supply chains (Cortazar et al., 2025). Ranking and labeling should therefore consider not only relevance but also identified impact intensities.

Return rates are high in the apparel e-commerce sector, significantly increasing environmental burdens. Recent evidence suggests that a significant proportion of returned items fail to reach a second user, meaning that embedded production and distribution emissions can outweigh transport emissions. Platforms should model the return probability and post-return disposition (resale, repair, reconditioning, or discard) at the SKU–user level. Nudges can target high-impact return cycles by surfacing sizing guidance, richer material, and fit information to raise fit confidence, giving visibility to slower shipping options, and signaling "lower return rate" items (Roichman et al., 2024).

Extending product lifetimes can significantly reduce carbon, water, and waste. Research and industry guidance emphasize that durability depends on material properties, stitching and construction, fabric weight, ease of care, repairability, and design timelessness. Emerging protocols and scorecards measure physical durability, and combining these signals with platform data enables ranking policies to shift exposure toward longer-lasting items. This supports an impact-per-conversion orientation and integrates with buy-back, repair, and resale programs (WRAP, 2012; WRAP, 2017; Guo et al., 2025).

These three metric families should feed directly into multi-objective optimization. At the platform level, the objective can be jointly optimized to maximize revenue, user satisfaction, fair exposure, and reduce environmental impact. Operational KPIs include Carbon-per-Conversion (average carbon per conversion), Impact@K (aggregate impact intensity of items shown in the top K), Return-Adjusted Impact (impact adjusted for embedded emissions of returns), and Durability-Weighted Exposure (impression share weighted by durability score). Bandit and RL policies can incorporate such metrics via constraints or explicit weights, and perceived transparency and autonomy should be tracked alongside to ensure ethical boundary conditions remain intact.

Finally, data governance and validation are essential. SKU-level LCA estimates require explicit provenance and quality ratings. Return and durability metrics should be cross-validated with field data. Standard terminology and methods should be translated into clear consumer-facing explanations so users understand what is being optimized and why, which helps build trust in the nudging strategy.

3. LAYERED ARCHITECTURE

This chapter proposes a four-layer architecture consisting of data, modeling, policy, and interface actions that make algorithmic nudging scalable and auditable in practice. Its purpose is to translate explicit sustainability objectives into a sustainable utility function and then into real-time decision policies under governance and explainability constraints. The architecture assumes versioned data and model assets, versioned policy decisions, and user-facing explanations that together form a coherent whole (Baylor et al., 2017; Mitchell et al., 2019; Manfredi et al., 2025).

3.1. Data Layer: Stated–Behavioral–Context–Sustainability Metadata; Feature Store and Versioning

The data layer is the foundation of any responsible algorithmic nudging system, as it determines what models can learn, what policies can enforce, and what explanations can be truthfully disclosed to users. In practice, this layer must combine four complementary families of signals: declared preferences, observable behavior, situational context, and SKU sustainability metadata. It must also guarantee reproducibility through a versioned feature store and protect user agency with explicit consent and low-friction controls. The following paragraphs describe these elements, their operational requirements, and the governance practices necessary to maintain the stack's audibility and respect for privacy.

Stated signals are the most direct expression of user agency. Persistent preferences, such as opting for low-carbon shipping, selecting an "ethical production" filter, or setting a preference for long-lasting items, should be explicitly captured and treated as high-priority inputs for personalization and policy decisions. Prioritizing declared choices reduces the need for sensitive inferences and strengthens autonomy by making the user's intent visible to the system and easy to edit.

Behavioral telemetry provides the empirical substrate for learning. Impressions, clicks, add-to-cart events, purchases, returns and their reasons, shipping selections, dwell time, and navigation depth all generate time-stamped events that feed both online decisioning and offline model training. To avoid training/serving skew and data leakage, every event must carry source and timestamp metadata, and support point-in-time joins; these engineering practices are essential for reproducible and auditable models (González–Cebrián et al., 2024).

Contextual variables determine when and where interventions should differ. Time of day, device type, traffic source, category composition, inventory availability, price promotions, and the carbon intensity of available shipping options are examples of situational features that meaningfully modulate nudge effectiveness. Incorporating these variables enables models to ask not only who should see an intervention but also when and under what circumstances a particular cue is appropriate.

Sustainability metadata converts product attributes into decision-ready signals. SKU-level life cycle indicators, such as carbon footprint, water use, chemical burden and waste, supplier certifications, historical return probability, and post-return disposition rates, as well as durability scores from standardized tests and repairability markers, all belong in this catalogue. These features must carry provenance and quality ratings so that policy decisions claiming environmental benefits can be audited against credible LCA standards (ISO, 2006; Al Aghbari, 2025; Niinimäki et al., 2020; WRAP, 2012, 2017; Guo et al., 2025)

Operationally, all of the above signals should be materialized in a feature store that supports both low-latency reads for serving and stable offline extracts for training. Each feature requires a precise definition, a computational recipe, a refresh cadence, access control, and a semantic version. Training and serving must reference the same feature schema and rely on historical snapshots so experiments are reproducible and audits can map outcomes back to exact data and model versions (Baylor et al., 2017; Mitchell et al., 2019; Gebru et al., 2021).

Finally, privacy and consent are non-negotiable. Collection and use should follow the principles of data minimization and purpose limitation, favoring explicit, stated signals over inferred sensitive attributes. The data layer must surface the controls users need, including concise "why am I seeing this?" explanations, easy opt-outs, and a clear path to edit persistent preferences, so that technical capability never substitutes for user agency.

3.2. Model Families: Relevance, Impact, and User-State Inference

The first family of models addresses preference and relevance. Production recommender stacks typically split the problem into retrieval and ranking: a retrieval stage provides a high-throughput shortlist using dual-tower embeddings, and a ranker orders that shortlist with pairwise or listwise objectives. Dual-tower architectures learn compact representations of users and items in a shared space, making retrieval tractable at scale, while supervised rankers refine ordering for relevance and conversion (Covington et al., 2016; Datta et al., 2025). Because logged interactions reflect previous policies, counterfactual correction and off-policy evaluation are essential for estimating how new ranking rules will perform. Methods such as counterfactual risk minimization and doubly robust estimators are therefore standard tools for bias correction and safe policy selection (Dudík et al., 2014).

A distinct but connected family operationalizes sustainability objectives by predicting impact-relevant quantities. Supervised regressions and ensemble learners to map SKU attributes to life-cycle indicators, such as carbon, water, and waste footprints. These predictions should expose calibrated uncertainty, allowing downstream policies to reason about risk. Returns are best modeled in two stages: first, estimate the probability that an item or order will be returned, then conditionally predict post-return disposition probabilities — for example, resale, repair, or disposal — together with their associated emissions. Longevity and durability require a different toolkit. Survival analysis and hazard models combine laboratory or protocolized durability tests with field usage patterns to estimate the expected use-phase duration. These impact estimators feed ranking and bandit layers as either soft weights or hard constraints so that the Impact@K profile of visible slots progressively aligns with pre-specified sustainability targets (WRAP, 2012, 2017; Acciai & Perez-Bou, 2025; Guo et al., 2025).

The third family infers user state, encompassing momentary beliefs and dispositions that determine the intensity with which an intervention should be applied. Perceived Consumer Effectiveness, the belief that one's actions matter, can be measured with brief questionnaire items or proxied behaviorally; higher PCE amplifies the effectiveness of norm cues and comparative feedback (Ellen et al., 1991). Signals of reactance and fatigue are detectable in interaction patterns such as repeated dismissals of prompts, rapid exits from flows, or serial ignores of badges; psychometric work provides calibration rules to translate these markers into intervention thresholds (Dillard & Shen, 2005; Dong et al., 2023). In contextual bandits and reinforcement learning setups, these inferred states serve as side information: models include them to modulate which nudge to show, how often, and at what strength, thereby protecting autonomy while optimizing long-run impact (Ye & Fu, 2024).

These three model families form a coherent stack in which retrieval and relevance secure discovery, impact models quantify the environmental stakes of choices, and user-state inference governs intensity and personalization. Integrating them requires careful versioning, uncertainty propagation, and governance so that optimization moves visibility and choice architecture toward measurable sustainability outcomes without compromising fairness or autonomy (Sutton & Barto, 2018).

3.3. Policy Layer: Sustainable Utility Function and Constraints

The policy layer determines how model outputs map to interface actions. The proposed Sustainable Utility Function (SUF) augments conventional objectives such as revenue and satisfaction with impact reduction, fair exposure, and autonomy:

$$\max_{\pi} E[\lambda_r R+\lambda_s S+\lambda_f F-\lambda_{viol} V]$$

Here R denotes revenue or CLV contribution, S denotes environmental reduction per conversion (for example, a decrease in Carbon-per-Conversion), F denotes a fair-exposure score, and V aggregates penalties for constraint violations. Weights λ are published and aligned with institutional goals. The policy is governed by three constraint families:

1. **Transparency and explainability:** At least a fraction χ of decisions must include a user-visible "why am I seeing this?" explanation that passes comprehension tests. Enforce an explainability coverage $\geq \chi$ and a transparency score $\geq \tau$ (Doshi-Velez & Kim, 2017; Mitchell et al., 2019).

2. **Fair exposure and outcomes:** The disparate impact ratio across demographic or socioeconomic groups is kept in the [0.8, 1.25] band. Monitor both exposure and outcomes. For ranking, apply exposure fairness constraints that account for position bias (Feldman et al., 2015; Singh & Joachims, 2018; Biega et al., 2018; Ekstrand et al., 2022).
3. **Autonomy and exit friction:** Opt-out friction $\leq \phi$ measured as a composite of clicks, time, and bounce-back likelihood required to disable interventions. If friction trends upward, automatically lower intensity and expand explanations.

Two solution patterns are practical.

- The epsilon-constraint approach maximizes revenue and satisfaction while imposing hard constraints on impact, fairness, and autonomy.
- The lambda-weighting approach combines all targets in a single utility and searches along the Pareto frontier.

In both cases, use off-policy evaluation and doubly robust estimators to assess new policies safely, and cap online exploration rates subject to group-fairness constraints (Dudík et al., 2014; Puranik et al., 2024). Document policy choices in Policy Cards that summarize the objective, constraints, models used, explanation texts, opt-out paths, audit cadence, and kill-switch procedures, aligned with Model Cards and Datasheets for Datasets (Mitchell et al., 2019; Gebru et al., 2021).

3.4. Interface Actions: Labeled, Logged, and Explainable Interventions

Interface actions are the final link in the nudge pipeline, where algorithmic decisions meet human judgment. These actions must be visibly labeled, recorded in audit logs, and explained in plain language so that users understand why an option appears and how to change it. Table 1 summarizes the intervention families, the psychological targets they aim to influence, the expected primary effects, and plausible side effects. Refer to this matrix for a concise overview of trade-offs and monitoring priorities (see Table 1).

- **Salience badges and info panels:** Surface low-carbon or low-water intensity, durability, and fair-trade attributes with references to data sources and clear rationales.
- **Eco-defaults:** Set the default shipping option to lower carbon or open ethical filters by default while preserving choice. Default effects are strong in environmental decisions (Pichert & Katsikopoulos, 2008; Ebeling & Lotz, 2015).

- **Ranking and re-ranking:** Operate under Impact@K and fair-exposure constraints.
- **Comparative feedback:** Show the environmental footprint of a chosen option relative to baselines; comparative feedback has robust evidence in energy and environment domains (Canlas et al., 2025).
- **Norm and identity cues:** Local and peer norms can be effective, especially in high-PCE segments (Goldstein et al., 2008; Ellen et al., 1991).
- **Light frictions:** Short confirmations, fit-verification prompts, or micro-pauses reduce errors and return risk without triggering reactance.
- **Commitment devices:** Reversible and easy-to-disable preferences such as "prefer long-lasting items" help bridge intentions and actions (Ariely & Wertenbroch, 2002).

Each intervention is logged with time, user context, display position, explanation text, and a unique identifier. The explanation layer exposes core signals and policy constraints in plain language. This supports auditability, strengthens user trust, and enables field testing of uplift-focused hypotheses developed later.

Table 1. Intervention family × target psychological variable × potential side effect matrix

Intervention family	Target psychological variable (salience, PCE, norm signal, attention)	Expected primary effect	Potential side effect (reactance, fatigue, misattribution)	Ethical or operational countermeasure	Relevant KPI
Salience badges (low-carbon, low-water, durability)	Salience, attention	Increase visibility and choice of lower-impact SKUs	Information overload; "green-sheen" misattribution	Show data source; concise badge tooltips; limit badge density	Impact@K; Carbon-per-Conversion
Eco-default shipping (slower/lower-carbon pre-selected)	Salience, attention	Higher adoption of low-carbon shipping	Reactance if default feels hidden; perceived coercion	Clear "why this default" text; one-click opt-out	Carbon-per-Conversion; Autonomy Cost Index
Re-ranking with impact weights	Salience	More exposure for low-impact items without removing choice	Exposure unfairness across groups	Position-bias-aware fair-exposure constraints	Impact@K; FairExposure

continued on following page

Table 1. Continued

Intervention family	Target psychological variable (salience, PCE, norm signal, attention)	Expected primary effect	Potential side effect (reactance, fatigue, misattribution)	Ethical or operational countermeasure	Relevant KPI
Comparative footprint feedback (choice vs baseline)	PCE, attention	Stronger conversion to lower-impact options	Fatigue from repeated prompts	Frequency caps; show only at high intent states	Carbon-per-Conversion
Local/peer norm cues ("X% in your area chose...")	Norm signal, PCE	Social proof nudges toward eco choices	Backfire if user differs from the norm	Segment by receptivity; avoid false precision	Carbon-per-Conversion
Fit-confidence assistant (size guides, try-on prompts)	Attention, salience	Fewer mis-sized purchases and returns	Friction; funnel drop	Inline micro-prompts; skip option	Return-Adjusted Impact
Durability scorecards (repairability, lifespan hints)	Salience, PCE	Shift demand to longer-lasting products	Misinterpretation of scores	Plain-language scales; link to test protocol	Impact@K; Carbon-per-Conversion
Light frictions (confirm step before "Buy Now")	Attention	Reduce impulsive purchases and returns	Reactance if overused	Trigger only on risky patterns; A/B throttle	Return-Adjusted Impact; Autonomy Cost Index
Commitment toggles ("Prefer long-lasting items")	PCE, attention	Persistent preference toward durable SKUs	Choice inertia, later regret	Reversible, visible toggle; reminder of setting	Impact@K; Carbon-per-Conversion
Explanations ("Why am I seeing this?" panels)	PCE, attention	Trust and acceptance of interventions	Cognitive load	Progressive disclosure; short, skimmable text	Autonomy Cost Index
Ethical filter presets (e.g., ethically produced ON)	Salience	Higher discovery of compliant items	Perceived paternalism	First-run consent; easy reset	Impact@K; Autonomy Cost Index
Slower-shipping visibility modules	Salience, PCE	Uptake of low-carbon delivery	Choice fatigue in checkout	Smart placement; pre-filled rationale	Carbon-per-Conversion

4. PSYCHOLOGICAL PATHWAYS: BRIDGING INTENTION AND ACTION

The gap between intention and action is one of the main obstacles to sustainable decision-making in fashion e-commerce. Algorithmic nudging seeks to narrow this gap, but its effectiveness depends on psychological mediators that operate through cognitive systems, self-determination motives, and the value–belief–norm (VBN) chain. This section integrates three theoretical pillars — dual-process theories, self-determination theory, and the VBN framework — to explain which interventions work, for whom, and under what conditions. Meta-analytic and experimental evidence shows that psychosocial determinants of pro-environmental behavior are robust and that well-designed interface cues can effectively activate them (Bamberg & Möser, 2007; Stern, 2000).

4.1. Dual-Process, Self-Determination, and Value–Belief–Norm Integration

Salience-based cues often trigger System-1 processing: attention capture, accessible comparisons, and ready value signals enable fast, heuristic evaluation (Kahneman, 2011). This route saves cognitive effort, but when users perceive a threat to autonomy, psychological reactance rises and resistance to "being steered" emerges. Interventions must therefore be designed to preserve the self-determination needs of autonomy and competence; otherwise, short-term gains in attention can undermine long-term acceptance and adherence (Deci & Ryan, 2000; Dong et al., 2023).

Four mediators are especially relevant in the intention–action bridge. Perceived Consumer Effectiveness (PCE) captures the belief that one's choices make a real difference, and it is a strong predictor of eco-behavior (Ellen et al., 1991). Moral elevation, the uplifting emotion elicited by witnessing exemplary conduct, increases prosocial motivation and can carry over to sustainable choices (Huang & Fang, 2024; Li et al., 2021). Anticipated guilt and anticipated pride function as self-regulatory forecasts—"how will I feel afterward?"—and robustly guide behavior in sustainable consumption contexts (Onwezen et al., 2014). These mediators translate salience into durable action by connecting attitudes with choice.

Within the VBN perspective, values (especially biospheric values) shape beliefs about environmental threats, which in turn activate personal norms and a felt obligation to act (Stern, 2000). Algorithmic interventions should not try to "implant values"; instead, they should reduce micro-costs of acting in ways congruent with existing values and norms. When the choice architecture lowers friction for value-consistent behavior, intention–action alignment becomes more stable.

4.2. Identity and Norm Cues: Local Social Proof and Identity-Consistent Choice

Social norms operate in two forms. Descriptive norms communicate what most people do, whereas injunctive norms signal what is socially approved. Field experiments demonstrate that norm messages can have constructive, destructive, or reconstructive effects, depending on their design. Poorly framed messages can produce "boomerang" effects among already low-consumption users; well-framed messages, on the other hand, leverage peer comparison and approval signals to strengthen pro-environmental behavior. Local and proximal-peer norms are typically more effective than distant or abstract references (Allcott, 2011; Cialdini, 2003; Schultz et al., 2007; Goldstein et al., 2008).

Identity cues align choices with answers to the question, "Who am I?" Research on identity-based consumption shows that options congruent with one's self-concept attract more attention, receive more favorable evaluations, and convert into behavior more reliably. As environmental self-identity strengthens, preference for lower-impact options and behavioral persistence increase. Evidence suggests that environmental self-identity is reinforced by biospheric values and past behavior, indicating that interface framing that surfaces identity-consistent options (for example, highlighting long-lasting products or local peer uptake) can help translate intentions into action (Eom & Choy, 2025; Capasso et al., 2025).

4.3. The Role of Transparency: Trust, Perceived Autonomy, and Adherence to Defaults Over Time

In algorithmic systems, transparency and explanation support two critical psychological outcomes: trust and perceived autonomy. Experiments show that "why am I seeing this?" explanations, when provided at the right level of detail, increase trust, whereas too much or too little information can erode it. Full disclosure of decision logic is not always beneficial; information overload can hinder error detection and lead to increased fatigue. Algorithmic nudging should therefore prefer moderate, comprehensible, action-oriented explanations and offer visible, low-friction opt-out and preference controls to bolster autonomy (Shen et al., 2025).

Transparent, autonomy-supportive design affects not only momentary acceptance but also long-run adherence to defaults. Meta-analytic work on defaults reveals that acceptance is driven by inertia and effort savings, as well as by implied endorsement and perceived justifiability. Defaults that preserve freedom of choice and clearly communicate their rationale tend to be more durable. At the same time, users may exhibit algorithm aversion after observing an error; one response is to grant minor but meaningful user adjustments, strengthening shared control and mitigating aversion. Together, these findings suggest that the explanation layer and control surface should be designed to optimize trust and perceived autonomy, alongside behavioral outcomes (Oh et al., 2025; Adam et al., 2024; Jachimowicz et al., 2019).

Inputs are interface interventions (salience badges, eco-defaults, re-ranking, comparative feedback, norm and identity cues, light frictions). These operate through cognitive–affective mediators: salience and attention engage System-1 processing; PCE, moral elevation, and anticipated guilt/pride bridge intention to action; trust facilitates acceptance; reactance provides a negative signal to modulate intensity. Behavioral outputs include selection of lower-impact products, adoption of lower-carbon shipping, and reduced return propensity. Two moderators shape effects: green orientation/environmental self-identity and baseline PCE. High identity and high PCE amplify norm and identity cues; when they are low, explanations and autonomy signals gain relative importance. A governance loop monitors reactance indicators and ties them to intensity reduction and visible opt-out.

5. ETHICAL BOUNDARY CONDITIONS AND GOVERNANCE

Algorithmic nudging in fashion commerce is only legitimate when its aims, constraints, and accountabilities are explicit, testable, and enforceable. This section outlines the boundary conditions and governance stack that enable sustainability-oriented nudging to be aligned with user autonomy and fairness, while remaining auditable in production. The approach integrates life-cycle impact accounting, autonomy protections against manipulative design, multi-level fairness testing, proportionality controls on intervention intensity, robust accountability artifacts, and safeguards against mission creep and greenwashing. It draws on established standards and emerging AI governance frameworks to translate ethical aspirations into operational rules (ISO, 2006).

5.1. Purpose Legitimacy: LCA-Based Objectives, Publishing the Objective Function, and Model/Policy Cards

Purpose legitimacy begins with environmental objectives that are measurable at the SKU level and grounded in Life Cycle Assessment (LCA). ISO 14040 defines the principles and framework for LCA, including goal and scope definition, inventory analysis, impact assessment, and interpretation (ISO, 2006). A chapter-level commitment to LCA means the optimization objective can be expressed in terms such as carbon per conversion, return-adjusted impact, water scarcity footprint, and waste intensity. These impact targets should be incorporated into the optimization objective and constraints, rather than being treated as post-hoc labels. Publicly stating the high-level objective function—what the system is trying to maximize under which constraints—helps align stakeholder expectations and supports external scrutiny (Mitchell et al., 2019).

Transparency about the system's goals and scope is strengthened by Model Cards for models and Datasheets for datasets, providing key information about data assets. Model Cards document the intended use, performance disaggregated across relevant subgroups, and known limitations; Datasheets record the dataset's motivation, composition, collection processes, and recommended uses. In this chapter's architecture, we add Policy Cards that summarize the sustainable utility function, fairness and autonomy constraints, explanation coverage requirements, and opt-out mechanics for each deployed policy. Together, these artifacts enable independent review and internal discipline (Sheil et al., 2026).

Finally, purpose legitimacy is not only a matter of documentation; it is a risk-management obligation under emerging governance frameworks. The U.S. NIST AI Risk Management Framework (AI RMF 1.0) and the EU AI Act both focus on risk identification, monitoring, and governance throughout the AI life cycle. Even when a fashion recommender is not "high-risk" in the EU sense, adopting these practices—clear risk registers, monitoring plans, and human oversight—raises the standard of care (NIST, 2023).

5.2. Autonomy Protection: Low-Friction Opt-Out, No Dark Patterns, Reversibility

Autonomy protection requires that users can understand and easily decline nudging. First, opt-out controls must be visible, reversible, and low-friction. Second, interfaces must avoid dark patterns that pressure or deceive, such as obstructive cancellation flows, disguised ads, or asymmetric consent. The U.S. Federal Trade Commission's 2022 staff report details how dark patterns manipulate choice and warns that such designs may be unfair or Deceptive (FTC, 2022a). In the EU, the European Data Protection Board's Guidelines 3/2022 describe deceptive patterns in social media interfaces that contravene GDPR's transparency and consent standards and provide concrete design recommendations to avoid them (EDPB, 2023).

Third, nudges should adhere to a reversibility principle: commitments, such as "prefer long-lasting items," must be clearly indicated and immediately revocable. The ethical literature on nudges stresses that influence must respect dignity and self-government, which is best served by reversibility and clear reasons for defaults. Publishing the rationale for eco-defaults and helping simple "one-click" opt-outs sustain trust over time (Sunstein, 2016).

5.3. Fairness and Discrimination Auditing: Exposure/Outcome Parity, Counterfactual Tests, Disparate-Impact Bands

Fairness in ranking-based systems encompasses two levels: exposure fairness (who is seen) and outcome fairness (who benefits). In recommender and search contexts, position bias can lead to systematic inequities, which motivates exposure constraints that ensure fair distribution of attention across items or providers subject to relevance. Research formalizes the concept of exposure fairness and provides efficient algorithms to optimize utility under fairness constraints; complementary work defines the equity of attention at the individual level across repeated rankings. These ideas extend naturally to fashion platforms, where sellers, brands, or product types can be disadvantaged by ranking dynamics unless guardrails are applied (Singh & Joachims, 2018).

At the group level, a pragmatic baseline is the disparate impact or "four-fifths" rule of thumb from U.S. equal employment guidance: if a protected group's selection rate falls below 80 percent of the highest group's, this flags potential discrimination and requires justification. While born in employment testing, the concept offers a screening band for exposure and conversion in platforms, for example by monitoring whether a demographic segment consistently receives materially lower exposure to sustainable offers. Importantly, any DI screen is a diagnostic, not a final legal conclusion; interventions must be validated and tailored to context (EEOC, 1979).

Beyond group parity, counterfactual fairness tests ask whether a decision would be the same if a user's protected attribute were different in a causal model of the data-generating process. Counterfactual analysis complements statistical screens by directly probing individual-level fairness. Additionally, individual-fairness principles formalize the intuition that similar individuals should be treated similarly, which is often operationalized through task-specific similarity metrics. In practice, a layered regimen that combines exposure fairness for rankings, DI band monitoring, and counterfactual checks gives stronger coverage than any single metric (Wang et al., 2024).

5.4. Proportionality and Intensity Control: From "Nudge İntensity" to İmpact Elasticity

Proportionality requires that the intensity of nudges is commensurate with their demonstrated social benefit and respectful of user experience. We define Nudge Intensity as the frequency and salience of interventions per session, adjusted for their intrusiveness. We define SKU-Impact Elasticity as the change in a sustainability impact metric (for example, reduction in carbon per conversion) per unit increase in nudge intensity. Intensity should be ratcheted up only while elasticity remains meaningfully positive and should be dialed down when marginal impact wanes or autonomy costs rise. This operationalizes the ethical requirement of proportional influence in contemporary debates on nudging.

Intensity control also serves the purposes of fairness and autonomy. If DI screens or exposure audits detect drift outside accepted bands, or if opt-out friction rises, the policy should automatically reduce intensity and expand explanations until indicators normalize. Moderation by reactance signals and perceived consumer effectiveness measures can further tailor the intensity: users with low PCE and higher reactance require lighter, more informational nudges; high-PCE users may benefit from stronger social-norm or identity cues. Although these psychological diagnostics are developed elsewhere in the chapter, proportionality ties them directly to governance (Ekstrand et al., 2022).

5.5. Accountability: Immutable Logs, Versioning, Independent Audit, and Human-in-the-Loop Kill Switch

Accountability depends on being able to reconstruct what happened, why it happened, and who approved it. Production ML guidance emphasizes the risks of hidden technical debt and silent pipeline drift, which make reproducibility difficult. A mature platform utilizes append-only logs, feature and model versioning, and policy version records to associate outcomes with specific training data, parameters, and constraints. Additionally, continuous pipelines with standardized components, as exemplified by TFX, reduce ad-hoc glue code and stabilize experimentation and rollbacks.

The accountability layer should include independent audits of both models and policies. An internal end-to-end audit framework, such as the one proposed by Raji et al. (2020), creates an auditable trail from design intentions to deployment, including documentation artifacts, review gates, and red-team tests. External audits can verify DI screens, exposure fairness, explanation coverage, and opt-out friction, as well as the correctness of LCA claims driving optimization. Crucially, there must be human-in-the-loop kill-switch procedures that allow for the rapid deactivation of a policy when thresholds are breached or new risks emerge. Risk-management standards, such as NIST AI RMF, reinforce these practices by framing continuous monitoring and human oversight as core to trustworthy AI.

5.6. Mission Creep and Greenwashing: Weight-Change Logs, Board Approval, and Spillover Monitoring

Mission creep occurs when a sustainability-oriented objective slides toward pure revenue optimization under the guise of "green" personalization. To prevent this, implement weight-change logs for the sustainable utility function, including timestamps, rationale, and approvals, and require governance-board sign-off for any material changes in weights that trade off impact reduction against revenue or engagement. This makes the direction and magnitude of shifts visible to auditors and stakeholders.

Guarding against greenwashing is equally important. The sustainability management literature documents incentives that lead firms to overstate environmental benefits, undermining trust. For fashion platforms, this means independently verifying LCA labels, disclosing data provenance, and monitoring whether nudges that advertise "eco" benefits actually reduce impact metrics. Consumer psychology research also warns about behavioral spillovers, including possible moral licensing or rebound effects, whereby an initial "green" choice licenses less sustainable follow-up behavior or reduces its net impact (Wang et al., 2025). The evidence is mixed, but the prudent course is to measure spillover and counteract it through complementary interventions rather than assuming monotonic benefits.

Practical Thresholds and Trigger Rules (τ, φ, χ, DI)

To operate sustainably and ethically at scale, platforms should adopt a small set of pre-specified operational thresholds that serve as early warning signals and automatic safety guards. These thresholds are not normative endpoints; they are pragmatic defaults intended to be calibrated in pilot studies and adjusted as evidence accumulates. The recommended defaults below strike a balance between transparency, explainability, user autonomy, and fairness, while enabling automated and auditable responses when violations occur.

Require a transparency comprehension score (τ) of at least 0.70 on a 0–1 task-based scale for the short "Why am I seeing this?" explanation. If the rolling average TCS for any user segment falls below τ, reduce the nudge intensity and improve the explanation clarity before resuming the prior exposure levels. Ensure explainability coverage (χ) of at least 0.80 for algorithmic decisions that alter defaults, rankings, or prompts; first-exposure inline explanations should be present for the vast majority of such actions. Cap opt-out friction (φ) so that median effort to opt out is no more than two clicks or ten seconds from the point of intervention; rising φ should trigger immediate throttling and a user-experience review. Maintain group exposure and outcome ratios within a disparate-impact band of [0.80, 1.25] relative to the best-served group as a diagnostic screen; breaches prompt fairness-aware re-ranking and root-cause analysis, while recognizing that this band serves as an operational signal rather than a legal determination. Finally, require a minimum nudge-intensity elasticity so that a one-standard-unit increase in intensity produces at least a 0.10 reduction in carbon per conversion. If elasticity falls below this threshold for two consecutive weeks or if the Autonomy Cost Index moves above its 95th percentile, reduce intensity and switch to explanation-first variants.

Operationally, any single hard breach (for example, DI band or opt-out friction) or two soft breaches (for example, τ, χ, elasticity) within a rolling seven-day window should trigger an automated rollback to the last compliant policy version and open a formal audit tied to the relevant Policy Card and versioned model artifacts. All thresholds and triggers should be preregistered with the experiment plan and continuously monitored, with revisions documented in light of pilot results and external audit findings (Kohavi et al., 2020; NIST, 2023). These measures align practical governance with consumer-protection guidance on coercive design and early diagnostic screening for disparate impact (FTC, 2022a; EEOC, 1978), while preserving proportionality and user agency (Sunstein, 2016).

6. MEASUREMENT, KPIS, AND EXPERIMENTAL FRAMEWORK

A sustainability-nudging system must be instrumented from end to end. The same pipeline that delivers interventions should also log exposures, choices, and context, and then aggregate them into interpretable metrics that can be tied to governance thresholds and business outcomes. This section organizes the measurement layer into primary behavior metrics, perception metrics, hybrid or composite metrics, an experimentation and policy-evaluation framework, and a reporting cadence with automated responses to threshold breaches.

6.1. Primary Behavioral Metrics

Primary behavioral metrics capture observable choices that directly affect environmental outcomes or reduce wasteful flows. These metrics should be tracked at the the session, order,, and user levels so that immediate responses and sustained behavioral changes can be evaluated. Proper instrumentation of these outcomes is the empirical foundation for determining whether interface interventions yield measurable life-cycle benefits.

Engagement with verified lower-impact products is a central family of outcomes. Two complementary indicators are handy. The eco-SKU click-through rate is the fraction of impressions of verified lower-impact items that lead users to the product detail page, and the eco-SKU basket share measures the share of cart units or value composed of those items. These indicators link exposure to eventual purchase, revealing whether ranking and presentation influence consumption composition. Because position bias in rankings can concentrate visibility and distort measured effects, platforms should monitor exposure and engagement by user segment to detect silent drift and to ensure that visibility gains are not confined to a narrow slice of traffic (Singh & Joachims, 2018).

Shipping choices provide a direct lever on fulfilment emissions. The low-carbon shipping adoption rate records the share of eligible orders where customers choose consolidated, slower, or otherwise lower-emission fulfilment options. When combined with SKU-level footprints and shipment-mode emission coefficients, changes in this adoption rate map cleanly into order-level carbon accounting, making this metric an operational bridge between interface nudges and carbon-per-conversion estimates (GHG Protocol, 2011).

Returns and their disposition account for a significant portion of apparel lifecycle waste. Measuring the return rate indicates how often orders result in reverse logistics, and a return-adjusted impact metric translates returns into net life-cycle effects by accounting for additional transport emissions and post-return disposition, such as resale, repair,, or disposal. Recent empirical work has documented that a substantial share of returned apparel does not reach a second consumer, and that production-phase emissions associated with those items often dominate post-return logistics. This underscores why preventing avoidable returns is a first-order sustainability strategy (Roichman et al., 2024).

Durability and longevity proxies help align short-term engagement with long-term environmental benefit. Durability-weighted exposure aggregates attention given to items with higher durability scores derived from standardized tests, warranty records, or validated review signals. A repeat-wear proxy, collected through panel follow-ups or opt-in app reporting, measures whether an item remains in use after a predetermined horizon. Longevity is widely recognized as a key determinant of clothing life-cycle impact, so these proxies are essential for connecting interface effects to material reductions over time (WRAP, 2012).

Instrumenting these metrics requires rigorous logging practices and careful experiment design. Events and aggregates must include stable denominators, consistent eligibility rules, and privacy protections such as randomized salts on identifiers. Production logs should tie impressions and actions to model and policy versions, ensuring that outcomes are reproducible and auditable. These engineering practices mitigate technical debt and support reliable causal analysis. Finally, retaining both intent-to-treat and treatment-on-the-treated views is crucial for uplift estimation and for separating exposure effects from compliance effects in randomized and bandit experiments (Kohavi & Longbotham, 2023).

6.2. Perceptual Metrics

Sustainable Interface interventions aimed at promoting sustainable choices are most effective when users understand what they are seeing, believe they can make a difference, and do not feel manipulated. Measuring these perceptual states is therefore essential both to evaluate the effectiveness of interventions and to regulate their intensity. I outline four complementary constructs that should be routinely measured in experiments and production monitoring: trust in the algorithmic interface, perceived consumer effectiveness, psychological reactance, and comprehension of transparency.

Trust in the interface refers to whether users perceive the system as procedurally fair and informationally reliable. Short batteries adapted from human–AI transparency research can assess both procedural trust and informational trust. These measures should be collected under varying outcome scenarios, as research shows that transparency can either bolster or erode trust, depending on cognitive load and the perceived usefulness of explanations (Miller, 2019). Comprehension-tested items and scenario questions help distinguish superficial acceptance from informed trust that is likely to persist.

Perceived consumer effectiveness, or PCE, is the belief that one's own actions have real consequences. PCE differs from general environmental concern and is a strong predictor of pro-environmental purchase behavior. Measuring PCE with brief, validated items and tracking its pre-/and post-change in targeted cohorts allows practitioners to test whether an intervention increases the sense that personal choices matter, which in turn mediates downstream behavioral shifts (Ellen et al., 1991).

Reactance and cognitive fatigue are key factors in controlling ethical intensity. Momentary feelings of threatened freedom or of being coerced predict avoidance and backlash, while fatigue reduces responsiveness and can make repeated nudges counterproductive. State reactance scales and brief trait measures provide complementary diagnostics. In addition, online markers such as repeated dismissals of prompts, rapid exits from decision flows, or serial ignores of badges should be validated against psychometric instruments so that inferred signals of reactance and fatigue map meaningfully onto user experience (Dillard & Shen, 2005; Steindl et al., 2015).

Finally, transparency comprehension is a task-based metric that measures whether users actually understand an explanation when they request it. A straightforward operationalization is a short quiz presented after a user opens a "Why am I seeing this?" panel, consisting of two or three multiple-choice items that test whether the user has grasped the rationale and knows how to change settings. Prior work cautions that disclosure alone is not sufficient; what matters is comprehensibility and actionable clarity, and measures of comprehension predict whether transparency improves acceptance or increases cognitive burden (Poursabzi-Sangdeh et al., 2021; Shin et al., 2023)

Collecting these perceptual metrics alongside behavioral outcomes creates a richer evaluation framework. Doing so makes it possible to test mediation hypotheses, segment users by susceptibility and autonomy preferences, and trigger governance responses—for example, reducing nudge intensity when reactance rises or switching to explanation-first modes when comprehension falls. These perceptual indicators, therefore, play a dual role: they are outcome measures and real-time safety signals for ethical operation.

6.3. Hybrid and Composite Metrics

We recommend four composite metrics that align closely with the chapter's governance thresholds and multi-objective optimization.

Carbon-per-Conversion (CPC)

A ratio expressing emissions per successful conversion, integrating product and logistics footprints:

$CPC = \mid \{o \in O{:}purchase\} \mid \sum o \in O(\sum i \in oPCFi{+}ShipCFo{-}Avoided\text{-}CFo, returns).$

$$f(x) = \frac{\sum_{o \in O}\left(\sum_{i \in O} PCF_i + ShipCF_O - AvoidedCF_{O,\,returns}\right)}{|\{\, o \in O{:}\text{purchase}\}|}$$

Product Carbon Footprints (PCFs) follow the GHG Protocol Product Standard and ISO-aligned LCA assumptions. Shipping terms use mode-specific factors; returns subtract avoided emissions when restock or resale occurs. CPC is sensitive to both product mix and fulfilment choices (GHG Protocol, 2011).

Impact@K (I@K)

Inspired by exposure-aware ranking measures, I@K aggregates the expected environmental impact of the top-K items shown in a session, discounted by a position-bias weight w_r (for example $w_r = 1/\,Log_2(\text{r}+1)$).

$$\text{I@K} = \sum_{r=1}^{K} w_r \,.\, \mathbb{E}\,[\text{Impact}(item_r)]$$

Lower values indicate that highly visible slots are populated with better options on average. This metric captures progress even when users browse without clicking and can be constrained jointly with utility-optimal ranking under fairness constraints (Singh & Joachims, 2018).

FairExposure (FE)

A group-parity ratio that tracks whether exposure to sustainable opportunities is equitably distributed across user or provider groups. For a set of groups g,

$$FE = \min_g \frac{Exposure_g}{Exposure_g^*},$$

where $Exposure_g^*$ is the target exposure proportional to relevance. Using exposure-aware fairness for rankings avoids the pitfall of measuring only outcomes while visibility remains unequal (Singh & Joachims, 2018).

Autonomy Cost Index (ACI)

A composite of interaction frictions and perceived control:

ACI=0.3Z(opt_out_clicks)+0.2Z(opt_out_time)+0.2Z(dismissals/100 exp.)−0.15Z(TCS)−0.15Z(perceived autonomy),

where Z denotes z-scores. Lower is better. ACI links directly to dark-pattern guidance by quantifying avoidance effort and comprehension. Thresholds should be calibrated in pilots and reviewed by governance (FTC, 2022a).

6.4. Experimentation and Policy Evaluation Framework

An experimentation and policy-evaluation framework is essential for reliably estimating causal effects and for managing the ethical, business, and environmental trade-offs that arise when AI-driven nudges are deployed in fashion e-commerce. This framework combines randomized A/B tests for causal identification, contextual bandits and off-policy evaluation for fast yet safe personalization, and uplift/ Individual Treatment Effect methods to target interventions where they will actually change behaviour. Robust metric hygiene, pre-specified guardrails, and fairness-aware ranking complete the stack, ensuring deployments remain auditable, replicable, and socially responsible.

A/B testing as the backbone: Online controlled experiments remain the standard for causal assessment of product changes. Large experimentation programs emphasize trustworthy metrics, pre-registration of guardrails, variance-reduction techniques, and protection against peeking. Sequential monitoring can be supported with "always-valid" p-values to maintain Type-I error control during continuous reads.

Contextual bandits for rapid learning: For intervention targeting in dynamic catalogs, contextual bandits learn which nudge works for whom and when. The classic Yahoo! news work shows that contextual bandits can be evaluated offline using randomized logs, enabling safe iteration before full rollout. Doubly robust estimators further improve accuracy by combining models of rewards with logged propensities.

Uplift and individual treatment effects (ITE): To minimize "wasted" nudges and avoid autonomy costs, target users whose behavior is likely to change because of the intervention. Differential response methods and uplift decision trees are well-documented, and modern ITE estimators such as causal forests allow valid inference about heterogeneous effects under standard assumptions. These tools support segment-of-one strategies that remain auditable (Rzepakowski & Jaroszewicz, 2012).

Off-policy evaluation (OPE) for safety: Before deploying a new policy broadly, estimate its value using historical logs from a different policy. Doubly robust OPE in contextual bandits and reinforcement learning reduces variance relative to importance sampling while retaining consistency if either the reward or behavior model is correct. High-confidence OPE provides lower bounds to support safe rollouts.

Fairness-aware ranking: Because exposure drives opportunity, experimental arms that change ranking or sorting should include exposure fairness constraints in their objective or as ex-post checks. Equity-of-attention and fairness-of-exposure frameworks provide implementable constraints that preserve task utility (Biega et al., 2028).

Metric hygiene: Use stable definitions, consistent denominators, and pre-specified guardrails. Audit for interference and carry-over effects in cohort-level tests. When KPIs are highly correlated, publish a primary outcome set and use the rest as secondary analyses to avoid garden-of-forking-paths problems (Kohavi & Longbotham, 2023).

6.5. Reporting Cadence and Automated Responses

Each week the governance team should publish a concise dashboard reporting four core areas: fairness (DI screens for exposure and outcomes by protected attributes or relevant segments, including FE and the minimum group ratio), autonomy (ACI distributions and trends plus opt-out friction histograms), transparency (TCS broken down by intervention type and user segment), and impact (CPC trend lines, I@K for top modules, and return-adjusted impact deltas). Definitions, formulas, example targets, and potential side effects for these KPIs are summarized in Table 2.

Weekly governance packet: Each week, publish a concise dashboard:

- **Fairness:** DI screens for exposure and outcomes by protected attributes or relevant segments; report FE and the minimum group ratio.
- **Autonomy:** ACI distributions and trends; opt-out friction histograms.
- **Transparency:** TCS by intervention type and user segment.
- **Impact:** CPC trend lines; I@K for top modules; return-adjusted impact deltas.

Trigger-based throttling: If the DI ratio falls outside the [0.80, 1.25] band or if median opt-out effort exceeds two clicks or ten seconds, throttle intervention frequency automatically, revert to the last compliant policy version, and open an investigation. If TCS falls below its threshold for any segment or ACI rises above its control limits, reduce salience and replace prompts with explanation-first variants until scores recover. The DI band draws on the four-fifths screening rule; although not dispositive in law, it serves as a practical early-warning indicator when combined with exposure-aware fairness (EEOC, 1979).

Table 2. KPI Dashboard

KPI	Definition	Formula	Example target	Potential side effect
Eco-SKU CTR	Clicks on verified lower-impact SKUs divided by their impressions	CTR_eco = Clicks_eco / Impressions_eco	+15% vs. baseline	Over-exposure may reduce diversity of options
Eco-SKU Basket Share (EBS)	Share of cart units or value from lower-impact SKUs	EBS = Units_eco / Units_total	≥ 30% of units	Cannibalization of essential basics if badges over-nudge
Low-carbon Shipping Adoption (LCSA)	Share of orders selecting low-carbon modes	LCSA = Orders_lowC / Eligible_orders	≥ 40% when available	Delivery-speed dissatisfaction; increased churn
Return Rate (RR)	Share of orders with any return	RR = Orders_returned / Orders_total	−20% YoY	Over-deterrence can reduce trial of new sizes
Return-Adjusted Impact (RAI)	Emissions after subtracting avoided impacts from successful restock/ resale	Sum_order(PCF + ShipCF − AvoidedCF_ returns)	−10% per quarter	Model misspecification if non-resale share mis-estimated
Durability-Weighted Exposure	Exposure to SKUs with higher durability scores	DWE = Σ Exposure_i × Durability_score_i	+25%	Supplier gaming of durability proxies
Carbon-per-Conversion (CPC)	Emissions per purchase	CPC as defined in §6.3	−12% vs. baseline	Incentivizes smaller carts without revenue guardrail

continued on following page

Table 2. Continued

KPI	Definition	Formula	Example target	Potential side effect
Impact@K (I@K)	Expected impact in top-K results, position-weighted	I@K = Σ_{r≤K} w_r·E[Impact(item_r)]	−20%	Hidden trade-offs if utility drops at lower ranks
FairExposure (FE)	Minimum parity ratio of exposure vs. target exposure	FE = min_g Exposure_g / Exposure_g^*	≥ 0.90	Over-correction can harm relevance for some users
Transparency Comprehension Score (TCS)	Task-based comprehension of explanations	% correct on 2–3 items after first exposure	≥ 0.70	Excess detail can reduce comprehension
Perceived Consumer Effectiveness (PCE)	Belief that personal choices matter	Mean of PCE items	+0.3 SD in targeted cohorts	Moral burden or guilt if overemphasized
Autonomy Cost Index (ACI)	Composite friction and control measure	Weighted z-score composite in §6.3	≤ 0 (centered) with tight CI	Gaming opt-outs by accidental clicks; measure with TCS too

Source: Authors' own elaboration based on empirical data (2025).

Notes. PCF follows the GHG Protocol Product Standard and ISO-aligned LCA, with water-footprint add-ons per ISO 14046 if water scarcity is in scope.

7. OPERATIONALIZING THE IMPLEMENTATION PLAN AND TECHNICAL ARCHITECTURE

This section explains how the conceptual architecture can be realized in production, focusing on the core data and model pipelines, policy orchestration, auditing requirements, and the user-facing control surface. The aim is to make deployment reproducible, auditable, and safe, while preserving the operational simplicity that teams need to run experiments and iterate.

Data collection begins as an event stream. Impressions, clicks, add-to-cart events, purchases, and return notices are emitted as durable events into a streaming backbone, typically implemented with a log-oriented system such as Kafka. The event stream feeds both low-latency consumers for online inference and batch consumers that populate the data lake and training sets for nightly retraining. This separation between online and offline consumers is essential to prevent training/serving skew and to ensure that production decisions are reproducible (González–Cebrián et al., 2024).

Features derived from these events are materialized in a feature store that records each feature's definition, computation method, refresh cadence, and provenance. Online inference servers query the feature store through low-latency APIs, retrieve the latest validated feature vectors, and feed them to the serving models: retrieval, ranking, impact estimators, and user-state predictors. The policy engine sits above these models as a microservice. It consumes model scores, evaluates the Sustainable Utility Function together with declared constraints, and emits a single decision object that the frontend can render. Treating policy as a versioned microservice preserves auditability and decouples policy logic from model implementations (Baylor et al., 2017).

Model lifecycle and CI/CD are structured around nightly retraining and staged rollouts. New training runs are recorded with explicit metadata: dataset snapshot, feature schema, hyperparameters, and random seeds. Candidate models undergo first-pass offline validation, then shadow tests in production, and only then conduct controlled experiments. Off-policy evaluation methods and doubly robust estimators are incorporated into the pipeline, allowing candidate policies to be assessed against logged data before any live exploration is permitted (Dudík, Erhan, Langford, & Li, 2014). This provides a safety-oriented predeployment barrier to policies that would otherwise risk ethical or performance regressions.

Auditability requires an append-only ledger that ties every exposure to the model hash, policy card identifier, and feature snapshot used to create that decision. Every impression or interaction entry should therefore contain those referents so investigators can reconstruct the exact chain of artifacts that produced any outcome. Policy Cards, automatically generated at deployment time, summarize the objective function, constraint thresholds, explanation texts, opt-out mechanics, audit cadence, and the administrator responsible for sign-off. These artifacts are the binding source of truth for both internal reviews and external audits (Raji et al., 2020).

User control and transparency must be visible and usable. A centralized interface module — the Sustainability and Privacy Control Center — provides insight into why items are displayed, how sustainability attributes are calculated, and how users can modify their preferences. This control center must offer immediate, low-friction opt-out options, a history of past preferences and toggles, and a one-click route to reverse any default. Offering such a control panel strengthens perceived autonomy and reduces the risk of algorithm aversion.

Security, privacy, and governance are threaded through the architecture. Sensitive inference is restricted by policy. Federated learning is supported as an option to reduce central data aggregation, with secure aggregation protocols protecting local updates (Fernández et al., 2025). Differential privacy mechanisms can be applied where aggregate signals leak individual behavior, with a clearly tracked privacy budget to manage trade-offs between utility and disclosure risk (Hou et al., 2025).

These pieces form a production topology in which event streaming, a feature store, online inference, a versioned policy microservice, append-only auditing, and a user control center operate in concert. This combination enables robust experimentation, accountable decisioning, and rapid rollback through human-in-the-loop kill-switch procedures when governance thresholds are breached.

8. METHODOLOGICAL AGENDA AND RESEARCH QUESTIONS

To evaluate short-term efficacy and long-term systemic consequences of sustainability-oriented nudging, the research program combines qualitative discovery, controlled experiments, large-scale field trials, and agent-based simulation. This mixed program is designed to uncover mechanisms, quantify heterogeneous effects, and stress-test policies under adversarial and long-horizon scenarios.

The first stage is qualitative. Semi-structured interviews, think-aloud sessions, and interaction diaries reveal how users interpret interface cues, how they reason about explanations, and how they experience autonomy while interacting with nudges. These insights are crucial for developing comprehension-tested explanation texts and for creating concise, valid psychometric instruments for PCE, trust, and reactance that will be utilized in subsequent quantitative studies. Qualitative work also refines segmentation criteria for randomized trials so that subgroup analyses are meaningful.

The second stage consists of randomized controlled trials. These experiments cross-intervention families with transparency modes and degrees of autonomy. For example, a factorial design might compare badge versus eco-default versus comparative feedback. Within each arm, explanation mode can vary from brief, action-oriented text to technical details to a no-explanation control. Autonomy conditions can vary from an immediate one-click opt-out to more complex preference menus. Mediator variables, such as PCE, moral elevation, anticipated guilt and pride, trust, and reactance, are measured to enable mediation analysis and to train uplift models for subsequent targeting. Because causal heterogeneity matters, trials also gather the data needed to estimate individual treatment effects and to validate uplift targeting strategies.

Stage three scales the most promising interventions into production with large-scale field experiments. A feasible strategy is to condition regions or cohorts on different policy portfolios — for instance, an eco-basket module in one cohort, an eco-default in another, and a returns-reduction package in a third — and then use difference-in-differences and off-policy evaluation to estimate the impacts on CPC, Impact@K, FairExposure, and ACI. These production experiments test external validity and operational constraints: whether an intervention that works in a controlled RCT still moves the needle when exposure volumes and inventory churn are high.

The final stage uses simulation and stress testing. Multi-agent reinforcement learning environments simulate repeated interactions, enabling researchers to study long-term dynamics, including mission drift, fairness erosion, and rebound effects. These simulations are particularly valuable for exploring the time path of Pareto trade-offs between revenue, impact reduction, and fairness, and for evaluating throttling and rollback heuristics before deployment in the wild (Sutton & Barto, 2018).

The program is organized around targeted research questions. Which psychosocial segments respond to which interventions? How sensitive are outcomes to small changes in SUF weights? How do different transparency modes affect comprehension, opt-out behavior, and long-run default adherence? Do bandit or RL adaptations produce fairness drift over long horizons, and if so, which brakes are effective? Ultimately, does uplift targeting increase the net environmental gain while keeping autonomy costs and disparate impact within acceptable bounds?

Each research question is paired with an experimental design, primary and secondary metrics, an analysis plan, and risk mitigations. Pre-registration and rigorous metric hygiene are standard practices across stages, and off-policy evaluation plays a continuous role in ensuring safety during staged rollouts.

9. SECTORAL IMPLEMENTATION GUIDE

Applying this architecture across retail verticals requires tailoring impact metrics, user flows, and logistic mappings to the domain. The core decision framework remains the same, but practical choices differ between categories such as groceries, electronics, and travel.

The starting point is a decision matrix that maps intervention family to segment readiness and SKU impact profile. For durable basics that score highly on durability tests, badges and commitment toggles are highly suitable. By contrast, fast-fashion trend items, which have low expected longevity and high resale risk, are poor candidates for durability-focused nudging and may carry reputational risk if presented as durable. The matrix helps product owners prioritize pilots by focusing on interventions where SKU characteristics and segment preparedness align to maximize impact per experimental dollar.

Policy Card templates are central to operational consistency. Each card should state the intended objective, the target KPIs, constraint thresholds (such as DI band and ACI limits), the exact explanation text to be shown to users, opt-out procedures, audit cadence, and rollback criteria. Example language for the "Why am I seeing this?" panel should be concise and actionable: "This badge appears because this product has a lower life-cycle carbon footprint than the category average. Data source: supplier LCA and third-party verification. Change this preference in the Sustainability & Privacy Center." Short, localized messages preserve comprehension while providing users with a clear path to adjust settings.

Product and procurement teams need an operational checklist to ensure claims are defensible. The checklist includes verified LCA sources, durability testing protocols, continuous monitoring of return flows and resale rates, policy card approval workflow, and a requirement for third-party validation when making public impact claims. Marketing and legal reviews are necessary before any consumer-facing sustainability label goes live.

Sector examples illustrate required adaptations. In grocery, perishability and cold-chain emissions mean slower shipping nudges may be infeasible; interventions should emphasize sourcing, seasonal choices, and packaging reduction. Electronics benefit more from repairability and trade-in nudges; refurbishment pathways must be integrated into return-adjusted impact models. Travel demands multi-leg accounting and special care around urgent booking contexts; here, minimal, highly salient comparisons are preferable to dense explanations.

In every vertical, the governance framework includes transparent objectives, easy opt-outs, fairness monitoring, immutable logs, and a human kill switch, and it remains constant. What changes are the KPI calibrations, the elasticity thresholds, and the operational definitions of durability or impact? Pilots should be run with vertical-specific KPIs and recalibrated governance thresholds before scaling.

10. IMPLICATIONS FOR POLICYMAKERS

Algorithmic nudging in fashion will only deliver genuine sustainability benefits when public policy aligns incentives, clarifies responsibilities, and requires verifiable evidence. The first implication is objective-function transparency. Platforms should disclose, in plain language, what their recommender policies are optimizing under, along with the relevant constraints. A concise statement of goals encompassing revenue, user satisfaction, impact reduction, fairness, and autonomy should be paired with a clear description of guardrails and trade-off logic. This disclosure is not a blueprint of proprietary models; it is a public commitment that enables oversight and comparison across platforms, consistent with broader AI governance principles that emphasize documentation and risk management (NIST, 2023; European Union, 2024).

Documentation must be concrete. Model Cards and Datasheets for Datasets should be mandatory for any model or dataset that materially affects ranking, default settings, or sustainability labeling (Mitchell et al., 2019; Gebru et al., 2021). We further recommend Policy Cards: one-page summaries that state the sustainable utility function, fairness and autonomy constraints, explanation coverage, opt-out mechanics, and audit cadence for each deployed policy. These artifacts make compliance and accountability auditable, and they create a common language for regulators, consumer groups, and technical teams.

Second, impact claims require robust, standardized evidence. Product-level environmental data should rely on recognized frameworks, such as ISO 14040/44 for life-cycle assessment and the GHG Protocol Product Standard, with water footprinting under ISO 14046 where relevant (ISO, 2006; GHG Protocol, 2011). Policymakers should expect platforms to report impact-linked KPIs, such as Carbon-per-Conversion and Impact@K, and to submit these to third-party assurance. Independent verification is essential to limit algorithmic greenwashing and ensure that optimization truly reduces impacts, rather than merely reshuffling labels.

Third, autonomy and anti-manipulation safeguards are essential components of consumer protection. Regulators have already flagged deceptive interface patterns as harmful. The FTC's analysis of dark patterns and the EDPB's guidance on deceptive design in social platforms provide practical criteria for evaluating consent flows, defaults, and opt-out frictions (FTC, 2022b; EDPB, 2023). Applying these standards to fashion platforms implies visible, low-friction opt-outs, reversible choices, and clear explanations of why a user is seeing a particular option or default.

Fourth, fairness must be measured where it actually matters—exposure and outcomes. Because ranking algorithms distribute attention, exposure parity should be monitored in conjunction with conversion parity. Research in ranking fairness provides implementable constraints and diagnostics, including equity-of-attention and fairness-of-exposure formulations (Pitoura et al., 2022). Policymakers can adopt a pragmatic screening band based on the disparate-impact ratio from employment testing practice, recognizing it is a diagnostic that triggers investigation rather than a legal conclusion.

Finally, auditability and human oversight should be required throughout the entire design and deployment process. Immutable logs, versioned features and models, and versioned policy records enable the reconstruction of decisions and the safe rollback when thresholds are breached (Baylor et al., 2017). Independent audits—internal or external—should confirm fairness screens, explanation comprehension, opt-out frictions, and the accuracy of impact data, while human-in-the-loop kill-switch procedures ensure timely intervention when risks escalate (Raji et al., 2020). Together, these measures align private optimization with public interest.

11. LIMITATIONS, TRANSFERABILITY, AND FUTURE RESEARCH

The framework presented in this chapter is designed for the fashion industry, but several limitations temper direct generalization. Data quality and access remain the most serious constraints. SKU-level life-cycle data are incomplete and heterogeneous; supplier claims may vary in scope, boundaries, and data provenance (Finkbeiner et al., 2006). Water scarcity and chemical impacts are especially context-dependent. Without standardized disclosures and third-party verification, optimization risks chase noisy proxies rather than genuine improvements (ISO, 2006; ISO, 2014; GHG Protocol, 2011).

A second limitation concerns long-horizon effects and behavioral spillovers. The benefits of longer-lasting products and slower shipping may materialize over months, whereas most online experiments are short. Moreover, sustainability interventions can produce moral licensing or rebound effects: an initial "good" action may license subsequent choices that offset gains (Maki et al., 2019). Platforms should therefore complement short-run A/B tests with longitudinal tracking and pre-registered spillover analyses.

Third, heterogeneity and cultural context complicate transferability, as norm and identity cues vary in effectiveness across segments and locales. Poorly framed norms can backfire, while identity-consistent framing often requires careful localization. The psychological moderators highlighted in this chapter, environmental self-identity and perceived consumer effectiveness, should be measured and modeled explicitly to avoid one-size-fits-all deployments (Tamlyn et al., 2025).

Fourth, algorithmic and governance risks remain. Bandit and reinforcement-learning policies can drift toward unintended objectives if feedback signals are biased, if logging is incomplete, or if SKUs change rapidly. Fairness in sequential decision-making poses additional challenges; exposure constraints and disparate-impact screens should be complemented by counterfactual fairness tests where feasible (Puranik et al., 2024; Peng & Mitra, 2024). Even with extensive logging, reconstructing causality from observational data remains challenging, which is why robust off-policy evaluation and staged rollouts are crucial (Dudík et al., 2014).

Finally, the transferability of this architecture to adjacent verticals such as electronics, grocery, and travel depends on how well impact metrics can be defined, verified, and linked to user-facing choices. Groceries, for example, involve perishability and cold-chain logistics; travel requires complex, multi-leg emissions accounting. Future work should develop sector-specific impact measures and interface patterns, while retaining the same core principles: objective-function transparency, autonomy, fairness, and auditable optimization.

Future research priorities include: better product-level durability measurement and standardization; improved ITE and uplift estimators that incorporate fairness and autonomy costs; explanation-comprehension instruments that predict long-term adherence rather than only momentary trust; and policy-aware experiment designs that combine A/B tests with contextual bandits under exposure constraints. These directions would deepen the empirical foundations of ethical algorithmic nudging and make its benefits more reliably transferable.

12. CONCLUSION

This chapter argues that algorithmic nudging can narrow the intention–action gap in fashion only under strict boundary conditions. The architecture links data, modeling, policy, and interface actions to measurable sustainability outcomes while embedding fairness and autonomy protections. Psychological mechanisms such as salience, perceived consumer effectiveness, anticipated guilt and pride, trust, and reactance explain how and when interventions sustain behavior rather than produce short-lived shifts. Governance elements, including objective function disclosure, auditable documentation, third-party assurance, fairness checks, explanation comprehension, low-friction opt-outs, and human kill switches, translate ethics into operational rules.

The core claim is conditional: algorithmic nudging produces significant environmental benefits only when autonomy, explainability, fairness, and accountability are treated as primary constraints rather than afterthoughts. When platforms disclose what they optimize, align impact metrics with recognized standards, verify claims independently, and design interfaces that respect user agency, optimization power is directed toward the public good. In the absence of these conditions, the same system fuels fast fashion impulses, entrenches opacity, and risks algorithmic greenwashing. The practical agenda is therefore to make optimization both legible and governable: define the goals, measure the trade-offs, publish the rules, and maintain human oversight.

REFERENCES

Acciai, E., & Perez-Bou, S. (2025). Exploring the role of digital product passports for supply chain traceability in the "Made in Italy" textile sector. *Asia Pacific Journal of Marketing and Logistics*, 1–17. Advance online publication. DOI: 10.1108/APJML-03-2025-0371

Adam, M., Diebel, C., Goutier, M., & Benlian, A. (2024). Navigating autonomy and control in human-AI delegation: User responses to technology- versus user-invoked task allocation. *Decision Support Systems*, *180*, 114193. DOI: 10.1016/j.dss.2024.114193

Aghbari, A. I. (2025, October 03). S., Mohammed, A., Zubairu, N., & Rahman, N. S. F. A. (2025). Exploring the social and environmental performance in fast-fashion supply chains: A comparative analysis between MNCs and SMEs. *International Journal of Productivity and Performance Management*, *74*(8), 2932–2958. Advance online publication. DOI: 10.1108/IJPPM-05-2024-0342

Allcott, H. (2011). Social norms and energy conservation. *Journal of Public Economics*, *95*(9–10), 1082–1095. DOI: 10.1016/j.jpubeco.2011.03.003

Ariely, D., & Wertenbroch, K. (2002). Procrastination, deadlines, and performance: Self-control by precommitment. *Psychological Science*, *13*(3), 219–224. DOI: 10.1111/1467-9280.00441 PMID: 12009041

Assaker, G., & O'Connor, P. (2023). The importance of green certification labels/badges in online hotel booking choice: A conjoint investigation of consumers' preferences pre- and post-COVID-19. *Cornell Hospitality Quarterly*, *64*(4), 401–414. DOI: 10.1177/19389655231184474

Ayabe, S., Otomo, T., Kera, H., & Kawamoto, K. (2025). Robustness evaluation of offline reinforcement learning for robot control against action perturbations. *International Journal of Advanced Robotic Systems*, *22*(4), 17298806251360454. Advance online publication. DOI: 10.1177/17298806251360454

Aydin, G. (2025). Status or sustainability, can we have both, please? Decoding the factors shaping eco-friendly fashion buying. *Journal of Fashion Marketing and Management*, *29*(3), 434–458. DOI: 10.1108/JFMM-02-2024-0061

Bamberg, S., & Möser, G. (2007). Twenty years after Hines, Hungerford and Tomera: A new meta-analysis of psycho-social determinants of pro-environmental behaviour. *Journal of Environmental Psychology*, *27*(1), 14–25. DOI: 10.1016/j.jenvp.2006.12.002

Baylor, D.. (2017). TFX: A TensorFlow-based production-scale machine learning platform. In *Proceedings of the 23rd ACM SIGKDD International Conference on Knowledge Discovery and Data Mining* (pp. 1387–1395). DOI: 10.1145/3097983.3098021

Biega, A. J., Gummadi, K. P., & Weikum, G. (2018). Equity of attention: Amortizing individual fairness in rankings. In *Proceedings of the 41st International ACM SIGIR Conference on Research & Development in Information Retrieval* (SIGIR '18) (pp. 405–414). Association for Computing Machinery. https://doi.org/DOI: 10.1145/3209978.3210063

Canlas, I. P., Plecerda, L. P., Panit, N. M., Sereno, R. M., & Gamez, A. L. (2025). Differential effect of environmental sustainability beliefs and norms on green consumption and energy conservation behaviors among pre-service teachers. *Human Ecology: an Interdisciplinary Journal*, *53*(3), 581–596. Advance online publication. DOI: 10.1007/s10745-025-00608-7

Cao, Y. S., Wang, W. Z., Zhang, Y. J., Deveci, M., Kadry, S., & Wang, L. M. (2025). Analyzing adoption factors of data-driven nudging for e-commerce platforms using an integrated decision model. *Electronic Commerce Research and Applications*, *71*, 101500. DOI: 10.1016/j.elerap.2025.101500

Capasso, M., Guidetti, M., Bianchi, M., Cavazza, N., & Caso, D. (2025). Enhancing intentions to reduce meat consumption: An experiment comparing the role of self- and social pro-environmental identities. *Journal of Environmental Psychology*, *101*, 102494. DOI: 10.1016/j.jenvp.2024.102494

Cialdini, R. B. (2003). Crafting normative messages to protect the environment. *Current Directions in Psychological Science*, *12*(4), 105–109. DOI: 10.1111/1467-8721.01242

Cortazar, L. O., Cachón-Rodríguez, G., Nebreda, L. P., & Medrano, M. L. (2025). Motivational dimensions of slow fashion to promote environmentally and socially sustainable consumption in the fashion industry. *Journal of Fashion Marketing and Management*, *29*(5), 761–780. DOI: 10.1108/JFMM-07-2023-0184

Covington, P., Adams, J., & Sargin, E. (2016). Deep neural networks for YouTube recommendations. In *Proceedings of the 10th ACM Conference on Recommender Systems* (pp. 191–198). https://doi.org/DOI: 10.1145/2959100.2959190

Datta, J., Rabbi, R., Saha, P., Zereen, A. N., Abdullah-Al-Wadud, M., & Uddin, J. (2025). Deep representation learning using layer-wise VICReg losses. *Scientific Reports*, *15*(1), 27049. DOI: 10.1038/s41598-025-08504-2 PMID: 40715190

Deci, E. L., & Ryan, R. M. (2000). The "what" and "why" of goal pursuits: Human needs and the self-determination of behavior. *Psychological Inquiry*, *11*(4), 227–268. DOI: 10.1207/S15327965PLI1104_01

Dillard, J. P., & Shen, L. (2005). On the nature of reactance and its role in persuasive health communication. *Communication Monographs*, *72*(2), 144–168. DOI: 10.1080/03637750500111815

Dong, Y. J., Li, W., & Chen, M. (2023). Personalization reactance in online medical consultations: Effects of two-sided personalization and health topic sensitivity on reactance. *Human Communication Research*, *50*(1), 66–78. DOI: 10.1093/hcr/hqad039

Dourado, P., Llovet-Rodríguez, C., & Gallego-Gómez, C. (2024). Social responsibility of designer fashion brands in Spain: Analysis of websites based on sustainability and transparency. *Revista Internacional de Relaciones Públicas*, *14*(28), 67–86. DOI: 10.5783/revrrpp.v14i28.871

Dudík, M., Erhan, D., Langford, J., & Li, L. (2014). Doubly robust policy evaluation and optimization. *Statistical Science*, *29*(4), 485–511. DOI: 10.1214/14-STS500

Ebeling, F., & Lotz, S. (2015). Domestic uptake of green energy promoted by opt-out tariffs. *Nature Climate Change*, *5*(9), 868–871. DOI: 10.1038/nclimate2681

Ekstrand, M. D., Das, A., Burke, R., & Diaz, F. (2022). *Fairness in information access systems. Foundations and Trends® in Information Retrieval, 16*(1–2), 1–177. https://doi.org/DOI: 10.1561/1500000079

Ellen, P. S., Wiener, J. L., & Cobb-Walgren, C. (1991). The role of perceived consumer effectiveness in motivating environmentally conscious behaviors. *Journal of Public Policy & Marketing*, *10*(2), 102–117. DOI: 10.1177/074391569101000206

Eom, K., & Choy, B. K. C. (2025). Is common behavior considered moral? The role of perceived others' motives in moral norm inferences and motivation about environmental behavior. *Journal of Experimental Social Psychology*, *116*, 104684. DOI: 10.1016/j.jesp.2024.104684

European Data Protection Board. (2023). *Guidelines 3/2022 on deceptive design patterns in social media platform interfaces*. Retrieved from, https://www.edpb.europa.eu/our-work-tools/our-documents/guidelines/guidelines-032022-deceptive-design-patterns-social-media_en

Federal Trade Commission. (2022a, September). *Bringing dark patterns to light* (Staff Report). Retrieved from, https://www.ftc.gov/reports/bringing-dark-patterns-light

Federal Trade Commission. (2022b, November 28). *FTC, states sue Google and iHeartMedia for deceptive ads promoting the Pixel 4 smartphone* [Press release]. Retrieved from, https://www.ftc.gov/news-events/news/press-releases/2022/11/ftc-states-sue-google-iheartmedia-deceptive-ads-promoting-pixel-4-smartphone

Feldman, M., Friedler, S. A., Moeller, J., Scheidegger, C., & Venkatasubramanian, S. (2015). Certifying and removing disparate impact. In *Proceedings of the 21st ACM SIGKDD International Conference on Knowledge Discovery and Data Mining* (pp. 259–268).

Felfernig, A., Jeran, M., Ninaus, G., Reinfrank, F., & Reiterer, S. (2013). Toward the Next Generation of Recommender Systems: Applications and Research Challenges. In Tsihrintzis, G., Virvou, M., & Jain, L. (Eds.), *Multimedia Services in Intelligent Environments. Smart Innovation, Systems and Technologies* (Vol. 24). Springer., DOI: 10.1007/978-3-319-00372-6_5

Feng, C. Y., Martinez-Lopez, F. J., Li, Y. C., & Campo-Fernandez, J. (2025). Personalize it, no return: Nudging online consumers towards product personalization that makes the product non-returnable with herd instinct and regret nudges. *Electronic Commerce Research and Applications*, *73*, 101525. DOI: 10.1016/j.elerap.2025.101525

Fernández, J. D., Willburger, L., Wiethe, C., Wenninger, S., & Fridgen, G. (2025). Scaling smart cities with federated learning. *Business & Information Systems Engineering*. Advance online publication. DOI: 10.1007/s12599-025-00957-z

Finkbeiner, M., Inaba, A., Tan, R. B. H., Christiansen, K., & Klüppel, H.-J. (2006). The new international standards for life cycle assessment: ISO 14040 and ISO 14044. *The International Journal of Life Cycle Assessment*, *11*(2), 80–85. DOI: 10.1065/lca2006.02.002

Gebru, T., Morgenstern, J., Vecchione, B., Vaughan, J. W., Wallach, H., Iii, H. D., & Crawford, K. (2021). Datasheets for datasets. *Communications of the ACM*, *64*(12), 86–92. DOI: 10.1145/3458723

Goldstein, N. J., Cialdini, R. B., & Griskevicius, V. (2008). A room with a viewpoint: Using social norms to motivate environmental conservation. *The Journal of Consumer Research*, *35*(3), 472–482. DOI: 10.1086/586910

González–Cebrián, A., Bradford, M., Chis, A. E., & González-Vélez, H. (2024). Standardised versioning of datasets: A FAIR-compliant proposal. *Scientific Data*, *11*(1), 358. DOI: 10.1038/s41597-024-03153-y PMID: 38594314

Guo, Y., Morris, K. E., Sumner, M., & Taylor, M. (2025). A framework for measuring physical garment durability. *Cleaner and Responsible Consumption*, *16*, 100245. DOI: 10.1016/j.clrc.2024.100245

Gutiérrez, P., & Gérardy, J.-Y. (2017). Causal inference and uplift modelling: A review of the literature. In *Proceedings of the 3rd International Conference on Predictive Applications and APIs* (pp. 1–13). PMLR.

Hansen, P. G., & Jespersen, A. M. (2013). Nudge and the manipulation of choice: A framework for the responsible use of the nudge approach to behaviour change in public policy. *European Journal of Risk Regulation*, *4*(1), 3–28. DOI: 10.1017/S1867299X00002762

Hou, Y. M., Song, Y. Q., & Wang, Z. J. (2025). Transfer learning for linear regression with differential privacy. *Complex & Intelligent Systems*, *11*(1), 100. Advance online publication. DOI: 10.1007/s40747-024-01759-8

Huang, M., & Fang, S. (2024). Mechanisms of self-control in the influence of moral elevation on pro-social behavior: A study based on an experimental paradigm. *Psychology Research and Behavior Management*, *17*, 537–552. DOI: 10.2147/PRBM.S446186 PMID: 38374937

Hyun, J., Lee, K., & Kim-Vick, J. (2021). Consumer responses to trade-offs in eco-friendly clothing: The moderating effects of fashion leadership and regulatory focus. *Journal of Retailing and Consumer Services*, *59*, 102365. DOI: 10.1016/j.jretconser.2020.102365

ISO. (2006). *ISO 14040: Life cycle assessment—Principles and framework*. International Organization for Standardization. Retrieved from, https://www.iso.org/standard/37456.html

ISO. (2014). *ISO 14046: Water footprint—Principles, requirements and guidelines*. International Organization for Standardization. Retrieved from, https://www.iso.org/standard/43263.html

Jachimowicz, J. M., Duncan, S., Weber, E. U., & Johnson, E. J. (2019). When and why defaults influence decisions: A meta-analysis of default effects. *Behavioural Public Policy*, *3*(2), 159–186. DOI: 10.1017/bpp.2018.43

Janson, A., & Barev, T. J. (2024). Making the default more legitimate: The role of autonomy and transparency for digital privacy nudges. *Information Technology & People*, *2024*. Advance online publication. DOI: 10.1108/ITP-04-2023-0334

Kahneman, D. (2011). *Thinking, fast and slow*. Farrar, Straus and Giroux.

Kapoor, P. S., Maggon, M., & Gangwani, K. K. (2025). Inform me or make me laugh: Influencer marketing and the role of emotional contagion and information value. *International Journal of Consumer Studies, 49*(1), e70005. DOI: 10.1111/ijcs.70005

Kohavi, R., & Longbotham, R. (2023). Online controlled experiments and A/B tests. In Phung, D., Webb, G. I., & Sammut, C. (Eds.), *Encyclopedia of Machine Learning and Data Science*. Springer., DOI: 10.1007/978-1-4899-7502-7_891-2

Kohavi, R., Tang, D., & Xu, Y. (2020). *Trustworthy online controlled experiments: A practical guide to A/B testing*. Cambridge University Press. DOI: 10.1017/9781108653985

Lee, S. H. N., Kim, H., & Yang, K. (2015). Impacts of sustainable value and business stewardship on lifestyle practices in clothing consumption. *Fashion and Textiles, 2*(1), 17. DOI: 10.1186/s40691-015-0043-8

Li, M., Tan, M., Wang, S., Li, J., Zhang, G., & Zhong, Y. (2021). The effect of preceding self-control on green consumption behavior: The moderating role of moral elevation. *Psychology Research and Behavior Management, 14*, 2169–2180. DOI: 10.2147/PRBM.S341786 PMID: 34992478

Lou, X. Q., & Xu, Y. J. (2024). Consumption of sustainable denim products: The contribution of blockchain certified eco-labels. *Journal of Theoretical and Applied Electronic Commerce Research, 19*(1), 396–411. DOI: 10.3390/jtaer19010021

Maki, A., Carrico, A. R., Raimi, K. T., Truelove, H. B., Araujo, B., & Yeung, K. L. (2019). Meta-analysis of pro-environmental behaviour spillover. *Nature Sustainability, 2*(4), 307–315. DOI: 10.1038/s41893-019-0263-9

Manfredi, R., Prontera, C. T., Mariano, F., Pugliese, M., Maggiore, A., Zizzari, A., Cinquino, M., Tarantini, I., Gigli, G., & Maiorano, V. (2025). Optimization of electron transport layer inkjet printing towards fully solution-processable OLEDs. *Materials (Basel), 18*(14), 3231. DOI: 10.3390/ma18143231 PMID: 40731441

Mattis, N., Masur, P., Möller, J., & van Atteveldt, W. (2024). Nudging towards news diversity: A theoretical framework for facilitating diverse news consumption through recommender design. *New Media & Society, 26*(7), 3681–3706. DOI: 10.1177/14614448221104413

Michels, L., Ochmann, J., Schmitt, K., Laumer, S., & Tiefenbeck, V. (2024). Salience, transparency, and self-nudging: A digital nudge to promote healthier food product choices. *European Journal of Information Systems, 33*(5), 717–747. DOI: 10.1080/0960085X.2023.2229787

Miller, T. (2019). Explanation in artificial intelligence: Insights from the social sciences. *Artificial Intelligence, 267*, 1–38. DOI: 10.1016/j.artint.2018.07.007

Mitchell, M., Wu, S., Zaldivar, A., Barnes, P., Hutchinson, B., Spitzer, E., Raji, I. D., & Gebru, T. (2019). Model cards for model reporting. In *Proceedings of the 2019 Conference on Fairness, Accountability, and Transparency* (pp. 220–229). https://doi.org/DOI: 10.1145/3287560.3287596

National Institute of Standards and Technology. (2023). *Artificial intelligence risk management framework (AI RMF 1.0)* (pp. 1–42). https://doi.org/DOI: 10.6028/NIST.AI.100-1

Niinimäki, K., Peters, G., Dahlbo, H., Perry, P., Rissanen, T., & Gwilt, A. (2020). The environmental price of fast fashion. *Nature Reviews. Earth & Environment, 1*(4), 189–200. DOI: 10.1038/s43017-020-0039-9

Oh, J., Nah, S., & Yang, Z. D. (2025). How autonomy of artificial intelligence technology and user agency influence AI perceptions and attitudes: Applying the theory of psychological reactance. *Journal of Broadcasting & Electronic Media, 69*(3), 161–182. DOI: 10.1080/08838151.2025.2485319

Onwezen, M. C., Bartels, J., & Antonides, G. (2014). The self-regulatory function of anticipated pride and guilt in a sustainable and healthy consumption context. *European Journal of Social Psychology, 44*(1), 53–68. DOI: 10.1002/ejsp.1991

Peng, C., & Mitra, U. (2024). Planning versus learning: Fair space-time scheduling for unwired networks. *IEEE Transactions on Wireless Communications, 23*(11), 16621–16634. DOI: 10.1109/TWC.2024.3444693

Perra, N., & Rocha, L. E. C. (2019). Modelling opinion dynamics in the age of algorithmic personalisation. *Scientific Reports, 9*(1), 7261. Advance online publication. DOI: 10.1038/s41598-019-43830-2 PMID: 31086228

Pichert, D., & Katsikopoulos, K. V. (2008). Green defaults: Information presentation and pro-environmental behaviour. *Journal of Environmental Psychology, 28*(1), 63–73. DOI: 10.1016/j.jenvp.2007.09.004

Pitoura, E., Stefanidis, K., & Koutrika, G. (2022). Fairness in rankings and recommendations: An overview. *The VLDB Journal, 31*(3), 431–458. DOI: 10.1007/s00778-021-00697-y

Poursabzi-Sangdeh, F., Goldstein, D. G., Hofman, J. M., Vaughan, J. W., & Wallach, H. (2021). Manipulating and measuring model interpretability. In *Proceedings of the 2021 CHI Conference on Human Factors in Computing Systems* (Article 1). DOI: 10.1145/3411764.3445315

Protocol, G. H. G. (2011). *Product life cycle accounting and reporting standard.* World Resources Institute. Retrieved from, https://ghgprotocol.org/product-standard

Puranik, B., Guldogan, O., Madhow, U., & Pedarsani, R. (2024). Long-term fairness in sequential multi-agent selection with positive reinforcement. *IEEE Journal on Selected Areas in Information Theory, 5*, 424–441. DOI: 10.1109/JSAIT.2024.3416078

Raji, I. D., Smart, A., White, R. N., Mitchell, M., Gebru, T., Hutchinson, B., Smith-Loud, J., Theron, D., & Barnes, P. (2020). Closing the AI accountability gap: Defining an end-to-end framework for internal algorithmic auditing. In *Proceedings of the 2020 Conference on Fairness, Accountability, and Transparency* (pp. 33–44). https://doi.org/DOI: 10.1145/3351095.3372873

Repenning, A. (2024). Speeding up, slowing down, losing grip: On digital media metronomes and timespace friction in the platformised temporalities of fashion design. *Environment and Planning A. Environment & Planning A, 56*(5), 1503–1520. DOI: 10.1177/0308518X241231691

Roichman, R., Sprecher, B., Blass, V., Meshulam, T., & Makov, T. (2024). The convenience economy: Product flows and GHG emissions of returned apparel in the EU. *Resources, Conservation and Recycling, 210*, e107811. DOI: 10.1016/j.resconrec.2024.107811

Roichman, R., Sprecher, B., Blass, V., Meshulam, T., & Makov, T. (2024). The convenience economy: Product flows and GHG emissions of returned apparel in the EU. *Resources, Conservation and Recycling, 210*, 107811. Advance online publication. DOI: 10.1016/j.resconrec.2024.107811

Rzepakowski, P., & Jaroszewicz, S. (2012). Decision trees for uplift modeling with single and multiple treatments. *Knowledge and Information Systems, 32*(2), 303–327. DOI: 10.1007/s10115-011-0434-0

Schultz, P. W., Nolan, J. M., Cialdini, R. B., Goldstein, N., & Griskevicius, V. (2007). The constructive, destructive, and reconstructive power of social norms. *Psychological Science, 18*(5), 429–434. DOI: 10.1111/j.1467-9280.2007.01917.x PMID: 17576283

Sheil, B., Anagnostopoulos, C., Buckley, R., Oryem Ciantia, M., Febrianto, E., Fu, J., Gao, Z., Geng, X., Gong, B., Hanley, K., He, P., & Kolomvatsos, K., de C.F.L. Lopes, B., Ninic, J., Previtali, M., Rezania, M., Ruiz-Lopez, A., Sun, J., Suryasentana, S., ... Zhang, P. (. (2026). Artificial intelligence transformations in geotechnics: Progress, challenges and future enablers. *Computers and Geotechnics, 189*, 107604. DOI: 10.1016/j.compgeo.2025.107604

Shen, Z., Hu, Y., & Yin, Y. (2025). Algorithm-generated identity labeling promotes identity-consistent product preferences. *Psychology and Marketing*, *42*(6), 1667–1679. DOI: 10.1002/mar.22195

Shen, Z. Y., Hu, Y. X., & Yin, Y. L. (2025). Algorithm-generated identity labeling promotes identity-consistent product preferences. *Psychology and Marketing*, *42*(6), 1667–1679. DOI: 10.1002/mar.22195

Shin, D., Kee, K. F., & Shin, E. Y. (2023). The nudging effect of accuracy alerts for combating the diffusion of misinformation: Algorithmic news sources, trust in algorithms, and users' discernment of fake news. *Journal of Broadcasting & Electronic Media*, *67*(2), 141–160. DOI: 10.1080/08838151.2023.2175830

Shin, D., Kee, K. F., & Shin, E. Y. (2023). The nudging effect of accuracy alerts for combating the diffusion of misinformation: Algorithmic news sources, trust in algorithms, and users' discernment of fake news. *Journal of Broadcasting & Electronic Media*, *67*(2), 141–160. DOI: 10.1080/08838151.2023.2175830

Singh, A., & Joachims, T. (2018). Fairness of exposure in rankings. In *Proceedings of the 24th ACM SIGKDD International Conference on Knowledge Discovery & Data Mining* (pp. 2219–2228). DOI: 10.1145/3219819.3220088

Steindl, C., Jonas, E., Sittenthaler, S., Traut-Mattausch, E., & Greenberg, J. (2015). Understanding psychological reactance: New developments and findings. *Zeitschrift für Psychologie*, *223*(4), 205–214. DOI: 10.1027/2151-2604/a000222 PMID: 27453805

Stern, P. C. (2000). Toward a coherent theory of environmentally significant behavior. *The Journal of Social Issues*, *56*(3), 407–424. DOI: 10.1111/0022-4537.00175

Sunstein, C. R. (2016). *The ethics of influence: Government in the age of behavioral science*. Cambridge University Press. DOI: 10.1017/CBO9781316493021

Sutton, R. S., & Barto, A. G. (2018). *Reinforcement learning: An introduction* (2nd ed.). MIT Press.

Tamlyn, K. A., Champine, V., Teel, T. L., Abrams, K. M., & Niemiec, R. M. (2025). From self to society: Comparing the social-psychological drivers of personal-sphere, social diffusion, and civic action behaviors in native plant gardening. *Society & Natural Resources*, *38*(9), 1003–1019. DOI: 10.1080/08941920.2025.2494011

Thaler, R. H., & Sunstein, C. R. (2008). *Nudge: Improving decisions about health, wealth, and happiness*. Yale University Press.

von Zahn, M., Bauer, K., Mihale-Wilson, C., Jagow, J., Speicher, M., & Hinz, O. (2024). Smart green nudging: Reducing product returns through digital footprints and causal machine learning. *Marketing Science*. Advance online publication. DOI: 10.1287/mksc.2022.0393

Wang, T., Liu, F. F., Xiong, S. S., & Wang, K. (2025). Getting licence or keeping consistent? The role of moral identity in subsequent pro-environmental behaviours. *Asian Journal of Social Psychology*, *28*(1), e12670. DOI: 10.1111/ajsp.12670

Wang, X. M., Li, Q., Yu, D., Li, Q., & Xu, G. D. (2024). Counterfactual explanation for fairness in recommendation. *ACM Transactions on Information Systems*, *42*(4), ART106. Advance online publication. DOI: 10.1145/3643670

WRAP. (2012). *Valuing our clothes: The evidence base* (35 pp.). Retrieved from, https://www.wrap.ngo/resources/report/valuing-our-clothes-true-cost-how-we-design-use-and-dispose-clothing-uk-2012

WRAP. (2017). *Valuing our clothes: The cost of UK fashion* (54 pp.). Retrieved from, https://www.wrap.ngo/resources/report/valuing-our-clothes-cost-uk-fashion#download-file

Ye, X. W., & Fu, L. Q. (2024). Joint codebook selection and UE scheduling for unlicensed mmWave NR-U/WiGig coexistence based on deep reinforcement learning. *IEEE Transactions on Mobile Computing*, *23*(9), 8919–8934. DOI: 10.1109/TMC.2024.3356442

KEY TERMS AND DEFINITIONS

A/B Testing: A/B testing is the randomized comparison of two or more versions of a web element or policy to estimate causal effects on user behaviour, and it serves here as the baseline method for validating interventions before wide deployment.

Algorithmic Nudging: Algorithmic nudging refers to the deliberate design of automated recommendation or interface cues that steer users toward certain choices while preserving freedom of choice; in this chapter it denotes AI-driven signals intended to promote more sustainable fashion behaviour.

Carbon-per-Conversion: Carbon-per-Conversion is an operational impact metric that divides estimated product lifecycle emissions by the number of conversions attributable to a policy, useful for comparing the environmental efficiency of alternative recommendation strategies.

Contextual Bandit: A contextual bandit is an online learning algorithm that selects personalized actions (e.g., which nudge to show) based on user and contextual features, balancing exploration and exploitation to maximize a reward such as sustainable conversions.

Fairness-Aware Ranking: Fairness-aware ranking denotes ranking or exposure algorithms that explicitly include constraints or corrective procedures so that items, vendors, or user groups receive equitable visibility and opportunity in the recommender output.

Guardrails: Guardrails are pre-specified rules, constraints, or monitoring procedures (ethical, fairness, or business) embedded into model deployment to limit harmful behaviours and to make trade-offs explicit and auditable.

Impact@K: Impact@K is a practical metric that aggregates the environmental or social impact (for example, carbon footprint avoided) associated with the top-K recommended items, enabling comparison of recommendation policies by their realized sustainability outcomes.

Individual Treatment Effect (ITE) / Uplift Modeling: ITE or uplift modeling estimates the causal effect of an intervention on individual users (who will change their behaviour if nudged), allowing targeted allocation of nudges to those most likely to respond positively and reducing wasted interventions.

Metric Hygiene: Metric hygiene refers to the disciplined practice of defining stable, consistent KPI definitions and denominators, pre-specifying primary outcomes, and auditing for interference or carry-over effects to ensure valid evaluation.

Off-policy Evaluation (OPE): OPE consists of statistical methods that estimate the value of a candidate policy using historical logs collected under a different policy, providing safety checks before full online rollout.

Opt-out Autonomy: Opt-out autonomy means designing interventions so users can easily decline or change personalization settings, thereby preserving user agency and minimizing perceived coercion or autonomy costs.

Transparency / Explainability: Transparency or explainability denotes the design and communication practices that make algorithmic decisions intelligible to users—why a recommendation was made and what impact it implies—thereby increasing trust and accountability.

Chapter 5
Ethical Personalisation in Fashion E-Commerce:
Leveraging AI for Sustainable Consumption

H. P. Ramya
http://orcid.org/0000-0002-2048-807X
Dayananda Sagar College of Engineering, India

Mohit Saundatti
http://orcid.org/0009-0002-2753-075X
Dayananda Sagar College of Engineering, India

ABSTRACT

This chapter explores the ethical implications of AI-driven personalization in fashion e-commerce and proposes an "Ethical Personalization Framework" that balances commercial success with societal and environmental responsibility. It critiques conventional personalization systems for promoting impulsive buying and unsustainable consumption. Drawing from ethical theories—Virtue Ethics, Utilitarianism, and Deontology—and case studies like Patagonia and Zalando, the chapter outlines principles of fairness, transparency, user autonomy, privacy, and sustainability. It recommends operational strategies and policy interventions for retailers, developers, and regulators to embed ethical design in AI systems, thereby supporting responsible consumption and aligning fashion retail with the UN Sustainable Development Goals.

DOI: 10.4018/979-8-3373-5525-2.ch005

1. INTRODUCTION

The apparel retail industry is facing a tremendous digital revolution fuelled by AI adoption in e-commerce channels. In the past decade, AI has transitioned from a buzzword to a strategic imperative for international retailers. Of all its uses, personalisation has become an effective agent for improving customer engagement, conversion, and loyalty. Personalization on the online fashion front means product, service, and experience tailoring to the individual's requirement by recommendation systems powered by AI. They scan customers' data—search history, purchases, and demographics—to provide personalized recommendations, prices, and offers. Leaders such as ASOS, Zalando, and Net-a-Porter set the tone, delivering ease-of-use, user-friendly shopping experiences. Where this creates business value, it does so with moral and sustainability considerations. They are led primarily by short-term profitability alone in most such systems, encouraging impulse buy and subsidizing fast fashion, as contrasted with climate goals and circular economy strategies. Studies reveal this double-edged sword—AI can streamline operations and build loyalty but also trigger overconsumption and ignore the planet.

The chapter focuses on the key question: How can AI fashion online shopping personalisation be re-conceptualised to promote more ethical and sustainable consumption? The discussion intersects AI ethics, marketing, and sustainability, highlighting that technology needs to be balanced with social and environmental obligations. As Millennial and Gen Z care about sustainability, brands are compelled to marry ethics and digital strategy. The chapter speculates ethical personalisation from multidisciplinary literature and critiques problems such as bias, privacy, manipulation, and loss of autonomy. It contends that AI can both mirror and shape greener consumer behaviour. In support of students with this, the chapter presents the cases of Patagonia, Zalando, and ThredUp, showing how sustainable products would be guaranteed through AI. With Virtue Ethics, Utilitarianism, and Deontological Ethics as its foundation, it deconstructs these models and learns lessons for ethical AI design. One of the key outputs is the Ethical Personalisation Framework, combining academic expertise and best practice. It provides a set of principles and design guidance for policy-makers, developers, and retailers—prioritizing justice, transparency, user control, and sustainability and aligning with the UN SDGs and circular fashion. Lastly, the chapter establishes governance strategies, regulation requirements, and avenues of future research to disentangle AI's impact on sustainability. Integrating ethics into fashion personalization, the chapter offers theory- and practice-informed insights to support ethically informed, sustainable consumption in the digital marketplace.

2. CONCEPTUALISING ETHICAL PERSONALISATION

As personalisation with AI becomes ever more integral to the business operations of fashion e-commerce businesses, the need arises to transcend its common description as an essentially profit-maximizing technical device. The theorization of ethical personalisation emerges from this critical eye as a reaction to reconsider personalisation practice to the advantage of models which honour and further to promote superior societal, ethical, and environmental goals in addition to business goals.

Ethical personalisation can be defined at its essence as:

"The creation and application of AI-driven personalisation systems that balance commercial interests of usefulness and efficiency with normative values of fairness, transparency, consumer autonomy, data protection, and sustainability, thereby promoting well-informed, aware, and responsible consumption patterns".

This working definition places ethical personalisation within the broader discussion on Responsible AI, recognizing that algorithmic systems have immense control over consumer decisions and, by proxy, consumption patterns with material social and environmental consequences. Traditional recommender systems are chiefly focused on maximizing engagement metrics and short-term volumes of sales, but an ethically informed approach reverses these priorities so as not to compromise on the long-term welfare of consumers and the environmental system.

2.1 Fairness

Moral personalisation is founded on fairness. Fairness in algorithms must minimize the possibility of machine learning algorithms and data sets promoting exclusionary or discriminatory outcomes. For fashion e-commerce, fairness means that algorithms for personalisation must avoid disproportionately targeting at-risk consumers and reinforcing consumption inequalities along the lines of income, gender, or culture. This is consistent with general AI ethics guidelines that call for minimizing bias and treating all parties fairly. For example, fairness metrics can be used to determine whether product recommendations are representative and available to different consumer segments.

2.2 Transparency

Transparency calls for the explanation of how personalisation systems operate, what data is gathered, how the data is processed, and how suggestions are produced to be clearly stated. Practically, what it means is retailers have to get away from impenetrable algorithmic rationality and put people in a position where they can see why particular products are being recommended to them. Transparency leads to trust, informed consent, and compliance with laws like the General Data Protection Regulation (GDPR) that give priority to people's right to know and contest machine-led suggestions. For since accountability researchers posit, explainable AI (XAI) plays an important role in ethical system design.

2.3 User Autonomy

For respect of user autonomy, personalisation systems need to empower consumers so that they can exercise considerable choice and control in their engagement with digital platforms. This feature is founded on the principle that consumers should not be pushed passively by hyper-personalized pushes but also have a certain level of autonomy to wade through personalized suggestions on their own values and tastes. Operational measures can include opt-out or opt-in provisions for specific types of recommendations, variable levels of personalisation control, and open access routes and erasure for information. Scholarship on Value-Sensitive Design (VSD) supports the belief that information artefacts need to be planned to convey and safeguard values like autonomy, dignity, and self-determination for human beings.

2.4 Privacy

Ethical personalisation has to be supported by robust data privacy measures. The extensive data accumulation process for personalisation seriously raises concerns about consumer surveillance, misusing personal data, and any eventual privacy violations. Best practice involves the minimisation of data, limitation of purpose, and secure storage controls, i.e., only necessary information is collected and its use is limited to the purpose agreed upon. The consent must be explicit, informed, and capable of being withdrawn at any time. The privacy-by-design principle, which is one of the axioms of Responsible AI, requires privacy concerns to be built into every phase of system design and deployment, and not addressed as an afterthought.

2.5 Sustainability

The most defining feature of ethical personalisation in the context of fashion is that it formally embeds sustainability imperatives within its design. This aspect acknowledges that AI personalisation mechanisms, if optimised for ultimate sales without foresight, could end up exaggerating the environmental footprint of fast fashion by encouraging excessive and compulsive consumption. Alternatively, ethical personalisation repositions the use of recommender systems: they need to be set up to nudge consumers towards more sustainable options, i.e., eco-labelled products, rental or second-hand products, and transparently supplied brands. The digital nudging process, if used ethically, can direct consumer choice towards waste avoidance, product longevity, and increased application of circular economy thinking.

2.6 Applicable Frameworks: Value-Sensitive Design, Responsible AI, and Digital Nudging

Ethical personalisation demands strong conceptual underpinning combining technology, ethics, and human values. Friedman et al.'s Value-Sensitive Design (VSD) insists on incorporating human values such as fairness, autonomy, and sustainability within system design even if it means compromising on efficiency. It offers tools for stakeholder identification, resolution of value conflicts, and management of normative challenges across a system's lifetime.

Accountable AI, as Floridi and Cowls (2019) point out, builds on this by proposing five fundamental principles: beneficence, non-maleficence, autonomy, justice, and explicability. They are transferred into policy, audit, and regulation of algorithms applied to ethical AI in fashion retail.

Digital Nudging, based on Thaler and Sunstein's (2008) behavioral economics, applies choice architecture to subtly nudge people toward sustainability without ever crossing the line of their autonomy. When applied ethically, it serves long-term purposes without compromising user autonomy.

2.7 Recommended Ethical Personalisation Framework

The integration of the above elements is a comprehensive Ethical Personalisation Framework that fashion e-commerce businesses can use as a pragmatic roadmap to system development and management. The framework positions fairness, transparency, user control, privacy, and sustainability as mutually dependent pillars, each underpinned by actionable guidelines and markers of implementation.

Figure 1.

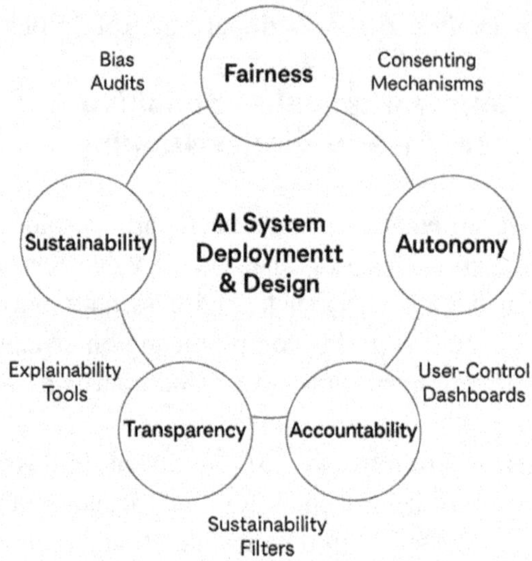

2.7 – AI System Deployment & Design

To put this into perspective, the accompanying diagram should show these five foundational pillars that intersect with each other at the point of AI system deployment and design. Each pillar can be encircled by functional items—like explain ability tools, consenting mechanisms, bias audits, sustainability filters, and user-control dashboards—depicting how ethical thinking pervades technical and operational domains.

The framework encourages multi-stakeholder collaboration among designers, developers, marketers, data scientists, and policymakers to bring ethical imperatives into the foreground instead of the periphery of AI innovation in fashion retailing. Through embedding these principles in the tech substrate and organisational culture, fashion businesses can not only control the risks associated with conventional personalisation models but also employ AI as an instrument of change for sustainable consumption practices.

As a whole, the vision of ethical personalisation across all these different dimensions reminds us of the necessity for an intentional paradigm shift: away from algorithmic platforms that take advantage of behavioural vulnerabilities towards those that honour people's rights, build trust, and advance the global sustainability agenda.

3. LITERATURE REVIEW

Scholarly research into AI-based personalization within fashion e-commerce is growing quickly, which indicates speeding up of the rate at which digital technologies are transforming consumer experience and industry value chains. This section of the paper critically synthesises existing academic literature, categorizing it into five interrelated thematic areas: (i) AI within fashion e-commerce innovation and market dynamics, (ii) the technological foundations of personalisation algorithms, (iii) novel ethical issues arising from their use, (iv) the sustainability impacts of traditional personalisation practice, and (v) new research and industry-led frameworks that set out solutions for responsible, ethical personalisation.

3.1 AI in Fashion E-Commerce: Use Cases, Market Trends, and Growth

Recent McKinsey (2024), Accenture (2025), and Global Fashion Agenda (2024) fashion industry reports highlight that AI personalization is not only a technological advancement but also a primary enabler of sustainable consumption, and generative AI can fuel such advancements.

In the last decade, AI has been a major part of the world's fashion e-commerce. McKinsey State of Fashion (2022) estimates that AI is widely used in trend and demand forecasting, inventory optimization, virtual fitting rooms, and hyper-personalized marketing. Among them, personalization is one of the most business-relevant applications of AI (Davenport et al., 2020).

Industry data reveal that AI significantly enhances conversions and customer satisfaction. Business of Fashion (2023) revealed that 74% of leading online fashion retailers use AI-powered recommendation engines. Jun et al. (2021) also cited higher adoption amid the COVID-19 pandemic as businesses adapted to store closures.

Even small DTC businesses today make use of AI for differentiation, since the plug-and-play apps and cloud-based systems are available (Kumar et al., 2021). But as these technologies move more profoundly into human existence, they more and more raise questions about their collateral social and environmental consequences—making it all the more necessary to explore their technical and ethical underpinnings.

3.2 Personalisation Algorithms: How They Work, Recommender Systems, Data Mining, Predictive Analytics

Personalization algorithm studies span broadly from collaborative and content-based filtering to hybrid and deep learning approaches (Ricci et al., 2011). They all basically depend on enormous, high-quality data—everything from user ratings and buying behaviour to indirect signals such as clickstreams and time spent on page—to suggest items personalized for every user.

Jannach (2022) categorize recommenders as three kinds: memory-based (such as neighbourhood methods based on similarity matrices), model-based (utilizing machine learning to discover latent action patterns), and hybrid systems that merge both to achieve more accuracy.

The latest predictive analytics technologies have further advanced personalisation systems to unprecedented degrees. Algorithms now interpret unstructured information—reviews, images, and social media posts—using NLP and computer vision (Sun & Zhang, 2023). Moreover, real-time data processing allows dynamic personalisation, updating recommendations automatically upon user interaction.

While these technologies improve customer experience and increase sales, they also have ethical implications. Sundar and Marathe (2021) warn that hyper-personalisation may include intrusive monitoring, eroding consumer privacy and autonomy if left unregulated.

3.3 Ethical Implications: AI Bias, Effects on Privacy, Psychological Manipulation

Current literature has considered the ethical issues with AI personalization in e-tailing critically, such as algorithmic bias being an overarching issue. Bias can occur either due to skewed training data or defective model design reflecting societal biases (Mehrabi et al., 2021). In online fashion shopping, this could lead to skewed product presentation within groups, even perpetuating stereotypes or neglecting underrepresented groups.

Data privacy is also at stake. As Acquisti et al. (2020) point out, personalisation initiatives depend heavily on rich customer data, frequently obtained passively in the absence of customers' explicit consent. Although legislation such as the EU's GDPR has intensified privacy walls, fashion retail is still largely under regulated internationally, leaving space for intrusive data collection and third-party trading.

Scholars like Yeung (2019) and Zuboff (2019) have posited that AI personalisation is able to take advantage of cognitive bias and hence subtly manipulate psychology. Fashion retail algorithmic nudging has the potential to make impulse buying respectable, invading consumer agency and raising ethical concerns around exploitative sales.

Empirical research justifies the discovery of increased consumer dissatisfaction. Awad and Krishnan (2022) discovered that users enjoy relevant suggestions but are concerned about algorithmic transparency and data control. These results highlight the necessity for increased transparency and user control in personalisation procedures.

3.4 Sustainability Impacts: Spontaneous Consumption, Fast Fashion, Waste Creation

The intersection of AI personalization and sustainability is emerging as a priority, especially given the poor environmental track record of fashion—accounting for nearly 10% of global carbon emissions, along with severe textile waste and water pollution (Ellen MacArthur Foundation, 2017).

Researchers such as Niinimäki et al. (2020) contend that AI personalization, normally Profit-based, amplifies these problems since they encourage overconsumption and fast fashion turnover cycles. Hyper-personalized guidance and flash sales encourage impulse buying, with high product turnover and increased wastage.

On the other hand, studies indicate that AI can facilitate sustainable consumption if it is developed using circular economy principles. Henninger et al. (2021) describe recommender systems focused on environmentally friendly products, second-hand resell marketplaces, and renting plans, lengthening product lifecycles and lowering resource consumption. Park and Armstrong (2020) promote sustainability filters for algorithms, allowing consumers to select more sustainable products.

Although such potential exists, real application of sustainability-focused personalisation in everyday life is minimal, with vast-scale examples being few and far between. Such a discrepancy necessitates strong ethical frameworks and regulations to ensure responsible AI utilization in fashion online shopping.

3.5 Responsible Personalisation: Academics' Key Models and Business Practice

In reaction to ethics and sustainability concerns, researchers and practitioners are crafting responsible personalisation models. One of these models is Value-Sensitive Design (VSD), a formal approach for embedding human values within technology design (Friedman & Hendry, 2019). Deployed to personalisation, VSD is interested in understanding how to co-design algorithms for prioritising fairness, explainability, and user agency.

Responsible AI theory, as Floridi and Cowls (2019) characterized it, suggests important principles like explain ability, accountability, and beneficence—now being used in fashion retail. Jiang et al. (2022) suggest applying explainable AI (XAI) to explain recommendation logic and thereby establish consumer trust and well-informed consent.

Industry practice also hints at future best practice. Brands such as Zalando and Patagonia have used recommender systems to display eco-label certified products and supply chain transparency. The Sustainable Apparel Coalition's (2023) whitepaper identifies that such systems can integrate AI personalisation and sustainability objectives, though even then scalability is an inherent challenge.

Lastly, digital nudging literature presents a positive moral solution in proposing, reflective decision architecture has the ability to make environmentally friendly options for consumers without limiting freedom of choice. Coupled with behavioural economics and Responsible AI, digital nudging presents a balanced approach towards achieving profitability alongside environmental and ethical considerations.

3.6 Summary of Literature Review

Lastly, the literature substantiates that AI personalization is both an imperative innovation driver in fashion online retailing and a potential source of ethical and sustainability threats if neglected. There is existing literature that demands the shift from profit-driven algorithmic designs to allow multi-dimensioned constructions comprising fairness, transparency, user agency, data privacy, and sustainability. This synergy provides the theoretical foundation on which the Ethical Personalisation Framework, as outlined in the following sections, is built and how the sustainable consumption of the world fashion industry can be augmented by AI technologies, given that these are appropriately designed and regulated.

4. OPERATIONAL CHALLENGES OF ETHICAL AI PERSONALISATION

Notwithstanding the revolutionary power of ethical AI-based personalisation in online fashion buying, the operational challenges of adopting it cross-cut levels across different regions. The challenges are disparate and, with a few exceptions, cross-cutting with more general data governance, business culture, and regulative preparedness issues. Southeast Asia provides a distinctive setting wherein digital adoption is high but data governance and industry practice diverge.

4.1 Data Limitations

The basis of personalisation is high-quality, large-data consumer insights. Yet in reality, most fashion brands are confronted with data silos, disconnected sustainability labels, and poor customer profiles. Inconsistent product metadata — i.e., conflicting definitions of "eco-friendly" or "sustainable" — make algorithmic recommendations problematic. Furthermore, AI models with Western consumer data as the predominant data pool overlook the cultural and behavioural micro-details of Southeast

Asian markets. These limits may create imbalanced or inaccurate personalization, undermining both ethical goals and consumer trust.

4.2 Organisational Culture Readiness

Issuance of ethical personalization requires more than technology infrastructure; it requires changing organizational culture. The majority of fashion companies are still ruled by short-term drivers of profit, making it hard to accord proper priority to sustainability-driven personalization. Resistance could be a result of leadership unwillingness to depart from conventional KPI measures like conversion rate and basket size or the lack of cross-functional collaboration among marketing, IT, and sustainability functions. Without organizational preparedness, AI systems built for ethical personalization are likely to be neither best deployed nor strategically aligned.

4.3 Regulatory Context in Southeast Asia

Southeast Asia will be a prime region for fashion e-commerce, but AI and customer data regulation remains patchy. Singapore's Personal Data Protection Act (PDPA), for example, has stringent data governance requirements, while Indonesia and Vietnam are developing policy on AI. This patchiness makes cross-regional rollouts of ethical personalization systems difficult. Moreover, enforcement mechanisms are yet to develop, and therefore, uncertainty exists in accountability for algorithmic decisions. These gaps in compliance present operational risks for overseas fashion retailers who seek to implement normalized ethical AI practices across various Southeast Asian markets.

5. RISK ANALYSIS OF TRADITIONAL PERSONALISATION

Though AI personalisation has generally been received as the pillar of convenience and business expansion for fashion online retailers, there is also mounting agreement that algorithmic personalisation models, optimised primarily for short-term sales and engagement metrics, pose huge sustainability and ethical risks. This section critically discusses the unwanted effects of conventional algorithmic personalisation utilizing empirical research and multidisciplinary studies to expose its contribution to unsustainable consumption patterns and societal consequences.

5.1 Over-Targeting and Impulse Purchasing Behaviour

Among the glaring issues with classic personalisation is how it contributes to consumers' impulse shopping. Through the processing of behaviourally relevant data, recommender systems make hyper-relevant, time-critical suggestions that leverage psychological signals like scarcity, urgency, and social proof. Although such strategies can yield higher short-term sales, they yield unplanned purchases that consumers do not necessarily need or subsequently regret.

Sundström et al. (2019) demonstrate that hyper-personalised suggestions trigger far more impulse buys than generic ones. Likewise, Kukar-Kinney et al. (2021) posit that algorithmic targeting disempowers cognitive controls so it is increasingly difficult for consumers to avoid instant gratification. Such manipulation of behaviour erodes responsible consumption efforts, a key focus of universal sustainability plans such as the UN's SDG 12.

5.2 Misuse of Data and Privacy Issues

Another widely debated risk of conventional personalisation is mass-scale, frequently black-boxed gathering and utilising customer information. These algorithms need to be continually tuned and thus depend on enormous, high-data—anything from browsing and buying behaviour to psychographic feedback from social media or third parties through to location (Acquisti et al., 2020).

Such a scale of mass data mining is serious in terms of privacy concerns. Awad and Krishnan (2022) established that consumers are generally unaware of the magnitude of surveillance by personalisation. Consent processes are generally not adequately explained, and this constrains scope for informed consumer choice. These practices are at odds with data minimisation and purpose limitation principles in models such as the EU General Data Protection Regulation (GDPR) (Voigt & Von dem Bussche, 2017).

In addition to privacy, data exploitation deepens power imbalances between consumers and large fashion companies. Zuboff (2019) calls this development "surveillance capitalism," where companies trade on personal data in order to predict and shape consumers' behaviour without responsibility or recourse. In internet shopping in fashion, this mechanism underpins an extractive regime that values profit over consumer agency and public interest.

5.3 Algorithmic Assistance for Unsustainable Consumption

Standard personalisation algorithms are generally calibrated for maximizing click-through, purchasing frequency, and basket size—the measurably quantifiable parameters that correspond to the traditional definition of retail success but aim to ignore downstream effects of higher consumption. Evidence from Niinimäki et al. (2020) show that such algorithmic improvements have the direct effect of speeding up the fast fashion cycle, with high product turnover, constant stock refresh, and intensive waste generation.

The unanticipated environmental ramifications of this dynamic are profound. The Ellen MacArthur Foundation (2021) reports that the fashion sector already produces around 92 million tonnes of clothing waste every year, as garment lifecycles shorten because consumers increasingly desire novelty. By fuelling such a drive for perpetual newness through relentless, tailored prodding, AI systems may play a part in a vicious cycle of unsustainable linearity's of production and consumption which is self-defeating to the circular economy's core principles.

Another recent work by Xu et al. (2022) illustrates how repeatedly exposed customers to algorithmic recommendations for fashion-driven buying are less likely to adopt repair, reuse, or recycling habits and therefore add to the industry's environmental footprint. This finding indicates that, left unchecked, classical personalisation not only speeds up environmentally unsound consumption behaviours but also weakens consumers' sensitisation toward the ecological implications of their decisions.

5.4 Social Impacts: Loss of Autonomy and Psychological Manipulation

Aside from environmental concerns, personalization has far-reaching social and psychological effects. Scholars such as Yeung (2019) and Helberger et al. (2018) argue that highly personal suggestions use cognitive biases, stripping consumers of agency over time. Implementing the application of "hyper nudging"—algorithms that adapt dynamically in line with real-time behaviour—can nudge individuals towards decisions incompatible with their long-term interest or values (Helberger, 2018).

Fashion tends to standardise overconsumption as the optimal standard, based on social comparison pressures within social commerce. Personalisation therefore enforces a hyper-material culture where self-perception and self-esteem are based on ongoing buying.

Algorithmic black boxing exacerbates these impacts by reducing consumers' capacity to question the reasoning behind recommendations. Ananny and Crawford (2018) illustrate that the cryptic "black box" character of the majority of recommender systems conceals why profiles are built and forecasts are generated. Inability to be transparent in this erodes trust and raises ethical issues regarding equity and responsibility within algorithmic markets.

5.5 Synthesis: The Call for a Paradigm Shift

The evidence indicates strongly that legacy AI-driven personalisation, business outcome narrowly optimised, poses risks to environmental sustainability and consumer well-being. It enables unhealthy impulse buying and profligacy; dark data behaviour undermines privacy and entrenches power imbalances; and algorithmic manipulation undermines independent, reflective consumption.

All of these risks underscore the imperative to transition to a fairer model of personalisation—a more sustainable one, based on ethics and justice. As subsequent sections detail, reframing personalisation on grounds of fairness, transparency, empowerment of users, data protection, and sustainability can redirect AI as a force for ethical, responsible fashion consumption. This will require technical re-design as well as redefining success in digital fashion retail.

6. EMPIRICAL CASE STUDIES

In order to better show how ethical personalisation theoretical bases can be applied, this section presents three empirical case studies of prominent fashion retailers—Patagonia, Zalando, and ThredUp (with comparative reflections from Net-a-Porter)—that have made sincere efforts to integrate ethical and sustainability considerations within their AI-facilitated personalisation practices. Each case study addresses organisational context, the corresponding AI applications utilised, implementation mechanisms, quantifiable effects, and the wider lessons to be found that can guide industry best practice.

6.1 Patagonia: Prioritizing Sustainability Filter and Conscious Purchase

Context

Patagonia, with its California headquarters and industry-leading outdoor apparel business, is also a global corporate responsibility and sustainability leader. Since it was established in 1973, Patagonia has been an anti-fast fashion pioneer in promoting product durability, repair, and environmental responsibility. In the past two years, Patagonia has employed strategic adoption of digital technologies such as AI software to coordinate its e-commerce personalization platforms with its vision for lessening environmental destruction and promoting ethical consumption.

AI Strategy and Implementation

Whereas other fashion retailers employ personalisation solely to create repeat business, Patagonia combines sustainability as a filter throughout its recommender algorithm's recommendation algorithms in its digital strategy. For instance, when customers shop online, the recommender system on the site favours products that use recycled content, Fair Trade products, or lower-impact supply chains. It does so by including sustainability metadata in products and assigning larger weights to these factors in the algorithm's ranking function.

In addition, Patagonia uses predictive analytics to reduce returns—a principal cause of fashion waste. Based on customers' preference for fit and reviews, the platform offers tailored fit recommendations and presents durability data so consumers can make informed choices likely to lead to product satisfaction and reuse.

The second distinguishing aspect of Patagonia's AI system is its intersection with the Worn Wear program, encouraging product repair and resale. In suitable cases, the site proactively provides refurbished models of an item, or steers buyers toward repair centers rather than new ones. The intersection is a clear deviation from the linear 'buy more' model, setting Patagonia apart as a sustainability leader.

Outcomes

Though complete proprietary data regarding conversion rates are not publicized, Patagonia in-house sustainability reports reveal extremely high levels of customer engagement with repairing and reselling. Secondary studies (Hawken, 2021) emphasize the way that Patagonia's sustainable personalisation reduces return rates and extends garment life, thus achieving massive savings in carbon emissions and textile waste.

Lessons Learned

Patagonia shows that sustainability filters may be incorporated into recommender systems without business compromise. By marrying algorithmic goals with its business intention, Patagonia has also built high brand affinity from environmentally minded consumers, showing how responsible consumption can lead to profitability in the long run. The case refers to the necessity of employing metadata tagging, in-built resale websites, and open consumer education in a bid to implement ethical personalisation.

6.2 Zalando: Leading Circular Fashion through AI and Transparency

Context

Based in Berlin, Zalando is Europe's biggest online fashion platform with over 45 million active customers in 23 markets. With its market leadership, Zalando has embraced sustainability as an intrinsic aspect of the business model, reflecting consumers' growing appetite for environmentally friendly fashion and transparency. Adopting the power of personalisation algorithms in shaping consumption habits, Zalando has invested in AI-powered innovations that seek to balance growth in sales with the needs of sustainability.

AI Strategy and Implementation

Zalando's ethical personalization is multi-faceted. Its recommender systems are first combined with a sustainability filter that favours products that fit the company's internal "Sustainability Criteria." Such criteria consist of certifications like the Global Organic Textile Standard (GOTS) and Leather Working Group (LWG) rating. Consumers can actively choose sustainability preferences that in turn influence the AI engine product recommendations.

Second, Zalando launched the Zalando Zircle platform, a special second-hand marketplace tied to its core website. The inclusion of resale choices to its recommendation streams demonstrates how AI can facilitate circular fashion. If a consumer expresses interest in a particular high-turnover category, the system will automatically suggest pre-owned alternatives if available.

Another notable aspect is Zalando's Sustainability Flag, an algorithmically prompted badge for products with lowered environmental effect that can be guaranteed. The flag comes with transparency instruments demonstrating supply chain traceability as well as material origin. The aspects are not only intended to push consumers towards sustainable options but also to create belief in the authenticity of the recommendation.

Outcomes

According to Zalando's 2023 Sustainability Progress Report, products marked with the Sustainability Flag have accounted for more than 20% of sales, a significant step towards lower-impact shopping. The second-hand platform, Zircle, has grown at high velocity with millions of goods traded since its introduction, extending the lifespan of clothing and reducing landfill contributions. Customer research shows that customers value transparent labelling and are able to link their consumption behaviour with their values. This research demonstrates that customers react favourably if the sustainability content is subtly integrated into the process of personalisation.

Lessons Learned

Zalando's experience supports the contention that personalisation is not just a case of backend algorithm calibration but also requires the backing of transparent communication and consumer empowerment. With its mix of sustainability filters, in-built resale features, and transparency aspects, it demonstrates how a mass-market platform powered by AI can spearhead circular economy principles. Zircle's success confirms the commercial case for hybrid models fusing new product sales and used product equivalents.

6.3 ThredUp and Net-a-Porter: Resale Business Models and AI-Powered Minimalism

Context

California-headquartered ThredUp, the world's largest online resale platform, marries technology, fashion, and sustainability since its establishment in 2009. Its circular business model supports garment life extension through resale and consignment. Upscale fashion brand Net-a-Porter has also ventured into the resale space through third-party partnerships to respond to sustainability needs from high-end consumers.

AI Strategy and Implementation

ThredUp's machine learning-powered personalization engine pair's second-hand goods with individual tastes. The uniqueness of each good demands accuracy in recommendation. The website considers history of purchases, fashion sense preference, and internet browsing in suggesting suitable options based on the fashion quotient and budget of each user.

ThredUp even employs predictive analytics to predict demand by style and brand, which optimizes curation of inventory and reduces waste. Its "Clean out Kit" product utilizes AI to tell sellers what products have the best potential to be resold, reducing unsold inventory and emissions.

Net-a-Porter's "NET SUSTAIN" platform employs AI to construct transparency around sustainably produced, low-carbon luxury products. Its resale strategy employs personalization recommendations, placing second-hand luxury alongside new products side by side, inspiring conscious consumption while preserving the luxury experience.

Results

ThredUp's 2023 Resale Report explains how its AI-driven features have saved more than 100 million clothing items from the landfill. Its resale predictive model has registered top-quartile sell-through rates through smarter curation of stock and customer guidance.

Net-a-Porter's resale experiment has already taken off among high-end consumers looking for sustainability, turning exclusivity and disposability on its head by placing resale at the Centre of the luxury shopping experience.

Lessons Learned

Both examples show how resale AI personalisation can make sustainable, scalable consumption possible. Intelligent recommendation systems are needed to manage individual inventory. Both examples show how extended product lifespan and minimalism is something that appeals to price-sensitive as well as high-end consumers alike when driven by responsive and transparent AI.

6.4 Synthesis: Lessons Learned from the Case Studies

Combined, these real-life cases demonstrate that ethical personalisation is far from an ideal but rather a feasible approach when brands match AI potential with sustainability goals. Common principles spanning cases are:

- Adding Sustainability Filters: Eco-friendly product labelling and eco-ranking within recommendation systems can direct consumer selection to less impactful alternatives.
- Transparency and Consumer Empowerment: Providing transparent data on supply chain traceability, product lifecycle, and sustainability certifications fosters trust and facilitates informed choice.
- Circular Economy Enablement: Including resale and repair in the recommendation stream nudges consumers towards alternatives to linear consumption.
- Alignment with Brand Identity: Successful deployment relies on reconciling AI personalisation with a brand's core mission and stakeholder expectations.

These lessons provide an empirical basis for the Ethical Personalisation Framework described in the following section and show how AI can be used not only to fulfil consumer demands but to cultivate a culture of responsible, conscious, and sustainable consumption around world fashion.

7. APPLICATION OF ETHICAL THEORIES

Having established the theoretical bases of ethical personalisation and mapped them through recent case examples, it is interesting to interrogate such findings using common theories of ethics. A rational ethical critique demonstrates how personalisation practices, when they are based on normative values, can at the same time affirm the rights of citizens, enhance stakeholder well-being, and ensure long-term sustainability. This chapter utilizes three well-known ethical methods—Virtue Ethics, Utilitarianism, and Deontological Ethics—to critically examine the moral obligations on which responsible AI personalisation in the fashion e-commerce industry is based.

7.1 Virtue Ethics: Fostering Long-Term Environmental and Social Virtues

Virtue Ethics, based on Aristotelian thought, is concerned with developing moral character and virtues that achieve human flourishing along with the common good. Unlike rule theories, Virtue Ethics is concerned with habitual activities that cause organizations and individuals to become aligned with values like honesty, integrity, and accountability to others.

Through fashion e-commerce personalization, Virtue Ethics requires a paradigm shift from profit-maximizing algorithmic approaches to virtue-influenced systems of environmental and social stewardship. Patagonia, for instance, designs recommender systems to encourage virtues such as moderation, attentiveness, and ecological sensitivity. By emphasizing durability, repair ability, and resale value, Patagonia's system supports the virtue of sustainability.

In addition, Virtue Ethics places special emphasis on organisational culture and leadership to enshrine such values. With the internalisation of ethical personalisation within brand positioning and everyday practice, fashion retailers can encourage sustainable consumption as a common virtue—sufficiently different from conventional models of personalisation that fuel short-term wants and overconsumption.

7.2 Utilitarianism: Maximising Net Positive Impact for Stakeholders

The Utilitarian ethical theory, as formulated by Bentham and Mill, weighs action on their utility—how much they contribute to total happiness. With AI personalisation, that is weighing business benefits such as increased sales against the loss of eating into overconsumption, privacy, and environmental degradation.

Cases such as Zalando and ThredUp illustrate how personalisation can be directed towards broader stakeholder interests. Zalando combines sustainability ratings and resale reminders to align fashion decisions with sustainable consumption, delivering collective wellbeing as well as waste minimisation.

On the other hand, personalisation for profit alone is sub-utilitarian. It provides immediate gratification but tends to bring long-term regret, over-consumption, and destruction of nature—lowering net happiness. The increasing carbon footprint and pollution of clothes in the fast fashion sector are an example of such negative externalities.

From a utilitarian moral perspective, AI personalization should seek to create the greatest good and minimize harm. Ethical algorithm design should reconcile user desires with social and environmental impact, as evidenced through ThredUp's used clothing resale model and Patagonia's Worn Wear program.

7.3 Deontological Ethics: Respecting Autonomy, Privacy, and Informed Consent

Deontological Ethics, as gleaned from Kantian philosophy, is concerned with the rightness of actions rather than duty compliance and respect for people's rights rather than consequences. In AI personalization, it guarantees consumer rights of autonomy, privacy, and informed consent.

Legacy personalization algorithms are resistant to these principles by covertly shaping choices through obfuscated recommendation methods. Zuboff (2019) laments this kind of "surveillance capitalism" profiting from user data without adequate privacy protection or genuine consent—an intrinsic moral violation from a deontological perspective.

Ethics-based personalisation needs to foster transparency and respect user rights. GDPR data protection principles—such as data minimisation, limitation of purpose, and explicit consent—are deontological standards necessary for AI adoption in fashion. Companies like Zalando and Patagonia demonstrate this by using transparent design and sustainability-oriented personalisation that enables informed choice.

Also, Deontological Ethics requires fairness and justice while creating algorithms. Recommender systems should not be biased, exploitative, or systemically discriminatory towards vulnerable users. Incorporating explain ability, fairness audits, and user-control features into AI systems is the ethical requirement to respect consumers as autonomous agents who must be respected.

7.4 Applying Ethical Theories to Sustainability and Corporate Responsibility

These ethical paradigms justify a common conclusion: AI personalization needs to look beyond short-term transactional objectives and be anchored on a heightened commitment to corporate social responsibility and sustainability. Virtue Ethics supports the embedding of pro-environment virtues in organisational culture and consumer conduct. Utilitarianism identifies the need to maximise net social and environmental well-being through regard for consumption externalities. Deontological Ethics believes that even the most revolutionary technology has to be in observance of basic consumer rights and the intrinsic dignity of individuals.

Case studies illustrated above uncover that such ethical stands are not in conflict but complementary pillars of a strong moral framework for AI personalisation. Retail fashion companies can formulate practicable guidelines based on these stances, balancing commercial pragmatism with environmental conservation and social justice.

In practice, this multi-theory framework instructs brands to do the following:

- Create Ethical Cultures: Encourage organisational values that focus on sustainability, justice, and openness as organising principles when creating algorithms (Virtue Ethics).
- Evaluate Net Impacts: Consider social and environmental benefits and harms of personalisation practices (Utilitarianism).
- Guard Rights: Enact robust governance for data privacy, explain ability, and consumer control (Deontological Ethics).
- Transferred to AI systems, such principles provide a strong trajectory for personalisation models that are significantly contributing to the United Nations Sustainable Development Goals (SDGs) and the shift to a circular fashion economy.

In total, ethical theory reasons why AI personalisation should be employed, if bounded by clear moral commitments, as not an overconsumption inducer but an incentive towards responsible, equitable, and sustainable consumption practices.

8. ETHICAL PERSONALISATION FRAMEWORK

Drawing from the aforementioned theoretical frameworks, normative theories, and empirical case studies, the following section provides an overall Ethical Personalisation Framework to help fashion e-commerce stakeholders balance AI personalisation practice with ideas of fairness, transparency, user autonomy, privacy, and sustainability. The framework seeks to change personalisation systems from transactional focused tools into tools that actively encourage responsible consumption and contribute to the global agenda of sustainability.

8.1 The Principles of the Framework

Essentially, the Ethical Personalisation Framework is built on five dependent principles:

- Fairness: Algorithms should be unbiased and should equally serve different consumer segments without reproducing social injustices.
- Transparency: Personalisation processes should be understandable and readable to inform consumers about how recommendations are being built and how their data are being processed.
- User Autonomy: Systems need to honour human agency through the granting of meaningful control over personalisation options, such as opt-in/opt-out and consent.
- Privacy: The collection and processing of data should be governed by minimisation, purpose limitation, and security principles so that consumers' rights to confidentiality are upheld during the entire lifecycle of the AI system.
- Sustainability: Personalisation needs to integrate green thinking, nudging consumers to lower-impact consumption and developing a culture for responsible, circular consumption.

These are inter-dependent and operate collectively as normative reference points for operationalization of the framework.

8.2 Ethical Personalisation Framework Conceptual Diagram

Figure 2.

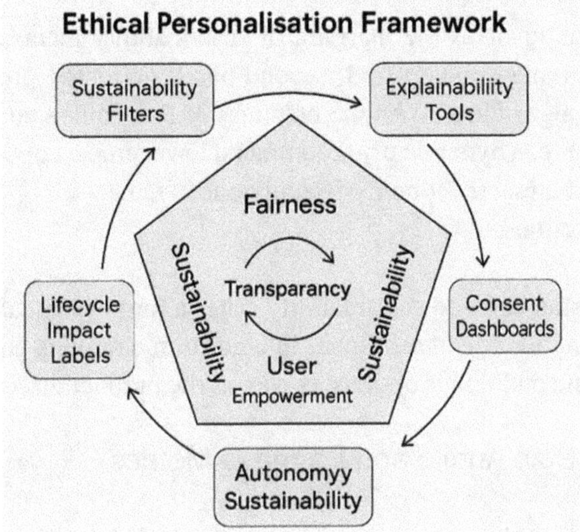

8.3 Ethical Personalisation Framework Conceptual Diagram

The background conceptual diagram would depict the system as an integrated system, and the five key principles a circular or pentagon model at the Centre. Around the Centre, practical aspects—like sustainability filters, explain ability tools, consent dashboards, bias audits, and lifecycle impact labels—can be depicted as functional layers that embed the principles into system design and engagement on a day-to-day level.

Arrows connecting the principles and functional components ought to show the dynamic loops of feedback to ensure ongoing monitoring, evaluation, and adaptation. This image highlights that ethical personalisation is not static checklist but a dynamic practice which has to be constantly refreshed in relation to stakeholder expectations as well as technology developments.

8.4 Operational Actions and Practical Applications

a) Merging Circular Economy and Sustainability Filters

Practically, this involves the merging of sustainability metadata with product databases and ranking eco-certified, second-hand, or rented products higher in recommendation algorithms. With the practices of Patagonia's and Zalando's, recommender systems can dynamically recommend lower-impact options, influencing consumers toward circular economy-friendly ones.

Operational Actions:

- Implement standardized sustainability criteria for product labelling.
- Rank sustainability features higher in algorithmic ranking equations.
- Include resale and repair options as part of the product discovery process.

b) Algorithmic Bias Audits and Fairness Metrics

For fairness, algorithmic biases should be audited from time to time in order to detect and neutralize those biases that would have a negative impact on a particular demographic or cultural group. Disparate impact analysis and equal opportunity measurement metrics should be included in system performance reviews.

Operational Steps:

- Utilize bias detection measures during model training.
- Perform fairness testing on representative data sets on a regular basis.
- Document mitigation steps and report outcomes to stakeholders.

c) Explain ability and Consumer Education

Transparency entails AI-driven recommendations being understandable in plain language. This entails offering justifications for suggestions, emphasizing sustainability factors, as well as offering supply chain traceability information.

Operational Steps:

- Implement easy-to-use "Why This Product?" interfaces.
- Embed interactive sustainability learning content on impacts.
- Create consumer-facing sustainability ratings or badges.

d) Consent Mechanisms and User-Control Dashboards

In order to maintain user control and privacy, traders must offer high-granularity control over data collection and preference for personalization. Consent has to be informed, explicit, and revocable at any time.

Operational Steps:

- Develop privacy dashboards enabling consumers to control personal data.
- Implement default settings that enable privacy-by-design values.
- Notify users of their rights on a regular basis with straightforward notices.

e) Continuous Monitoring and Impact Assessment

A personalisation ethics framework would incorporate feedback mechanisms to review its social and environmental effects. This would involve the establishment of key performance indicators (KPIs) that go beyond sales data to encompass outcomes for sustainability.

Steps in Operation:

- Establish KPIs like reduction in carbon footprint per transaction or take-up in resale.
- Use real-time analytics to track consumer reaction to green nudges.
- Publish regular impact reports with consumers and stakeholders.

8.5 Executable Rules for Stakeholders

For AI Developers:

- Incorporate fairness and bias detection modules into data inputs and model training.
- Incorporate explain ability tools via methods like local interpretable model-agnostic explanations (LIME) or SHAP values.
- Create algorithms with modular sustainability filters that evolve as criteria change.

For Retailers:

- Align personalisation goals with company sustainability goals and company values.

- Invest in consumer education programs to situate sustainability attributes within context.
- Balance short-term profit goals with long-term loyalty creation through ethical value differentiation.

For Policymakers and Industry Associations:

- Set cross-industry standards on sustainability labelling, transparency disclosures, and algorithmic accountability.
- Enforce algorithmic impact assessments as a standard requirement for large retailers.
- Encourage cross-sectorial learning to share best practices and innovative solutions.

8.6 Managing Trade-offs: Profit Optimisation vs. Sustainability

Ethically personalizing inherently requires compromises—especially in short-term profit and long-term sustainability balance. Heritage measures like basket size and conversion rate need to be re-thought in light of the new drivers of ecological and social footprint.

Patagonia demonstrates that profitability is possible alongside discouraging overconsumption through building trust and brand affection. Likewise, Zalando's coupling of resale with new product sales demonstrates that circular business models can be profitable and eco-emancipated.

However, trade-offs are situation-dependent. For high-turnover volume retailers, sustainability recommendations first will reduce frequency of purchase. That is why there is a necessity to construct a long-term value proposition—customer retention, regulatory compliance, managing risk, and brand reputation.

The Ethical Personalisation Framework requires a transformation from transactional to relational consumer interaction. By creating AI systems that respect consumers and enable sustainable decision-making, brands can engage more constructively with conscious consumers. By doing so, they build longer-term competitiveness and resilience in a growing sustainability-aware marketplace.

8.7 A Living Framework

Lastly, it should be noted that the Ethical Personalisation Framework is not a final answer but a living framework of adaptation. The breakneck speed of technology, shifting consumer values, and novel regulatory regimes require continuous evolution. Continuous cross-disciplinary research, stakeholder conversations, and incremental improvement must be undertaken in order to keep AI personalisation an instrument of good, guaranteeing a fair, and transparent, respectful, and sustainable fashion retail environment.

Lastly, this framework charts a realistic trajectory to operationalizing ethical personalization in the e-fashion commerce sector, transforming AI from a tool of overconsumption to a catalyst for mindful, sustainable shopping habits that promote people's and planet's welfare.

9. IMPLEMENTATION ROADMAP & BEST PRACTICES

While the previous sections have outlined the conceptual and empirical basis for ethical personalisation, its real-world success hinges on the translation of such principles into action. What follows is a framework of systematic implementation, which outlines phases fashion brands can adopt in designing, implementing, and running ethical AI-facilitated personalisation systems. Further, it also establishes operational governance, transparency, and impact measurement best practices whereby sustainability and ethical requirements are integrated into levels of the personalisation process.

9.1 Step 1: Define Ethical Objectives and Stakeholder Alignment

The foundation of any ethical personalisation approach is a proper definition of the organisation's ethical obligations and sustainability goals. Top management needs to specify how fairness, transparency, user autonomy, privacy, and sustainability would be given priority in the brand's personalisation goals.

Organize a cross-functional working group comprising data scientists, AI engineers, sustainability officers, marketing teams, and legal advisors to collaborate on an Ethical AI Charter. The charter must include commitments to bias minimization, privacy-by-design, sustainability goals, and explain ability requirements.

9.2 Step 2: Data Mapping and Governance

Good data governance is the premise of ethical AI. Organizations need to conduct a sound audit of data sources, collection processes, and storage infrastructures to verify continuous compliance with privacy legislations as well as ethical standards.

Best Practice:

- Apply data minimisation by keeping only data required for personalisation purposes.
- Utilize purpose limitation principles to limit data use strictly to its intended usage.
- Enshrine clear data retention policies and secure storage facilities to ensure user confidentiality.

In addition to that, brands must incorporate easy-to-use privacy dashboards to enable consumers to change consent settings and see, correct, or erase their data.

9.3 Step 3: Ethical Algorithm Design and Testing

After deciding on the governance structures, technical staff must include ethical considerations in algorithmic design. This includes:

- Fairness Audits: Test algorithms for disparate impact and representation bias across representative, diverse data sets.
- Sustainability Filters: Incorporate sustainability metadata and impact scores into the recommendation logic.
- Explain ability Features: Develop features through which consumers can view why some recommendations are being brought up.

Best Practice:

Utilize an iterative design process, testing algorithm prototypes for unexpected bias or sustainability misalignments before full-scale deployment. Having independent audits from external experts will lend authenticity.

9.4 Step 4: Transparency Measures and Consumer Communication

Effective functioning relies on consumers being informed, empowered, and confident to use the personalisation system. Transparency statements must make it evident that:

- What kind of personal data is collected and why.
- How recommendation algorithms work to produce recommendations.
- What sustainability aspects are emphasized in the recommendation engine?

Best Practice:

Implement explainable AI (XAI) features like "Why this product?" tags, transparent sustainability labels, and traceability data throughout the supply chain. Back them up with consumer education initiatives on the fashion industry's impact on the environment.

9.5 Step 5: Deploy, Track, and Refine

Deployed personalisation platforms should be tracked continuously to check for adherence to promised targets. Brands need to set Key Performance Indicators (KPIs) that move beyond traditional conversion rates in tracking wider social and environmental impacts.

Consumer Satisfaction KPIs:

- User trust scores and transparency feedback.
- Opt-in rates for sustainability-driven recommendations.
- Consumer sentiment on data privacy and control.
- Sustainability Outcomes KPIs:
- Percentage of purchases adhering to sustainability standards.
- Boosting rate of resale or rental conversions.
- Decrease in return rates, wastage, or carbon footprint per sale.

Best Practice:

Make it a habit to publish impact reports to report back to stakeholders, and thus establish accountability and consumer confidence.

9.6 Governance and Continuous Improvement

Personalisation is not a single static activity but an evolving process which reacts to technological innovations, consumer pattern, and policy change. Brands need to create governance frameworks to instil accountability within teams.

Governance Measures:

- Appoint an Ethical AI Officer or a sustainability lead for algorithmic governance.
- Provide regular in-house and third-party audits of personalisation systems.
- Maintain open complaint and redress channels for consumers, so concerns regarding privacy, bias, or manipulation can be fast-tracked.
- Join multi-stakeholder forums and industry working groups in sharing good practices and adopting new norms. Involvement of actors other than

Government, such as policy-makers and NGOs, can also add muscle to a brand's voice for bringing responsible AI practices to the fashion sector.

9.7 Implementation Roadmap Summary

The suggested roadmap is the one above, and it can be summarized as follows:

- Establish the clear ethical goals consistent with the brand vision for sustainability.
- Map and regulate data flows to honour privacy and users' consent.
- Develop algorithms that put fairness first, transparency second, and sustainability third.
- Be transparent in communications to enable consumers.
- Track and improve performance through longer KPIs that measure not just consumer well-being but also green footprint.
- Govern with provisions for accountability, audit, and ongoing learning.

9.8 Forward Thinking

Ethical personalisation will need brands to reconcile short-term commercial urgency with longer-term drivers of sustainability and consumer trust. While such action will entail cultural change and upfront expense, it allows fashion retailers to get ahead in anticipation of intensifying regulatory pressures and changing consumer ethics. Finally, by an open, step-by-step process supported by good governance and impact measurement, brands can use AI personalisation not just as a driver of sales but also as a source of smarter, more ethical, and more sustainable consumption habits.

10. POLICY & GOVERNANCE IMPLICATIONS

The behavioural operationalization of accountable AI personalisation of fashion online shopping cannot be left to the good intentions of corporate goals but requires a conducive framework of effective policy norms, industry practice, and regulation. With AI technologies driving consumer behaviour and consumption patterns, there is a need for policymakers, regulators, and trade associations to come forward and take a leadership role in upholding public interest and facilitating sustainability objectives.

10.1 Developing Digital Consumer Rights

At the centre of ethical AI personalisation is the principle that users need to have meaningful control over how their personal data is collected, processed, and used. Although the European Union's General Data Protection Regulation (GDPR) has established a global gold standard for data privacy and consent, loopholes exist in the majority of legal systems, most notably with regard to transparency on algorithmic decision-making.

Policymakers therefore need to attempt to harmonise and consolidate digital consumer rights by:

- Enlarging legal obligations for clear, informed consent with AI personalization systems.
- Making transparent disclosures of automatic suggestion logic, meaning, and implications.
- Granting consumers actionable rights of access, rectification, and erasure for their personal data employed in personalization models.

These steps will assist in combating information and power asymmetry that have a tendency to typify the consumer-big online retailer relationship.

10.2 Demanding Algorithmic Transparency and Accountability

Algorithmic transparency is a foundation of morally correct AI regulation. The regulators can help by enacting legislation that will hold businesses accountable for providing understandable explanations of how personalisation algorithms work, such as:

- The types of data utilized.
- The most influential factors that affect recommendations.
- Whether or not there are any sustainability criteria or impact scores.
- New law proposals, like the EU's Artificial Intelligence Act, are useful blueprints for defining high-risk AI systems and laying out minimum transparency and accountability requirements.
- Industry trade associations and country regulators should make sure recommender systems that have significant consumer effects are subject regularly to impact assessments and third-party audits for detection of bias, manipulation, or unwanted social and environmental harms.

10.3 Creating Sustainability Certifications for AI Personalisation

To connect AI personalization to wider environmental ambitions, industry associations and certifiers can create sustainability labels or certifications that signal digital retailing destinations with sustainable AI practices. These can require that:

- Sustainability filters are included in recommendation engines.
- Supply chain traceability and product life cycle information are visible to customers.
- Resale, rental, or repair capabilities are actively promoted along the user journey.
- Just as successful physical supply chain eco-labels such as Fairtrade or the Global Organic Textile Standard (GOTS) are able to foster consumer confidence and act as a competitive spur for brands to engage in ethical personalisation, so can digital sustainability certificates.

10.4 Fostering Industry Cooperation and Standardisation

Industry associations like the Sustainable Apparel Coalition and Digital Responsibility organizations can play a vital role by creating sectorial codes of conduct and technical standards regarding responsible use of AI. Common frameworks for bias detection, explain ability, and sustainability scoring would prevent fragmentation and promote consistency instead of patchworks of rival solutions.

Policy-makers should encourage collaboration between fashion retailers, technology firms, academia, and civil society in a co-creation of such standards and best practices. Public–private partnerships and innovation sandboxes can provide test beds for experimenting with innovative ways of responsible AI personalisation, i.e., new methods of digital nudging conducive to sustainable consumption without limiting consumer freedom.

10.5 Global Conformity and Regulation Cooperation

With the international nature of digital fashion business, international regulatory harmonization is an imperative. Inconsistent regulatory regimes may provide loopholes for companies to escape stricter systems by shifting activities to weaker jurisdictions. Inter-state cooperation—through mechanisms like the OECD, G20, or UN working groups—is most likely to enhance compatibility on matters such as:

- Algorithmic transparency requirements.

- Cross-border data flows and privacy protection.
- Harmonised sustainability reporting and certification models.

This global harmonisation will assist in levelling the playing field and ensure that ethical brands are not placed at a competitive disadvantage for maintaining a higher ethical and environmental standard.

10.6 Finalising Governance View

Overall, strict policy and governance steps are needed to make ethical personalization a standard and not the exception in the fashion e-commerce industry. Through enhancing digital consumer rights, enforcing algorithmic transparency, triggering sustainability through certification, and enabling industry cooperation, regulators and policymakers can formulate a regulatory environment that keeps brands in line while enabling sustainable and responsible innovation.

11. FUTURE RESEARCH AGENDA

Longitudinal university studies and cross-industry collaboration are an urgent need, as AI-based personalisation is developing further. Although this chapter has given a conceptual and applicative grounding to personalisation for fashion e-commerce with ethical considerations, a number of critical questions remain open and must be studied systematically.

11.1 Measuring the Real Sustainability Impact

One of the largest gaps in the literature on research is a lack of strong methodologies to pick up actual sustainability gains that are the result of AI personalisation interventions. Although case studies report encouraging results—e.g., greater take-up of resale or fewer returns—there is not much empirical evidence to show that particular algorithmic building blocks correlate with concrete reductions in carbon emissions, water consumption, or material waste. Future research should therefore establish standardised impact assessment models and life-cycle analysis tools that allow brands to monitor and report the environmental performance of their personalisation systems in a credible and comparable way.

11.2 Scaling Ethical AI Models Profitably

Future research should also be employed to build on the scalability of ethical AI models across varying market contexts. Though lead firms such as Patagonia, Zalando, and ThredUp illustrate that commercial feasibility could be reconciled with sustainability-driven personalisation, difficulties lie in extending these strategies to high-volume, thin-margin mass-market retailers. Trans disciplinary research cross-listing AI engineering, sustainable business strategy, and economics needs to be conducted to identify scalable design patterns, cost–benefit trade-offs, and governance arrangements accommodating profitability and ethical demands.

11.3 Consumer Trust and Engagement Building

The success of ethical personalisation then hinges on consumer trust, understanding, and participation. Pilot testing with clear tools and understandable AI interfaces has been promising, and further empirical research is required to investigate whether consumers engage with and react favourably to sustainability content embedded within recommendations. Behavioural economics and digital nudging research can inform valuable insights regarding the ways in which interface design, framing, and feedback loops can enhance greater engagement without diminishing control.

11.4 Interdisciplinary Directions

Resolving these open questions will necessitate a truly interdisciplinary research agenda in several domains:

- AI Ethics and Responsible Innovation: Ongoing investigation into fairness, accountability, and transparency mechanisms in new algorithmic architectures.
- Fashion Sustainability and Circular Economy: Increasing incorporation of sustainability science, supply chain management, and lifecycle thinking into design and governance of personalisation systems.
- Consumer Behaviour and Digital Psychology: Examining the impact of customized digital spaces on long-term consumer behaviour, identity formation, and corporate social responsibility orientations.
- Policy and Regulation Studies: Comparative study of new regulation approaches and their implications for innovation, consumer protection, and competitiveness in the industry.

11.5 Closing Note on Research Imperatives

Looking ahead, the rapid advancement of generative AI is expected to reshape personalization paradigms, enabling hyper-contextual recommendations while also raising fresh ethical questions around authenticity, transparency, and consumer autonomy (MIT Sloan, 2024; Nature Machine Intelligence, 2023).

More generally, the construction of ethical personalisation involves not just technological advance but also inter-disciplinary research, stakeholder engagement, and empirical validation. Closing these gaps enables researchers, businesses, and policymakers to construct AI personalisation models that are technically advanced and commercially successful, yet ethically sound and environmentally friendly.

12. CONCLUSION

This chapter has argued the revolutionary potential that can be brought to the fashion e-commerce sector by artificial intelligence-powered personalization—if created in an ethical and sustainability-focused environment. Based on conceptual analysis, ethical theory, and best-practice firm case studies such as Patagonia, Zalando, and ThredUp, the research delineates how traditional personalisation—replete with commercial success—tends towards instant gratification consumption, unsustainable methods, and exploitative data use.

The chapter sketched out an Ethical Personalisation Framework based on five interconnected principles: fairness, transparency, user autonomy, privacy, and sustainability. Far from a prescriptive model, it is an adaptive, pragmatic set of recommendations for retailers, AI developers, and policymakers to balance digital retail systems with social and environmental requirements. Utilitarian components like sustainability filters, explain ability tools, bias audits, and consumer consent mechanisms make these ethical principles concrete design and governance choices.

The suggested rollout schedule and supporting best practices offer an exemplar of responsible AI deployment in the real world, with particular emphasis on robust data stewardship, ongoing impact assessments, and open communication. Maybe more than anything else, the chapter suggests a new measure of success—beyond short-term return on investment—into consumer well-being and material sustainability indicators.

It also emphasizes the need for facilitating policy environments, in terms of additional digital consumer protection rights, required algorithmic explain ability, sustainability labelling, and cross-border regulatory harmonization. These interventions in combination with coordinated industry action can make ethics-first personalization become the norm for the fashion e-commerce industry.

Last but not least, the moral improvement of AI personalisation is not merely an entrepreneurial imperative but an ethical social responsibility. Industry, academia, and policymakers alike must understand that innovation must be specifically designed to minimize harm and increase equity. Ethical AI personalisation development and regulation can generate more conscious, transparent, and sustainable consumption—driving the world faster toward a circular fashion economy and universal Sustainable Development Goals.

It is our shared responsibility to act with bravery—creating systems that are human rights-respecting, doing no harm, and enabling consumers to make choices that benefit humanity and the planet.

REFERENCES

Accenture. (2025). *Technology Vision 2025: Reinventing retail with AI.* Accenture Research. https://www.accenture.com

Acquisti, A., Taylor, C., & Wagman, L. (2020). The Economics of Privacy. *Journal of Economic Literature*, *54*(2), 442–492. https://www.aeaweb.org/articles?id=10.1257/jel.54.2.442. DOI: 10.1257/jel.54.2.442

Ananny, M., & Crawford, K. (2018). Seeing Without Knowing: Limitations of the Transparency Ideal and Its Application to Algorithmic Accountability. *New Media & Society*, *20*(3), 973–989. DOI: 10.1177/1461444816676645

Armstrong, C. M. J., & Park, H. (2020). Online clothing resale: A practice theory approach to evaluate sustainable consumption gains. *Journal of Sustainability Research*, *2*(1), 17. Advance online publication. DOI: 10.20900/jsr20200017

Davenport, T., Guha, A., Grewal, D., & Bressgott, T. (2020). How Artificial Intelligence Will Change the Future of Marketing. *Journal of the Academy of Marketing Science*, *48*(1), 24–42. DOI: 10.1007/s11747-019-00696-0

Ellen MacArthur Foundation. (2017) A New Textiles Economy: Redesigning Fashion's Future. https://www.ellenmacarthurfoundation.org/assets/downloads/publications/A-New-Textiles-Economy_Full-Report.pdf

Floridi, L., & Cowls, J. (2019). A Unified Framework of Five Principles for AI in Society. *Harvard Data Science Review*, *1*, 2–15. DOI: 10.1162/99608f92.8cd550d1

Friedman, B., & Hendry, D. G. (2019). *Value sensitive design: Shaping technology with moral imagination.* The MIT Press., DOI: 10.7551/mitpress/7585.001.0001

Global Fashion Agenda. (2024). *Fashion CEO agenda 2024: Scaling sustainability in fashion*. Global Fashion Agenda. https://globalfashionagenda.org

Hawken, P. (2021). *Regeneration: Ending the climate crisis in one generation.* Penguin Books.

Helberger, N., Pierson, J., & Poell, T. (2018). Governing online platforms: From contested to cooperative responsibility. *The Information Society*, *34*(1), 1–14. DOI: 10.1080/01972243.2017.1391913

Jannach, D. (2022). Massimo Quadrana, Paolo Cremonesi: Session-based Recommender Systems. In Ricci, (Eds.), *Recommender Systems Handbook* (3rd ed., pp. 301–333). Springer. DOI: 10.1007/978-1-0716-2197-4_8

Kumar, V., Dixit, A., Javalgi, R. G., & Dass, M. (2021). Digital Transformation and AI Adoption in Marketing and Sales: Opportunities and Challenges. *Industrial Marketing Management*, *95*, 48–60. DOI: 10.1016/j.indmarman.2021.03.008

Mehrabi, N., Morstatter, F., Saxena, N., Lerman, K., & Galstyan, A. (2021). A survey on bias and fairness in machine learning. *ACM Computing Surveys*, *54*(6), 1–35.

MIT Sloan Management Review. (2024). *Generative AI in business: Balancing opportunity and responsibility*. MIT Sloan Management Review. https://sloanreview.mit.edu

Nicolaï, M., & Grange, C. (2021). The digital transformation of retail during the Covid-19 pandemic: A comparative study in Canada, China, and France. In E. Mazaheri (Ed.), *The impact of Covid-19 on e-commerce* (pp. xx–xx). Proud Pen. https://doi.org/DOI: 10.51432/978-1-8381524-8-2_1

Niinimäki, K., Peters, G., Dahlbo, H., Perry, P., Rissanen, T., & Gwilt, A. (2020). The Environmental Price of Fast Fashion. *Nature Reviews. Earth & Environment*, *1*(4), 189–200. DOI: 10.1038/s43017-020-0039-9

Radhakrishnan, S. (2014). The Sustainable Apparel Coalition and the Higg Index. In Muthu, S. S. (Ed.), *Roadmap to sustainable textiles and clothing: Regulatory aspects and sustainability standards of textiles and the clothing supply chain* (pp. 23–57). Springer Science & Business Media., DOI: 10.1007/978-981-287-164-0_2

Ricci, F., Rokach, L., & Shapira, B. (2011). Introduction to Recommender Systems Handbook. In Ricci, F., Rokach, L., Shapira, B., & Kantor, P. (Eds.), *Recommender Systems Handbook*. Springer., DOI: 10.1007/978-0-387-85820-3_1

Shyam Sundar, S., & Sampada, S. (2010, July 1). Marathe, Personalization versus Customization: The Importance of Agency, Privacy, and Power Usage. *Human Communication Research*, *36*(3), 298–322. DOI: 10.1111/j.1468-2958.2010.01377.x

Sundström, M., Hjelm-Lidholm, S., & Radon, A. (2019). Clicking the boredom away – Exploring impulse fashion buying behavior online. *Journal of Retailing and Consumer Services*, *47*, 150–156. DOI: 10.1016/j.jretconser.2018.11.006

Voigt, P., & von dem Bussche, A. (2017). *The EU General Data Protection Regulation (GDPR): A practical guide*. Springer International Publishing., DOI: 10.1007/978-3-319-57959-7

Yeung, K. (2017). 'Hypernudge': Big Data as a mode of regulation by design. *Information Communication and Society*, *20*(1), 118–136. DOI: 10.1080/1369118X.2016.1186713

ADDITIONAL READING

Patagonia. (2023). *Environmental & Social Responsibility Report.* Retrieved from https://www.patagonia.com

ThredUp. (2023). *Annual Resale Report.* Retrieved from https://www.thredup.com/resale

Zalando. (2023). *Sustainability Progress Report.* Retrieved from https://corporate.zalando.com/en/sustainability

Chapter 6
Mediation of Sustainable Consumption Between Ethical Personalization and Fashion E-Commerce

Shashi Kant
http://orcid.org/0000-0003-4722-5736
DMI-St.Eugene University, Zambia

Wako Jio
http://orcid.org/0009-0003-6192-459X
Bule Hora University, Ethiopia

Rituraj Singh
http://orcid.org/0009-0008-0452-9303
O.P. Jindal Global University, India

Nitu Nimbrain
http://orcid.org/0000-0001-5585-3287
Maharshi Dayanand University, India

ABSTRACT

In this chapter, the author discusses how to mediate sustainable consumption, referring to ethical personalization and e-commerce in the realm of fashion. Incorporating 390 study participants, we resorted to qualitative methods of quantitative investigation in showing interaction between these variables. The paper will commence with justifying the significance of sustainable consumption as a growing dimension of the modern fashion industry, in which the ethical individualization of style is in demand among consumers. We found that ethical personalization has a noteworthy impact

DOI: 10.4018/979-8-3373-5525-2.ch006

on the behavior of sustainable consumption in fashion e-commerce environments. Moreover, the approach reveals that the relationship is mediated by consumer trust and perceived value, and this aspect emphasizes the importance of a differentiated approach to marketing. The chapter adds value to the existing body of literature by presenting empirical evidence of the mechanisms through which ethical personalization leads to sustainable consumption.

INTRODUCTION

The factor of sustainable consumption has received a worldwide concern in an age where people are getting more concerned with the environment and their needs are also changing (Lo & Lin, 2024; Mangudhla, 2025). The fashion industry has a long history of negative environmental impact issues and ethical concerns and has increasingly been getting pressure to embrace greener practices (Sardianou & Briana, 2025). Sustainable consumption is a notion that was created in the 1980s, which focuses on the necessity of a compromise between the depletion of resources and conserving the environment (Rana, 2024; Ashuro et al., 2025). With the increasing awareness of the consumer on the ethical aspect of their purchases, there has been increased demand on ethical personalization (Mukherjee et al., 2024), that is, on the products and marketing strategies to suit individual's values (Shao et al., 2024). In the empirical literature, there is an increased synergy between consumer behavior and sustainability that suggests that personalized marketing can bring about the sustainability choices (Cossatin et al., 2024; Lemi et al., 2025). Researchers also observe that when people believe that products and services are compatible with their own views, then they will be willing to take part in sustainable consumption (Allahverdiyev, 2025). Nonetheless, there are practical obstacles such as the fact that it is hard to execute ethical personalization strategies effectively and to quantify the effect they have on consumer behavior (Zubaidah et al., 2024). Striking the balance between personalization and sustainability is a challenge most fashion retailers face, and are met with skepticism by consumers (Wasilewski & Zgrzywa-Ziemak, 2024).

In this chapter, the author seeks to deal with these dilemmas through examining how sustainable consumption is mediated between ethical personalization and fashion e-commerce. Although the literature has provided a starting point on the subject matter, there remain a lot of gaps on how the relationship is facilitated. Our research is aimed at bridging these gaps by using statistically sound models that can be used to acquire data on the effect of ethical personalization on sustainable consumption as mediated by mediators such as consumer trust or perceived value. The main research question that informs the study involves: ***How ethical personalization mediates sustainable consumption behaviors in the case of fashion e-commerce?***

The explanations of the present question will help the researchers and policymakers formulate their further actions in the way of advancing ethical and sustainable trends of fashion industry development. In addition to the theoretical discussion on the topic of the chapter, the work also provides helpful guidelines to the industry stakeholders trying to negotiate the maze of the sustainable consumer engagement.

BACKGROUND

The fashion industry finds itself at an epical juncture in facing the twofold task of sustainability in fashion and the demand of the consumers towards individualization (Rana, 2024). Sustainable Consumption is the use of products and services, which satisfy the current generation without undermining the ability of the future generations to satisfy their needs (Shao et al., 2024). The name is derived out of the concept sustainable development, Sustainable consumption has both environmental and environmental strains and goes beyond the traditional portfolio of sustainability to include social and economic concerns such as unethical sourcing and lack of social equity (Sardianou & Briana, 2025). Ethical Personalization is a prerequisite in the delivery of products and marketing to meet ethical concerns and interests of the consumers. The idea came into existence due to the combination of personalization of marketing and the increased demand of ethical consumption. Ethical personalization can help consumers by ensuring they have options that they can connect with in ways that make sense and are valuable to them, which will allow them to connect even more with brands (Lo & Lin, 2024). Consumer Trust defined as the trust people have in their brands and their integrity, reliability, and adherence to ethical ways of doing business. Its origin can be traced to the literature of relationship marketing and brand management, where the key importance of trust has been stressed in building consumers loyalty over the long term. In sustainable consumption terms, consumer trust is important, and instills ideas about brand authenticity, and the credibility of brand statements around sustainability (Shao et al., 2024). Perceived Value refers to the judgments made by the consumer concerning the gains an individual gets through product or service relative to the cost. It is an economic theory, which relates to the marketing concept that has a great impact on the behavior of consumers. The perceived value in sustainable fashion does not only involve the functional value of a product but also the moral connotations of a product and impact on the environment, which makes consumers willing to pay more money to have a sustainable product (Al-Olfi et al., 2025).

With an increasing level of awareness surrounding global environmental issues, so have the light beheld on fashion brands in regard to their procedures of production and ethics (Shao et al., 2024). This context imposes a compelling necessity of a strategy of sustainable consumption that can appeal to the consumers, especially in the case of fashion e-commerce where competition is stiff, and differentiation is the one (Cossatin et al., 2024). The idea of sustainable consumption is to change the purchasing patterns to more responsible ones, that focus on environmental and societal dimensions of shopping. Nonetheless, there are many challenges to rendering this idea into workable strategies (Lo & Lin, 2024). An example of the company can be provided, when the case study of the popular retailer of fast fashion is reproduced. The company released a so-called sustainable collection and targeted environmentally conscious customers (Sardianou & Briana, 2025). The initiative received initial interest but customers became against it once they realized that the overall processes produced did not change much (Mukherjee et al., 2024). This discrepancy between the claims by the marketing and actual practices eventually resulted in the allegations of the green washing which further compromised the reputation of the brand, and it lost credibility with the consumers (Allahverdiyev, 2025).

One more example can be related to the industry of luxury fashion brands that have also tried to include ethical personalization into their products (Al-Olfi et al., 2025). Along with the financial means of developing a sustainable line, high-end brands are weak in the adaptation of personalized services, which would consider the values of the consumers (Kant et al., 2025). As another example, one of the luxury brands launched a customization service, which provided a chance to tailor clothing (Niguse et al., 2026). Nevertheless, the environmental consequences of manufacturing processes were not sufficient, which caused the complaints of consumers who also cared about sustainability (Cutinha & Mokshagundam, 2024). These case studies highlight the complexities of the procedure of implementing the practices of sustainable consumption (Zubaidah et al., 2024). Brands are in a dilemma between satisfying consumer demand on personalization and practice sustainability (Wasilewski & Zgrzywa-Ziemak, 2024). Besides, the inability to provide specific metrics to assess the efficiency of ethical personalization strategies makes it even more complicated to deploy them (Cunha, 2025).

The chapter seeks to exploit such issues and understand how sustainable consumption can be conducted through ethical personalization that can act as an intermediary. Through the prism of consumer trust, subjective value and ethical reasoning, we attempt to offer our understanding of how could fashion retail companies surpass these challenges and even turn them into the opportunities towards creating a more personalized experience to consumers and a more sustainable company.

PROBLEM STATEMENT

The shift of the fashion industry towards sustainable consumption is also characterized by a sophisticated network of the obstacles posing a challenge to the desired future where irresponsible consumer behavior does not exist in the market (Mukherjee et al., 2024). Nothing is better than a future in which consumers are well informed on ethical purchases, and incorporate sustainability into their lifestyles easily (Shao et al., 2024). Contrary evidences however tend to emerge meaning that with the increased awareness (Al-Olfi et al., 2025), many consumers still tend to give preference to convenience and price above ethical ground, thus producing a paradox of manifested intention versus action (Lo & Lin, 2024). The previous empirical research provides various, at best inconclusive evidence, about the effectiveness of the ethical personalization strategy in stimulating sustainable consumption (Sardianou & Briana, 2025). Although there is evidence to show that personalized marketing strategies are more likely to result in sustainable choices, others indicate that consumers become dubious of brands that do not live up to their sustainability claims (Rana, 2024). Such inconsistency leaves theoretical gaps as the processes behind the ethical personalization effects on consumer behavior have not been studied sufficiently, especially within the framework of the fashion e-commerce industry (Mukherjee et al., 2024). In addition, there is a remaining area of knowledge gaps on which mediators facilitate this relationship (Cossatin et al., 2024). As an example, consumer trust and perceived value are often mentioned, but their applications in the context of ethical personalization and sustainable consumption have not been studied in detail yet (Allahverdiyev, 2025). The presence of gaps is also contextual as a lot of the research done in the past has failed to develop the dynamics of the various market segments or geographical regions adequately and this lack can have significant impacts on consumer behavior (Cutinha & Mokshagundam, 2024).

The practical difficulties also create an even more complex picture as despite the fashion retailer's willingness to use ethical personalization strategies, many cannot do it effectively and create the personalization strategies that truly become well-matched with consumers (Zubaidah et al., 2024). Such factors as the limited availability of resources, the high complexity of supply chains, and green washing risk limit the capacity of the brands to be in tune with the consumer expectation in regard to sustainability (Wasilewski & Zgrzywa-Ziemak, 2024). This paper seeks to fill these multidimensional gaps by examining the intervening role of ethical personalization in enhancing sustainable consumption of the fashion e-commerce industry.

THEORETICAL FOUNDATION

Theory of Planned Behavior (TPB): It presents that the attitude, subjective norm, and perceived behavioral control will influence an individual to engage or not engage in a behavior. This theory is especially important when interpreting sustainable consumption since it reveals how our opinions and those of the society impact our consumer choices. According to the e-commerce environment, consumption intention to make sustainable choices would be driven by positive perceptions of sustainable behavior and a sense that social norms encourage them to do so. Factors that hinder them are barriers e.g. one may not have information or find access to such services. Taking the perspective of ethical personalization, such as confirmed by PB, a framework of investigation can be developed to see the influence of ethical personalization on consumer intentions by incorporating marketing strategies with values and perceived control of consumers (Lo & Lin, 2024).

Social Identity Theory: It explains how individuals derive their sense of identity based on the group affiliations that they have, which can strongly determine their behavior, and decisions that they make. The theory would be applicable to sustainable consumption because consumers tend to belong to a particular group of people who propagate ethical lifestyles. This issue of fashioning people to behave in a certain way is also applicable in the concept of sustainable consumption being undertaken by people who consider themselves environmentally conscious should there be a set of perceived beliefs held through this perceived notion that this is what the rest of the world is doing. Ethical personalization has a potential to tap into these social identities by designing unique experiences that appeal to a consumer's social affiliation in a way that would encourage a maintained behavior (Rana, 2024).

Value-Belief-Norm Theory (VBN): It draws attention to the association that exists between the personal values and beliefs about environmental problems and pro-environmental behaviors. It is more likely that individuals would take sustainable actions according to VBN that individuals will familiarize themselves with good environmental attitudes, combined with a belief that it is possible to have a certain impact. This theory places a lot of importance on the application of ethical personalization on convincing consumers of their values and beliefs therefore encouraging sustainable forms of consumption behavior. Marketing messages that emphasize common ground and the effect of personal choices are best done on a more individual level, furthermore this personalization of the marketing message also does not have to be costly to implement (Sardianou & Briana, 2025).

Consumer Culture Theory (CCT): It is the approach to the study of the role of culture in the construction of consumption patterns, compared to any program, is that analyses of consumption patterns are accompanied by an analysis of the social and cultural context. This theory is more relevant in explaining the dynamics underlying sustainable consumption in the fashion industry since the cultural standards or norms and values work to influence the consumer expectations. CCT can aid in determining the cultural story lines of sustainability and how such story lines can be harmonized with ethical personalization in order to achieve overall consumer responsibility. The cultural context should be taken into account to ensure that brands develop more profound relationships with consumers, which is critical to the success of their sustainable products (Mukherjee et al., 2024).

In this work, it is the ***Theory of Planned Behavior (TPB)*** to be used as a main theoretical framework. The attention TPB gives to the formation of intentionality under the influence of attitudes, norms, and perceived control is complete enough to be able to study how ethical personalization can influence sustainable consumption in fashion e-commerce. By examining how personalized marketing can influence the consumer intentions, the given study would help to explain exactly how ethical personalization can drive sustainable behaviors, eventually contributing to theory and practice improvement.

In this framework, ethical personalization is the starting point: when consumers experience product offerings and messages that genuinely reflect their ethical values, they begin to see the brand as more **trustworthy** and feel that it offers superior value relative to alternatives. Higher trust and perceived value then translate into more favorable attitudes toward sustainable options and stronger intentions to choose such options in their fashion purchases. As these intentions are enacted, consumers shift their actual behavior toward sustainable consumption, which deepens their ongoing engagement with the brand and its sustainability initiatives, creating a reinforcing cycle of ethical personalization, trust, and responsible consumption.

In the framework, ethical personalization can be the origin of the message, and when consumers receive product offers and communication that reflect their true values, people begin to perceive the brand as trustworthy and feel it even provides better value compared with alternatives. Higher trust and perceived value in turn is then translated into more favorable attitudes towards the sustainable options and increased intentions to choose such options when purchasing their fashion. As these intentions are put into action, the consumers change their actual behavior to sustainable consumption, increasing the consumers engagement with the brand and its sustainability initiatives on a continuous basis creating an increasing cycle of ethical personalization, trust and responsible consumption.

EMPIRICAL LITERATURE REVIEW

Ethical Personalization and Fashion E-Commerce

The nexus between ethical personalization and fashion e-commerce has accumulated much interest in the recent empirical studies due to rising consumer preference of brands that resonated with their value ethics (Lo & Lin, 2024). Research shows that ethical individualization has a substantial effect on the purchase behavior of the consumer by increasing brand adherence and integrity (Sardianou & Briana, 2025). To give another example, another study revealed that customers tend to relate to brands that promote a personalized experience with a focus on sustainability and ethical sourcing (Rana, 2024). This indicates that by aligning their products and customer service to the ethical stand of the customers, the brands not only increase customer satisfaction but also build lasting loyalty among them (Mukherjee et al., 2024). Furthermore, there is empirical evidence how ethical branding influences the consumer perceptions in the environment of e-commerce (Shao et al., 2024). A study conducted revealed that ethical branding does have a positive influence on emotional reactions in consumers by instilling higher purchase intentions (Allahverdiyev, 2025). This emotional appeals are essential in the fashion industry where customers are sometimes interested in brands with which they can identify themselves with their personal values (Al-Olfi et al., 2025). The results show that ethical personalization may establish a differentiating selling point to separate brands in a crowded market (Zubaidah et al., 2024). Beyond this, the influence of Sustainable Consumption as a mediating factor in the connection between ethical personalization and consumer behavior has been investigated (Cutinha & Mokshagundam, 2024). As an illustration, a research found that ethical personalization impacts the way individuals feel about sustainability, and this aspect will drive their buying behavior (Wasilewski & Zgrzywa-Ziemak, 2024). The discussed mediation indicates the prominence of sustainability as one of the characteristics that brands should take into account when adopting ethical personalization techniques (Mangudhla, 2025). The study recommends that ethical appeals would work better together with sustainable practices to give them the best impact on the consumer decision-making.

In the field of technology, empirical research has been done on how innovations in the data analytics and artificial intelligence allow the realization of ethical personalization in fashion e-commerce (Deng et al., 2024). As an example, found that the personalized approach to crafting ethical-value-based market messages using consumer data could be seen as an important factor improving staff engagement (Kant et al., 2025). The power to understand consumer preference and behavior means the brand can effectively customize their communications towards its audience which results in a more effective connection (Niguse et al., 2026).

H1: Ethical Personalization and Fashion E-commerce having empirical association

Ethical Personalization and Sustainable Consumption

According to studies, ethical personalization has a great impact on the devotion among consumers to adopt sustainable consumption practices (Al-Olfi et al., 2025). One example of the findings shown is the study that when brands tailor their offering to reflect the ethical concerns of the consumer such as environmental sustainability and social responsibility, a significant boost is experienced about the consumer intents to buy sustainable products (Allahverdiyev, 2025). This result indicates that ethical personalization is a facilitating factor that helps persuade consumers to act in more sustainable ways (Zubaidah et al., 2024). Besides, consumer attitudes towards sustainability have been widely discussed in the literature as the mediating factor (Shao et al., 2024). The research found out that ethical personalization increases positive attitudes of consumers towards sustainable consumption, and such influences boost their purchase intentions (Cutinha & Mokshagundam, 2024). This mediation provides emphasis on the need to match marketing strategies with values held by the consumers (Rana, 2024). Whenever brands are able to convey their ethical practice, they can create a better attitude towards sustainable alternatives, and as a result, persuade buyers to choose them (Sardianou & Briana, 2025).

Along with individual attitudes, the effect of social influences has been studied on the link between ethical personalization and sustainable consumption (Wasilewski & Zgrzywa-Ziemak, 2024). It was found out that when the consumers think that their peers appreciate ethical practices, they tend to participate in sustainable consumption more frequently. The study demonstrated that ethical personalization would allow increasing social norms through the display of consumer testimonies and social proof in the marketing campaigns (Mukherjee et al., 2024). This also helps with the sustainability choices becoming desirable and ethical consumption as a collective responsibility which would encourage people to join (Lo & Lin, 2024). Transparency on ethical personalization strategy is also needed in the literature (Cunha, 2025). A report reveals that consumers tend to adopt sustainable solutions in case brands share information regarding sourcing, production processes, and the effect their products have on the environment (Niguse et al., 2026).. Transparency does not only create trust but enables the ethical personalization to be more effective as it makes a consumer more secure in his/her personalization purchasing decisions because he/she is aware of the ethical impact of particular choice (Jio et al., 2025).

H2: Ethical Personalization and Sustainable Consumption having empirical association

Sustainable Consumption and Fashion E-Commerce

There is stable research evidence that consumers are increasingly focusing their purchasing decisions in the fashion sector on the basis of sustainability issues (Rana, 2024). One study showed that customers are more likely to switch to brands that had a commitment to sustainable processes, including the use of environmentally friendly materials, ethical labor practice, etc (Shao et al., 2024). The tendency is an indication that sustainability is becoming a common driving force in consumer trends in fashion e-commerce (Al-Olfi et al., 2025). In addition, consumer attitude to sustainability has been an area, which has been greatly explored (Cutinha & Mokshagundam, 2024). A research study found out that positive perceptions of sustainable consumption in consumers greatly boosts the intentions to buy ecofriendly fashion products (Wasilewski & Zgrzywa-Ziemak, 2024). The research shows, the more perceptions of sustainability in fashion as an expensive and atypical style decreases, the more consumers are willing to take a sustainable consumption behavior (Niguse et al., 2026) This observation is indicative of the fact that brands should demonstrate their sustainable practices by communicating them appropriately to develop positive consumer attitudes. Technology is also a key element in providing sustainable consumption in fashion e-commerce (Kant et al., 2025). It is also pointed out in a research that digital modes are effective in building awareness about sustainability and in making people have access to green products (Jio et al., 2025). The research shows that online stores focusing on green products in their advertisement can win a market share because they will capture the attention of the earth lovers. Furthermore, data analytics can be used to make recommendations, which can be personally tailored to each consumer depending on their specific preferences towards more sustainable products to further encourage use and purchase behavior (Cunha, 2025).

Another important factor that affects sustainable consumption in fashion e-commerce's is transparency of the supply chains (Lo & Lin, 2024). One particular study highlights that customers are becoming asking more and more questions about how their fashion products are made and manufactured (Sardianou & Briana, 2025). These findings indicate that brands who best communicate their sustainability measures relating to issues like sourcing materials with responsibility and fair working conditions are most likely to win the hearts of consumers (Mukherjee et al., 2024). Transparency does not only build brand credibility but also builds the commitment of consumers to engage in sustainable consumption (Shao et al., 2024). The barriers to adoption of sustainable consumption approaches in fashion practiced by consumers as cited in the literature are also mentioned (Allahverdiyev, 2025). According to research, some of the factors that delay the adoption of sustainable choices include increased cost of the same, scarcity of availability of sustainable alternatives, and ignorance to this change (Zubaidah et al., 2024).

H3: Sustainable Consumption and Fashion E-commerce having empirical association

Ethical Personalization, Fashion E-COMMERCe and Sustainable Consumption

Studies show that ethical personalization is a major factor in promoting sustainable consumption behaviors within the fashion e-sphere business (Niguse et al., 2026).. Specifically, one study conducted identified a significantly high growth in the tendency of sustainable products consumption when brands incorporate in their marketing strategies the ethical interests of consumers including environmental sustainability and social responsibility (Jio et al., 2025). This shows that ethical personalization will not only increase consumer engagement but also lead to more sustainable consumer behavior (Kant et al., 2025). A major characteristic of this relationship is that it is mediated by the attitude towards sustainability on the part of the consumer (Cunha, 2025). A research study showed that ethical personalization has a positive effect on consumers and their attitudes, which subsequently leads to promotion of the intentions to make sustainable consumption (Wasilewski & Zgrzywa-Ziemak, 2024). This mediation outcome is critical in regard to ensuring marketing messages are in line with the values of consumers and implies that an effective ethical messaging has the potential of developing positive attitudes which can be used in enhancing sustainable purchasing behavior (Zubaidah et al., 2024). The results depict how companies can ethically use personalization to shape a longer-lasting consumer attitude (Cutinha & Mokshagundam, 2024). Furthermore, empirical studies have examined the role of social norms in moderating such mediation process. found that people are more prone to endorsing ethical consumption behaviors when they feel that their peers highly appear in ethical practices (Al-Olfi et al., 2025). Their paper implies that ethical personalization would be able to engage these social influences by displaying testimonials and likes of other consumers with similar views (Allahverdiyev, 2025). Brands may incorporate social proof in their marketing campaigns and by so doing, they can build a circle of ethically- conscious consumers, which will continue to encourage people to join consumption of rarely consumed products (Cossatin et al., 2024).

Transparency in the brand practices would also play a paramount role in supporting the mediation between the amiable personalization with sustainable consumption (Shao et al., 2024). One study concluded that consumers will gravitate more to brands that actively engage in ethical practices and sustainability efforts and will communicate clearly the actions being taken (Mukherjee et al., 2024). The results indicate that transparent information on brands regarding sourcing, production and its relationship to the environmental impact can be a useful strategy to build credibility and gain consumer trust that is vital in influencing sustainable consumption (Rana, 2024). The efficiency of ethical personalization is further boosted by this transparency because consumers understand better and are more willing to make responsible purchase decision (Sardianou & Briana, 2025). The existence of these insights notwithstanding, the literature also presents some barriers that could impede the efficacy of ethical personalization to encourage sustainable consumption (Lo & Lin, 2024).

H4: Sustainable Consumption Mediation across Ethical Personalization and Fashion E-commerce having an empirical association

Figure 1. Conceptual Framework

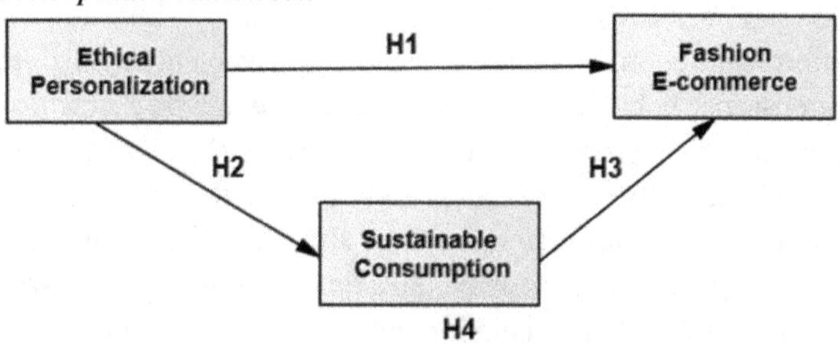

METHODOLOGY

This chapter involved a quantitative research design to examine interrelations between ethical personalization, fashion e-commerce and sustainable consumption. A group of 390 sample participants was selected across a wide variety of demographics in order to create a good representation of the target population. The structured questionnaires were used to collect the data in terms of measuring constructs of interest. The Kaiser-Meyer-Olkin (KMO) test was done before the analysis to determine the adequacy of the sample to be used in factor analysis since KMO above 0.7 indicates sufficient sample size. Exploratory Factor Analysis (EFA) was conducted next to determine the underlying sub-dimension of the constructs given the statements contained in the questionnaire. This was carried out via extraction of factors through Principal Component Analogy and varimax rotation to effect better gird structures. The results of EFA were used to revise the measures of the scales under consideration by removing an item that did not contribute to the constructs because of being irrelevant or insignificant. After EFA, the proposed relationships to be tested were done with Structural Equation Modeling (SEM) using AMOS software. SEM enabled the consideration of the model fit and the robustness of the relationships giving an opportunity to identify the mediation of ethical personalization on the sustainable consumption in fashion e-commerce.

Scale Development

The scale development process was based on comprehensive review of pertinent literature on ethnical personalizing, use of online as a channel of fashion shopping and sustainable consumption. Questions used in the scales were based on the previously validated elements and therefore they were relevant and reliable. Concepts like ethical awareness, consumer trust, perceived value and sustainable consumption behavior were found to be imperative to the structure of the study. All the items were effectively phrased to capture the semantics of the constructs with emphasis on considering clarity and applicability to the target group. Subjecting the initial pool of items to expert reviews also aimed at developing content validity through which it was ensured that the items were capturing what they were meant to capture. The initial scale was composed after taking into consideration the feedback and then piloted with a smaller sample of the respondents to test its clarity and reliability. The results of the pilot study facilitated subsequent improvements to its contents resulting in the final version of items that was adopted by the main study. This stringent scale development procedure did not only amplify the validity of the scales but also created a solid framework on which the statistical analysis could be performed, and hence, a satisfactory investigation of the mutual relationship was established between ethical personalization, fashion e-commerce and sustainable consumption.

Customer data for ethical personalization in fashion e-commerce poses key ethical and privacy considerations that need to be specifically addressed. First, companies must adhere to data minimization so that companies collect only the data strictly needed to personalize sustainable offers and avoid intrusive or unsolicited profiling which could harm consumer autonomy. Second, just rely on transparent consent: customers must be informed about what data is collected and how algorithms use this data to provide personalized and sustainability-oriented recommendations and whether there are third parties involved. Third, strong protection, such as secure storage, restricted access and clear retention practices are necessary to minimize the risks of misuse or leak of data, particularly where sensitive ethical or value-based preferences can be inferred from that data. Finish along with alignment above with sustainability must extend for argumentation to data practices themselves, ensuring that personalization honors consumer rights, is devoid of manipulativeness "dark patterns" and offers opt-out or data deletion options to maintain trust on ethical personalization wants together with a sustainable approach to consumption.

DATA ANALYSIS

Table 1. Data Adequacy

Adequate sample		.908
Bartlett Test o	Chi-Square	19484.673
	df	780
	p-value	.000

Source: Authors

Table 1 shows the values of the data adequacy tests. The value of KMO is indicated to be 0.908 showing a very high level of adequate sampling of the information. KMO values over 0.7 are normally acceptable and values that are near 1 indicate that the data is appropriate to use in factor analysis. This large value of KMO indicates that the correlations among the items that are involved in the research are reasonable and that the sample has the appropriate size which is necessary to perform the relevant analyses. Moreover, the Test results in a chi-square = 19,484.673; df = 780; p = 0.000. The large p-value ($p < 0.001$) shows that the correlation matrix is not an identity matrix, so that there are essential relations among the variables. This finding is another support to the relativeness of having factor analysis of the data. Taken together, these results demonstrate that the sample size is sufficient and that the data is proper to test the underlying constructs using factor analysis, and hence strengthen future analyses like Exploratory Factor Analysis (EFA) and Structural Equation Modeling (SEM).

Table 2. Variance Illuminated

Sum Variance Explained									
Factor	Initial Eigenvalues			Extraction			Rotation		
	Sum	% of Variance	Cumulative %	Sum	% of Variance	Cumulative %	Sum	% of Variance	Cumulative %
1	2.7	26.7	26.76	2.7	26.7	26.7	8.7	21.9	21.9
2	1.9	14.9	41.71	1.9	14.9	41.7	6.0	15.0	37.0
3	1.3	10.9	52.68	1.3	10.9	52.6	4.6	11.6	48.6

Source: Authors

The table 2 demonstrates the results of variance explained. The first factor has an initial eigenvalue of 2.7 with percentage of variance at 26.7 percent and this shows that this is the leading factor adding up to the construct. The overall contribution of such a factor is 26.76% making the latter less than a quarter of the proportional variation in responses attributable to the single dimension. The second factor has an initial eigenvalue at 1.9 determining 14.9 percent of the variance and the cumulative percentage to 41.71. This is to the effect that the combination of the first two factors explains a very high percentage in the analysis indicating its importance. The third factor has an initial eigen value of 1.3, accounting for 10.9 percent of the Variance giving a total cumulative total of 52.68 percent. This is indicative that the three factors that were identified explain more than half of the variance in the data which is a good basis on which analysis can proceed. The sums of the squares of loadings parallel the original eigenvalues assuring stabilization of the factor structure. The rotation sums, likewise reveal a clearer picture of the data, with the first three factors begetting 21.9%, 15.0 chaque, and 11.6 eper cent of the variance, respectively. On the whole, these findings support the idea that the EFA managed to extract the relevant factors which are supposed to be further analyzed and confirmed during the further studies.

Table 3. Covariances

Covariance			**Estimate**	**S.E.**	**C.R.**	**P**	**Hy.**
Sustainable Consumption	**<-->**	**Ethical Personalization**	**.563**	**.094**	**5.989**	**.00**	**H2**
Sustainable Consumption	<-->	Fashion E-commerce	.493	.056	8.803	.00	**H3**
Ethical Personalization	<-->	Fashion E-commerce	.652	.105	6.209	.00	**H1**

Source: Authors

Table 3 gives the estimates of the covariance between the constructs of Sustainable Consumption, Ethical Personalization and Fashion E-commerce with their C.R. and P-values. The covariance between Sustainable Consumption and Ethical Personalization is 0.563 with standard error = 0.094 and C.R. = 5.989. The p-value associated indicates that the relationship is highly significant as it is equal to 0.00, which supports H2. This robust positive correlation signifies that when the level of ethical personalization is high, correspondingly, the sustainable consumption of the consumers will go up. In the same manner, the covariance estimate of Sustainable Consumption and Fashion E-commerce is 0.493 with a standard error of 0.056 and C.R. of 8.803. The large p-value of 0.00 supports H3 and this shows that the consumers who are using fashion e-commerce are inclined toward greater sustainable consumption behavior. Finally, the covariance between Ethical Personalization and Fashion E-commerce is 0.652, the standard error of such covariance is 0.105 and the C.R. is 6.209. A p-value of 0.00 is a significant relationship, therefore the result supports the H1. This positive high-covariance indicates that ethical personalization is a central point of consumer involvement in fashion e-commerce.

Figure 2. Structural equation model

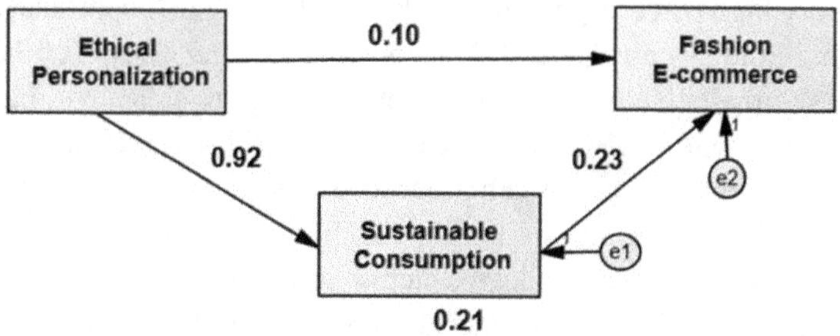

Table 4. Regression

Relative			Approx.	S.E.	C.R.	P	Ass.
Sustainable Consumption	**<---**	**Ethical Personalization**	**.716**	**.405**	**1.767**	**.06**	**H2**
Fashion E-commerce	<---	Sustainable Consumption	.651	.197	3.304	.00	H3
Fashion E-commerce	<---	Ethical Personalization	.563	.105	5.361	.00	H1

Source: Authors

The table 4 provides the results of the regression analysis. The initial regression path looks at the impact of Ethical Personalization on Sustainable Consumption and as it turns out, the coefficient is 0.716. The standard error of this estimate is 0.405 and this gives a C.R. of 1.767. The p-value is generated as 0.06, barely above the commonly observed level of significance (0.05), implying that though there is positive correlation, it probably cannot be shown to be significant at traditional level of significance. This result corroborates H2, which denotes a close relationship, albeit not that significant. The second regression link tests how Sustainable Consumption relates to Fashion E-commerce, and it returns a 0.651 coefficient and a 0.197 standard error. A C.R. of 3.304 with corresponding p-value of 0.00 strongly indicates a positive relationship that is highly significant thus validating H3. This finding indicates that those more involved in sustainable consumption practices will be more likely to enter the fashion e-commerce. The last path looks into the direct effect of Ethical Personalization on the Fashion E-commerce, and it revealed a coefficient of 0.563 with a standard error of 0.105. The independent C.R. is 5.361 and p-value = 0.00 is highly significant and gives strong support to H1. The above finding implies that the ethical personalization levels were related to the high levels of consumer engagement in fashion e-commerce.

Table 5. Mediation

	Coefficient
Ethical Personalization → Fashion E-commerce	.10
Ethical Personalization → Sustainable Consumption → Fashion E-commerce	.93*.23=.21
	.21

Source: Authors

The mediating effect of Sustainable Consumption working through the relationship between Ethical Personalization and Fashion E-commerce is illustrated in Table 7. The two important paths shown in the table are the direct effect of the Ethical Personalization on the Fashion E-commerce and the initial effect on the Sustainable consumption, in turn, having impact on the Fashion E-commerce. The direct relationship between Ethical Personalization and Fashion E-commerce is a low .10, which means that their influence is insignificant. This implies the notion that Ethical Personalization in Fashion E-commerce on its own has no great effect towards consumer engagement. On the contrary, the indirect path demonstrates a greater impact. The product of the path coefficient is as reflected: Ethical Personalization positively influences Sustainable Consumption (0.93), Sustainable Consumption Influences Fashion E-commerce (0.23). The indirect effect thus determined is 0.93* 0.23 = 0.21. This value shows that, Sustainable Consumption is a powerful mediator between Ethical Personalization and Fashion E-commerce. In this case, the detection of such mediation effect is suggested as Partial mediation meaning that all the impact of Ethical Personalization on Fashion E-commerce is mediated through the Sustainable Consumption, as opposed to being directly levied. This observation shows the relevance of the development of sustainable consumption behaviors as a central passage to convert ethical considerations into a bigger involvement in Fashion E-commerce.

DISCUSSION

The results of the current research can be used to gain better understanding of interconnections between Ethical Personalization, Sustainable Consumption, and Fashion E-commerce. The positive correlations above the 0.900 mark in the covariance analysis also indicate that the consumers, being the same people, who adopt ethical personalization tend to embrace sustainable consumption subsequent to doing so. This does not go against recent trends in consumer behavior due to the undeniable ethical factor in the purchasing aspect of the fashion industry, where sustainability has been making itself heard significantly. The regression analysis also supports the significance of the Sustainable Consumption as the mediator of significant connection between Ethical Personalization and Fashion E-commerce. Ethical Personalization was insignificant in affecting Fashion E-commerce directly but had a significant effect on it indirectly, through sustainable practices, as it is a proxy of the contributions of ethical conducts. This research implies that companies need to pay more attention to combining the concepts of ethics with their marketing efforts since this can result in improved consumer involvement and retention within the context of fashion e-commerce. Furthermore, the ability of the model to fit well as indicated by the statistics on model fitness provides further support in the validity of the relationships postulated. The results provide a contribution to the existing literature in portraying that ethical personalization may also play a significant role in influencing the behaviors of consumers when positioned in the framework of sustainability. This is an indication that brands are not only required to ensure they engage in ethical practices, but they should also communicate these messages to their consumers which leads to the creation of a more sustainable fashion system.

CONCLUSION

The paper presents important knowledge on the interrelationships between Ethical Personalization, Sustainable Consumption, and Fashion E-commerce. Based on the findings it has been revealed that though Ethical Personalization as a sole factor does not have significant impact on Fashion E-commerce, it is a key in promoting Sustainable Consumption, which then promotes consumer engagement in the fashion-related purchases. This highlights the role of sustainability as a mediating variable, so that the brands cannot rely only on making their marketing solely, as a marketing strategy, but also as a sales practice and business model. The fact that a great part of the constructs in use in the analyses showed affinities and the finding that these relationships are substantial support the validity of these constructs and their usefulness in consumer behavior today. As consumers are growing more discerning about the brands that they associate themselves with in relation to their ethical mandates, companies within the fashion industry can use such information to improve on their marketing initiatives and thus developing a closer relationship between consumers and the company. Overall, this study demonstrates that the fashion industry needs to incorporate ethical issues in their production and in their messages. In such a way, they will be able not only to satisfy the increased interest in sustainable practices but also to cultivate loyalty among the customers. The paper acts as a wake-up call to fashion retailers to drive industry-focused ethical personalization to sustainability to lead a greener future in fashion e-commerce.

MANAGERIAL IMPLICATIONS

The results of the present study provide valuable managerial insights to brands that conduct their business in the fashion e-commerce industry. The first one is that the importance of Ethical Personalization in stimulating Sustainable Consumption highlights the need of companies to embrace and promote ethical actions. The focus of the management must be to be as transparent as possible in sourcing, production, and marketing endeavors because consumers now tend to buy brands they connect with. This may include highlighting environmentally friendly materials, use of fair trade, and the manufacturing process being ethical to promote in marketing. It is also found that the identified mediation effect stands out to indicate that brands should come up with strategies that would not only focus on ethical considerations but also kind of informing the consumers about how their purchase decision contributes to sustainability. It is possible to implement such initiatives as informative contents, workshops or engagement activities in the community to increase awareness of consumers and promote sustainable behaviors. Moreover, managers ought to seek to introduce feedback tools to evaluate consumer perceptions on ethical conduct and the sustainability initiatives. This can assist brands in shaping their strategies to be more aligned to the anticipated expectations of the consumers and build a sense of community that aligns with shared values. Lastly, because ethical and sustainable practices are gaining prominence in terms of consumer choices, efforts should be put in research and development of sustainable-based innovations. When integrated within the scope of business strategies, ethical consumerism trends do not only help e-commerce fashion brands become more competitive in the market but they also allow ensuring a positive effect on the environmental and social ends. All these implications offer a guide to managers advancing on a more responsible and involved fashion e-commerce environment.

PRACTICAL IMPLICATIONS

The lessons of this article have a range of practical implications in the context of fashion e-commerce business that wants to boost its presence within the market and across its consumers. Above all, brands must proactively engage and demonstrate the responsible brand personalization process, with their marketing collateral bearing witness to respecting sustainability. This may include the development of customized experiences to encourage the consumers to buy such eco-friendly products and businesses operating in an ethical manner and thus directly offer the message to the value of environment- conscious consumers. In addition, brands have the advantage of adding the concept of sustainability to their product development cycle. This involves using sustainable materials, streamlining their supply chains to be as environmentally conscious as possible, and practicing circular economy (like recycling and upcycling). When these practices are prioritized, companies can not only stand out in an otherwise saturated market, but they can also comply with the increased demand of consumers consumable clothing that is based on practices of responsibility. Moreover, they can establish collaboration with nonprofit companies or sustainability lobbyists to strengthen the perception of credibility and expand outreach activities. Partnership with the communities or community campaigns can also build a common cause and get the consumer interested in organizations that are good in terms of ethical treatment. Lastly, establishing feedback mechanisms to gather consumer feedback on ethical preferences and sustainable practices can be used to set up future strategies. This cycle of feedback can help brands to refine their products and ways to market them to have a more consumer-relevant approach. By performing these practical actions, fashion e-commerce companies can ensure that they implement the ethical factors in their operations, thereby, encouraging sustainability and improving customer loyalty as a whole.

THEORETICAL IMPLICATIONS

The implications of the current study in terms of theory are important to consumer behavior and marketing research, especially in environmental friendly consumption and eco products. This study is valuable to the existing bodies of knowledge because it shows how a particular concept, Sustainable Consumption mediates between ethically mindful personalization and fashion e-commerce. This is an indication of the need to measure not only direct relationships, but also the relationships between different constructs. Additionally, the work confirms the validity of the Theory of Planned Behavior, according to which the behavioral intentions are influenced by the attitudes, subjective norm, and perceived behavioral control. The findings have identified that ethical attitudes stand a good chance of influencing consumer intentions to purchase in a sustainable manner belting the Ethical Personalization and Sustainable Consumption. This will give perspective to the theoretical framework because it shows how ethical values can be implemented in marketing practices so as to contribute to sustainable consumption. Moreover, the study highlights the necessity of the closer-knit exploration of ethical consumer behavior. Future research is encouraged to investigate other mediators/moderators that can have an impact on the correlation between ethical considerations and consumer behaviors in diverse settings. This study can advance the theoretical discussion of ethical personalization and sustainability to initiate additional research on what exactly brands can do to engage consumers successpartialy and in a more sustainable way.

RECOMMENDATIONS

A number of recommendations can be advanced based on the findings of the present study to guide the fashion e-commerce companies in their bid to boost their ethical operations and develop sustainable consumer behaviors. To begin with, the brands must pay primary attention to incorporating ethical personalization in the marketing strategy. This may be done with the help of the data analytics approach to learn more about consumer values (e.g. sustainability and ethical sourcing) and to provide product recommendations that communicate those values. Individualized message has a potential to build customer relationship and loyalty. Besides, the brands are advised to invest in educational programs that would create awareness of the need to practice sustainable consumption. That may include the production of content that focuses on impacts caused by fashion choices and promoting environmentally and socially responsible consumption. With the help of workshops, webinars, or social media campaigns, the consumers could be affected and made to change their behavior and become more sustainable. The cooperation with sustainability organizations and influencers can also enhance the effect of a brand, its reach and credibility. Collaborations with reputable organizations would help brands improve their communications and prove that; such partnerships have the capacity of ensuring community involvement, a feeling of responsibility among the consumers. Last, the brands must also integrate sound feedback systems that will constantly monitor consumer perception and preference as far as ethical practices is concerned. It can help in product development and marketing strategies and enable brands to be dynamic and flexible to the changes in consumer demands. By incorporating these suggestions, fashion online retailers will be able to project themselves as leaders in terms of ethical and sustainable standards, and eventually develop a more responsible industry.

FUTURE DIRECTIONS

The direction of the work to be undertaken in the field of ethical personalization and sustainable consumption in fashion e-commerce should go in several directions subsequent to the results of this work. First, longitudinal studies are likely to give us an idea about the development of consumer attitudes and behavior, especially in response to increasing attention to sustainability places. By comprehending these dynamics, brands are more likely to be prepared in the future when consumer expectations change and create more of a challenge to deal with. Furthermore, the researchers are encouraged to examine how different demographics, including age, gender, and socio-economic status, affect how consumers react to having their personalization being done ethically and having their purchasing practices support sustainability. This might provide subtle information on the way that the various groups of consumers view and interact with ethical fashion providing brands with the opportunity to address them in a more specific manner. The discussion on the part played by technology in supporting ethical personalization is also deserving of investigation. For example, artificial intelligence and machine learning have the potential to be implemented to allow brands to personalize the offerings further to promise better alignment with the values and preferences of the individual consumers. Lastly, inter-industry comparisons would help to make the knowledge on ethical consumer behavior even richer as it explores how the precepts of ethical personalization and sustainability in other industries are put to use. The experiences in other sectors such as food, technology, or home products can be used to enlighten the fashion e-commerce brand about which practices and strategies are the best and most innovative. In focusing on these future directions, scientists can help inform the issues that adventure between ethics, sustainability and consumer behavior in the fashion industry.

REFERENCES

Al-Olfi, S. A. A., Song, Y., & Al-Hajj, Y. M. (2025). The Impact of Sustainable Supply Chain Strategies on E-Commerce Consumer Purchasing Behavior: Considering the Moderating Effect of Big Data Analytics. *Journal of the Knowledge Economy*, •••, 1–36. DOI: 10.1007/s13132-025-02671-3

Allahverdiyev, K. (2025). Leveraging AI for Enhancing Sustainable Marketing and Consumer Experience in E-Commerce. *Journal of Emerging Trends in Marketing and Management, 1*(1), 49–59.

Ashuro, T., Kant, S., & Adula, M. (2025). Multi-Stakeholder Collaboration Effect on Sustainable Supply Chain Optimization by Mediation of Vendor Managed Inventory in the Horn of Africa. In *Multi-Stakeholder Collaboration for Sustainable Supply Chain* (pp. 203–224). IGI Global Scientific Publishing. DOI: 10.4018/979-8-3693-8925-6.ch009

Cossatin, A. G., Mauro, N., & Ardissono, L. (2024). Promoting green fashion consumption through digital nudges in recommender systems. *IEEE Access : Practical Innovations, Open Solutions, 12*, 6812–6829. DOI: 10.1109/ACCESS.2024.3349710

Cunha, M. N. (2025). Transforming Online Retail: The impact of augmented and virtual reality on consumer engagement and experience in e-commerce in the context of the Sustainable Development Goals (SDG). *Journal of Lifestyle and SDGs Review, 5*(3), e4816–e4816. DOI: 10.47172/2965-730X.SDGsReview.v5.n03.pe04816

Cutinha, Z. P., & Mokshagundam, D. S. (2024). Sustainability practices in E-commerce: Opportunities and challenges for digital marketers. *International Journal of Research Publication and Reviews, 5*(2), 1068–1075. DOI: 10.55248/gengpi.5.0224.0435

Deng, Y., Shen, H., & Ji, X. (2024). Exploring virtual fashion consumption through the emotional three-level theory: Reflections on sustainable consumer behavior. *Sustainability (Basel), 16*(13), 5818. DOI: 10.3390/su16135818

Jio, W., Kant, S., & Lemi, K. (2025). Ethical Leadership: Effect on Future of Organizational Citizenship Behavior by Mediation of Organizational Culture in Ethiopia. In *Generation Alpha and Next Generation Leadership for Greener Futures* (pp. 41-62). IGI Global Scientific Publishing.

Kant, S., Adula, M., & Jio, W. (2025). Consumer Neuroscience in the Perception of AI and Market Orientation. In *Advancing Medical Research Through Neuroscience* (pp. 21–46). IGI Global Scientific Publishing. DOI: 10.4018/979-8-3693-5464-3.ch002

Kant, S., Niguse, T., Olubiyi, T. O., Adula, M., & Kebede, K. (2025). Sustainable Fashion-Based Innovations and Consumer Behavior in Ethiopia. In *Global Impacts and Sustainable Practices in Fast Fashion* (pp. 167–196). IGI Global Scientific Publishing. DOI: 10.4018/979-8-3693-7853-3.ch007

Kant, S., Toma, F., Niguse, T., & Adula, M. (2025). Eco-Friendly Packaging Effect on the Future of Consumer Shopping Habits by Mediation of Consumer Awareness in Retail Industries in the Horn of Africa. In *Sustainable Practices in the Fashion and Retail Industry* (pp. 179–202). IGI Global Scientific Publishing. DOI: 10.4018/979-8-3693-9959-0.ch008

Lemi, K., Kant, S., & Jio, W. (2025). Greener Hospital Future in the Horn of Africa by Transactional Leadership: Outcome on Altruism Through Adaptability. In *Generation Alpha and Next Generation Leadership for Greener Futures* (pp. 1-22). IGI Global Scientific Publishing.

Lo, C. H., & Lin, L. F. (2024, July). Personalized E-Shopping Recommendations for Sustainable Consumption. In *2024 16th IIAI International Congress on Advanced Applied Informatics (IIAI-AAI)* (pp. 585-588). IEEE. DOI: 10.1109/IIAI-AAI63651.2024.00111

Mangudhla, T. (2025). Sustainable E-Commerce Platforms: Integrating Green Marketing Strategies in Digital Marketplaces. In *Regulatory Frameworks and Digital Compliance in Green Marketing* (pp. 259-290). IGI Global Scientific Publishing.

Mukherjee, S., Thapliyal, K., Manchanda, M., & Jha, S. (2024, November). Sustainable E-Commerce Through Customer Emotion Recognition with Machine Learning. In *2024 3rd Edition of IEEE Delhi Section Flagship Conference (DELCON)* (pp. 1-7). IEEE. DOI: 10.1109/DELCON64804.2024.10866879

Niguse, T., Kant, S., Kebede, K., & Alemu, Z. K. (2026). Effect of Green Branding on Sustainable Competitive Advantage With Mediating Role of Continuous Learning in the Case of Luxury Products, Ethiopia. In *Technology-Driven Market Transformations for Digital Fashion and Smart Luxury* (pp. 93–120). IGI Global Scientific Publishing.

Niguse, T., Kant, S., Kebede, K., & Alemu, Z. K. (2026). The Role of Co-Marketing on the Digital Fashion Integration in Smart Product by Mediation of Cross-Cultural Marketing in Ethiopia. In *Sustainable Branding, Cultural Intelligence and Co-Marketing* (pp. 75-100). IGI Global Scientific Publishing.

Rana, N. (2024). Ethical AI Integration in Marketing Strategies for Sustainable E-Commerce Fashion Designing. In *Contemporary Management and Global Leadership for Sustainability* (pp. 218–233). IGI Global Scientific Publishing. DOI: 10.4018/979-8-3693-1273-5.ch013

Sardianou, E., & Briana, M. (2025). Platform-Driven Sustainability in E-Commerce: Consumer Behavior Toward Recycled Fashion. *Recycling*, *10*(4), 161. DOI: 10.3390/recycling10040161

Shao, J., Feng, Y., & Liu, Z. (2024). The impact of big data-driven strategies on sustainable consumer behaviour in E-commerce: A green economy perspective. *Sustainability (Basel)*, *16*(24), 10960. DOI: 10.3390/su162410960

Wasilewski, A., & Zgrzywa-Ziemak, A. (2024). Multi-variant e-commerce user interfaces for business sustainability. *Operations Research and Decisions*, *34*(4), 211–229. DOI: 10.37190/ord240412

Zubaidah, T. R., Muzdalifah, L., Boyas, J. R., Mustaqim, M., Sholikhah, A., Violita, C. E., & Putrihadiningrum, D. C. (2024, September). Sustainable Business of E-Commerce in the Smart Economy: A Systematic Review of Roles and Challenges for Future Research. In *2024 International Conference on ICT for Smart Society (ICISS)* (pp. 1-7). IEEE. DOI: 10.1109/ICISS62896.2024.10751282

KEY TERMS AND DEFINITIONS

Ethical Personalization: The trend of customizing marketing and product offerings to the various ethical values and undesirables of the consumers, especially to sustainability and social responsibility.

Sustainable Consumption: The consumption of products and services that have little or no harm to the environment and society where the concern is sound decisions made in purchase to strive for ecological status quo and social justice.

Fashion E-commerce: The online selling of fashion items, such as, clothing, accessories, and footwear, operated through digital media that enables the consumer to browse, choose and buy fashion items online.

Consumer Behavior: The research on the behavior of citizens to invest their possession in consumption-based sections depending on the psychological and social and economic driving forces.

Mediation: The special case of statistical relationship when a third variable (mediator) describes the association between an independent and a dependent variable, typically employed to learn mechanisms.

Transparency: A brand that is transparent about the way it sources, the way it produces and also the ethical standards pumped into its products will enable a consumer to make an informed choice, based on the available information.

Circular Economy: A model intended to reduce wastes and maximize use of the resources through encouraging recycling, reusing, and making other products marketable, again through refurbishments in order to increase their lifecycle.

Chapter 7
Digitally Mediated Wardrobes:
Advancing Sustainable Consumption in the Fashion Ecosystem

Meghna Gupta
http://orcid.org/0000-0002-4812-6740
Lovely Professional University, India

Amit Kakkar
Lovely Professional University, India

ABSTRACT

The fashion industry is facing a pivotal transformation shaped by digital innovation and sustainability demands. Digitally mediated wardrobes, including AI-powered outfit planners, virtual wardrobe platforms, and AR/VR fitting tools, are redefining how consumers interact with clothing. By promoting mindful consumption, rewearing, and optimized apparel use, these technologies reduce waste and encourage circular practices. This chapter explores the intersection of technology, consumer behavior, and sustainability, analyzing their impact on consumption patterns, infrastructure, and environmental outcomes. Ethical issues of data privacy, inclusivity, and digital access are critically examined. Drawing from academic research, case studies, and sustainability reports, the chapter argues that digital wardrobes are not only reshaping the fashion ecosystem but also creating pathways for systemic change. Positioned at the crossroads of culture, policy, and technology, they offer a viable route toward a more sustainable and circular fashion model.

DOI: 10.4018/979-8-3373-5525-2.ch007

1.INTRODUCTION

A significant turning point has occurred in the global fashion industry. According to the Ellen MacArthur Foundation (2017), the fashion industry's environmental impact has reached a critical point, making it completely unsustainable. This industry is responsible for about ten percent of the world's carbon emissions and is the second-largest consumer of the world's water supply. As climate change accelerates and ecological boundaries are crossed, it is becoming increasingly indisputable that the sector must undergo systemic reform. Due to the low-cost, high-turnover production model employed by fast fashion, hyper consumption and the disposability of garments have become the norm. This has resulted in the development of a culture in which clothing is regarded as inconsequential rather than precious. The United Nations Environment Programme (UNEP) reports that every second, the amount of textiles disposed of in landfills or burned is equivalent to that of one garbage truck carrying waste (Stevenson, 2023).

In addition to the environmental damage it causes, the fashion industry has also been criticized for its social impact. Exploitation of workers, hazardous working conditions, and unfair distribution of profits are all issues that continue to plague global supply chains. Additionally, the opaque structure of production networks and the outsourcing of manufacturing to countries in the Global South, where laws are less stringent and enforcement is frequently limited, both contribute to the worsening of these problems (Sugadev et al., 2024).

These vulnerabilities were brought to light by the COVID-19 epidemic, which also served as a driving force toward the digital revolution. Both customers and marketers enthusiastically welcomed E-commerce, virtual fashion shows, and remote styling services while the traditional retail industry came to a standstill. Even more significantly, a large number of people reevaluated their spending patterns, leading to an increase in interest in minimalism, resale platforms, and sustainable alternatives. This convergence of crises environmental, economic, and public health has intensified the desire for new solutions that match fashion with larger sustainability goals. Specifically, this convergence has occurred in the fashion industry.

Within the framework of this discussion, digitally mediated wardrobes have emerged as a promising invention. Users can manage, assess, and improve their clothing collections more effectively with the assistance of these systems, which utilize digital technology to enhance their experience. At their essence, they encourage consumers to maximize the value of what they already possess, shifting the focus away from purchase while simultaneously boosting use. These platforms not only encourage users to cultivate more purposeful connections with fashion but also have the potential to significantly change consumer behavior, providing them with opportunities to plan outfits, track their wardrobe, and monitor sustainability data (Sun et al., 2022).

The purpose of this chapter is to investigate how these technologies carry out their functions not only as applications but also as interventions in cultural and behavioral patterns. On the other hand, they provide a new interface through which fashion may be experienced, one that integrates sustainable practices into everyday activities. As an illustration, a user who is prompted to wear an item they have not worn before or to refrain from acquiring a garment similar to one they already possess is interacting with a form of digital nudging that has its origins in behavioral economics.

Additionally, digital wardrobes are fully compatible with the principles that underpin the circular economy. These activities support a closed-loop system in which fashion goods are kept in use for as long as possible. These practices include enhancing the lifetime of garments, making it easier to resell and donate clothes, and improving clothing care methods. In addition, brands can reap the benefits of these insights by utilizing aggregated data to estimate demand, reduce overproduction, and meet the standards for sustainability reporting. This compatibility with the circular economy offers a promising path towards a more sustainable fashion industry (Szatkowski et al., 2024).

The many obstacles that need to be addressed in order to harness the full potential of these instruments are also acknowledged in this chapter. One of the persistent obstacles is accessibility, particularly in areas with limited digital infrastructure. Data privacy, algorithmic bias, and the risk of greenwashing are all aspects that need to be controlled to preserve consumer confidence and comply with regulations. Furthermore, the success of these technologies depends not only on innovation but also on their widespread adoption at scale. To achieve this outcome, it will be necessary to collaborate across different sectors, have supportive legislative frameworks, and adopt a cultural mindset that is open to change.

The purpose of this chapter is to illustrate that digitally mediated wardrobes are more than just a specialized niche in the realm of technology. It represents a paradigm shift in the way we think about fashion consumption. They present a model for a more ethical and ecologically resilient fashion future by enabling consumers to make more sustainable choices through the use of data, customization, and convenience capabilities. In the following sections, we will examine the historical progression of fashion consumption, explore the technology that enables it, assess the behavioral processes involved, and investigate real-world implementations of digital wardrobe platforms (Wardani et al., 2022).

The following research questions guide this chapter:

(1) How do digitally mediated wardrobes influence fashion consumption behavior toward sustainability?

(2) Which digital technologies most effectively support circular fashion practices at both consumer and industry levels?
(3) What ethical, economic, and cultural challenges limit the scalability of digital wardrobes globally?

By addressing these questions, the chapter positions digitally mediated wardrobes not merely as technological tools, but as systemic interventions within the sustainable fashion ecosystem.

Despite growing interest in digital wardrobes, existing research remains fragmented. Most studies examine isolated technologies or consumer attitudes, leaving a gap in understanding how **technological affordances interact with behavioral mechanisms to drive sustained sustainable consumption**. This chapter addresses this gap by integrating technological, behavioral, and ethical perspectives into a unified conceptual understanding.

2. THE EVOLUTION OF FASHION CONSUMPTION

The evolution of fashion consumption reflects the broader sociocultural, economic, and technological transformations that have shaped contemporary civilization. These transitions have been made possible by technological advancements. In cultures that existed before the Industrial Revolution, clothing had a practical purpose. It was frequently created from materials taken from the immediate area and infused with symbolic cultural values. The garments were handed down from generation to generation and mended as required, which encouraged usage that was both deliberate and long-lasting. The beginning of industrialization brought about a significant shift in this regard (Zhong et al., 2022).

It was during the Industrial Revolution that clothing began to be manufactured in large quantities and became a commodity. As a result of advancements in textile production and the proliferation of automated factories, clothing could be manufactured rapidly and at an affordable price. This not only made fashion more accessible to people outside of the elite, but it also accelerated the process of detaching clothes from the customs and artistry that had previously been associated with them. Department stores and global fashion centers emerged throughout the twentieth century, redefining shopping as a leisure activity and clothing as a means of self-expression and social signaling (Kosiba et al., 2020).

Starting in the 1990s and continuing into the early 2000s, fast fashion businesses such as Zara, H&M, and Forever 21 began to utilize global supply chains to deliver new trends at a pace and volume that had never been seen before. Micro collections were distributed to customers on a weekly or biweekly basis, which encouraged a faster turnover of apparel and the disposal of unwanted items. The consumption pattern standardized by fast fashion was one in which clothing was no longer considered an investment, but rather a temporary commodity. The average customer today purchases sixty percent more apparel than they did twenty years ago, and they retain each item for fifty percent of the time (MacArthur 2017).

Although it has been economically successful, this strategy has had significant repercussions. As a result of its reliance on low-cost manufacturing in countries with poor labor rights, it has exacerbated environmental degradation by consuming excessive amounts of resources and producing vast quantities of textile waste. Additionally, it has firmly established worker exploitation. At the same time, it has contributed to the development of a psychological connection with clothing that is characterized by impulsivity, a desire for novelty, and a desire to showcase one's status.

It is essential to acknowledge that social media platforms have played a significant role in accelerating these trends. Both Instagram and TikTok have become digital runways due to their emphasis on visuals and algorithmic selection. These platforms enable users and influencers alike to showcase their ensembles and establish their unique aesthetic identities. The culture of "outfit of the day" (OOTD), fuelled by rapid content cycles, encourages individuals to refresh their wardrobes regularly. Due to the proliferation of fashion hauls and unboxing videos, the desire for quantity over quality has become even more ingrained in society (Mallon 2024).

However, there has also been a rise in opposition to these rules that cannot be maintained. The concept of slow fashion prioritizes the ideals of sustainability, ethics, and environmental responsibility in the fashion industry. It motivates customers to purchase fewer items, make more informed decisions, and extend the lifespan of their clothing. Brands such as Patagonia, Eileen Fisher, and Stella McCartney have been at the forefront of this industry by including repair services, ethical sourcing, and transparency into their respective business strategies.

Concurrently, the sharing economy has given rise to peer-to-peer resale platforms, including Depop, Poshmark, and Vinted, as well as apparel rental businesses such as Rent the Runway. To create a hybrid model that combines circularity with fashion involvement, these platforms cater to customers seeking affordable, unique, and ethically sound products. Both the user experience and the decision-making process are being improved as a result of the increased integration of digital wardrobe technologies into these ecosystems (Kim & Seo 2023).

Wardrobes that are mediated by digital technology are located at the crossroads of these historical and current developments. Through providing insight into one's existing wardrobe, encouraging re-wearing, and establishing connections between users and circular services, these technologies rethink what it means to interact with fashion. They reframe the process of purchasing fashion as a discipline that involves creativity, awareness, and sustainability, shifting the focus from "what is new?" to "what can I do with what I have?"

Upon closer inspection of the development of fashion consumption, it becomes abundantly clear that technology solutions alone are not sufficient. Another thing that needs to change is the cultural myths surrounding identity, success, and desirability. Education, storytelling, and community efforts will all play significant roles in transforming consumption habits. The further development of digital wardrobes necessitates combining these wardrobes with larger initiatives that aim to address the fundamental principles and structures that influence fashion behavior (Manzo et al., 2025).

3. TECHNOLOGIES ENABLING DIGITALLY MEDIATED WARDROBES

The confluence of developing technologies is firmly based in the creation and functionality of digitally mediated wardrobes. Each of these technologies contributes specific capabilities to support sustainable fashion practices, which in turn supports the sustainability of the fashion industry. Artificial Intelligence (AI), Augmented Reality (AR), Virtual Reality (VR), Blockchain, Digital Product IDs, and the Internet of Things (IoT) are all components that comprise this ecosystem. The transition of passive wardrobe ownership into an interactive, data-driven fashion engagement is made possible by the deployment of these technologies in a synergistic manner, meaning they work together in a coordinated and complementary way. Industry trials of AR-based virtual try-on tools report return rate reductions ranging from 15 to 40 percent, particularly in size- and fit-sensitive product categories, translating into lower transport emissions and reduced reverse logistics waste. The figure below illustrates the technological ecosystem that supports digitally mediated wardrobes, highlighting the interaction between core digital tools and fashion processes.

Figure 1.

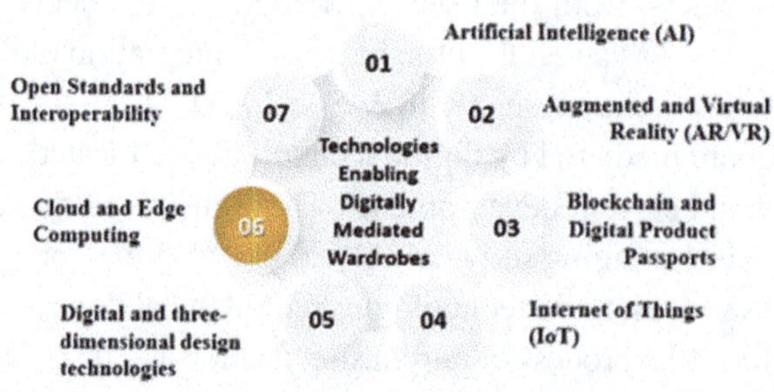

3.1 Artificial Intelligence (AI)

Personalization in digital wardrobes is powered by artificial intelligence (AI), which is the engine that drives the process. To recommend outfits and predict requirements, artificial intelligence systems examine user preferences, previous behavior, seasonal patterns, and contextual variables such as weather or calendar events. This is accomplished using deep learning and pattern recognition. The use of artificial intelligence in applications like Whering and Save Your Wardrobe not only helps users plan their outfits but also provides recommendations for eco-friendly style alternatives and cost-per-wear statistics, assisting users in making informed decisions that extend the lifespan of their garments. Beyond the realm of personal style, artificial intelligence is being utilized at the corporate level to forecast demand for clothing, manage inventory, and reduce overproduction. This initiative aims to address one of the most inefficient aspects of the fashion industry. Tools such as Vue.ai and Stylumia collect real-time data from customers to provide designers and merchants with assistance in designing items that align with actual usage trends, thereby reducing waste (Mesjar et al., 2023).

3.2 Augmented and Virtual Reality (AR/VR)

By allowing consumers to envision clothes in virtual worlds, augmented reality (AR) and virtual reality (VR) technologies are redefining the buying experience. To replicate how clothing fits and looks in real-time, augmented reality apps utilize the cameras on smartphones or smart mirrors. This technology enhances purchasing trust, which in turn reduces return rates, one of the most significant contributors to carbon emissions in the fashion e-commerce industry (Mesjar et al., 2023).

On the other hand, virtual reality (VR) provides immersive showrooms, virtual runways, and interactions based on avatars. Companies such as The Fabricant and DressX are at the forefront of establishing virtual fashion lines. These lines may be "worn" in digital pictures, gaming settings, or social media, therefore detaching the expression of style from the purchasing of material goods. The necessity for resource-intensive production is reduced as a result of these innovations, which lay the groundwork for fashion interaction in the metaverse.

3.3 Blockchain and Digital Product Passports

Blockchain technology offers a secure and immutable record that can be used to track clothing throughout their entire life. It promotes openness in the management of ownership, disposal, manufacture, and procurement of materials. In circular fashion systems, where several people may wear items, have different tasks, or appear on multiple platforms, this is an especially significant feature.

Digital Product Passports, also known as DPPs, are digital representations of physical garments that contain metadata about the garment's origin, materials, care instructions, and sustainability ratings. Examples of projects that demonstrate how these capabilities facilitate recycling, resale, and compliance with evolving regulatory frameworks include the CircularID Protocol and Eon's Connected Products. Users can access extensive histories of their clothing by scanning a QR code or an NFC chip, which fosters trust and facilitates informed decision-making (Morandi, & Tonelli 2023).

3.4 Internet of Things (IoT)

The Internet of Things enables real-time interaction between different types of garments and their wearers using RFID tags or integrated sensors. The data that these devices collect on garment usage, care frequency, and wear patterns may subsequently be used to notify users when it is appropriate to clean, mend, or retire their apparel. One example is the Project Jacquard collaboration between Google and Levi's, which investigated the use of touch-sensitive fabric to incorporate control interfaces into clothing.

IoT-enabled wardrobes have the potential to significantly reduce waste, offering a hopeful and optimistic view of the future of fashion. These wardrobes help track wear frequency and identify misused goods, enabling platforms to send nudges for re-wearing and discouraging wasteful purchases. Accumulated data from Internet of Things devices can be used to inform product development and circular strategies by highlighting real usage habits. This is a significant step towards a more sustainable and efficient fashion industry (Kosiba et al., 2020).

Digital and three-dimensional design technologies have seen notable advancements in recent years, including the development of 3D clothing design tools such as CLO3D, Browzwear, and Adobe Substance. With the use of these technologies, designers can create, alter, and envision clothes digitally before they are physically manufactured. This prevents the waste of samples, shortens development cycles, and enables the conduct of more experiments with a smaller environmental impact. A fully digital fashion pipeline is created when these models are combined with augmented reality and virtual reality, revolutionizing the way fashion is designed, produced, and consumed.

3.5 Cloud and Edge Computing

A Robust computer infrastructure is essential for digital wardrobes because it enables them to provide real-time responsiveness and accessibility across several devices. Computing on the cloud enables the storage and retrieval of data related to wardrobes, picture libraries, and outfit combinations. On the other hand, edge computing helps to minimize latency for applications such as smart mirrors and artificial intelligence stylists. As the use of 5G networks becomes more widespread, these capabilities will become increasingly accessible to people worldwide and will also become faster, enabling seamless and real-time interactions with digital wardrobes (Murugesan et al., 2024).

3.6 Open Standards and Interoperability

Integrating these technologies across different platforms and brands is one of the most significant challenges they face. It will be essential to have interoperability through open standards, such as common garment information formats or universal style taxonomies, in order to scale digital wardrobe solutions across various apps, merchants, and user demographics. This is necessary to ensure smooth transitions between digital fittings, resale platforms, and sustainability dashboards (Orisadare et al., 2025).

While existing studies consistently highlight the potential of AI, AR/VR, and blockchain to enhance sustainability outcomes, findings remain uneven. For example, while Mesjar et al. (2023) report reduced return rates through AR-enabled try-ons, other studies caution that rebound effects such as increased browsing and impulse purchases may offset environmental gains. Similarly, blockchain-based transparency initiatives improve traceability, yet their effectiveness depends heavily on consumer literacy and regulatory enforcement. These tensions suggest that technology alone cannot guarantee sustainability outcomes without supportive behavioral and policy frameworks.

3.7 Conceptual Framework for Digitally Mediated Wardrobes

This chapter proposes a conceptual framework in which enabling technologies (AI, AR/VR, blockchain, IoT) influence consumer behavior through mediating mechanisms such as nudging, gamification, and feedback loops. These mechanisms shape outcomes including extended garment use, reduced consumption, and increased circular participation, while being moderated by ethical safeguards, cultural context, and access equity.

4. BEHAVIORAL SHIFTS AND SUSTAINABLE CONSUMPTION

Digital wardrobes, far from being mere tools, are catalysts of behavioral change. They are designed to fundamentally alter the way individuals engage with their clothing. These platforms leverage a blend of psychological concepts, data-driven insights, and persuasive technologies to steer individuals towards more sustainable fashion practices. By offering the benefits of visibility, interaction, and social reinforcement, digital wardrobes aim to shift consumer behavior from impulsive, trend-driven consumption to conscious, value-driven participation. The figure presents a behavior-oriented model that explains how digital wardrobe features influence sustainable consumption decisions.

Figure 2.

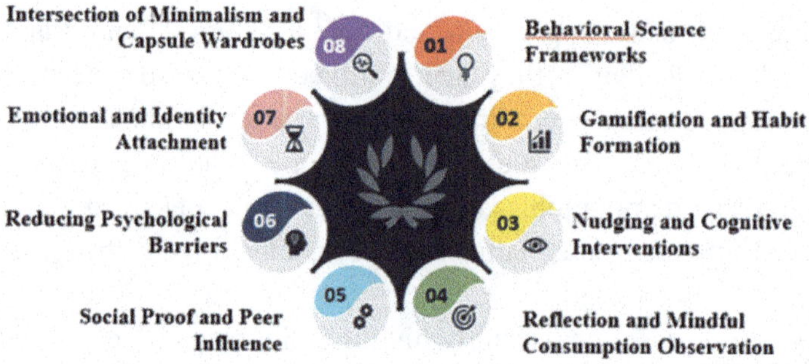

4.1 Behavioral Science Frameworks

When attempting to understand the impact that digital wardrobes have on behavior, it is essential to consider recognized behavioral models. According to Ajzen's Theory of Planned Behavior (published in 1991), factors such as attitudes, subjective norms, and perceived behavioral control influence behavioral intentions and actions. All three of these goals are accomplished by digital wardrobes: they encourage good attitudes about re-wearing, they mainstream sustainable habits through social aspects, and they provide users with the tools they need to put their intentions into action.

In a similar vein, the COM-B paradigm (which stands for capacity, opportunity, and motivation–behavior) proposes that in order for individuals to alter their behavior, they must possess the psychological and physical capability, the social and physical opportunity, and the drive to take action. These issues are addressed by digital wardrobes, which make wardrobe administration more intuitive (capacity), provide simple-to-use platforms (opportunity), and deliver motivated feedback through dashboards and achievements (motivation).

4.2 Gamification and Habit Formation: The Role of Gamification in Creating Sustainable Habits

Digital wardrobes play a pivotal role in transforming sustainable fashion into an engaging and rewarding activity. By incorporating gamification elements such as sustainability scores, daily outfit challenges, and milestone badges, these platforms encourage the development of sustainable routines and habits. For instance, users may receive feedback when they refrain from purchasing products that are already in their closet, or they could earn points for wearing all the items in their wardrobe within a predetermined time frame. These mechanisms, when combined with notifications and reminders, foster sustained user involvement and habit formation.

According to Vitola the concept of consistency is another factor that contributes to the formation of habits. Once users start tracking their clothing and engaging with sustainability features, they are more likely to continue doing so in order to maintain their self-image as responsible consumers. This means that they are more likely to continue using the app. According to Cialdini et al (2006), this psychological mechanism, referred to as the commitment and consistency principle, plays a crucial role in maintaining behavior (Ornati 2023).

4.3 Nudging and Cognitive Interventions

Both cognitive interventions and nudging are employed. A common feature of digital wardrobes is the use of "nudges," which are subtle indications that guide behavior without limiting the individual's freedom of choice. For example, if a user is trying to buy a new black shirt, the app can alert them to the fact that they already have other comparable products. This takes advantage of the status quo bias and the endowment effect, which encourages users to place a higher value on things they currently have.

Additionally, platforms can provide sustainability indicators (such as carbon or water savings) during decision-making moments. This can be achieved through the use of framing effects, which highlight the benefits of making sustainable decisions. These interventions are implemented at the moment of action, which makes it simpler to make sustainable decisions, makes them more noticeable, and makes them more rewarding (Kim & Seo 2023).

4.4 Reflection and Mindful Consumption Observation: Observing Consumption With Contemplation

Users of digital wardrobes are encouraged to consider their personal fashion preferences. By utilizing usage dashboards, wear counts, and style history records, these platforms promote a greater awareness of the patterns and decisions that users make. This introspective process, characterized by a connection with reduced impulsivity and greater congruence between ideals and behavior, helps to build awareness and encourages thoughtful, mindful consumption.

Additional help for mindful consumption comes from features that allow for self-monitoring. Users can establish objectives (for example, "wear every item at least five times"), monitor their progress, and review their previous choices. For behavior change to occur, it is necessary to have this feedback loop consisting of awareness, intention, and feedback. This is especially true in situations such as the fashion industry, where deeply ingrained habits prevail (Pal & Jayarathne 2022).

4.5 Social Proof and Peer Influence

Digital wardrobes capitalize on the social nature of fashion by facilitating social sharing, community interaction, and influencer relationships. Fashion inherently involves interaction with others. By encouraging users to publish their clothing and ideas for their style, platforms such as Whering create an atmosphere that is rich in feedback and encourages rewearing and remixing of different ensembles. The social evidence that comes from seeing peers and aspirational figures follow sustainable fashion guidelines helps to eliminate the stigma associated with wearing the same outfit repeatedly.

Through the incorporation of collaborative elements such as "wardrobe swaps" or peer challenges (for example, "no-new-clothes month"), several applications provide a sense of community accountability and shared drive. Research has shown that behavior is more likely to change in group settings, particularly when it is linked with identity and shared values. These dynamics are consistent with evidence that supports this hypothesis (Liu & Liu 2025).

4.6 Reducing Psychological Barriers: Overcoming Psychological Obstacles

A lack of understanding, fear of making a fashion faux pas, or choice fatigue are psychological obstacles that consumers frequently encounter when it comes to sustainability. Digital wardrobes, through the provision of organized alternatives, individualized advice, and confidence, act as a reassuring support system. By simplifying outfit planning and reducing cognitive burden, these platforms boost style confidence and make sustainable fashion less intimidating and more accessible to consumers (Rathore 2019).

4.7 Emotional and Identity Attachment: Attachment to One's Emotions and Identity

Digital wardrobes have the potential to develop emotional durability, which is the tie that exists between a user and their apparel. This is one of the most significant characteristics of digital wardrobe collections. Through the process of documenting memories, digitally customizing garments, or revisiting previous ensembles, users can construct identity-linked connections that support preservation and durability. Since emotional connection is a well-established predictor of prolonged product usage, it is an effective method for minimizing the amount of waste produced by the fashion industry.

4.8 Intersection of Minimalism and Capsule Wardrobes

Capsule wardrobes and minimalism intersect in this combination. There are also minimalist fashion techniques that may be made easier with digital wardrobes. One example of this is the capsule wardrobe, a carefully curated collection of versatile apparel that maximizes possibilities with a limited number of pieces. The concepts of minimalism are made more applicable and interesting via the use of digital tools, which assist users in recognizing essentials, avoiding repetition, and experimenting with different combinations of outfits. In addition to enhancing one's lifestyle and appearance, this aligns with the goals of ecological sustainability.

4.9 Final Thoughts

Behavioral research, design innovation, and user engagement methods are the three components that make up digital wardrobes, which act as accelerators for sustainable fashion behavior. The consumption of fashion is transformed from an unconscious habit into a conscious practice as a result of its ability to encourage consumers to act with awareness, creativity, and responsibility. In the next section, we will examine how these behavioral consequences translate into observable, sustainable results by utilizing digital evaluation methods and measurements (Raza et al., 2023).

Studies indicate that users of wardrobe digitization apps increase average wear-per-garment by approximately 20–30 percent compared to non-users, suggesting a measurable shift toward prolonged garment use and reduced redundancy in purchases.

5. MEASURING SUSTAINABILITY THROUGH DIGITAL TOOLS

The ability to quantify sustainability is crucial for validating claims, monitoring progress, and informing decision-making in the fashion industry. Digital wardrobes have emerged not only as behavior-shaping interfaces but also as rich data ecosystems capable of tracking, measuring, and visualizing environmental impacts at both individual and systemic levels. These tools integrate metrics related to carbon emissions, water usage, circularity performance, material durability, and other key sustainability indicators. Platform-generated sustainability dashboards suggest that extending a garment's use by as little as nine additional months can reduce its carbon footprint by roughly 20–30 percent, depending on material composition and care practices. The following figure depicts how digitally mediated wardrobes align with circular economy principles by extending garment lifecycles and reducing waste.

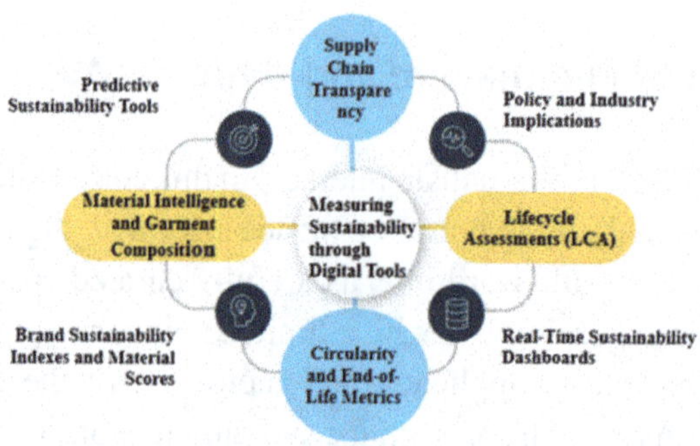

5.1 Lifecycle Assessments (LCA)

Lifecycle Assessment (LCA) is a methodological framework used to evaluate the environmental impacts associated with all stages of a product's life from raw material extraction through processing, manufacturing, distribution, use, and eventual disposal. Digital wardrobes are increasingly incorporating simplified LCA tools that allow users to estimate the footprint of garments in their collections. These estimates often include metrics such as:

- CO2 emissions per wear
- Water consumption per garment
- Energy intensity across the supply chain

By presenting this data in intuitive dashboards, digital wardrobes inspire users to adopt sustainable habits. They can gain a better understanding of the environmental cost of underused items versus frequently worn pieces, creating an incentive to wear garments more frequently and to consider environmental impact when making future purchases (Shaw & Duffy 2020).

5.2 Real-Time Sustainability Dashboards

One of the most impactful innovations in digital wardrobe platforms is the integration of real-time sustainability dashboards. These dashboards allow users to view:

- Number of wears per garment
- Total emissions saved from rewearing
- Comparisons between digital users and national/international sustainability benchmarks
- Avoided waste through donations or recycling

Such dashboards foster transparency and accountability. Users gain a comprehensive picture of their fashion habits and can make informed choices that align with sustainability goals. Gamified elements such as 'footprint reduction streaks' (which reward users for consistently reducing their environmental footprint) or weekly eco-challenges (which encourage users to take on specific sustainability tasks each week) can further engage users in improving their metrics.

5.3 Circularity and End-of-Life Metrics

Digital wardrobes are particularly valuable in tracking circularity the flow of garments through reuse, resale, repair, recycling, or donation. Features that support this include:

- Integration with resale platforms (e.g., Depop, ThredUP)
- Logging repair history or customizations
- Tracking the lifespan and number of owners per item
- Auto-suggestions for donation, resale, or recycling based on wear frequency

These metrics enable users to engage more easily and clearly in the circular economy. Moreover, they offer insight into how digital tools can reduce the average lifecycle impact of garments by extending their use and redistributing them across multiple users.

5.4 Brand Sustainability Indexes and Material Scores

Some digital wardrobe platforms incorporate third-party data on brands' environmental and social performance. Ratings from organizations such as Good On You, the Higg Index, or Fashion Transparency Index are embedded into the shopping or logging experience. Users can:

- See sustainability scores when adding new items to their wardrobe
- Filter collections by brand ethics or material impact
- Receive alerts about brands that fail to meet environmental criteria

This level of integration not only bridges the gap between individual action and corporate responsibility but also empowers consumers. It allows them to vote with their wardrobe, supporting brands that align with their values and influencing the industry towards sustainability.

5.5 Material Intelligence and Garment Composition

Knowing what garments are made of is essential for both care and end-of-life processing. Platforms may assess:

- Biodegradability of fibers
- Recyclability of blended fabrics
- Durability ratings based on material properties and usage patterns

This data can be sourced from digital product passports, which are comprehensive digital records of a product's materials, manufacturing process, and environmental impact, or brand disclosures and presented to users when they log in or evaluate clothing. It informs how garments should be washed, stored, or retired, thereby improving longevity and reducing unintended environmental damage (e.g., microfiber pollution).

5.6 Predictive Sustainability Tools

Advanced platforms utilize machine learning models to forecast sustainability outcomes based on user behavior. For example:

- Forecasting the carbon savings of buying secondhand instead of new
- Estimating the impact of delaying a new purchase by six months
- Modeling the lifecycle extension from proper garment care

These tools help translate abstract sustainability principles into concrete, personalized predictions. They allow users to simulate the effect of different choices, fostering proactive engagement.

5.7 Supply Chain Transparency

Digital wardrobes can also connect users with the broader garment supply chain. Through integration with blockchain or verified databases, users can:

- Trace the origin of raw materials
- View worker conditions and factory audits
- Understand emissions at each stage of production

Such transparency fosters deeper consumer-brand trust and supports emerging legislation (e.g., EU digital product passports, mandatory due diligence laws).

5.8 Policy and Industry Implications

As sustainability metrics become standardized, they will play an increasingly significant role in regulatory compliance and corporate reporting. Governments may require brands to disclose carbon footprints or provide QR-code-based sustainability information on garments. Digital wardrobes can facilitate this compliance by serving as repositories and validators of garment-level data.

Additionally, anonymized aggregate data from digital wardrobe platforms can inform industry reports, consumer trend analyses, and policy planning. For example, aggregated wear data could inform municipalities in designing effective textile recycling programs or influence procurement guidelines for sustainable uniforms.

For digitally mediated wardrobes to scale, financial sustainability is essential. Platforms increasingly rely on hybrid business models combining subscriptions, brand partnerships, resale commissions, and premium analytics services. For independent designers, digital wardrobes and 3D design tools reduce sampling costs and enable made-to-order production, aligning economic resilience with sustainability goals.

6. INDUSTRY CASE STUDIES

The adoption of digitally mediated wardrobes by enterprises and platforms is a testament to the tangible benefits and applications of modern technologies in the real world. The case studies presented here demonstrate how various stakeholders in the fashion ecosystem are leveraging digital technologies to promote environmentally responsible purchasing, enhance the user experience, and align themselves with the principles of the circular economy movement.

6.1 ThredUP: Scaling Resale with Sustainability Insights

ThredUP is one of the world's largest online thrift stores, specializing in the resale of secondhand fashion. Beyond simply facilitating resale, ThredUP has developed tools that quantify the environmental impact of choosing secondhand over new. Its "Fashion Footprint Calculator" allows users to understand the CO2 and water savings associated with purchasing pre-owned garments. Through partnerships with brands like Madewell and Gap, ThredUP has also integrated branded resale shops, encouraging legacy retailers to participate in the circular economy.

ThredUP's annual 'Resale Report' provides data-driven insights into consumer behavior, garment lifespans, and sustainability metrics, influencing public discourse and corporate strategy. ThredUP's success is a testament to the potential of resale platforms, when combined with educational features and data analytics, to mainstream sustainable fashion habits, inspiring the industry to follow suit.

6.2 Whering: Wardrobe Digitization for Everyday Use

Whering is a mobile app that allows users to digitize their wardrobes and receive AI-generated outfit recommendations. It emphasizes "shopping your closet" by creating a virtual inventory of existing clothing, helping users discover new styling combinations without making new purchases. Sustainability features include cost-per-wear tracking, alerts for underused items, and integration with eco-conscious brands.

Whering's community features, where users can share outfit ideas, reinforce sustainable norms through social validation. Its partnerships with organizations like Fashion Revolution amplify advocacy around conscious consumption. By combining personalization with sustainability education, Whering has successfully engaged a digitally native audience, making them feel part of a larger, sustainable fashion community.

6.3 Save Your Wardrobe: Bridging Digital Tools with Physical Services

Save Your Wardrobe extends the concept of digital wardrobe management by integrating with physical repair, cleaning, donation, and resale services. The app enables users to connect with local providers, promoting circular practices that extend beyond the digital space. Its backend AI monitors wear frequency and garment conditions, triggering reminders for care and repair.

This platform's strength lies in its holistic approach treating wardrobe care as an ongoing cycle rather than a one-time digitization task. Save Your Wardrobe has collaborated with sustainability-focused fashion councils and government initiatives, illustrating how digital tools can support national and regional textile circularity agendas.

6.4 Gucci and Balenciaga: Virtual Fashion and the Metaverse

Luxury brands are experimenting with digital fashion to explore low-waste, high-engagement alternatives to traditional design. Gucci's "Virtual 25" sneakers were explicitly designed for digital environments and can be worn in AR apps or gaming platforms, such as Roblox. Balenciaga has released digital-only fashion drops and used virtual runways for collection previews.

These innovations reduce the environmental footprint associated with physical samples, runway shows, and marketing, while introducing new revenue models based on digital ownership. Although still in the early stages, these initiatives demonstrate the exciting potential of digital wardrobes to evolve into immersive, avatar-based fashion ecosystems, sparking anticipation for the future of fashion.

6.5 DressX: Fashion Without Fabric

DressX is a digital fashion platform offering virtual-only clothing. Users upload photos and select digital garments, which are rendered onto their images for social media use. This approach eliminates the need for physical production entirely, replacing consumption with visual expression.

DressX quantifies environmental savings such as CO2 emissions avoided compared to conventional garments and provides educational content about the benefits of digital fashion. Its collaborations with high-profile designers and brands help mainstream this futuristic model, while its marketplace introduces circularity into virtual fashion through the resale of digital pieces.

6.6 Eon and the CircularID Initiative: Infrastructure for Transparency

Eon's Connected Products Platform enables garments to carry digital identities that store and share information across their lifecycle. Through QR codes or embedded NFC chips, consumers can access details on materials, care instructions, origin, resale eligibility, and recycling options.

The CircularID Protocol, developed by Eon in collaboration with the fashion industry, provides a standardized system for digital product passports. These IDs empower consumers and enable companies to meet regulatory requirements for transparency and circularity. Eon's partnerships with retailers like H&M and Target signal scalability and industry readiness.

6.7 Patagonia: Digital Engagement for Sustainable Loyalty

Patagonia integrates digital storytelling with traceability tools to educate consumers about its supply chain. Through "The Footprint Chronicles," users can explore the origins and environmental journey of products. The brand's Worn Wear initiative promotes repair and resale through an online platform that tracks product life and shares user stories.

These efforts are supported by Patagonia's commitment to environmental activism and open-source sustainability practices. The brand utilizes digital tools not only to inform but also to create an emotional connection between the consumer and the garment, thereby enhancing product longevity and reducing churn.

6.8 Challenges and Lessons Learned

These case studies highlight several key challenges:

- **Integration**: Building interoperable systems between digital tools and physical services remains a complex challenge.
- **Accessibility**: Digital literacy and smartphone access vary significantly globally, which limits adoption in underserved regions.
- **Verification**: Claims of sustainability must be backed by standardized metrics to avoid greenwashing.
- **User Retention**: Maintaining long-term engagement in wardrobe apps requires continual updates, community features, and personalized insights.

The global online resale market has consistently outpaced traditional apparel retail, with annual growth rates exceeding 10–15 percent in recent years, signaling a structural shift rather than a niche consumer trend.

7. ETHICAL AND SOCIAL CONSIDERATIONS

As digitally mediated wardrobes gain traction, they present not only technological opportunities but also a series of ethical, cultural, and social dilemmas. The intersection of digital innovation and fashion raises questions of equity, surveillance, representation, and systemic transformation. For these tools to make a meaningful contribution to sustainable development, their deployment must be inclusive, respectful of privacy, and sensitive to diverse cultural contexts. The figure presents a framework for understanding the ethical, social, and regulatory dimensions associated with digitally mediated wardrobes.

Figure 4.

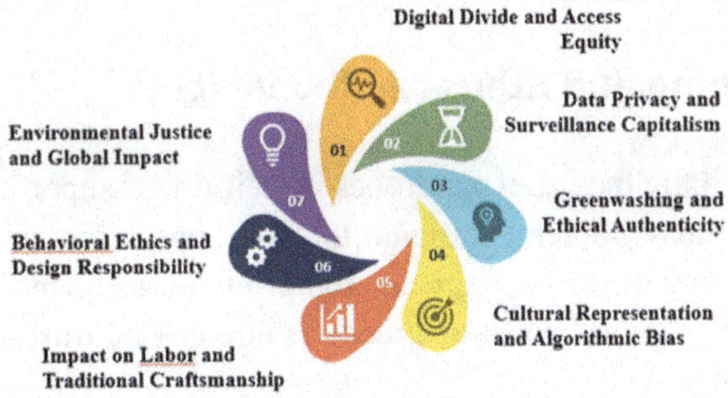

7.1 Digital Divide and Access Equit

Despite the increasing ubiquity of smartphones and internet connectivity, access to digital wardrobe platforms is far from universal. Individuals in the Global South, low-income households, and remote regions often lack access to the necessary infrastructure, digital literacy, or compatible devices, which hinders their ability to benefit from these tools. The risk is that digital fashion innovations become concentrated in affluent, urban populations, exacerbating global disparities in sustainability participation.

To ensure inclusivity, developers must prioritize affordability, language diversity, low-data usage, and mobile-first designs. Collaborations with community organizations can also help bridge access gaps, enabling the broader adoption of sustainable fashion practices. Equitable access is not only a moral imperative it is essential to the scalability and legitimacy of digitally mediated wardrobes.

7.2 Data Privacy and Surveillance Capitalis

Digital wardrobes collect sensitive personal data, including user images, style preferences, shopping habits, and potentially even biometric information through AR interfaces. Without robust governance, this data could be monetized, misused, or compromised. Fashion platforms increasingly operate within the logic of surveillance capitalism, where user behavior is commodified to drive targeted advertising and sales.

Platforms must adopt privacy-by-design principles, including clear consent protocols, data minimization, end-to-end encryption, and user control over data retention and deletion. Regulatory compliance with frameworks such as the GDPR and emerging digital rights laws must be paired with proactive transparency regarding data practices (Dhama, et al., 2024).

7.3 Greenwashing and Ethical Authenticity

One risk of digitally mediated wardrobes is their use as superficial sustainability tokens. Brands may implement digital tools to appear eco-conscious without substantively reducing their environmental footprint or transforming their business models. This phenomenon known as greenwashing erodes trust and undermines genuine innovation.

To guard against this, transparency and independent verification are critical. Metrics must be publicly auditable, methodologies must be transparently disclosed, and sustainability claims must align with industry benchmarks. Consumers also need education to critically interpret sustainability dashboards and differentiate between genuine ethical leadership and marketing spin (Gautam, et al., 2023).

7.4 Cultural Representation and Algorithmic Bias

Many wardrobe platforms rely on machine learning models trained on Western fashion aesthetics, body types, and cultural references. As a result, non-Western dress traditions, diverse body shapes, and marginalized style expressions may be underrepresented or misinterpreted. This creates both a practical limitation (users cannot see themselves accurately) and an epistemic injustice (cultures are made invisible).

Diverse datasets, inclusive design practices, and participatory modeling can mitigate this issue. Developers should collaborate with designers, scholars, and users from underrepresented communities to create algorithms that accurately reflect the richness and diversity of global fashion. Representation must also extend to marketing, leadership, and UX (Glogar, et al., 2025).

7.5 Impact on Labor and Traditional Craftsmanship

The digital transformation of fashion, while reducing material waste, may displace workers in traditional garment manufacturing sectors. Automation, digitization, and the virtualization of fashion experiences risk devaluing human labor, particularly in countries where garment production is a key economic sector.

A just transition is essential. Investments should be made in reskilling programs, digital literacy, and community-based innovation hubs that allow workers to participate in new digital value chains. Moreover, digital fashion should not be positioned as a replacement for all physical production but as a complementary tool that elevates craftsmanship, care, and repair (Guliyev, et al., 2025).

7.6 Behavioral Ethics and Design Responsibility

The persuasive technologies embedded in digital wardrobes can shape behavior sometimes subtly, sometimes decisively. Designers wield significant influence over user habits, and this power must be exercised in an ethical manner. Features that encourage compulsive logging, constant feedback checking, or conformity to idealized body images may cause harm.

Ethical UX practices emphasize agency, reflection, and well-being. Users should be able to customize their engagement, pause or reset usage, and access mental health support where relevant. Nudges should support autonomy and align with long-term values, rather than focusing on short-term dopamine rewards (Hardadi, et al., 2021).

7.7 Environmental Justice and Global Impact

Finally, digital wardrobes must be evaluated within the broader framework of environmental justice. Climate change and ecological degradation disproportionately affect vulnerable populations who have contributed least to the problem. Ensuring that digital fashion tools reduce emissions, foster solidarity, and support circular economies globally, not just in affluent markets is crucial.

Ethical sustainability means centering those most affected and co-creating solutions that reflect their realities. Whether through data-sharing protocols that support rural artisans or recycling networks spanning continents, digital wardrobes must be designed with planetary equity in mind (Carrera-Rivera, et al., 2022).

While digital wardrobes reduce material waste, their enabling technologies are not impact-free. Data centers, blockchain validation processes, and AR rendering consume energy and contribute to emissions. Without renewable energy integration and efficient computing practices, digital fashion risks shifting rather than eliminating environmental burdens. A net-positive sustainability outcome therefore depends on responsible digital infrastructure design.

8. FUTURE DIRECTIONS AND POLICY IMPLICATIONS

The future of digitally mediated wardrobes is not just a possibility, but a promising reality that is poised to be shaped by several converging trajectories: technological advancement, regulatory frameworks, cultural shifts, and institutional partnerships. To realize their full transformative potential, these systems must evolve beyond standalone apps into integrated lifestyle ecosystems supported by policy, infrastructure, and public engagement (Blazquez, M., 2024). The following figure outlines potential future directions for digitally mediated wardrobes, integrating technological, policy, and cultural dimensions.

Figure 5.

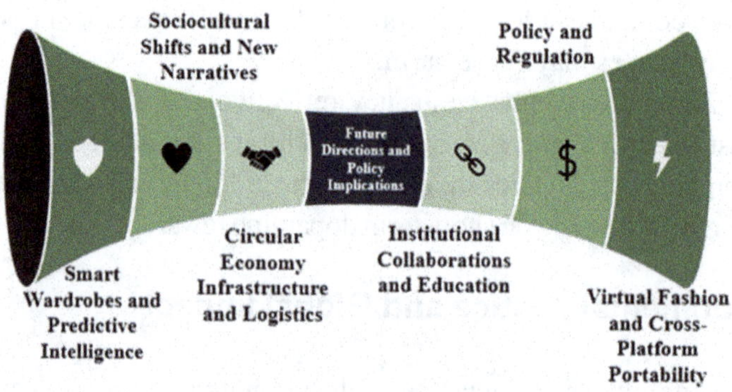

8.1 Smart Wardrobes and Predictive Intelligenc

Future wardrobe systems will likely integrate with broader digital ecosystems, syncing with calendars, weather apps, personal fitness trackers, and even mental health platforms. AI will deliver predictive styling based not only on fashion preferences, but also on mood, energy levels, and social contexts. This dynamic interface will not only guide users to dress efficiently, ethically, and expressively, but also make their daily routines more convenient.

Smart wardrobes may also include automated inventory management through RFID tagging or visual recognition. These features can suggest capsule wardrobe optimizations, identify overrepresented categories (e.g., too many jeans or shoes), and trigger repair or recycling prompts based on usage wear (Choufan, 2022).

8.2 Virtual Fashion and Cross-Platform Portability

As more consumers interact with digital avatars and metaverse environments, the virtual fashion industry is expected to continue growing. The ability to create, buy, trade, and style virtual garments across gaming, social media, and augmented reality platforms introduces a new paradigm of identity construction. This future raises questions about the ownership, licensing, and interoperability of digital assets.

Developing open standards for digital garments ensuring that a piece bought in Roblox could also be worn in Instagram filters or used in VR meetings will be key. Interoperability protocols, digital asset wallets, and sustainable design standards for virtual clothing will shape the future value of these garments (Choi, 2022).

8.3 Circular Economy Infrastructure and Logistics

To support wardrobe circularity, digital systems must be linked to robust infrastructure for take-back, repair, upcycling, and recycling. Governments and cities can foster this through reverse logistics programs, textile hubs, and public-private partnerships that connect wardrobe apps with drop-off centers or community repair services.

Blockchain and IoT can streamline chain-of-custody tracking and verify sustainable handoffs, enabling precise audits and certifications. Circular wardrobe ecosystems may also involve community co-ownership of shared digital or physical clothing libraries, supported by digital management tools (Che, et al., 2022).

8.4 Policy and Regulation

Regulatory support will play a vital role in normalizing digital wardrobes and incentivizing sustainable practices. Key policy levers include:

- **Digital Product Passports**: Mandatory tracking of materials, sourcing, and lifecycle metrics.
- **Sustainability Labeling**: Requiring QR codes or NFC chips on garments linked to environmental impact data.
- **Extended Producer Responsibility (EPR)**: Obligating brands to manage post-consumer waste.
- **Data Privacy Laws**: Ensuring user control over personal wardrobe data.

- **Circular Procurement Standards**: Governments prioritizing digital tools in public fashion sourcing.

National strategies, like the European Union's "Strategy for Sustainable and Circular Textiles," will increasingly integrate digital wardrobe technologies into broader climate action and waste reduction mandates (Casciani, et al., 2022).

8.5 Institutional Collaborations and Education

Universities, cultural institutions, and nonprofits can serve as vital partners in scaling digital wardrobe adoption. Fashion schools can embed digital wardrobe literacy into their curricula. Museums and galleries can use digital fashion exhibits to educate the public. NGOs can co-create platforms with marginalized communities to ensure accessibility and relevance (Akram et.al., 2022).

Moreover, collaborations between tech developers and public agencies can lead to nationally recognized platforms that serve both educational and regulatory functions, similar to how government health apps provide both personal and population-level data.

8.6 Sociocultural Shifts and New Narratives

At the heart of sustainable fashion transformation lies cultural change. Narratives of success, beauty, and identity must evolve to celebrate reuse, creativity, and sufficiency. Storytelling campaigns, influencers embracing repetition and repair, and celebrities normalizing the reuse of digital fashion can accelerate this shift.

Media and entertainment will increasingly portray digital wardrobes as aspirational, empowering, and ethical, influencing mainstream fashion culture. Public discourse must reframe sustainability from a constraint to a canvas for innovation, autonomy, and community (Bang, H., & Su, J., 2022).

Emerging experiments in India, Southeast Asia, and parts of Africa demonstrate how digital wardrobes can intersect with traditional repair cultures, informal resale networks, and artisanal production, suggesting alternative pathways to sustainability beyond Western consumption models.

9. CONCLUSION

Fashionable wardrobes that are mediated by digital technology represent the intersection of innovation, ethics, and sustainability within the ever-evolving fashion industry. A crucial frontier for sustainable development is the ability of digital infrastructure to modify consumer behaviors, including what we buy, how we wear, and when we dispose of items. This possibility has been more prevalent as digital infrastructure becomes more integrated into everyday life. The multiple aspects of this transition have been investigated in this chapter, shedding light on the fact that digitally mediated wardrobes serve not only as convenience aids but also as agents of behavioral, cultural, and institutional change.

Whether it is the advent of personalized artificial intelligence or immersive augmented reality and virtual reality interfaces, the wardrobe has become a site of innovation. This is due to historical transformations in consumption that were driven by industrialization and rapid fashion trends. There is more to this change than just technological advancement; it is also symbolic. Previously a private and unchanging space, the conventional wardrobe has transformed into a dynamic digital interface that not only educates, directs, and even nudges people toward more environmentally responsible behavior. The transformation of fashion from a disposable experience into a conscientious practice is facilitated by digital wardrobes, which provide consumers with information on garment consumption, environmental impact, and opportunities for reuse.

Artificial intelligence, blockchain, the Internet of Things, and digital passports are examples of technologies that are not goals in themselves, but rather enablers of new interactions and experiences. They provide an unparalleled level of transparency, enabling consumers and companies alike to see sustainability measures and make informed decisions based on facts. These technologies also facilitate the adoption of circular models, such as resale, repair, and leasing, by making them more accessible, quantifiable, and incorporated into everyday activity. This helps to speed the adoption process.

However, changing one's behavior is a difficult task. The practicality of digital wardrobes is not enough; they must also have a behavioral design that acknowledges and honors individual sovereignty while also encouraging awareness. It is possible to encourage meaningful engagement through the use of features such as gamified incentives, social sharing, use alerts, and wear monitoring; however, these features must be supplemented with education and support for long-term habit development. However, to be effective, digital wardrobes must be designed in a way that prioritizes user agency and wellness. The potential for digital wardrobes to motivate behavior change is enormous.

It is also vital to consider the social and ethical implications of this transformation for the future. Inclusion and fairness are essential qualities for digital technologies. It is essential to acknowledge that the digital gap, algorithmic bias, data privacy, and cultural representation are all significant concerns addressed in this chapter. To address these issues, it is necessary to co-design with disadvantaged populations, to have diverse data sets, to have clear policies, and to adhere to open standards.

Achieving sustainability is impossible without first achieving fairness. The exact issues that a digital wardrobe seeks to address are exacerbated by the fact that it caters only to wealthy customers, exploits workers from around the world, and overlooks other clothing cultures.

Real-world applications were also demonstrated in this chapter through the use of industry case studies. These case studies included resale giants such as ThredUp, as well as virtual pioneers like DressX. The aforementioned instances provide evidence that digital wardrobes are not only a theoretical concept; instead, they are actively transforming retail, user behavior, and brand tactics. Each of the cases provides an example of how digital wardrobes may be used to demonstrate how environmental integrity can be aligned with corporate innovation.

Looking ahead, the support of policies and institutions will be crucial. In addition to mandating transparency, enforcing digital product passports, encouraging sustainable design, and providing support for circular infrastructure, governments are required to do so. Learning in the classroom and participating in public exhibitions are both examples of how educational systems and cultural organizations can contribute to the development of digital wardrobe literacy. Narratives in the media must adapt to highlight re-wearing and responsible ownership, therefore normalizing digital fashion as a norm that is both creative and sustainable.

Further investigation should be conducted to investigate the linkages between health, psychology, urban design, and climate resilience in the future. On the other hand, how might digital wardrobes interact with health applications to make recommendations for temperature-regulated clothing? Can they be integrated with smart cities to maximize textile recycling? Where do they stand in terms of their ability to alleviate anxiety or decision fatigue associated with fashion?

As we synthesize the results of this chapter, it becomes clear that digitally mediated wardrobes are not just a solution to reducing the environmental impact of fashion; they are a transformative force. By balancing fashion with planetary constraints, they shift consumption into stewardship, replace opaqueness with knowledge, and establish connections between consumers and larger sustainability systems. Their adoption prompts a shift in values, transitioning from novelty to necessity, from ownership to access, and from individual style to societal style. This transformative potential should inspire us all, as we look towards a future where fashion is not extractive, but expressive, and not linear, but regenerative.

In conclusion, digitally mediated wardrobes are not just about reducing the environmental impact of fashion; they are about redefining what fashion means. In their vision of the future, fashion will not be extractive, but expressive, and it will not be linear, but regenerative. However, this future is not guaranteed. It will depend on our collective determination to continue innovating, aligning policies, and dressing consciously in a more digital world. This is a responsibility we all share, and it is within our power to shape the future of fashion.

This chapter contributes to fashion sustainability scholarship by bridging technology studies, behavioral science, and ethical analysis. It offers a systems-level perspective valuable to researchers, designers, policymakers, and educators seeking actionable pathways toward circular fashion. By framing digital wardrobes as behavioral infrastructures rather than mere applications, the chapter advances both theoretical understanding and practical relevance.

As we conclude this chapter, the call is not just to produce more tools, but to construct technical, social, and ethical frameworks that will enable a flourishing future for fashion. When we view the wardrobe through this lens, it is transformed from a mere closet into a compass, guiding us towards a future where fashion is not just beautiful, but also sustainable and ethical. This is a vision that should motivate us all to commit to the collective effort of building a better future for fashion.

REFERENCES

Ajzen, I. (1991). The theory of planned behavior. *Organizational Behavior and Human Decision Processes*, *50*(2), 179–211. DOI: 10.1016/0749-5978(91)90020-T

Akram, S. V., Malik, P. K., Singh, R., Gehlot, A., Juyal, A., Ghafoor, K. Z., & Shrestha, S. (2022). Implementation of digitalized technologies for fashion industry 4.0: Opportunities and challenges. *Scientific Programming*, *2022*(1), 7523246. DOI: 10.1155/2022/7523246

Bang, H., & Su, J. (2022). Who uses virtual wardrobes? Investigating the role of consumer traits in the intention to adopt virtual wardrobes. *Sustainability (Basel)*, *14*(3), 1209. DOI: 10.3390/su14031209

Blazquez, M. (2024). The Metaverse and its potential for digital sustainability in fashion. *Journal of Global Fashion Marketing*, *15*(3), 303–319. DOI: 10.1080/20932685.2024.2339236

Carrera-Rivera, A., Larrinaga, F., & Lasa, G. (2022). Context-awareness for the design of Smart-product service systems: Literature review. *Computers in Industry*, *142*, 103730. DOI: 10.1016/j.compind.2022.103730

Casciani, D., Chkanikova, O., & Pal, R. (2022). Exploring the nature of digital transformation in the fashion industry: opportunities for supply chains, business models, and sustainability-oriented innovations. Sustainability: Science. *Sustainability*, *18*(1), 773–795. DOI: 10.1080/15487733.2022.2125640

Che, F., Zhou, Y., & Liu, Y. (2022). Social quality, knowledge hiding, and community capacity: A study on multi-ethnic communities in Chinese cities. *Journal of Business Research*, *144*, 1024–1038. DOI: 10.1016/j.jbusres.2022.02.041

Choi, K. H. (2022). 3D dynamic fashion design development using digital technology and its potential in online platforms. *Fashion and Textiles*, *9*(1), 9. DOI: 10.1186/s40691-021-00286-1

Choufan, L. (2022). Fashion you do not own, fashion you cannot feel: Toward a new paradigm of sharing fashion in the digital age. *Fashion Theory*, *26*(3), 307–328. DOI: 10.1080/1362704X.2021.1912954

Cialdini, R. B., Demaine, L. J., Sagarin, B. J., Barrett, D. W., Rhoads, K., & Winter, P. L. (2006). Managing social norms for persuasive impact. *Social Influence*, *1*(1), 3–15. DOI: 10.1080/15534510500181459

Dhama, A., Kaur, A., Döngül, E. S., & Singh, N. (2024). Artificial intelligence and sustainable green fashion industry. In *Handbook of Artificial Intelligence Applications for Industrial Sustainability* (pp. 74–91). CRC Press. DOI: 10.1201/9781003348351-6

Gautam, P., Maheshwari, S., Kausar, A., & Jaggi, C. K. (2023). Sustainable retail model with preservation technology investment to moderate deterioration with environmental deliberations. *Journal of Cleaner Production, 390*, 136128. DOI: 10.1016/j.jclepro.2023.136128

Glogar, M., Petrak, S., & Mahnić Naglić, M. (2025). Digital technologies in the sustainable design and development of textiles and clothing—A literature review. *Sustainability (Basel), 17*(4), 1371. DOI: 10.3390/su17041371

Guliyev, E., Ramirez, J. S., De Caigny, A., & Coussement, K. (2025). Improving B2B customer churn through action rule mining. *Industrial Marketing Management, 125*, 1–11. DOI: 10.1016/j.indmarman.2024.12.005

Hardadi, G., Buchholz, A., & Pauliuk, S. (2021). Implications of the distribution of German household environmental footprints across income groups for integrating environmental and social policy design. *Journal of Industrial Ecology, 25*(1), 95–113. DOI: 10.1111/jiec.13045

Kim, B., & Seo, S. (2023). EfficientNetV2-based dynamic gesture recognition using transformed scalogram from triaxial acceleration signal. *Journal of Computational Design and Engineering, 10*(4), 1694–1706. DOI: 10.1093/jcde/qwad068

Kosiba, J. P., Acheampong, A., Adeola, O., & Hinson, R. E. (2020). The moderating role of demographic variables on customer expectations in airport retail patronage intentions of travellers. *Journal of Retailing and Consumer Services, 54*, 102033. DOI: 10.1016/j.jretconser.2020.102033

Liu, S., & Liu, C. (2025). Mapping the digital transformation in the fashion industry: The past, present and future. *Journal of Fashion Marketing and Management, 29*(7), 1292–1319. DOI: 10.1108/JFMM-09-2024-0380

MacArthur, E. (2017). Beyond plastic waste. *Science, 358*(6365), 843–843. DOI: 10.1126/science.aao6749 PMID: 29146782

Mallon, S. (2024). Digital Clothes and the Future of Fashion. In Technology, Sustainability and the Fashion Industry (pp. 1-15). Routledge. DOI: 10.4324/9781032658506-1

Manzo, D. S. H., Jiang, Y., Elyan, E., & Isaacs, J. (2025). Artificial intelligence-based conversational agents used for sustainable fashion: Systematic literature review. *International Journal of Human-Computer Interaction, 41*(8), 4640–4652. DOI: 10.1080/10447318.2024.2352920

Mesjar, L., Cross, K., Jiang, Y., & Steed, J. (2023). The intersection of fashion, immersive technology, and sustainability: A literature review. *Sustainability (Basel), 15*(4), 3761. DOI: 10.3390/su15043761

Morandi, A., & Tonelli, C. (2023). The impact of 3D technology on sustainability in fashion luxury product design: evidences from an exploratory analysis (Doctoral dissertation, Master's Thesis, Scuola di Ingegneria Industriale e dell'Informazione, Milano).

Murugesan, B., Jayanthi, K. B., & Karthikeyan, G. (2024). Integrating Digital Twins and 3D Technologies in Fashion: Advancing Sustainability and Consumer Engagement. In *Illustrating Digital Innovations Towards Intelligent Fashion: Leveraging Information System Engineering and Digital Twins for Efficient Design of Next-Generation Fashion* (pp. 1–88). Springer Nature Switzerland. DOI: 10.1007/978-3-031-71052-0_1

Orisadare, E. A., Achukwu, O. E., Ogunyemi, A. A., Adedeji, D. O., Diyaolu, I. J., Ugwu, E. I., Oluwatope, A. O., Bakare, K. O., & Awoyelu, I. O. (2025). Digitalisation and green strategies: A systematic review of the textile, apparel and fashion industries. *Circular Economy and Sustainability, 5*(4), 1–53. DOI: 10.1007/s43615-025-00555-x

Ornati, M. (2023, July). A Conceptual Model of Dress Embodiment and Technological Mediation in Digital Fashion. In International Conference on Fashion communication: between tradition and future digital developments (pp. 57-67). Cham: Springer Nature Switzerland. DOI: 10.1007/978-3-031-38541-4_6

Pal, R., & Jayarathne, A. (2022). Digitalization in the textiles and clothing sector. In *The digital supply chain* (pp. 255–271). Elsevier. DOI: 10.1016/B978-0-323-91614-1.00015-0

Rathore, B. (2019). Fashion sustainability in the AI era: opportunities and challenges in marketing. Eduzone: International Peer Reviewed/Refereed Multidisciplinary Journal, 8(2), 17-24..

Raza, A., Asif, M., & Akram, M. (2023). Give your hunger a new option: Understanding consumers' continuous intention to use online food delivery apps using trust transfer theory. *International Journal of Consumer Studies, 47*(2), 474–495. DOI: 10.1111/ijcs.12845

Shaw, D., & Duffy, K. (2020). Save Your Wardrobe: Digitalising Sustainable Consumption: Further Insights.

Stevenson, T. (2023). Virtual Fashion: Digital Representations of Materiality and Time (Doctoral dissertation, Open Access Te Herenga Waka-Victoria University of Wellington).

Sugadev, M., Niranjana, S., Deepa, N., Dhaarani, T. G., Giri, J., & Samhan, A. A. A. (2024, December). A Novel Development of Virtual Wardrobe Design Based on Artificial Intelligence and Internet of Things Enabled Technologies. In *2024 International Conference on Innovative Computing, Intelligent Communication and Smart Electrical Systems (ICSES)* (pp. 1-6). IEEE. DOI: 10.1109/ICSES63760.2024.10910343

Sun, C., Fang, Y., Kong, M., Chen, X., & Liu, Y. (2022). Influence of augmented reality product display on consumers' product attitudes: A product uncertainty reduction perspective. *Journal of Retailing and Consumer Services*, *64*, 102828. DOI: 10.1016/j.jretconser.2021.102828

Szatkowski, S., Jaen-Sola, P., & Oterkus, E. (2024). An Efficient Computational Analysis and Modelling of Transferred Aerodynamic Loading on Direct-Drive System of 5 MW Wind Turbine and Results Driven Optimisation for a Sustainable Generator Structure. *Sustainability (Basel)*, *16*(2), 545. DOI: 10.3390/su16020545

Vitola, L. S. Digital Innovation for Sustainable Fashion: Virtual Fitting Rooms as a Strategy to Minimize Waste and E-commerce Returns (Doctoral dissertation, Toronto Metropolitan University).

Wardani, J., Bos, J. J., Ramirez-Lovering, D., & Capon, A. G. (2022). Enabling transdisciplinary research collaboration for planetary health: Insights from practice at the environment-health-development nexus. *Sustainable Development*, *30*(2), 375–392.

Zhong, Y., Liu, J., Zhou, Y. W., Cao, B., & Cheng, T. E. (2022). Robust contract design and coordination under consignment contracts with revenue sharing. *International Journal of Production Economics*, *253*, 108543. DOI: 10.1016/j.ijpe.2022.108543

Chapter 8
Behavioural AI for Sustainable Wardrobes: Insights and Innovations in Fashion Tech

Razia Nagina
http://orcid.org/0000-0002-0305-8393
Lovely Professional University, India

ABSTRACT

This chapter explores how behavioural science and AI can be integrated to foster sustainable wardrobes by addressing overconsumption and high return rates in fashion e-commerce. It pursues four objectives: linking behavioural theories (nudges, habits, social influence) to AI design; assessing tools like virtual try-ons, recommender systems, and sustainability apps; identifying interventions to reduce excess buying and returns; and providing strategic brand guidelines. Using literature, industry cases (ASOS, Zalando, H&M, Patagonia, Nike), and a survey of 300 shoppers, the study finds fit uncertainty, promotions, and social influence drive unsustainable behaviours. Consumers respond positively to AI-driven size tools and try-ons, with moderate willingness to pay premiums for verified sustainable products. The chapter offers actionable recommendations to align commercial objectives with measurable sustainability outcomes.

INTRODUCTION

Fashion is a dynamic industry that represents the value of art linked with the prevailing culture. It is one of the most pollution-generating sectors across the entire planet (Garcia 2022). The boost in fast fashion trends along with the expansion of

DOI: 10.4018/979-8-3373-5525-2.ch008

the e-commerce industry and high return rates on the products has further increased the pollution effects associated with this industry. It has turned into a major concern across the entire planet with regards to sustainable consumption (George 2024). As reported by the United Nations Environmental Program, the fashion industry contributes nearly 10% of the entire carbon emissions on a global scale along with 20% of the entire wastewater created across the planet. Millions of tons of fashion waste are produced annually with the short lifespan of the products created within the fashion industry (UNFCCC 2018).

Conventional sustainability initiatives practiced in the fashion sector, including eco-labeling schemes, recycling initiatives, and corporate social responsibility initiatives, have raised awareness but not enough to induce behavior change among consumers (Wijewardena & Bhowmik, 2025). Despite the growing awareness of the environment, consumers are still engaging in impulse purchases, over-purchasing, and return deliveries that work against the sustainability agenda. To bridge the gap between intention and behavior, sustainable fashion needs not only the provision of information answers but also needs to appeal to the cognitive, emotional, and social dimensions that govern the behavior of consumers. Such demands from the field have encouraged the current literature on the adoption of AI in sustainable fashion behavior (Koul & Jasrotia, 2025).

Behavioral science offers important information regarding the discrepancy between the behavior and the values that consumers hold regarding the environment (Mahmoodi et al., 2021). Behavioral principles like nudging, habit, choice, and social influence are utilized to create sustainable behaviors without undermining personal choice and freedom (Prits, 2023). For example, highlighting social proof, like the number of people choosing environmentally responsible goods, can normalize eco-friendly behaviors, and default options like focusing on environmentally responsible clothing can nudge customers towards environmentally responsible clothing choices (Tran, 2024).

Artificial intelligence raises these behavioural strategies to higher levels by providing real-time interventions. These AI-related systems help make recommendations to consumers using data from past users and work on virtual trials that can decrease uncertainties. They use predictive analytics and help promote purchasing and return actions before they happen (Singh, 2024). Recommendation systems that use style preferences and behavioural actions can help modulate purchasing actions, while virtual trials help diminish overpurchasing and returning products. The integration of AI algorithm capacity and behavioural strategies has the power to create a new behavioural pattern regarding consumerism among individuals as well as groups.

Empirical work and real-world applications illustrate the engagement AI can have with the process of consumer choice transformation (Abrardi et al., 2022). Virtual try-on applications enable consumers to see how clothes fit and look, decreasing the likelihood of purchasing multiple copies for different sizes (Samy et al., 2025). Personalization initiatives boost confidence and engagement with the process through improved visibility and accessibility for sustainability metrics like ethical sourcing and carbon emissions (Bashynska, 2023). Finally, mobile applications like the one based on gamification encourage sustainability through competition and recognition, while AI-powered messaging encourages practices for the prolonged life of garments.

One of the most pressing issues in fashion e-commerce is related to overconsumption and excessively returned items (Brolin & Lundgren, 2024). The convenient nature of online shopping contributes to size ambiguity and impulse buying, thereby causing excessively higher rates of returns (Kumar & Taneja, 2025). AI-assisted predictive analytics can identify risky patterns of product returns and invoke immediate intervention strategies, such as size advice and cost of environment notifications, to induce more reflective behavior (von Zahn et al., 2025).

Nonetheless, incorporating behavioral AI within plans for sustainable fashion has been linked to issues concerning ethics and consumer trust (Rana et al., 2025). Well-designed nudges must empower rather than manipulate individuals and promote transparent communication concerning recommendations and how these can relate to sustainability objectives (Bhagat, 2024). It is necessary that brands guarantee that recommendations from AI do not contribute to environment degradation but instead reduce consumerism fueled by personalized recommendations (Bashynska, 2023).

This chapter integrates the secondary literature and the data available to the consumer in regard to the concept of sustainable consumption behavior in fashion by means of behavioral science and artificial intelligence. The chapter is driven by behavioral knowledge and artificial intelligence techniques, supplemented by case studies and findings generated by means of surveys, and its main significance is in connecting the idea of sustainability awareness for consumers with their actual behavior in terms of purchases by leveraging behavioral artificial intelligence for fulfilling sustainability aims while aligning them with business strategies.

THEORETICAL FOUNDATIONS AND LITERATURE REVIEW

This chapter adopts a review-based approach to examine how behavioural science and artificial intelligence (AI) jointly inform sustainable fashion consumption. While recent literature has rapidly expanded on AI-enabled fashion technologies and sustainability initiatives, much of this work remains fragmented and descriptively oriented. To address this gap, the literature is reorganized into three coherent thematic blocks: (i) foundational behavioural theories relevant to consumption and technology use, (ii) behavioural AI in fashion consumption, and (iii) sustainability and circular fashion models. Together, these streams provide a structured theoretical foundation for understanding how AI-driven interventions can influence consumer behaviour toward sustainability.

Behavioural Theories Relevant to Sustainable Fashion Consumption

Classic behavioural theories offer essential explanatory power for understanding why consumers frequently fail to act in line with their sustainability intentions. The Technology Acceptance Model (TAM) has been widely used to explain adoption of digital tools based on perceived usefulness and ease of use. In the fashion context, TAM helps explain consumer acceptance of AI-enabled features such as virtual try-ons, size recommendation tools, and sustainability dashboards. When such tools are perceived as reducing uncertainty, effort, or decision risk, consumers are more likely to engage with them, creating indirect pathways toward reduced returns and more deliberate purchasing (Roy, 2024).

The Unified Theory of Acceptance and Use of Technology (UTAUT) extends this perspective by emphasizing social influence and facilitating conditions. Fashion consumption is strongly shaped by peer norms, influencer culture, and digital platform design. Research indicates that AI systems using social cues such as popularity indicators and peer comparisons can normalize sustainable choices. These cues reduce the perceived trade-off between fashionability and responsibility. Facilitating conditions, including intuitive interfaces and seamless mobile integration, further encourage continued use of AI-enabled sustainability features (Khanh Linh et al., 2025).

The COM-B model (Capability, Opportunity, Motivation–Behaviour) offers a broad Behavioural perspective that is specifically relevant in the context of sustainability interventions. The Capability aspect can be improved by AI-driven solutions like virtual try-ons and size prediction technology that enhance consumers' capabilities to make better-informed decisions. Opportunities are influenced by digital choice architecture, which encompasses default sustainable filters and recommendations. The Factor of Motivation can be sustained by nudges, feedback, and rewards that emphasize ecological or social approval benefits. The COM-B model has been widely quoted in literature related to sustainability studies in that it spans individual cognitive elements combined with broader design considerations (Chang & Hsu, 2022).

Further, the Fogg Behavior Model onder the significance of timing to effect behavioral change when motivation, ability, and triggers meet. The model is applicable to AI-based nudging within the fashion ecommerce space, including reminders at the point of completion related to the environment impact of returns. Taken together, these theories convey that fashionable sustainability is the result of interactions among psychological and digital environments that are not solely information-based deficiencies (Prathibhani & Lakshika, 2023).

Behavioural AI in Fashion Consumption

Current research is increasingly concerned with the use of behavioural AI, which is described as AI designed to both forecast preference and influence the decision-making process of the customer based on behavioural knowledge. For fashion consumption, behavioural AI is employed through recommendation systems, virtual try-ons, predictive analysis, and targeted communication (Kemi & Zilahy, 2025). The recommendation system mitigates choice overload by aligning style choices with sustainability criteria, while virtual try-ons mitigate size uncertainty and bracketing and returns for larger sizes. Post-purchase interventions by AI technology, including reminders for product maintenance or repair as well as resale, amplify sustainability beyond the point of purchase and aid habit formation (Nablsi, 2024). Conversely, too much nudging is seen by researchers as inducing fatigue or autonomy loss, thus implying the use of transparent and ethical AI technology.

Sustainability and Circular Fashion Models

The third thematic bloc establishes the context for behavioural AI research by linking it to sustainability and circular fashion concepts. The conventional linear approach to fashion consumption has been widely questioned for its sustainability, which instigates a more circular approach based on longevity, returnability, repairability, resellability, and recyclability (Musova et al., 2021). However, for the success of circular systems, considerable behavioural compliance is required from consumers.

Studies in circular fashion have discussed the contribution of the virtual space and AI tools in the resale market, the second-hand alternatives, and the process of advising people on the possibility of refurbishing the product, focusing on the ethical consumption of fashion using the sustainability label and third-party scores, fighting against the problem of information asymmetry, allowing the individual to behave in line with their values and ethics (Gwa et al., 2025). The application of Behavioural Sciences relates to the processes described in the study of Li & Lorenzo, focusing on the power of defaults, social norms, and the feedback system in the continuous process of using the circular economy system (Li & Lorenzo, 2025).

Conceptual Framework

By integrating these currents, this chapter proposes a conceptual framework in which the role of behavioral theories (TAM, UTAUT, COM-B, and Fogg Behaviour

Model) occupies a foundational stance, which underpins AI technology mechanisms (virtual try-ons, recommendation systems, nudges, and predictive models). These mechanisms lie mid-stream and affect consumer decision-making and sustainable fashion outcome improvements such as improved returns, sustainable purchases, habit formation, and support for fashion circularity, among others.

OBJECTIVES

- To study how behavioural insights inform AI design in sustainable fashion applications.
- To evaluate the impact of AI-powered virtual try-ons, recommendations, and sustainable fashion apps on consumer choices.
- To explore ways of leveraging behavioural insights to reduce returns and overconsumption in fashion e-commerce.
- To formulate strategic recommendations for fashion brands to integrate behavioural AI solutions for sustainability goals.

METHODOLOGY

In this study, to explore the use of behavioural science and AI to facilitate sustainable fashion consumption, the review strategy will use a review methodology with a mixed descriptive approach. Firstly, to fulfill Objectives 1, 2, and 4, a systematic literature review will be conducted. This review will focus on literature explored within 2022 to 2025 and will centre on topics of behavioural theories (TAM, UTAUT, COM-B, Fogg Behaviour Model), usage of behavioural AI, and fashion circular systems. Secondly, to fulfill Objective 3, the research will include data gathered through a primary survey of fashion consumers conducted through a questionnaire with single-item, closed-response, and ordinal questions. This will focus on 300 online fashion consumers residing within Indian metropolises.

RESULTS

Objective 1: Behavioural Insights and AI Design in Sustainable Fashion

The fashion industry is currently undergoing a paradigm shift due to the growing needs of sustainability and advancements in technology (Ikram, 2022). AI has penetrated the fashion industry through recommendation systems, virtual try-on tools, and consumer application systems that are designed to provide benefits to consumers (Aakash et al., 2024). Technology, however, will not necessarily bring about sustainability. This is because AI systems work well only when aligned with the human factor, which often contradicts the intended environmental goals. Consumers may demonstrate growing concern about the need to look after the planet; however, consumers are still concerned with fast fashion consumption, impulse purchases, and return purchases (Hogh et al., 2025).

Behavioural science explains consumer decision-making as a process shaped by heuristics, habits, emotions, and social norms rather than rational evaluation (Escandón & Mejía, 2022). When applied to fashion technology, behavioural insights inform the design of AI algorithms and interfaces that can subtly guide decisions toward sustainability. Key frameworks—nudging, habit formation, and social influence—offer conceptual foundations for AI systems that encourage sustainable consumption while preserving consumer autonomy (Lata & Rana, 2025).

Nudging Sustainable Choices through AI

Nudging, as described by Thaler and Sunstein (2008), is the process of creating choice environments to direct behavior while preserving the ability to make choices (Viale, 2022). For the fashion e-commerce industry, nudges are applied via AI recommendation systems, filtering, default options, and prominent user interfaces (Rinne, 2025). Studies have already proven that sustainability nudges are more efficient when integrated into the path of habit decisions and not as a call for morality.

The application of default sustainability filters and visibility of eco-labels by Zalando illustrates the impact of algorithm-driven integration of the Higg Index on redirecting consumer attention towards environmentally positive alternatives without undermining personalization needs (Gossen et al., 2022; Cossatin et al., 2024). For instance, the balanced presentation of H&M's "Conscious Collection" through AI-powered "green tags" overcomes cognitive hurdles blocking environmentally positive choices (Mukherjee et al. 2025; Baker, 2024). ASOS's in-checkout calls to action to encourage consolidation of shipments from consumers demonstrates the significance of temporal factors related to consumer behavioral cues.

Across these cases, the key insight lies in the mechanism rather than the application: nudges are most effective when sustainability is positioned as the easy or default choice. However, behavioural research cautions that excessive repetition may reduce effectiveness over time, resulting in nudge fatigue or disengagement, particularly in promotion-intensive fast fashion contexts.

Habit Formation and Behavioural Consistency

Although nudges have the ability to affect individual behaviors, for environmentally and sustainably produced fashion, the change in behavior should be regular. As a matter of fact, for effective change in behaviors, repetition, feedback, and reinforcement are imperative, based on the theory of habit formation (Prashar & Kaushal, 2025). AI technology is appropriate for helping the formation of good behaviors since the technology is capable of reflecting on previous behaviors.

For instance, the "Move to Zero" campaign created by Nike using the Nike App showcases how "anticipatory prompts" through AI, such as "care instructions and repairs," could work towards extending the life cycle of products and making "sustainability" the norm (Asghar, 2023). However, the gamification approach provides a measure of how much has been accomplished towards "sustainable living" through the actions of consumers. For example, the "Good On You" app allows consumers to form the habit of examining the "sustainability" label even before the final purchasing process, as supported by the feedback approach provided to consumers through the "AI-rated" app itself. However, the "Worn Wear" campaign created by "Patagonia" showcases how "circular behavior" conducted through "AI insights" about "repair and resale" could make "sustainability" the norm (Pham, 2024).

Critically, the literature also notes potential rebound effects. Consumers may perceive sustainable actions as moral compensation, justifying increased consumption elsewhere. This underscores the need to integrate habit-based interventions with broader moderation strategies rather than treating sustainability as an add-on.

Social Influence and Norm Activation

Social influence is also deeply embedded in fashion consumerism, where identity, membership, and social approval heavily inform purchasing decisions. Behavioural studies have consistently shown the importance of norms, social evidence, and social comparisons in shaping consumer decision-making, phenomena further enhanced by the addition of social information by AI. Zalando's regional-based 'popular sustainable choices' exemplify the uptake of social influence in the promotion of sustainable actions. The collaborative project between Adidas and Allbirds highlights the uptake of transparency, influence, and social communication to offer collective action on sustainable, low-carbon versions, further promoted by social influence via AI-driven recommendations (Ghosal, 2025). Gamified social influence, such as Nike's Run Club social comparators, also exhibits the social influence drives further motivational behaviour. Social influence platforms, such as Depop, position pre-owned fashion further through AI-driven, social-narrated social influence, exemplifying second-hand fashion for desirable, positive aspiration (Panju, 2024), yet with risk of social influence effecting empty, superficial, or performative sustainability.

Designing Behaviourally Informed Algorithms and Interfaces

Effective AI design for sustainable fashion requires integrating behavioural principles into both algorithms and interfaces. Algorithms must balance personalization with sustainability objectives to avoid reinforcing overconsumption patterns (Fruttaldo, 2024). Interface design further shapes decision-making by reducing cognitive load and increasing the visibility of sustainability cues.

Zalando's integration of Higg Index data into recommendation logic demonstrates how sustainability metrics can be embedded without compromising relevance. H&M's visually salient Conscious Choice tags and Farfetch's "Positively Conscious" badges illustrate how transparency and labeling enhance trust and facilitate faster decision-making (Mekkaoui, 2022). Stitch Fix's use of explanatory notes accompanying sustainable recommendations highlights the importance of explainability; consumers are more likely to accept AI guidance when the rationale aligns with their values.

Critical Reflection

There are several clear limitations to the implementation of behavioural AI interventions. Nudging effects may fade away with repeated exposure, excessive personalisation undermines autonomy, and algorithmic optimisation for engagement perpetuates a risk of consumption rather than moderation. These challenges highlight the need for adaptive design, ethical safeguards, and ongoing evaluation.

Overall, behavioural insights provide a robust conceptual basis for the design of AI systems that link consumer psychology to sustainability objectives. When better implemented, behavioural AI has the potential to reduce waste, lower return rates, and make sustainable fashion normal. But balanced design is required for its success: it needs to focus on empowerment rather than persuasion and on long-term behaviour change rather than short-term engagement.

Objective 2: Evaluating the Impact of AI-Powered Virtual Try-Ons, Recommendations, and Sustainable Fashion Apps on Consumer Choices

As sustainability increasingly shifts from a niche concern to a core consumer expectation and corporate responsibility, artificial intelligence (AI) has emerged as a critical driver reshaping consumer experiences in the fashion industry (Dhiwar, 2024). Among the most influential AI-enabled tools are virtual try-ons, recommendation engines, and sustainable fashion applications. These technologies not only enhance convenience and personalization but also influence decision-making in ways that can support environmentally responsible consumption. Evaluating their impact therefore requires moving beyond functional benefits to examine how they reduce uncertainty, alter behavioural pathways, and encourage sustainability-oriented choices (Nichifor et al., 2025).

Virtual Try-Ons and Sustainable Decision-Making

Virtual try-on (VTO) technologies represent one of the most visible applications of AI in fashion retail. By allowing consumers to visualize garments on their bodies before purchase, VTOs directly address fit uncertainty—one of the primary causes of excessive returns in online fashion retail. High return rates not only undermine profitability but also generate significant environmental costs through reverse logistics, packaging waste, and additional emissions. By reducing size-related errors and bracketing behaviour, VTOs indirectly contribute to environmental sustainability (Gao & Liang, 2025).

This can be seen clearly in the applications of the mechanism by various industries. For instance, Zara's application of augmented reality-based virtual try-on allows consumers to make judgments about fitting by means of computer-based interfaces, thus reducing the risk of misfit. ASOS's 'See My Fit' service, where it presents apparels on models with differing body shapes, has been seen to increase consumer confidence and decrease returns, synchronizing efficiency with sustainability goals (Okur & Saricam, 2025). Amazon also offers Virtual Try-On for Shoes, where consumers can see their foot models with footwear through mobile software. While these technologies mean to promote consumer experience, the ultimate outcome is the reduction of unwanted purchasing and returns, accountable for specific waste decrement. In all these applications, the central mechanism does not lie in innovation itself, where a decrease in uncertainty leads to a decrease in overpurchased products.

AI-Powered Recommendations and Consumer Behaviour

AI-based recommendation algorithms further drive consumer decisions by offering product selection based on consumers' preferences and browsing patterns, and even sustainability, which increasingly shapes consumption decisions. Choice overload, which has been identified as a key driver of impulse buying, has been improved by such algorithms, which narrow down consumer options and direct them to products of their preference. When such sustainability factors are incorporated into AI algorithms, consumers' consumption patterns could be driven without being persuaded directly.

For example, the recommendation system at H&M uses AI to recommend products based on the "Conscious Collection," so customers are exposed to sustainable alternatives without bombarding them with too many options at once. Also, the Stitch Fix recommendation system uses AI to recommend clothing based on the consumer's taste and lifestyle, but also works towards combining ethical material and sustainable resource considerations into the recommendation process over time. This model has concluded that these recommendation systems increase consumer satisfaction and decrease the likelihood of overbuying, thereby lowering return rates (Kim et al., 2022). Farfetch takes it a step further by offering the consumer the chance to make informed decisions based on the "Positively Conscious" filter range, implementing the ethical shopper into the design of the purchase decision process.

Sustainable Fashion Apps and Consumer Awareness

Outside of retail platforms, applications of sustainability in fashion have become important influencers of consumer awareness and post-purchase behavior. Sustainability applications leverage artificial intelligence, together with transparency mechanisms, to enable value-aligned decisions. Good On You, an example of a sustainability app, rates brands based on their performance concerning labor practices, the environment, and animal conservation. Incorporation of this app into the Zalando platform allows consumers to make decisions based on third-party sustainability ratings.

Other applications extend sustainability beyond purchasing. Save Your Wardrobe (SYW) enables users to digitize wardrobes and receive AI-based suggestions for repair, resale, or donation, promoting durability and circularity while discouraging excessive consumption (Scaraboto et al., 2022). Nike's AI-supported Nike Refurbished program similarly encourages reuse by facilitating the return, refurbishment, and resale of gently used shoes. These applications highlight how AI can support sustainability across the product lifecycle rather than solely at the point of sale.

Impact on Consumer Decision-Making

Throughout these tools, the pattern is clear: AI-based solutions remove key behavioral hurdles for sustainable consumption. Virtual try-ons remove the uncertainty and waste associated with returns. Recommendation systems increase the accessibility of sustainable choices, reducing impulse purchasing. Sustainable fashion apps provide greater transparency and trust, making it easier for consumers to integrate personal values with actual behavior (Ali, 2025). There is evidence for the above points. ASOS showed reduced return rates with the implementation of the "See My Fit" feature, leading to reduced logistics emissions. Zalando showed considerable usage of sustainable collections with the inclusion of Good On You scores. Stitch Fix with its sustainable-focused personalization approach showed enhanced satisfaction and loyalty, proving that sustainable compatibility does not have to be mutually exclusive with success.

However, there is a case for critical reflection here. These technologies could have differing effects for varying groups of consumers, and in relying upon technological solutionism, there might be a tendency to overlook more fundamental, structural causes of the problem of overconsumption.

In conclusion, the use of AI virtual try-ons, recommendations, and eco-fashion apps is transforming how consumers make decisions regarding the fashion industry (Burnstine, 2025). They fill the gaps left by issues of uncertainty, overload, and information that hinder individuals from being behavioral and actual pro-sustainability individuals. As these tools continue to develop, they will offer great milestones and options to make the way consumers behave within the fashion community more effective and satisfying.

Objective 3: Leveraging Behavioural Insights to Reduce Returns and Overconsumption in Fashion E-Commerce

High Return Rates and Overconsumption are now pressing sustainability concerns for the fashion e-commerce retail sector (Sarkar, 2023). These two sustainability concerns are now further exacerbated by the growth of the internet as a shopping platform, as customers often indulge in impulse buying of multiple products because of the ease of purchase, bargain, or seductive consumer advertising (Kathuria & Bakshi, 2024). The Litmus test for items sent back or unsold, size irregularities, dissatisfaction with the promised performance, and the tendency to buy with the intention to return, also named 'bracketing,' are the three most prominent factors that contribute to 'Return Rates' (Langåsdalen, 2024). The role of reverse logistics, additional boxing, and the disposal of unsold products represent some of the distinct contributors through which such practices, besides generating diminished retail profitability, increase CO2 emissions to unprecedented proportions. In this respect, the integration potential with AI technology stands as the only 'Behavior Change' solution for such wasteful consumer practices.

Behavioural Patterns Behind Overbuying and Returns

According to behavioral science, a large portion of the overconsumption observed in fashion e-commerce is caused by cognitive biases. For example: Because they fear missing out on opportunities, consumers with loss aversion tend to overbuy during flash sales.

- Due to choice overload, consumers purchase a variety of options in anticipation of regretting their decision.
- Present bias encourages instant satisfaction at the expense of long-term financial or environmental repercussions.
- When consumers are exposed to popular products and peer endorsements, social proof increases the likelihood of overbuying.

In a similar vein, excessive confidence in product fit, reliance on deceptive images, or routine behaviors promoted by lax return policies are frequently associated with high return rates. When included in AI-driven systems, behavioral interventions like nudges, commitment devices, and default options can assist in resolving these problems (Mohammadian, 2024).

AI Interventions in Addressing Wasteful Consumer Behaviour

AI technologies can harness behavioural insights to develop systems that subtly guide consumers toward more sustainable decisions:

1. Predictive Analytics for Fit and Returns: AI-driven size recommendation systems are used by Zalando and ASOS, among other companies, to more precisely predict fit by analyzing customer demographics, purchase history, and return data. These tools drastically reduce return rates by lowering uncertainty.
2. Dynamic Nudges and Tailored Messaging: Bracketing can be decreased by AI-powered nudges; such as prompts that highlight the environmental impact or the number of returns the customer has made in the past. H&M, for instance, has tried using eco-labels and digital prompts that highlight clothing's sustainability ratings.
3. Personalized Recommendations: Platforms like Farfetch encourage eco-conscious choices while still catering to consumer preferences by using AI to promote sustainable product alternatives, such as recycled fabrics or versatile basics.
4. Commitment Mechanisms: Some platforms, like Zalando, are experimenting with “preference locking” features, which allow users to choose sustainability filters that stay in effect for subsequent sessions, thereby gently encouraging consistent environmentally friendly behavior.
5. Virtual Try-Ons: AI-powered try-ons are used by retailers like Gucci (through Snapchat AR lenses) and Nike (through the Nike Fit app) to lessen size un-

certainty and overbuying. These technologies reduce needless returns while simultaneously boosting confidence.

Empirical Data: Survey Insights

The study employed a descriptive survey design to support the review-based analysis of behavioural AI in fashion e-commerce. Data were collected from 300 active online fashion consumers aged 18–45 from Indian metropolitan cities using purposive sampling, ensuring respondents had recent experience with online fashion purchases and returns. The questionnaire consisted of single-item, closed-ended questions and ordinal response categories capturing distinct behavioural aspects such as purchase frequency, reasons for returns, influence of return policies and social media, and perceived effectiveness of AI interventions (e.g., virtual try-ons, size recommendations, and nudges). As no multi-item latent constructs were measured, internal consistency reliability testing was not required; instead, content validity was ensured through alignment with established behavioural science and fashion e-commerce literature. Findings are interpreted descriptively, acknowledging limitations associated with self-reported data.

Table 1. Frequency of Online Purchases per Month

Purchases per Month	Frequency	Percentage
1–2 items	95	31.7%
3–4 items	110	36.7%
5–6 items	60	20.0%
7 or more	35	11.6%

(Source: Authors' Survey Results)

Table 1 indicates that nearly one-third of consumers purchase 5 or more items monthly, highlighting the prevalence of frequent buying behaviour.

Table 2. Reasons for Returning Products

Reason for Return	Frequency	Percentage
Size/fit issues	120	40.0%
Product not matching description	70	23.3%
Impulse buying/regret	60	20.0%

continued on following page

Table 2. Continued

Reason for Return	Frequency	Percentage
Better alternatives elsewhere	30	10.0%
Defective product	20	6.7%

(Source: Authors' Survey Results)

As per Table 2, the majority of returns (63.3%) are attributed to **fit issues and mismatched expectations**, aligning with global findings from retailers like ASOS and Zalando.

Table 3. Consumer Perception of AI Tools in Reducing Returns

AI Intervention	Very Effective	Moderately Effective	Not Effective
Virtual try-ons (e.g., AR fitting)	140 (46.7%)	110 (36.7%)	50 (16.6%)
Size recommendation algorithms	160 (53.3%)	100 (33.3%)	40 (13.4%)
Sustainability nudges in interface	120 (40.0%)	130 (43.3%)	50 (16.7%)
Eco-labeling and transparency tools	100 (33.3%)	140 (46.7%)	60 (20.0%)

(Source: Authors' Survey Results)

Survey findings given in Table 4 suggest that AI-powered fit prediction and virtual try-ons are perceived as the most effective solutions to reduce return behaviour, while sustainability nudges and eco-labels influence consumer consciousness but may require stronger reinforcement to change purchasing patterns.

Table 4. Reasons for Returning Products

Reason for Return	Frequency	Percentage
Size/Fit Issues	132	44%
Product Not as Expected	96	32%
Better Options Available	42	14%
Change of Mind	30	10%

(Source: Authors' Survey Results)

As per Table 4, Fit and size issues (44%) are the leading cause of returns, followed by product mismatch with expectations (32%). This suggests that AI-driven virtual try-ons and personalised size recommendations could directly reduce a large proportion of returns.

Table 5. Openness to AI Nudges for Sustainable Shopping

Response	Frequency	Percentage
Strongly Agree	84	28%
Agree	138	46%
Neutral	54	18%
Disagree	18	6%
Strongly Disagree	6	2%

(Source: Authors' Survey Results)

As per Table 5 statistics, a combined 74% of respondents are open to AI nudges that encourage sustainable shopping, such as reminders about carbon footprints or prompts to avoid unnecessary returns. This demonstrates a positive consumer mindset towards behavioural interventions.

Table 6. Consumer Views on AI Helping with Sizing & Returns

Response	Frequency	Percentage
Very Effective	102	34%
Somewhat Effective	138	46%
Neutral	42	14%
Ineffective	18	6%

(Source: Authors' Survey Results)

Table 6 shows that a majority (80%) believe AI-powered size recommendations and virtual try-ons can be effective in reducing returns. This reinforces the potential of AI in directly addressing size-related challenges, which are the biggest drivers of returns.

Table 7. Impact of Return Policies on Buying Behaviour

Perception	Frequency	Percentage
Encourages More Purchases	156	52%
No Impact	96	32%
Encourages Cautious Purchases	48	16%

(Source: Authors' Survey Results)

Table 7 indicates over half the respondents (52%) admitted that lenient return policies encourage them to buy more. This validates the idea that overly flexible policies inadvertently promote overconsumption.

Table 8. Influence of Social Media/Influencers on Purchase Decisions

Influence Level	Frequency	Percentage
Very High	78	26%
Moderate	132	44%
Low	60	20%
No Influence	30	10%

(Source: Authors' Survey Results)

Table 8 results shows nearly 70% of respondents admitted that social media and influencer content moderately to strongly influences their purchase decisions. This shows that social comparison and aspirational buying significantly drive overconsumption in fashion e-commerce.

Table 9. Willingness to Pay Slightly More for Sustainable Products

Response	Frequency	Percentage
Strongly Willing	72	24%
Somewhat Willing	108	36%
Neutral	66	22%
Unwilling	36	12%
Strongly Unwilling	18	6%

(Source: Authors' Survey Results)

Table 9 indicates around 60% of consumers are willing to pay a small premium for sustainable products, while only 18% remain unwilling. This indicates a significant market opportunity for brands to integrate behavioural AI strategies that highlight sustainability without compromising on affordability.

Table 10. Preferred AI Interventions for Reducing Returns

AI Intervention	Frequency	Percentage
Personalised Size Guidance	126	42%
Virtual Try-On Features	96	32%
Predictive Style Suggestions	54	18%
Sustainability Nudges	24	8%

(Source: Authors' Survey Results)

As per Table 10, consumers showed the strongest preference for AI tools that directly tackle fit issues (42%) and virtual try-ons (32%). Sustainability nudges were less preferred (8%), indicating that practical problem-solving tools must take precedence, while nudges can work as complementary measures.

Inferences from Survey

An extensive understanding of the behavioral patterns causing overconsumption and product returns, as well as their receptiveness to AI-driven interventions, is provided by the survey of 300 fashion e-commerce customers. Many respondents said they shopped online at least three or four times a month, and a smaller but significant 14% said they shopped online seven or more times a month, making them particularly susceptible to overspending. 70% of respondents acknowledged that influencers and digital platforms have a significant impact on their purchasing behavior, making discounts, flash sales, and social media influence the main causes of overconsumption. Returns became a significant problem, with 40% of customers reporting that they occasionally send items back, and 44% citing size or fit issues as the most frequent cause.

Furthermore, 52% of respondents said that easy return policies encouraged them to buy more than they needed, demonstrating how convenience can lead to unsustainable habits. Positively, 74% of respondents said they were receptive to AI nudges that help them make sustainable decisions, and over 80% thought AI handled sizing and fit issues well. The most helpful features, according to respondents, were virtual try-ons (32%) and personalized size recommendations (42%). Price sensitivity continued to be a barrier for some consumers, even though 60% of them were willing to pay a little bit more for sustainable products. The survey concluded by highlighting the significant impact of social influence on consumption patterns and pointing to the necessity of AI systems that can help consumers avoid rash, comparison-driven decisions by guiding them toward more environmentally friendly and thoughtful options.

The findings show that psychological biases like social influence and FOMO, as well as structural factors like steep discounts, lax return policies, and recurring size mismatches, are the main causes of overconsumption and high return rates in fashion e-commerce. At the same time, customers showed a great willingness to accept AI-driven behavioral solutions, especially those that deal with product visualization and fit accuracy. The results show that personalized sizing and virtual try-ons can drastically lower returns, and predictive analytics can help prevent overbuying by deterring impulsive purchases brought on by sales or trends influenced by influencers. Furthermore, the majority of consumers around 60% may be persuaded to make more sustainable purchases by behavioral nudges that emphasize environmental costs. AI messaging in conjunction with balanced return policies can further reduce waste without sacrificing customer satisfaction. All things considered, fashion e-commerce can minimize overconsumption and needless returns, lessen its environmental impact, and preserve customer trust by combining behavioral insights with AI.

Objective 4: Strategic Recommendations for Fashion Brands: Integrating Behavioural AI for Sustainability

The fashion industry of today stands at a crucial juncture, being forced to balance and reconcile their business expansion with sustainability and environmental considerations. The fashion industry has faced criticism for being resource-intensive, with processes and attitudes of overconsumption (Khagokpam et al., 2025). Even with AI offering technology that has a great impact on consumers, consumer behavior theory could explain why, with greater consumer knowledge of sustainability, consumers end up overbuying, returning their purchase, or simply ignoring sustainable options (Mahajan et al., 2025). By incorporating consumer behavior principles and psychology into AI technology, fashion brands can utilize fashion technology platforms to support sustainability without ultimately impacting their profitability (Andre, 2024).

The strategic use of behavioural AI is based on its ability to optimize multiple, simultaneously related goals. From a commercial standpoint, it can help cut costs related to return negotiations, ensure minimal unsold merchandise, and maximize long-term customer loyalty. From the viewpoint of consumers and individuals, it improves confidence and optimal decision-making alignment. From a macro perspective, it helps in promoting appropriate consumption and thereby minimizes waste and damage to the environment (Peng et al., 2023). The strategic recommendations below are formed by integrating all relevant aspects of behaviour theory and AI techniques.

1. Prioritise Fit Accuracy Through AI-Powered Visualisation Tools

Fit uncertainty remains one of the primary drivers of returns and overconsumption. Brands should prioritise AI-driven virtual try-ons and size recommendation systems that enhance consumer capability at the point of decision. Tools such as Zalando's size recommendation engine and ASOS's "See My Fit" demonstrate how predictive analytics and visualisation can reduce uncertainty, improve confidence, and lower return rates. Importantly, these tools should be seamlessly integrated across platforms and supported by explainable AI features that clarify why specific sizes or styles are recommended. This dual focus on accuracy and transparency improves trust while directly reducing the environmental cost of reverse logistics.

2. Use Behavioural Nudges to Discourage Impulsive Overbuying

Impulse buying, flash sales, influencer marketing, and fear,EPROM Of missing out remain a challenge in the structure of the fashion ecommerce market (Faulhaber, 2023). Behavioral nudges can introduce moments for reflection. Examples include nudges concerning the likelihood of returns when checking out, delay timers for urgency, and sustainability metrics on the effect of purchases on the environment. Examples include the pilot initiated by Zalando's eco-indicators. Brands should be cautious since nudging can result in disengagement when frequently used.

3. Make Sustainable Options the Default or Highlighted Choice

Behavioural default effects are a subtle and highly effective means of reshaping consumption behaviour (Houf et al., 2024). The influence of default visibility is already evident in e-commerce sites such as Farfetch, with its 'Positively Conscious' search option, and H&M, whose 'Conscious Collection' is given default visibility. In this case, additional personalisation is possible based on consumers' former preferences using artificial intelligence, and this will further reduce the cognitive cost while maintaining freedom of choice. Default options, however, should adapt to avoid being coercive and green-washed.

4. Embed Sustainability Metrics Transparently

Trust in BHAI relies significantly on transparency (Jestratijevic, et al., 2022). When consumers are able to relate to the data, they are likely to rely on those links. Third-party sustainability ratings, as offered in Good On You and incorporated into sites such as Zalando, can increase trust. The Worn Wear initiative of Patagonia illustrates the impact of storytelling and performance measurement with regard to sustainability. Dashboards showing personal consumption data could be an important tool in this regard.

5. Foster Habit Formation Through Post-Purchase Engagement

Behavioral consistency with respect to consumption needs to extend beyond the point of sale itself (Owusu & Omari-Sasu, 2025). AI-assisted interventions after a purchase, like reminding consumers of fabric maintenance, or encouraging them to repair or resell an item, go a long way in building behavioral habits. Nike's "Move to Zero" campaign is a great example of the potency of simple and timely signals in making low-carbon practices a new norm. Rewarding consumer loyalty relating to repair, recycle, or resell practices can help make these a habit, provided the rebound impact of sustainability does not lead consumers to over-consume.

6. Leverage Social Proof to Normalize Sustainable Behaviour

Social norms are very influential when it comes to fashion, which makes social proof an important strategic move (Bollinger et al., 2023). Aggregated information, for instance, geographical indicators of popularity used in Zalando, provide an indication that many people support eco-friendly choices. Community-led sites, for example, Depop, demonstrate how social validation and storytelling bring secondhand fashion into the aspirational area (Panju, 2024). Joint projects, including Adidas and Allbirds' eco-friendly sneakers, understand the power to magnify the sustainability story with the help of social influencers.

7. Balance Return Policies with Sustainability Imperatives

Easy return policies might, in some cases, inadvertently promote overconsumption (Srivastava, 2024). It has to be seen if brands could conceptualize tiered return options that ensure fairness without promoting returns as a habit. They could offer some benefit for responsible custody of products, better returns for better environments, or even better returns through better communication of returns-related emissions.

8. Measure Impact Through Continuous Feedback Loops

The success of behavioral AI approaches relies on constant evaluation (Sjödin et al., 2021). This involves monitoring shifts that occur within return rates, sustainable products chosen, and levels of trust amongst consumers after AI-powered intervention implementation. Feedback cycles that use analytics and consumer research provide continuous improvements to ensure that the approach works and remains consumer-focused.

In conclusion, the integration of behavioral AI and fashion strategy provides the means to resolve the issue between the attainment of sustainability and commercial feasibility. Such systems, if ideally designed and critically developed, have the potential to make sustainable fashion the norm rather than the exception.

ETHICAL, REGULATORY, AND METHODOLOGICAL CONSIDERATIONS

The growing integration of behavioural artificial intelligence (AI) into fashion platforms necessitates careful examination of ethical, regulatory, and methodological considerations. While behavioural AI offers powerful mechanisms to reduce over-consumption, lower return rates, and promote sustainable choices, its influence on consumer autonomy, privacy, and fairness has generated significant academic and policy debate. Addressing these concerns is essential to ensure that sustainability-oriented AI systems remain trustworthy, responsible, and socially legitimate.

From a morality panel, the guidelines for ethical AI include transparency, explainability, and the process of informed consent. Customers can be more readily persuaded when they comprehend how their recommendations result from algorithm steps, and how sustainability measures can be integrated. These AI models tend to focus on giving a good explanation for the process, like providing information related to their past activities, purchases, and sustainability results. In fashion, unexplained methods for developing a successful process may increase the distrust associated with greenwashing.

A closely related issue concerns the boundary between behavioural empowerment and behavioural manipulation. Behavioural interventions are intended to guide choices without eliminating freedom; however, when combined with highly personalized AI systems, nudges may become coercive or exploitative. Scholars caution that excessive reliance on emotionally targeted messaging or default settings may undermine consumer agency, particularly in fast fashion environments characterized by impulse buying and social comparison. Ethical deployment therefore requires proportionality, opt-out options, and alignment with consumer welfare rather than purely commercial objectives.

Data privacy and bias within AI algorithms are important considerations. Behavioural AI relies heavily on data that concerns consumers. This data includes the surfing habits and purchasing patterns of consumers. This data also involves personal demographics. The deficiency of data governance strengthens the menace of data privacy and bias. This will have negative impacts on various consumer groups. This could also alter the recommendations on the impact of AI on the environment and will favour certain groups of consumers.

These ethical concerns are increasingly reflected in global AI governance frameworks. The European Union's AI Act establishes a risk-based regulatory approach emphasizing transparency, accountability, and human oversight. The United States has advanced AI governance through executive guidance and sector-specific regulations focusing on consumer protection and civil rights. China has introduced centralized AI governance measures, including mandatory labeling of AI-generated content and strict oversight of algorithmic systems. Japan and South Korea have adopted trust-based and risk-oriented AI laws promoting ethical deployment, while India, through the Digital Personal Data Protection Act and emerging AI governance initiatives, emphasizes consent, data security, and responsible innovation.

Collectively, these regulatory developments underscore a shared global emphasis on human-centered AI governance. For sustainable fashion platforms, aligning behavioural AI with these ethical and regulatory principles strengthens legitimacy, mitigates risks of manipulation, and ensures that sustainability-driven interventions respect consumer rights while advancing long-term environmental goals.

FUTURE CHALLENGES AND FAILURE RISKS

Although behavioural artificial intelligence (AI) is a great opportunity for the promotion of sustainable fashion consumption, it is highly dependent on solving some new and potential failures in the future. A future study reveals that, with lack of proper design and applications, some new negative consequences can be resulted because of the applications of behavioural AIs.

First, there is the issue of bias. Fashion AI systems are trained using past consumer behavior data that is tainted with existing inequalities. For example, some consumers might have limited access or afford certain brands. Consequently, the AI fashion system would favor certain brands. This issue also arises when the AI system favors sustainability. It might limit the inclusivity of the sustainability initiative. For example, the AI system might not favor consumers who have diverse body shapes.

A new emerging risk could be nudge fatigue. Behavioral nudges work well when they are targeted and context-driven, but they may be detrimental when they become redundant and targeted to individuals in a persistent manner. A sustainability nudge may become spam or appear insincere within very commercial fashion platforms, such as fashion applications, causing users to ignore targeted sustainability nudge efforts and even turn against them.

The threat of greenwashing could also increase with the use of personalization through AI technology. Sustainability issues may be incorporated within recommendations without any concrete validation or measure. This could cause AI technology to perpetuate deception. Consumers may be left confused and skeptical about the usage of environmental markers, creating distrust between brands and platforms.

Lastly, scalability within emerging markets proves to belong to a structural domain, as factors such as digital literacy, infrastructure, cost, and cultural contexts might inscribe limitations regarding AI-driven interventions in behavioral change. When the purchase pattern sees price sensitivity as primarily significant, applying sustainability nudges might not work unless they incorporate economic motivations and drivers, leaving scope for improvements related to inclusive AI designs and their proximity to sustainability aims.

Together, these challenges underscore the importance of cautious, reflexive, and context-sensitive deployment of behavioural AI in sustainable fashion.

OVERALL FINDINGS AND DISCUSSION

The findings of this chapter integrate information from industry practices, secondary literature, and a survey of 300 online fashion buyers to show why fashion e-commerce is still dominated by unsustainable consumption and how Fashion Tech, especially AI based on behavioral science, can provide useful solutions. The well-established intention–behavior gap is at the heart of these findings: although consumers frequently assert that they value sustainability, their real actions—impulse buying, buying multiple sizes, and returning items frequently—undercut these claims.

Purchase frequency and return behavior, which continue to be major sustainability challenges, are the subject of the first important finding. A sizable portion of customers said they shopped more than once a month, and size and fit mismatches accounted for 40–44% of returns. This illustrates a structural flaw in online fashion retail: sizing uncertainty raises emissions from packaging, logistics, and reverse supply chains in addition to frustrating customers. This problem is already being addressed by fashion tech solutions. AI-driven size recommendation engines and augmented reality tools like "See My Fit" have been introduced by platforms like ASOS and Zalando, showing quantifiable decreases in return rates. These illustrations demonstrate that innovations related to fit constitute a breakthrough in both operations and the environment.

A second set of results emphasizes the significance of social influence and promotional strategies. Nearly half of respondents cited discounts as a reason for impulsive purchases, and 70% acknowledged the significant influence of social media. These three factors were found to be the main causes of overconsumption: discounts, flash sales, and influencer-driven marketing. These actions are consistent with the concepts of social proof, scarcity, and loss aversion found in behavioral economics. These strategies do, however, contribute to unsustainable cycles of waste and overbuying, even though they are successful in increasing short-term sales. This emphasizes the necessity of behavior-sensitive promotional design, where fashion platforms use technology to strike a balance between sustainability goals and sales growth.

Third, the study reveals nuanced but promising evidence of consumer openness to AI interventions. With personalized recommendations (42%) and virtual try-ons (32%) emerging as the most valued features, more than 80% of respondents thought AI sizing tools and virtual try-ons were effective. On the other hand, 74% of participants were still receptive to sustainability nudges and eco-labels, despite their perceived moderate effectiveness. In order to create space for sustainability nudges to subsequently influence deeper behavioral change, Fashion Tech adoption must start with useful problem-solving tools that foster convenience and trust, like fit guidance and visualization.

Fourth, although it is still price-sensitive, there is a willingness to pay for sustainable fashion. Approximately 60% of consumers were willing to pay a modest premium, typically between 0% and 10%. As long as they convey clear value propositions, this implies a chance for brands to incorporate sustainability into product positioning. In a competitive market, integrations such as Zalando's collaboration with Good On You show how third-party validation can foster trust and support small premiums.

Return policies are another important finding that both facilitate and promote consumption. Over 50% of participants acknowledged that having easy return policies prompted them to make additional purchases. Flexible returns increase waste and emissions even though they are essential for boosting consumer confidence. Innovations in fashion technology, like AI-powered repair, resale, and refurbishment initiatives (like Nike Refurbished and Patagonia's Worn Wear), show how businesses can rethink return policies to maintain convenience while minimizing environmental harm.

Lastly, the results highlight how crucial algorithmic trust and transparency are. When explanations are given, such as recommendations based on environmental impact or past fit, consumers are more likely to interact with AI recommendations. Transparency fosters credibility, as demonstrated by Farfetch's "Positively Conscious" badges and Stitch Fix's annotated recommendations.

The evidence points to a staged Fashion Tech strategy: first, use AI to solve immediate consumer pain points (fit, visualization); second, integrate sustainability cues and behavioral nudges after trust is built; third, rethink promotions and returns to cut down on unnecessary incentives; and fourth, use third-party systems to ensure transparency and validation. Together, these actions enable Fashion Tech to balance profitability and sustainability, lowering waste and raising customer satisfaction.

IMPLICATIONS

The study's ramifications suggest that fashion technology will undergo a radical change in the future as AI and behavioral science combine to rethink sustainability tactics, business models, and consumer interaction. Behavioral AI integration into fashion platforms is becoming essential to creating sustainable wardrobes as fashion consumption continues to move toward online and digital-first models. The implications that follow show how managers, technologists, policymakers, and brands can use these insights.

Operational and Technological Implications

Size mismatches continue to be one of the main reasons for returns and waste, so fashion tech companies need to give AI-driven fit and visualization tools top priority. As demonstrated by ASOS's See My Fit and Zalando's recommendation systems, virtual try-ons, body-scanning apps, and personalized size engines have been shown to lower return rates while lowering reverse logistics expenses and emissions. Adoption is increased by making sure these tools are available on web and mobile platforms. Furthermore, explainable AI fosters long-term use and trust by making recommendations that are supported by cues like fit profiles or past purchases.

Marketing and Customer Engagement Implications

Overconsumption is fueled by conventional promotional tools like influencer campaigns and flash sales. In order to change behavior without detracting from the shopping experience, fashion tech must incorporate behavioral nudges into AI systems. Eco-badges, sustainability meters at the register, or prompts alerting customers to environmental costs are a few examples. Subtle interface design can influence preferences toward sustainable options, as demonstrated by initiatives like Zalando's eco-labels and Farfetch's Positively Conscious filter. Sequencing is crucial: platforms should address consumer annoyances like sizing first, and then, after trust has been built, implement eco-friendly nudges.

Managerial and Organizational Implications

Fashion tech's use of behavioral AI necessitates cross-functional cooperation. To make sure algorithms optimize not only for sales but also for sustainability outcomes like fewer returns and longer product lifespan, managers must coordinate data scientists, UX designers, sustainability specialists, and commercial teams. Performance systems should provide incentives for circular practices, such as refurbishing, repairing, and reselling. Rethinking loyalty programs to incentivize eco-friendly behaviors like product repair or recycling is another option. Nike's Refurbished and Patagonia's Worn Wear programs offer tested routes.

Supply Chain and Logistics Implications

Predictive analytics driven by AI can optimize logistics processes and forecast high-risk returns, lowering emissions from needless transportation. By providing incentives for exchanges, donations, or repairs rather than returns, tiered return policies can cut waste while preserving customer confidence. By communicating these policies through dynamic AI messaging at checkout, platforms and customers can share responsibility for sustainability.

Policy and Governance Implications

Frameworks for transparency and data standards must be promoted by industry associations and policymakers. AI-enabled sustainability labeling reduces the risk of greenwashing and boosts brand credibility when verified through collaborations with rating systems like the Higg Index or Good On You. In order to ensure that behavioral AI upholds consumer rights and promotes sustainability, regulation must also protect privacy and equity.

Ethical and Consumer Trust Implications

Fashion tech needs to strike a balance between empowerment and nudging. AI that is too manipulative runs the risk of undermining trust, especially in an industry that is already being accused of greenwashing. Opt-out choices, explainability, and transparency are essential. Clarity increases consumer acceptance, as demonstrated by Stitch Fix's annotated recommendations, which make behavioral AI seem encouraging rather than coercive.

Strategic and Long-Term Implications

Instead of being viewed as a side project, behavioral AI should be viewed as a fundamental sustainability enabler. Aligning profitability and ecological responsibility is ensured by incorporating KPIs like lower return rates, longer product lifespans, and sustainable purchase ratios into long-term strategies. Through collaborations with tech companies, resale marketplaces, and sustainability organizations, smaller businesses can implement scalable solutions, fostering a cooperative ecosystem where behavioral AI becomes commonplace.

Thus, the ramifications show that fashion technology lies at the nexus of sustainability, digital innovation, and consumer psychology. In order to effectively incorporate behavioral insights into algorithms, interfaces, and engagement models, the industry must go beyond superficial eco-labels. It is evident from the sizing innovations of ASOS and Zalando, the circular initiatives of Patagonia and Nike, and the transparency tools of Farfetch that, when properly designed, behavioural AI can make sustainable wardrobes both profitable and useful.

CONCLUSION

This chapter emphasizes how fashion brands can effectively address unsustainable consumption while retaining their competitiveness thanks to the convergence of behavioral science and artificial intelligence. Three major findings are highlighted by the analysis, which draws from a synthesis of literature, industry cases (ASOS, Zalando, H&M, Patagonia, Nike, Farfetch, and Stitch Fix), and survey data from 300 online shoppers. First, psychological triggers like social proof, scarcity bias, and FOMO, as well as structural enablers like discount mechanisms, lax return policies, and uneven sizing, are what propel unsustainable behaviors. Second, once trust is established, consumers show a moderate level of acceptance for sustainability nudges, but they are receptive to AI solutions that address immediate shopping frictions like fit and visualization. Third, consumers are much more inclined to select and pay small premiums for sustainable options when there are clear metrics and reliable third-party validation.

Practically, these insights point to a staged, human-centred strategy. Fashion tech should first focus on reducing friction through size algorithms, virtual try-ons, and clear visualization tools, as these directly cut down on returns—a primary source of environmental and financial waste. Once functional trust is established, behavioural nudges such as eco-badges, checkout impact prompts, and social cues can be introduced to reinforce sustainable habits. Complementary measures—redesigning promotions, recalibrating return policies, and incentivizing repair and resale—are needed to shift commercial incentives away from disposability toward circularity.

The governance and ethical aspects are equally significant. Instead of being manipulative, AI must continue to be explainable, private, and empowering. Transparent dashboards and third-party sustainability ratings can reduce the dangers of greenwashing and boost customer confidence. Managers can make sure AI is used for both business and environmental goals by integrating sustainability-focused KPIs and encouraging cooperation among technology, design, and sustainability teams. Scaling these practices will require supportive regulation, consumer education, and industry-wide data standards at the systemic level.

In conclusion, fashion tech can balance sustainability and profitability thanks to behavioral AI. It decreases returns, stops overconsumption, and promotes a robust, ethical fashion ecosystem by making greener choices easier, more understandable, and more rewarding. The strategy is straightforward: start by addressing customer concerns, establish trust via openness, and then progressively implement behavioral levers that make sustainability the norm when it comes to digital fashion consumption.

REFERENCES

Aakash, V. B., Akmal, A., Chandrababu, A., & Vijay, A. (2024). A Comprehensive Survey on AI-Driven Fashion Technologies: Clothing Detection, Recommendation Systems, and Virtual Try-On Solutions. *International Journal of Advances in Engineering and Management, 2024*(11), 6. DOI: 10.35629/5252-0611247252

Abrardi, L., Cambini, C., & Rondi, L. (2022). Artificial intelligence, firms and consumer behavior: A survey. *Journal of Economic Surveys, 36*(4), 969–991. DOI: 10.1111/joes.12455

Ali, A. (2025). *Influence of Perceived Uniqueness on Purchase Intention in a Virtual Try-on Store* (Master's thesis, Itä-Suomen yliopisto).

André, J. A. (2024). *Ai-Driven Personalization in Fast Fashion and Its Implications for Consumer Behavior and Sustainability* (Master's thesis, ISCTE-Instituto Universitario de Lisboa (Portugal)).

Asghar, M. (2023). Consumer perception of Nike green business strategy and implementation of profitable and sustainable products.

Baker, C. (2024). *Obsolete: How change brands are changing the world*. Bloomsbury Publishing. DOI: 10.5040/9781399416634

Bashynska, I. (2023). AI-driven personalization in advertising: Transforming consumer engagement through sustainability and circular economy. *Scientific Journal of Bielsko-Biala School of Finance and Law, 27*(4), 106–112.

Bhagat, C. (2024). Greenwashing vs. genuine efforts: The role of transparent communication in building corporate credibility. *Journal of Jurivox, 1*(2), 51–62.

Bollinger, B., Gillingham, K. T., & Wight, K. G. (2023). Making prosocial social: The effectiveness of social proof for energy conservation using social media. *Journal of the Association for Consumer Research, 8*(3), 290–300. DOI: 10.1086/725031

Brolin, S., & Lundgren, I. (2024). Return handling practices and strategies: Towards sustainable e-commerce in the fashion and electronics industries.

Burnstine, A. (2025). The Role of Artificial Intelligence in Transforming Physical and Online Fashion Retail: Enhancing Experiences, Driving Sustainability, and Fostering Innovation. *International Journal of Business and Management, 20*(2), 144. DOI: 10.5539/ijbm.v20n2p144

Chang, Y. W., & Hsu, Y. (2022). The factors that affect members' use of a beauty industry matchmaking platform: Validation of the COM-B extended model. *Frontiers in Psychology, 13*, 976109. DOI: 10.3389/fpsyg.2022.976109 PMID: 36300047

Cossatin, A. G., Mauro, N., & Ardissono, L. (2024). Promoting green fashion consumption through digital nudges in recommender systems. *IEEE Access : Practical Innovations, Open Solutions, 12*, 6812–6829. DOI: 10.1109/ACCESS.2024.3349710

Dhiwar, K. (2024, January). Artificial intelligence and machine learning in fashion: reshaping design, production, consumer experience and sustainability. In *2024 ASU International Conference in Emerging Technologies for Sustainability and Intelligent Systems (ICETSIS)* (pp. 1766-1775). IEEE. DOI: 10.1109/ICETSIS61505.2024.10459436

Escandón, P. A., & Mejía, G. M. (2022). Decision-making using heuristic evaluation in design for behaviour change. *Journal of Desert Research, 20*(3), 209–229.

Faulhaber, M. E. (2023). *A nudge-based social media intervention to improve impulse buying, problematic social media usage, and self-regulation*. Iowa State University. DOI: 10.31274/td-20240617-356

Fruttaldo, S. (2024). *Design for behavioural change: study of a concept and recommendations for information systems supporting eco-driving* (Doctoral dissertation, Loughborough University).

Gao, Y., & Liang, J. (2025). The Impact of AI-Powered Try-On Technology on Online Consumers' Impulsive Buying Intention: The Moderating Role of Brand Trust. *Sustainability (Basel), 17*(7), 2789. DOI: 10.3390/su17072789

Garcia, C. C. (2022). Fashion forecasting: An overview from material culture to industry. *Journal of Fashion Marketing and Management, 26*(3), 436–451. DOI: 10.1108/JFMM-11-2020-0241

George, A. S. (2024). The Hidden Cost: Understanding the Environmental Impact of Online Purchase Returns. *Partners Universal Innovative Research Publication, 2*(1), 132–149.

Ghosal, S. (2025). Transforming Retail. *Sustainable Practices in the Fashion and Retail Industry*, 1.

Gossen, M., Jäger, S., Hoffmann, M. L., Bießmann, F., Korenke, R., & Santarius, T. (2022). Nudging sustainable consumption: A large-scale data analysis of sustainability labels for fashion in German online retail. *Frontiers in Sustainability, 3*, 922984. DOI: 10.3389/frsus.2022.922984

Gwa, J. M., Shirazi, F., Nisar, T. M., & Hajli, N. (2025). Promoting circular practices in fashion: Strategies for sustainable business growth. *Strategy and Leadership*, •••, 1–25. DOI: 10.1108/SL-06-2025-0149

Hogh, N., Braun, J., Watermann, L., & Kubowitsch, S. (2025). I Don't Buy It! A Critical Review of the Research on Factors Influencing Sustainable Fashion Buying Behavior. *Sustainability (Basel)*, *17*(9), 4015. DOI: 10.3390/su17094015

Houf, L., Szymkowiak, A., & Shepherd, L. A. (2024). Promotion of sustainable products: Can sustainability labels promote user selection of environmentally friendly products? *Sustainability (Basel)*, *16*(13), 5390. DOI: 10.3390/su16135390

Ikram, M. (2022). Transition toward green economy: Technological Innovation's role in the fashion industry. *Current Opinion in Green and Sustainable Chemistry*, *37*, 100657. DOI: 10.1016/j.cogsc.2022.100657

Jestratijevic, I., Uanhoro, J. O., & Creighton, R. (2022). To disclose or not to disclose? Fashion brands' strategies for transparency in sustainability reporting. *Journal of Fashion Marketing and Management*, *26*(1), 36–50. DOI: 10.1108/JFMM-09-2020-0182

Kathuria, A., & Bakshi, A. (2024). Influence of promotional factors on online impulse buying: Exploring the mediating role of impulse buying tendency. *Current Psychology (New Brunswick, N.J.)*, *43*(44), 34035–34051. DOI: 10.1007/s12144-024-06911-8

Kemi, A. P., & Zilahy, G. (2025). Sustainable post-purchase behaviour of consumers of fashion textile products. *Discover Sustainability*, *6*(1), 94. DOI: 10.1007/s43621-025-00888-5

Khagokpam, D., Sharma, A., Sharma, R. S., & Mishra, V. (2025). Corporate Social Responsibility: A Pathway to Sustainability in the Fashion Industry. In *Circular Economy and Environmental Resilience: Solutions for a Sustainable Tomorrow* (Vol. 1, pp. 343–369). Springer Nature Switzerland. DOI: 10.1007/978-3-031-93091-1_14

Khanh Linh, C., Tung Lam, N., & Tram Anh, N. (2025). Motivating Gen Z to Adopt AI Chatbots for Sustainable Consumption on Fashion E-Commerce Platforms: An Integrated Model.

Kim, J., Kang, S., & Bae, J. (2022). The effects of customer consumption goals on artificial intelligence driven recommendation agents: Evidence from Stitch Fix. *International Journal of Advertising*, *41*(6), 997–1016. DOI: 10.1080/02650487.2021.1963098

Koul, S., & Jasrotia, S. S. (2025). How much is too much? Journey from compulsive buying to addiction of fashion products. *Social Responsibility Journal*, *21*(8), 1686–1703. DOI: 10.1108/SRJ-02-2025-0122

Kumar, S., & Taneja, N. (2025). Flow-induced impulse buying and return intentions: Strategic implications for live streaming entrepreneurs. *Journal of Small Business and Enterprise Development, 32*(6), 1–27. DOI: 10.1108/JSBED-12-2023-0592

Langåsdalen, I. L. (2024). *Bracketing in Online Shopping: An Investigation of the Underlying Psychological and Contextual Factors* (Master's thesis, University of South-Eastern Norway).

Lata, S., & Rana, K. (2025). AI's influence on young consumer behavior: Fostering sustainable consumption. *Young Consumers, 26*(5), 848–864. DOI: 10.1108/YC-05-2024-2081

Li, L., & Lorenzo, L. C. (2025). Case Project Paper on the Promoting Brand Transparency, Consumer Trust, and Purchase Decisions in an Apparel Business in Fujian Province, China. *European Journal of Business. Economics & Management, 1*(2), 97–119.

Mahajan, A., Sharma, S., Agrawal, V., & Nikalje, V. (2025). Influence of artificial intelligence on consumers' lifestyle product choices and the key to driving sustainable behaviour. *Young Consumers, 26*(5), 808–830. DOI: 10.1108/YC-10-2024-2307

Mahmoodi, J., Patel, M. K., & Brosch, T. (2021). Pay now, save later: Using insights from behavioural economics to commit consumers to environmental sustainability. *Journal of Environmental Psychology, 76*, 101625. DOI: 10.1016/j.jenvp.2021.101625

Mekkaoui, S. (2022). *The Role and Impact of the Influencer Marketing Strategy in Fashion Companies: Farfetch Case Study* (Master's thesis, ISCTE-Instituto Universitario de Lisboa (Portugal)).

Mohammadian, B. (2024). Smart Nudge Marketing: Ai-Driven Behavioural Interventions For Sustainable Tourism. In *Proceedings of the International Management Conference* (Vol. 18, No. 1, pp. 529-539). Faculty of Management, Academy of Economic Studies, Bucharest, Romania.

Mukherjee, A., & Bharti, L. (2025). Present Challenges and Future Opportunities of Sustainable Retailing in the Apparel Industry. In *Sustainable Apparel Retailing* (pp. 59–95). Springer Nature Switzerland. DOI: 10.1007/978-3-031-83875-0_4

Musova, Z., Musa, H., Drugdova, J., Lazaroiu, G., & Alayasa, J. (2021). Consumer attitudes towards new circular models in the fashion industry. *Journal of Competitiveness, 13*(3), 111–128. DOI: 10.7441/joc.2021.03.07

Nablsi, R. (2024). "Buy Now, Think Later?": The AI Product Recommendations Effect: From Impulse Buying to Post-Purchase Emotions.

Nichifor, B., Zait, L., & Timiras, L. (2025). Drivers, barriers, and innovations in sustainable food consumption: A systematic literature review. *Sustainability (Basel), 17*(5), 2233. DOI: 10.3390/su17052233

Okur, N., & Saricam, C. (2025). Modern Tools in Fashion Retailing and Consumer Perspective. In *Changing Textile and Apparel Consumption in Transformative Era of Sustainability and Digitalization* (pp. 163–223). Springer Nature Switzerland. DOI: 10.1007/978-3-031-97419-9_5

Owusu, P., Li, Z., & Omari-Sasu, A. Y. (2025). Optimizing consumer engagement and repurchase intentions: The role of strategic post-purchase communication. *Journal of Retailing and Consumer Services, 82*, 104095. DOI: 10.1016/j.jretconser.2024.104095

Panju, M. (2024). What Goes Around Comes Around?: The Sustainability Paradox of Second-Hand Clothing Marketplaces in a Cross-Cultural Context. *East African Journal of Interdisciplinary Studies, 7*(1), 1–27. DOI: 10.37284/eajis.7.1.1799

Peng, K., Feng, K., Chen, B., Shan, Y., Zhang, N., Wang, P., Fang, K., Bai, Y., Zou, X., Wei, W., Geng, X., Zhang, Y., & Li, J. (2023). The global power sector's low-carbon transition may enhance sustainable development goal achievement. *Nature Communications, 14*(1), 3144. DOI: 10.1038/s41467-023-38987-4 PMID: 37253805

Pham, D. T. (2024). *Ethos, Identification, and the Environment: Patagonia's Narrative Approach to Sustainability* (Master's thesis, San Diego State University).

Prashar, A., & Kaushal, L. A. (2025). Nudging sustainable fashion choices: An experimental investigation on generation Z fashion consumers. *Acta Psychologica, 253*, 104727. DOI: 10.1016/j.actpsy.2025.104727 PMID: 39837072

Prathibhani, H. K. K., & Lakshika, V. G. P. (2023). Sustainable consumer behaviour in clothes disposal in the Sri Lankan context. *Asian Journal of Marketing Management, 2*(02). Advance online publication. DOI: 10.31357/ajmm.v2i02.6471

Prits, E. (2023). From intentions to actions: nudging Generation Z towards sustainable fashion choices through service design.

Rana, K., Banerjee, S. P., Agarwal, V., & Chadha, P. (2025). Examining the Role of Artificial Intelligence in Influencing Consumer Preferences and Purchase Intentions toward Green Fashion. *Metallurgical and Materials Engineering, 31*(4), 982–992. DOI: 10.63278/1542

Rinne, K. J. A. (2025). *AI-Powered Customer Engagement: How Personalization.* Chatbots, and Recommendation Systems Influence E-commerce Customer Satisfaction.

Roy, A. (2024). Fashion Innovation Driven by AI: Transforming Design, Manufacturing, and Customer Experience. *Applied IT & Engineering*, *2*(1), 1–8.

Samy, T. M., Asham, B. I., Slim, S. O., & Abohany, A. A. (2025). Revolutionizing online shopping with FITMI: A realistic virtual try-on solution. *Neural Computing & Applications*, *37*(8), 6125–6144. DOI: 10.1007/s00521-024-10843-6

Sarkar, M. (2023). Environmental sustainability under E-commerce: A holistic perspective. *European Journal of Development Studies*, *3*(3), 1–6. DOI: 10.24018/ejdevelop.2023.3.3.252

Scaraboto, D., Shaw, D., & Duffy, K. (2022). Save your wardrobe: Supporting sustainable and mindful clothing consumption. *NIM Marketing Intelligence Review*, *14*(1), 54–59. DOI: 10.2478/nimmir-2022-0009

Singh, S. (2024). Artificial intelligence in the fashion and apparel industry. *Tekstilec*, *67*(3), 225–240. DOI: 10.14502/tekstilec.67.2024001

Tran, A. (2024). Consumer Culture in the Fashion Industry: Understanding Consumption Patterns and Sustainability Efforts.

UNFCCC. (2018, September 6). *UN helps fashion industry shift to low carbon.* United Nations Framework Convention on Climate Change. https://unfccc.int/news/un-helps-fashion-industry-shift-to-low-carbon

Viale, R. (2022). *Nudging.* MIT Press. DOI: 10.7551/mitpress/14437.001.0001

von Zahn, M., Bauer, K., Mihale-Wilson, C., Jagow, J., Speicher, M., & Hinz, O. (2025). Smart green nudging: Reducing product returns through digital footprints and causal machine learning. *Marketing Science*, *44*(4), 954–969. DOI: 10.1287/mksc.2022.0393

Wijewardena, M., & Bhowmik, A. (2025). Green Tags, Real Impact: A study on the impact of Eco-Labeling on Swedish Consumers' Purchase Intentions: A mixed method study in the fashion industry.

ADDITIONAL READING

Bieńkowska, J. (2025). The effects of artificial intelligence on the fashion industry—Opportunities and challenges for sustainable transformation. *Sustainable Development (Bradford)*, *33*(3), 3774–3790. DOI: 10.1002/sd.3312

Candeloro, D. (2020). Towards sustainable fashion: the role of artificial intelligence--H&M, Stella McCartney, Farfetch, Moosejaw: A multiple case study. *ZoneModa Journal, 10*(2), 91–105.

Manzo, D. S. H., Jiang, Y., Elyan, E., & Isaacs, J. (2025). Artificial intelligence-based conversational agents used for sustainable fashion: Systematic literature review. *International Journal of Human-Computer Interaction, 41*(8), 4640–4652. DOI: 10.1080/10447318.2024.2352920

Rathore, B. (2019). Fashion sustainability in the AI era: opportunities and challenges in marketing. *Eduzone: International Peer Reviewed/Refereed Multidisciplinary Journal, 8*(2), 17-24.

Rathore, B. (2019). From trendy to green: Exploring AI's role in sustainable fashion marketing. *International Journal of New Media Studies: International Peer Reviewed Scholarly Indexed Journal, 6*(2), 12–22. DOI: 10.58972/eiprmj.v6i2y19.120

KEY TERMS AND DEFINITIONS

AI: Artificial Intelligence refers to computer systems designed to perform tasks that typically require human intelligence, such as learning, reasoning, problem-solving, and decision-making, through algorithms, data analysis, and adaptive automation.

Behavioural Nudges: Behavioural nudges are subtle interventions that influence individuals' decisions and actions without restricting their choices, encouraging socially or environmentally responsible behavior through cues, defaults, or framing techniques.

Sustainable Fashion: Sustainable fashion refers to the design, production, and consumption of clothing in ways that minimize environmental impact, promote ethical labor practices, conserve resources, and encourage longevity, recycling, and responsible consumer behavior throughout the product lifecycle.

Sustainable Consumption: Sustainable consumption involves using goods and services in ways that meet present needs while minimizing environmental harm, reducing waste, and ensuring resources remain available for future generations.

Virtual Try-Ons: Virtual try-ons use augmented reality (AR) or artificial intelligence (AI) technologies to allow consumers to visualize how products like clothing, accessories, or cosmetics will look on them before purchase, enhancing convenience and reducing product returns.

Chapter 9
Promoting Sustainable Consumption in Fashion With AI:
Empowering Sustainable Fashion Through Virtual Digital Wardrobe Technologies

I. Nivetha
http://orcid.org/0009-0000-3851-219X
Velalar College of Engineering and Technology, India

V. Kavitha
http://orcid.org/0000-0002-5222-4781
Velalar College of Engineering and Technology, India

M. Parimala Devi
Velalar College of Engineering and Technology, India

S. Russia
Velalar College of Engineering and Technology, India

P. Ravi
KGiSL Institute of Technology, India

T. Suresh Kumar
http://orcid.org/0009-0001-1644-6678
AVS Engineering College, India

ABSTRACT

Artificial intelligence-powered virtual digital wardrobes encourage sustainability by enabling customers to make better decisions about their wardrobe management and fashion consumption. These platforms encourage less waste, longer product usage, and responsible purchasing by combining AI with personalized suggestions, lifecycle evaluation, gamification, and integration with circular models like resale and leasing. The chapter describes system architectures that facilitate industry-wide

DOI: 10.4018/979-8-3373-5525-2.ch009

data sharing, platform-level analytics, and consumer-level nudges for supply chain efficiency and transparency. Scalability, data protection, and the requirement to democratize these technologies globally are major obstacles.

1 INTRODUCTION

For a long time, people have noticed the importance of the fashion industry in the global economy, culture, and society. Nevertheless, it is now facing the greatest challenges, such as human rights violations, resource use, and pollution. The eco-friendly aspect of fast fashion's corporate practices is a disaster for the planet, as it leads to waste, production of carbon dioxide, and killing of rivers. Furthermore, the consumer's tendency to buy faster is not helping the earth. The fashion industry has not yet achieved a proper balance between satisfying customers, earning money, and producing clothes in an environmentally friendly way despite the rising consciousness of the issue among both consumers and lawmakers. It is quite obvious that the future of digital technology as the enabler of change in the manner consumers purchase and the businesses' interaction with their supply chains will be more prominent as the demand for change grows.

Among the different technologies, one of the most noticeable is the virtual digital wardrobe powered by AI, which is allowing the consumers to buy clothes as well as keep their wardrobes supplied without harming the environment. Besides, this virtual digital wardrobe is fostering customer interactions through the unification of both digital and physical wardrobes. It further aims to tackle immense consumption and prolong the life cycle of garments. Furthermore, the tech of virtual digital closets paves the way for circular business models which comprise resale, licensing, and upcycling, thus allowing the consumers as well as the companies to participate in the eco-friendly systems together.

The young ethical consumers are pushing the brands to be green and truthful. This is allowing the companies to improve their lead times, and the incorporation of the gamification and educational features in the new technologies is the putting of the consumers in a position to make the right choices when it comes to fashion and consumption. By the economic obstacles that the resale and rental marketplaces have created, the consumer is being empowered to turn their unused clothes into cash, and at the same time, the eco-friendly behavior is being promoted. However, the advancement of technology has also opened up new problems such as the privacy of data, the digital divide, and the environmental impact of digital systems like data centres.

Additionally, the large-scale adoption and simple operation of virtual digital wardrobe platforms are key factors in the process of making fashion available to everybody, since they are designed for different kinds of user communities around the world, even those that have been less favoured. In order to have safe, interoperable, and inclusive digital ecosystems, it will take the work of various stakeholders like clothing companies and lawmakers alongside tech developers and consumers. This chapter discusses the futuristic characteristics of virtual digital wardrobe technologies (with AI) and their role in circular fashion. Besides, the possibility of a total change of the fashion sector and the simultaneous decrease of its ecological footprint by altering consumer behaviours is signalled.

1.1 Motivation

The research that is being conducted is motivated by the necessity to deal with the increasing environmental and social problems caused by the fashion industry. To improve sustainability, companies usually focus on purifying the whole production process by using eco-friendly materials and following labour rights practices. As a result, the question of how to give consumers appropriate tools to control their clothing consumption sustainably has not been very often asked. People often do not have access to their wardrobe use statistics, and have duplicates of the same clothing. Usually, when a customer buys something new, they tend to forget about the old one, which results in the reduction of their clothing usage and eventually, unattended disposal. The problem of consumers losing track of their clothing is solved by the artificial intelligence-enabled digital virtual wardrobes. The users can keep a record of, sort and maximize the use of their existing wardrobes, which in turn very much helps in the waste reduction and clothing lifespan extension. Besides that, these technologies can be linked to resale and rental platforms at a closer distance to the circular economy model where the issue of the whole life-cycle of fashion products gets solved. This research is powered by the prospect of digital technology to shift the consumers' attitudes and behaviours thus making the sustainable fashion ecosystem which is coaxing the users to change their behaviour over time and making them accountable.

1.2 Statement of the Problem

Even if the awareness of the negative impact to the environment caused by the fast-fashion model of the industry is rising, that same model is still widely used. It is the main reason for degradation of the environment, cutting down of trees, and manufacturing more than what the market can consume. Most of the consumers do not have the knowledge about the production process of their apparel which leads to their inability to practice eco-friendliness, their having impulsive purchasing habits, and they're not having accessibility to resources that could help them in making more sustainable choices is also a contributing factor. Furthermore, brands find it difficult to synchronize their strategies with the aims of the circular economy due to poor inventory management and lack of consumer interest. Our understanding of the systematic use and acceptance of AI-powered virtual digital wardrobe technologies to foster sustainable production and consumption in the fashion value chain is extremely limited.

2 BACKGROUND STUDIES

Digital doppelgangers are AI-generated virtual avatars representing users (Hussain &Waheed, 2025) real body shapes. This may help consumers visualize garments accurately before purchase. Also, it reduces size-related product returns and associated waste. This technology supports more efficient online shopping and reduces overconsumption. Here it contributes to sustainability by minimizing physical trials and logistic emissions.

This chapter (Theodore Tarnanidis, 2024)explains how green marketing strategies influence sustainable consumer choices. This highlights the use of digital tools AR, VR, virtual models to promote eco-friendly fashion. Transparent digital communication improves trust in sustainability claims. Brands can use digital experiences to reduce dependency on physical samples. The positions of digital fashion as a key tool in sustainability-focused marketing.

This chapter discusses (Mohit, 2025) global environmental impacts of fast fashion. It identifies overproduction and excessive waste as major sustainability challenges. In digital design and virtual sampling are suggested to reduce material usage. The Virtual fashion minimizes physical prototypes and supports better forecasting. Here the authors argue digital tools must be paired with broader sustainable reforms.

The article presents (Yu, 2021)a system for remote virtual fitting in online fashion retail. The platform uses digital measurement and 3D simulation to recommend accurate sizes. Accurate virtual fitting minimizes returns and reverse logistics waste. It also improves customer experience and reduces unnecessary inventory movement. This tool supports sustainability through reduced transportation and material waste.

This chapter explores (Ross, 2017)how digital tools enable the co-creation between brands and consumers. Virtual design platforms let users customize garments digitally before production. Such co-creation supports on-demand manufacturing, reducing unsold stock. Digital prototypes replace physical samples, lowering resource consumption. The approach encourages slower, higher-value, and more sustainable fashion consumption.

This book explores (Ozuem, 2018)how to digital technologies reshape branding and consumer engagement in fashion and luxury sectors. It highlights strategies like omnichannel communication, immersive digital experiences, and influencer campaigns. This work emphasizes how digital tools can support sustainable marketing by reducing wasteful physical advertising. This also analyzes changing consumer expectations driven by online fashion culture. Overall, the book links technology adoption with improved brand loyalty and responsible communication.

This handbook examines (Noris, 2016) global fashion management practices across supply chains, marketing, and retailing. It discusses digital transformation and how virtual tools can improve efficiency and sustainability. This book includes research on consumer behavior in international fashion markets. It highlights the challenges faced by the industry, including environmental concerns and fast-fashion waste. Overall, it provides frameworks for adopting sustainable fashion merchandising strategies.

This chapter explains (Arantes, 2022) how digital marketing can support sustainability goals in fashion and retail. It emphasizes reducing environmental impact by shifting from physical to digital promotional methods. This author highlights consumer awareness, green branding, and digital transparency tools. It covers how to brands can use social media, analytics, and virtual campaigns responsibly. Overall, it shows how sustainability and digital transformation can work together.

This article explores (Adanyin, 2024) ethical issues around AI use in retail environments, including fashion. It focuses on data privacy, algorithmic fairness, and responsible AI adoption. This study highlights risks such as biased recommendations or intrusive data collection. It stresses the importance of transparency and consumer trust in AI-powered fashion systems. Overall, it provides guidelines for ethical AI use to support sustainable and fair retail practices.

This review analyzes(Glogar et al., 2025) how the digital technologies contribute to sustainable textile and clothing development. It covers the tools such as 3D simulation, digital prototyping, and virtual fashion design. The authors highlight how these technologies are reduce material waste, energy use, and sampling costs. It also identifies the research gaps in adopting digital sustainability practices. Overall, the study shows how digitalization supports circular and eco-friendly fashion systems.

Although not directly related to fashion, this review (Belen'kii et al., 2024) summarizes recent advances in heterocyclic chemistry. It discusses chemical structures, synthesis methods, and applications in materials science. Some heterocyclic compounds are relevant for developing smart textiles and functional fabrics. This chapter provides insights into chemical innovations influencing future textile materials. Overall, it contributes the scientific background for sustainable and advanced textile production.

This systematic review (Faludi, 2025)studies how the consumer behaviour influences sustainable and circular fashion practices. It highlights the barriers to circularity, including fast-fashion habits and limited awareness. This article proposes policy strategies and social marketing approaches to shift consumer choices. It also identifies digital tools that educate consumers about sustainability. Overall, it offers a roadmap to promote responsible consumption in the fashion ecosystem.

This Deep Fashion introduces the Deep Fashion dataset (Liu et al., 2016) for clothing recognition and retrieval using deep learning. It includes the rich annotations enabling advanced fashion AI applications such as virtual try-on. The technology supports sustainable fashion by improving digital cataloging and reducing physical sampling. It also enhances the online shopping accuracy, reducing returns and waste. Overall, Deep Fashion is a foundational AI resource for modern digital fashion systems.

This study analyses how virtual fitting applications (Zhang et al., 2024) can be optimized using Kano and QFD models. It also identifies customer expectations for digital fashion tools and prioritizes design requirements. This research highlights how virtual fitting reduces garment returns, waste, and resource use. It emphasizes the need for accurate 3D visualization and real-time customization. Overall, it shows how well-designed virtual fitting systems can support sustainable digital fashion.

This review compares the 50 years of fashion and textile industry trends with climate realities (Badhwar et al., 2025). It highlights how to unsustainable production and fast fashion have accelerated environmental damage. The study of contrasts Australia's progress with global sustainability practices. It emphasizes the digital transformation as a key enabler of greener fashion systems. Overall, it provides long-term evidence linking industry behavior with climate consequences.

This article discusses (Periyasamy&Periyasami, 2023)how digital fashion and the metaverse shift the consumption from physical to virtual. It argues that virtual clothing's reduces textile wastes, pollution, and overproduction. The authors explore a new business model like NFT fashion and digital showrooms. It also highlights challenges such as energy use in metaverse platforms. Overall, the study presents the digital fashion as a pathway toward sustainable future practices.

This paper (Werdayani&Widiaty, 2021)examines the development and functionality of virtual fitting room (VFR) systems. It explains how 3D body scanning and garment simulation enhance user experience. The technology reduces the need for physical samples and lowers return rates. The study emphasizes VFR's contribution to sustainability by minimizing fabric waste. Overall, it positions VFR as a valuable digital tool in modern fashion design.

This study explores consumer attitudes toward recycled fashion in digital e-commerce platforms (Sardianou& Briana, 2025).It analyses how platform design influences sustainable purchasing decisions. The authors highlight factors such as trust, transparency, and eco-label visibility. It shows that digital platforms can encourage environmentally conscious shopping. Overall, the research demonstrates how online systems can drive circular fashion behaviour.

This article (Copeland, 2024) investigates how young consumers view sustainable practices of the fashion brand and it identifies the gaps between brand messaging and consumer expectations. This study shows that transparency, authenticity, and ethical sourcing shape perceptions. It highlights the role of digital communication in influencing youth attitudes. Overall, it explains how brands must adapt sustainability strategies to meet young consumers' values.

This study uses of the Emotional Three-Level Theory to explain why consumers engage in virtual fashion (Deng et al., 2024). It identifies sensory, affective, and cognitive drivers behind choosing digital garments. The research links virtual fashion use with more sustainable consumer behaviour by reducing physical purchases. It highlights how emotional satisfaction from digital clothing can shift the consumption patterns. Overall, it provides a psychological basis for promoting virtual fashion as a sustainable alternative.

This article explores (Bang &Su, 2022) which consumer traits influence intention to use virtual wardrobe applications. It shows that how sustainability awareness, tech-savviness, and fashion involvement increase adoption. The virtual wardrobes help users track clothes, reduce overbuying, and make mindful fashion decisions. This study highlights their potential to support circular consumption habits. Overall, it demonstrates how digital wardrobe tools can influence sustainable lifestyle choices.

This study analyses (Jiang & Macintyre, 2025) the user reviews to understand how to wardrobe apps impact sustainability and well-being. It also finds that users experience reduced impulse buying, better outfit planning, and improved garment use. Unexpected benefits include the emotional well-being and reduced decision-making stress. These apps indirectly promote the sustainability by encouraging thoughtful clothing management. Overall, the wardrobe apps support both environmental and personal well-being outcomes.

This research examines (Arantes& Barbosa Costa, 2025) how luxury brands adapt the sustainable practices across different cultures. It highlights the global variations in consumer expectations for environmentally responsible luxury. This study shows that the culture shapes how sustainability messages are interpreted. Digital tools help luxury brands personalize sustainability communication. Overall, it explains how cultural adaptation strengthens sustainability in the luxury sector.

This paper investigates (Arantes& Ferreira, 2025) how digital transformation enables the innovative sustainability strategies in organizations. It identifies the technologies such as AI, digital twins, and virtual design as key drivers. This study emphasizes that digitalization improves efficiency, transparency, and resource optimization. It argues that digital solutions accelerate environmental and social responsibility goals. Overall, it shows that the strong synergy between digital transformation and sustainability progress.

This work analyzes how digital marketing influences tourism behaviour in Barcelos, Portugal(Arantes& Sousa, 2021). It shows that digital strategies improve visitor engagement and promote cultural heritage. Although not fashion-focused, the study demonstrates how digital tools shape consumer decisions. The findings highlight sustainability potential through targeted digital communication. It illustrates broader applications of digital marketing that can inform fashion practices.

This article examines how digital marketing affects visitor behaviour (de Amorim et al., 2024) at historic sites. It highlights how digital engagement enhances user experience while supporting cultural sustainability. The study demonstrates how online communication that encourages responsible tourism. It provides the insights into digital behavior that can be translate to sustainable fashion practices. Overall, the research shows how digital tools reinforce sustainable consumer engagement.

3 PROPOSED RESEARCH

The research under consideration investigates how the use of Artificial Intelligence (AI) powered virtual digital wardrobe technologies could be beneficial to the environment in the fashion industry. Unlike the traditional methods of making the industry more sustainable which are mainly focused on the manufacturing process, the study highlights the empowerment of the consumer as a result of new technology that gives them the power to decide intentionally through eco-friendly ways their selection of fashion products. The technologies make it easier for consumers to buy less and keep more through their awareness of wardrobe usage and sustainable impacts. Thus, they become less of a direct consumer and more of a circular user by participating in resale, rental, and other sustainability-related practices.

3.1 Principal Objectives

Examine Sustainability Challenges: The research starts with identifying the modern-day environmental and social problems in the fashion world like resource overconsumption, accumulation of textile waste, and exploitation of workers. This study is the base point for open up the development of solutions for sustainability straight away.

Research Evolution and Typologies: Next, the authors bring together research that has looked into the past of virtual digital wardrobe platforms by categorizing them according to their traits, such as AI personalization, the integration of circular economy services (including selling second-hand items, rentals, repairs), and the level of consumer involvement. The typology is used to assess the technology's maturity and its possible ramifications.

***Demonstrate Real-World Impact*:** Virtually stocked and fullfillment models have been shown to contribute to the reduction of overconsumption, the return rates and the longevity of clothing practices. Such scenarios are an eye-opener on how mistakes can turn into a boon for the companies and even lead to their victory.

Embrace Adoption Frameworks: Market readiness frameworks and methods for adoption at both industry and consumer levels are mentioned in the research as going through adoptions post facto. Consumers' trust and experience are addressed by the ways such as incentive systems (of the likes of loyalty programs and giving discounts), learning interventions, design principles, and the like. Also, it looks at ecosystem-wide adoption by the help of collaboration among legislators, tech providers, and brands.

***Imagining the upcoming difficulties and areas of attention*:** There is significant promise, accompanied by the ecological digital infrastructure's footprint and the data privacy issue of digital inequalities as the main obstacles. In favour of creating responsible AI and gaining better service quality and thus an increase in access to technology and stronger environment-friendliness, the authors suggest that crucial research gaps exist through their paper.

Figure 1 shows the integration of virtual digital wardrobes into the larger ecosystem of sustainable fashion. Through a linked digital platform, it illustrates how customers, designers, retailers, and recycling facilities interact. The virtual wardrobe serves as a focal point for users to monitor, control, and maximize their use of apparel. Reuse, repair, recycling, and resale are examples of circular fashion activities that the ecosystem promotes. Data flows show how digital wardrobes encourage sustainable decision-making and lower consumption. All things considered, the diagram depicts a closed-loop fashion system that uses technology to encourage environmentally sustainable behaviour.

Figure 1.

4 FUNCTIONAL LAYERS AND SYSTEM ARCHITECTURE

The suggested outline has three levels, namely, the consumer level, which deals with the development of behaviour and individual user experiences.The platform level, which acts as an intelligent orchestration hub for processing data and integrating services and the industry level, which allows for, among other things, considerable changes to business models, distribution, and production. The synergy that comes out of well-coordinated decision-making processes and an uninterrupted flow of data among the players is to the benefit of all, as each player brings his/her own unique skills.

In Figure 2 represents a proposed system architecture for circular fashion and virtual wardrobes utilizes digital tools to encourage sustainable clothing practices and minimize waste. The system connects consumers, designers, and retailers via a shared digital platform. This platform monitors the lifecycle and usage of garments. Virtual wardrobe technologies enable users to digitize their clothing, create outfits virtually, and make informed purchasing decisions. The system facilitates circular practices, including reuse, resale, repair, and recycling, by suggesting sustainable options.

Figure 2.

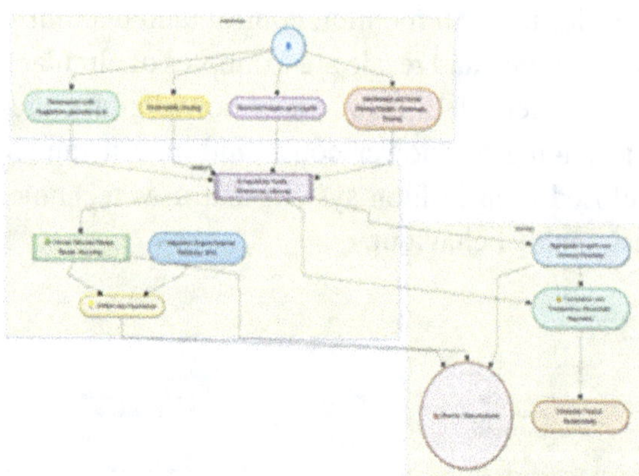

4.1 The Customer Level: Large-Scale Customized Sustainability

a) Improved Wardrobe Organization Powered by AI

Surpassing the conventional fashion applications is an intelligent garment management system which is essential for exceptional client experience. The technology is based on complex computer vision algorithms that effectively analyze and classify every piece of clothing thus resulting in the creation of extensive digital stocks which form the basis of all forthcoming recommendations and insights. Our system does not just focus on the fabrics, colour, season, and occasion attributes of the garments as traditional cataloguing applications do. It looks at all these and more when putting together garments for different scenarios.

b) Fundamental Algorithms for Wardrobe Intelligence

The Convolutional Neural Network (CNN) Architecture enables the identification of garments. It is built based on the ResNet-152 model which was already trained on a large dataset of fashion images. The approach taken involves the adoption of the transfer learning technique utilizing ImageNet models that have already been trained and then modified to fashion-oriented feature extraction. Images are passed through several convolutional layers with ReLU activation functions applied at every step.

Convolutional layers cast garment affinity and style orientation to higher dimensions from such basic outlines and textures. The Style Compatibility Matrix Algorithm measures how well the clothes look together by using the multi-dimensional vector representations. Each piece of clothing gets a feature vector that contains its colour palette, style category, formality level, and seasonal suitability. By the use of cosine similarity, compatibility scores are calculated while adjusting contextual factors.

$$C(A,B) = \alpha . S(A,B) + \beta . H(A,B) + \gamma . O(A,B) \tag{1}$$

In equation 1 Where α, β, and γ are learned weights that are enhanced by user feedback and remarks from fashion experts.

The Style Compatibility Matrix Algorithm is this really super cool algorithm that is able to find the similarity between two clothes based on their visual attributes through the use of multi-dimensional vector representations. The system is continuously updating dynamic user profiles, which are displayed as weighted combinations of style archetypes. The profiles are constructed using a combination of explicit and implicit feedback.

$$S_u(t) = \sum_{i=1}^{k} W_{i,u} . \vec{A}_{i_i} + \lambda . T(t) + \mu . R\left(t\right) \tag{2}$$

In equation 2 the term ($S_u(t)$) represents the user's overall score or state at time (t), calculated using multiple contributing factors. The summation $\sum_{i=1}^{k} W_{i,u}$shows the weighted influence of different activities or attributes on the user. The additional terms $\lambda . T(t)$include time-based and reward-based $\mu . R(t)$adjustments to produce the final score.

The temporal model provides personalized recommendations by considering an individual's taste and the fashion trends prevailing at that time through recognizing the stable personal preferences and the changing fashion trends.

c) Evolutionary-Based Behaviour Modification

The client experience calls for a feedback system that is precise and eco-friendly and can handle the difficult green ideas and convert them into useful information. With the user's closet, every single piece of clothing has a detailed sustainability profile where its whole life cycle is narrated starting from the raw material sourcing to its production, distribution, consumption, and finally waste management.

d) The Algorithm of the Sustainability Impact

The Life Cycle Assessment (LCA) Algorithm is popular because it enables environmental impact to be quantified by means of a multi-dimensional scoring system that considers several sustainability parameters. The subsequent steps should be taken to determine the overall sustainability grade of each garment.

$$\sum_{i=1}^{n} \left(w . i * Impact_i * NormalizationFactor\_i\right) = SustainabilityScore\left(g\right) \tag{3}$$

Impacti is a single category that combines and represents all the above-mentioned important issues of biodegradability, chemical impact, water consumption, and carbon footprint in equation 3.All metrics have been brought to a common standard, and w, i is a scientifically tested set of weights.The formula adds up the weighted effects of all n factors to determine a garment's Sustainability Score (g). To ensure fair comparison across various sustainability qualities, each factor's contribution is modified using a normalization value.

e) The Carbon Footprint Estimation Algorithm

This algorithmfollows a process-based method in order to estimate a product's total life cycle emissions.

$$Carboon\ footprint(g) = \sum_{i=1}^{n} \begin{pmatrix} E_{Material,i} + E_{\text{Production},i} \\ +E_{\text{Transport},i} + E_{Use,i} + E_{\text{End},i} \end{pmatrix} \quad (4)$$

The equation 4 formula adds up all of the emissions produced during a garment's lifecycle to determine its carbon footprint (g). Emissions from material extraction, manufacturing, transportation, use, and end-of-life procedures are among them.Each part is estimated using emission factors and supply chain data, which are of a high standard in the industry and are later quantified with uncertainty so as to provide confidence intervals for the estimates.

f) The Behavioural Nudge Optimisation Algorithm

Determines the most effective methods for each user to become more environmentally friendly through reinforcement learning. Response models are stored in the system for each user, which predict the likelihood of them adopting sustainable behaviours based on the type of message, the timing, and the format of the message. This model is perpetually evolving in response to user feedback. This approach enables individuals to discuss sustainability in a manner that is distinctive to them, thereby achieving the most favourable behavioural changes without becoming monotonous.

g) Participating in the Community and Developing Games

The consumer layer incorporates loads of highly sophisticated gamification (and gaming) features that make sustainability result in being socially enjoyable and plausibly compelling. This is predicated on the notion that in order to modify behaviour in a more sustainable manner, it is necessary to provide encouragement and reinforcement. The system monitors the performance of users in a variety of sustainable fashion consumption areas by awarding points for activities such as creative ensemble remixing, effective item exchanging, garment repair projects, and reduced overall consumption.

One aspect of the community component that transcends individual accomplishment is the determination of the overall effect. The prevailing belief in the power of the group helps the users to feel stronger, more motivated, and more purposeful because they can see that their collective efforts are making it possible to achieve wider sustainable goals. This approach acknowledges that the fashion industry must undergo both individual behavioural changes and cultural transformations at the local level in order to be sustainable.

4.2 Intelligent Service Integration and Orchestration at Platform State:

a) AI-Powered Analytic Engine

The platform level is the location where the most data is stored and the most valuable insights are generated for all users. The data is derived from a variety of sources within the industry. The AI analytics engine utilizes proprietary, modular components that are distinctive to each aspect of fashion sustainability and enhance the user experience.

b) Core Platform Algorithms

The system can provide much better predictions of the change in fashion trends by applying different learning methods together with data from multiple sources. Sentiment analysis, image recognition, and time series analysis are all integrated into the system.Long Short-Term Memory networks (LSTM) are used in the time dimension of fashion data. The computer vision technique is applied to analyse the images and determine the visual aspects of the fashion trends, while the transformer models are used for analysing the language from social media. The program uses machine learning to determine with high accuracy the customers' preferences for different items, locations, and times.

In the clustering and segmentation approach, unsupervised learning is used to detect groups of users with common interests and activities. Document segmentation can be done using K-means clustering with cosine similarity. The next step is fitting a Gaussian Mixture Models (GMMs) to try to separate out the clusters. The algorithms for dynamic clustering are capable of altering user segments immediately in the event of changes in their tastes, and thus, they can apply personalized strategies that change according to the requirement.

c) Roundabout: An Effortless Shift in Integration

The biggest benefit of the platform layer is that it can link the services of the circular economy, which means that the friction points that have been around for a long time preventing the use of sustainable fashion practices will be taken away. The network is continuously connected to all the sources of the textile waste recyclers, repair services, upcycling services, rental markets, and resale markets. The connection, in turn, creates a cycle where the clothes can easily move between different ownership and usage types.

The recommendation-generating algorithm is based on both matrix factorization and deep learning methods. The team gave the options of singular value decomposition-genre-based polynomial algorithm (SVDG) and social referencing via culture algorithm (OIDM). This combined model can be utilized for the analysis of both simple and more complex relationships between users and products.

d) Algorithms for the Circular Economy Optimization

To evaluate the operability of ENP in all pathways in the circular economy concurrently, various approaches are used. This facilitates the identification of the most advantageous path. The valuation algorithm is employed to solve the multi-objective optimization model through dynamic programming. The optimization will consider the resale value, rental value, upcycle value, and recycling value. It will also establish regulations regarding the necessary logistics, demand, and circumstances.

The Condition Assessor is a computer vision and machine learning application that inspects clothes images for quality. The condition assessment technique uses a CNN architecture that works at different dimensions to detect different kinds of wear and tear and damage. Pilling, fading, decay, and other types of wear can all be detected by the device. After that, it will give short, clear, and unbiased assessments of the condition that can be used for setting prices and determining the logistics.

The semantic similarity matching and collaborative filtering are employed by the peer-to-peer transaction Match-Making Algorithm. Preferring predictability, the algorithm checks the compatibility of a company for size, style, and location. The social networks of people and products are being analyzed through the use of graph neural networks by the system to make predictions about the quality of matches and the outcome of exchanges.

Figure 3 represents the Digital wardrobe technologies enable users to manage, view, and improve their clothing selections via digital platforms. These systems digitize clothing items, allowing individuals to monitor their usage and decrease superfluous purchases. Artificial intelligence-based suggestions promote outfit reuse and sustainable styling. Users can identify infrequently worn items and opt to donate, exchange, or resell them, thereby supporting circular fashion practices. This technology diminishes textile waste by encouraging conscious consumption. It also increases awareness of the environmental impact of fashion choices. In general, virtual wardrobes assist users in adopting more sustainable, mindful, and environmentally friendly fashion behaviours.

Figure 3.

e) Digital Persona Construction for Eco-Friendly User Profiling

A detailed digital persona that includes, among other things, the user's ecologically friendly objectives, engagements, measuring details, and favourite designs is built by the identity management system. After that, the user can see what data they want to pass on based on privacy policies. The users can assign different levels of access to the different services, thus, creating customized interactions while still keeping their private information under control. A user who can manage his or her personal data is more likely to trust and accept the platform.

4.3. Artificial Intelligence for Personal Wardrobe Management

People's closet management habits are being revolutionized by Artificial Intelligence (AI), which is to a great extent accomplished through the adoption of smart visualization, data-driven suggestions, and usage statistics making the whole fashion process eco-friendlier. VTO system is one of the most important technologies to emerge in this area. By combining augmented reality (AR) and 3D body scanning, it allows shoppers to see how the garments will look on digital avatars before proceeding further with the purchase.Among the most advanced AI models, the Generative Adversarial Networks (GANs) and the Pixel-Aligned Implicit Functions (PIFu) are capable of converting clothing into life-like representations by excelling at simulating the characteristics of the fabric like fit, drape, and feel. Vogue Business reports that return rates of retailers using AI-based virtual try-ons have been cut down by as much as 30%. This scenario benefits both the economy and the planet.

The implementation of AI technology is seen in the progress of intelligent clothing recommendation systems that are based on AI. When integrating AI into retail analytics, it selects the most sale-productive merchandise to be featured on sale, with the sale being a design of a great unit of an item. The algorithms are considering not only the user's preferences and the local weather but also their body shape and what they have worn before in order to suggest the best combinations. FashionBERT and the likes of it are using both the image and the text data in their determination of the meaning of an item's existence, as well as the harmony between its parts. GNNs (Graph Neural Networks) are effectively modelling the interconnections among fashion items that not only enhance the visually appealing sides but also the whole speaking and their relationships. With this personalization, the mixing and reusing of the clothes people already own are encouraged, thus giving the consumers the power to make better fashion choices. This is not only a win for the environment but also for the slow fashion movement.

According to Juan Milan, co-founder of Las Vegas-based Infinite AI Inc., AI enhances efficiency, precision, and low-cost production in creating highly personalized images. Save Your Wardrobe and other similar apps are using machine vision that is trained on data sets such as DeepFashion2 to find and sort clothes by category, colour, and fabric. AI constantly watching over the fashion items is able not just to indicate the rate of wearing but also to single out the less worn ones. Afterward, the predictive models would recommend sustainable practices, e.g. upcycling, donating, or restoring clothing to make it last longer and support a circular fashion economy. With this method people can be eco-friendly without any hassle and still get a personalized service.

It is building an AI-driven wardrobe ecosystem made up of the combined pieces of Virtual Try-On, Smart Outfit Recommendation, and Wardrobe Utilization Tracking. The user experience is improved, overproduction is cut down, and responsible consumer behaviour is encouraged, and thus they play the role of facilitators to a more responsible and circular digital fashion culture.

4.4 The Industry Level: Circular Business Models and Supply Chain Transformation

4.4.1 Flexible Production and Smart Demand Forecasting

Among all the elements at the industry level, the most important one is system architecture and this shapes the fashion firms' operations decisively. The fashion industry, which is still stuck in an old fashion, polishes its seasonal forecasts and goes for mass production, leading to the three issues of overproduction, wasted products, and a supply that does not match demand. System architecture, on the other hand, already collects data on people's behaviour when they want something and brings up a solution to these very inefficient systems, which have been around for a long time.

4.4.2 Algorithms That Generate Predictions at the Industry Level

The Hierarchical Demand Forecasting Algorithm has the ability to generate demand forecasts of varying degrees of detail. The algorithm primarily works in a top-down fashion, but it is nonetheless able to perform bottom-up operations as well. An ensemble technique, which is very sophisticated, is employed to combine several of forecasting models which include ARIMA for time series analysis, Random Forest for revealing non-linear relationships, and, lastly, Neural Networks for the modelling of complex interaction effects.

The Supply Chain Optimization Algorithm finds the best solution to the problem of multi-objective optimization.

4.4.3 Transparency and Traceability Enhanced by Blockchain Technology

The transparency of the supply chain is a key factor for the fashion industry to become more sustainable as it is so much easier for consumers to take the right actions by following the law. Nowadays, there are global blockchain-based traceability systems that keep records of every phase in the life cycle of a garment from obtaining the raw materials to finishing its production and distribution, processing, and disposal.

4.4.4 Blockchain and Algorithms for Traceability

The Consensus Algorithm for a Distributed Ledger makes sure that the entire historical supply chain network of fashion retains data authenticity always. The network of the system consists of Proof-of-Authority (PoA) consensus mode, which is best for closed networks where only select people are given access. The smart contracts operate automatically verifying compliance and signalling in case the sustainability standards are not met or quality tests drop below the established thresholds.

The Risk Assessment Algorithm of the Supply Chain is developed to identify sustainability defects and disruptions in the supplier network. Then, the graph neural networks are utilized to solve these issues considering the complex intertwining of supplier relationships. Some of the risk factors being studied are the financial health of the suppliers, adherence to environmental regulations, labour conditions, and political situation. Then, the propagation effects are utilized to estimate the extent to which supplier networks are impacted by these risks.

This Impact Attribution Algorithm distributes environmental and social impacts in complex supply chains with the help of ACTIVITY COSTING concepts. It is capable of performing very accurate lifecycle assessments for each garment by managing multi-production.

4.4.5 Innovative Circular Business Models

Architecture at the industry level enables the development of innovative business models that are beneficial for both the economy and the environment. When the logistics management system that enables subscription inventory services, which includes product curation, delivery, cleaning, maintenance, and rotation, is considered, the product-as-a-service business model becomes viable.

4.4.6 Business Model Optimization Algorithms

The Subscription Optimization method uses multi-objective optimization to get the best wardrobe mixes for one subscriber. The method considers the rotation schedules and the garment lifecycle stage in enhancing operational efficiency and user preference. The Revenue Sharing Algorithm utilizes the principles of cooperative game theory to ensure a fair distribution of profits all along the circular value chain. Moreover, the program grants a fee to all the members of the circular economy for their work, which in turn encourages them to be eco-friendly.

The Performance-Based Contract Algorithm sets up contracts between manufacturers and brands that are based on product performance rather than sales amounts. Long-lasting, consumer delight, refurbishment, and recycling at end of life all deliver upon the sustainable design and manufacturing components.

The Asset Utilization Optimization Algorithm, with the help of dynamic programming, extracts the highest value from fashion assets during their whole lifetime. The algorithm not only maximizes the value of assets but also meets sustainability goals by selecting the best time for their shifting from one use phase to another (new retail, rental, resale, upcycling, recycling).

4.5 Technical Implementation and System Integration Framework

a) Distributed Computing Architecture

To get the most out of it, it needs a very high-tech computer infrastructure that has the capability to process a lot of data and at the same time keep it private, secure, and fast. The design follows the best edge computing practices to assure data security and also to deliver users a personalized experience by treating each user's data at the edge of the user's device.

b) Core System Algorithms

Federated Learning Algorithm is the core technology empowering different parties' model cooperation without needing to store the sensitive data in a single place. By using differential privacy techniques, the system ensures that individuals' privacy is preserved, and at the same time, the group's intelligence can be tapped:

By employing adaptive algorithms, the Load Balancing Algorithm allocates the computation tasks to the distributed system in a deterministic manner considering the system load, distance, and data location. The algorithm applies reinforcement learning to the degree that it is not only aimed at global network resource utilization maximization but also quick in reacting to changes in the system.

c) Standards for Interoperability and Integration

The system's requirement for robust integration standards is a must to guarantee that the different parts and outside services will be able to talk to each other without any problems. In addition, the system architecture consists of complex algorithms to manage data transfer, security, and performance across all integration points.

The Auto-scaling Algorithm is a smart one that determines automatically how much computing power is gone be needed next based on demand prediction by using resource optimization and time series forecasting. It's a win-win situation where the program perfectly manages the cooling down and heating up of different parts of the system in terms of demand, thus preventing both resource wastage and performance degradation.

d) Security and Integration Algorithms

The API Rate Limiting Algorithm utilizes token bucket algorithms with burst capacity via regular intervals to stop the system from becoming overloaded and to make sure that all users get equal access. User behaviour patterns and system traffic are used to determine the rate at which the adaptive rate limiting will be applied to prevent the abuse of the system and keep it responsive.

The Data Privacy Algorithm uses differential privacy for each transaction of data sharing, putting in noise that is already determined to be enough to keep the privacy of every single individual. The system can also automatically assign privacy and sensitivity budgets for different kinds of searches, thus offering very high privacy guarantees with very little effect on data utility.

e) Consequence and Significance

The system-wide view of this research is the basis for the study's great importance which enables linking the consumer behaviour of people to the technology development in the industry through easier way of using. Through the combination of circular business ecosystems with personalized AI solutions, virtual fashion closets can change the linear structure of the fast fashion industry and bring forth a new sustainable and responsible fashion economy. Not only does this method reduce the damage done to the environment, but it also creates new economic and social value for the production and consumption of sustainable fashion.

The implementation of two-phase commit protocols along with timeouts and recovery methods in distributed transactions guarantees that the Data Consistency Algorithm does not violate the ACID properties. The system will persistently ensure that all its data is consistent across its different regions, even faced with network partitions and outages.

5 TECHNOLOGIES FOR VIRTUAL TRY-ON

Virtual Try-On (VTO) is one of the most obvious uses of AI in the fashion retail and personal care sectors. VTO gives the customers an option to 'try-on' the outfit on 3D avatars or even on their own real-time pictures before they decide to buy it thus cutting down the number of returns and eliminating the doubt related to online shopping. AI technologies such as Generative Adversarial Networks (GANs), Neural Radiance Fields (NeRF), and Pose Estimation Models are all capable of accurately and realistically dressing people with virtual clothes.

One of the upsides of VTO is that it can help to cut-down-in-waste significantly. Vogue Business reports that fashion companies that embrace AI-driven virtual try-ons have already seen a 30% decrease in the return of products which makes less logistics, shipping, and textile waste.

5.1 Architecture of Technology

5.1.1 Virtual Try-On Models Frequently Employ

- ***3D Body Scanning*:** It is a method that employs depth sensors along with computer vision to determine the body's size measurements in the most precise way.

- ***Garment Simulation*:** It is a procedure that utilizes the synergistic effect of neural rendering and material visualization to show the draping and shaping process of the fabric.
- ***AR Integration*:** A merging that provides the consumers with a possibility to immediately see the products either on their mobile devices or through a mirror.
- ***Personalization Engine*:** A mechanism that makes use of the previous sales data to suggest changes in size and fit as recommendations.

As an example, both Amazon's "Made for You" service and H&M's virtual fitting rooms rely on AI-powered body mapping and physics simulations to create a very realistic appearance. In 2024, Chen introduced the Pixel-Aligned Implicit Function (PIFu) framework which proved its worth by being able to modify fabric and fit garments much better than the usual 2D models.

Furthermore, the adoption of VTO technologies accelerates the action of digital-first fashion which means that the garments will be first shown in digital format before being made physically. It not only helps to get rid of the samples but also makes it easier to forecast the demands.

AI-based rendering may be utilized by brands as a means of exploring new concepts within a virtual environment, discovering the preferences of the consumers, and producing only those products that have a high probability of being sold. This practice supports their sustainable production goals.

5.2 Intelligent Outfit Recommendation Systems

The outfit selection system is, indeed, the second most essential part of AI-based wardrobe management. The system uses machine learning techniques and prompts the users to select the clothing that is both fashionable and of the least environmental impact. The systems provide the user with recommendations based on the analysis of various data including the user's physique, the calendar events, the weather, and the user's past fashion choices, etc.

a) Machine Learning and Fashion Semantics

The recommendation systems of today rely on deep learning methods to determine the visual and verbal relevance of fashion items. The Fashion BERT model suggested by unites the visual and textual embeddings to expose the intricate relationships between color, texture, and context. Also, Graph Neural Networks (GNNs) can find out which clothing items are compatible with each other by inspecting learned aesthetic patterns.

b) Sustainability Consequences

The constant and deliberately made fashion became the gods of the AI recommendation systems, which the latter supported by providing more and more suitable outfits made from already existing items. For instance, a recommendation engine could spot a consumer's black blazer that is good for many occasions and, instead of suggesting more items, to just "give" the consumer different methods in which he or she could combine the blazer with various accessories. This also serves to build a circular fashion economy as well as decrease the number of clothes made in the course of time.

Moreover, these systems may consider factors like the weather or social situation in a particular area in order to promote people dressing according to the climate, thereby minimizing the necessity of having multiple wardrobes. The use of AI-based recommendation engines has already been adopted by the likes of Cladwell and Save Your Wardrobe, which motivate consumers to wear their existing clothes more often.

c) Behavioural AI and Personalization

AI is not limited to just giving recommendations but rather is able to create connections through emotions and behaviours, at least in the case of fashion. One of the methods used is reinforcement learning which allows the system to change over time according to user feedback. If a user, for instance, prefers particular color palettes or extremely uncomplicated styles, the AI will recognize this and adjust its future recommendations in line with that.This kind of personalization that adapts to the user's tastes not only prolongs the clothes' life but also increases the satisfaction of the users, thus helping in reaching the sustainability goals.

5.3 Methods for Monitoring and Utilizing Your Wardrobe

The way people wear and take care of their garments is an often ignored but very important part of sustainable fashion. The clothing monitoring systems that are based on AI give a lot of information in real-time about how often the clothes are worn, how fast they lose their quality, and even about the wearer's feelings towards them. The systems make use of very small sensors and computer vision to create a digital version of a user's wardrobe and track how often and for how long each item is used.

a) Services for Digital Wardrobes

The first apps that used AI image classification were Save Your Wardrobe and Smart Closet which had been trained on large datasets such as DeepFashion2. The models automatically recognize the clothing type, colour, and material from the images. They are then transferred into a virtual inventory. The users can see their whole wardrobe, mix and match outfits, and avoid buying things that are either not needed or already owned.

b) Eco-Friendly Choices and Frequency of Use

AI algorithms monitor the frequency of usage for every item and determine the sustainability metrics such as CO2 emission and cost per use. The method encourages environmentally friendly practices such as giving away, reselling, or upcycling. The tremendous effect of merging behavioural insights into wardrobe management apps and reported a maximum of 25% per yearly user clothing waste reduction.

c) Partnering With Circular Economy Platforms

Presently, several closet management tools can be linked to resale and recycling platforms like Vinted, ThredUp, and Depop. In case a garment is not used often, the AI may propose its selling or recycling. This technique based on data is linking the person's clothing management with the world's sustainability goals, thus making the closed-loop fashion ecosystem easier to establish.

d) Artificial Intelligence and the Circular Fashion Economy

The circular fashion economy is a model where the products' reuse, repair, resale, and recycling are the main activities throughout the product's life cycle. AI is one of the main players in this transition as it, among other things, provides analytics, forecasting, and optimization according to the life cycles of the products.

5.4 Predictive Analytics in Fashion Life Cycles

The AI algorithms can study the different layer of a product and its durability, type of fabric, and wear to make the best recommendation for the garment's usage. Some predictive models can help people know when a product is about to finish its life cycle or even give suggestions on how to prolong the product's life. In the industry, AI-backed data enlightens the producers on how to set the production number that closely matches the customer's actual demand. Hence it avoids the production of unwanted goods and their subsequent disposal, which results in a waste reduction of sorts and overproduction minimization of around unsold items.

Figure 4 represents a Performance Evaluation Analysis graph illustrates the behaviour of a system, model, or procedure under various circumstances. It facilitates the comparison of several performance indicators, including efficiency, speed, accuracy, and precision. The graph draws attention to patterns, trends, and variances that could be difficult to see in raw data. It makes it possible for researchers to pinpoint advantages, disadvantages, and areas for improvement. Because the results are presented in an intelligible fashion, this type of visual analysis also aids in decision-making. All things considered, the graph offers a concise overview of system performance for assessment and comparison.

Figure 4.

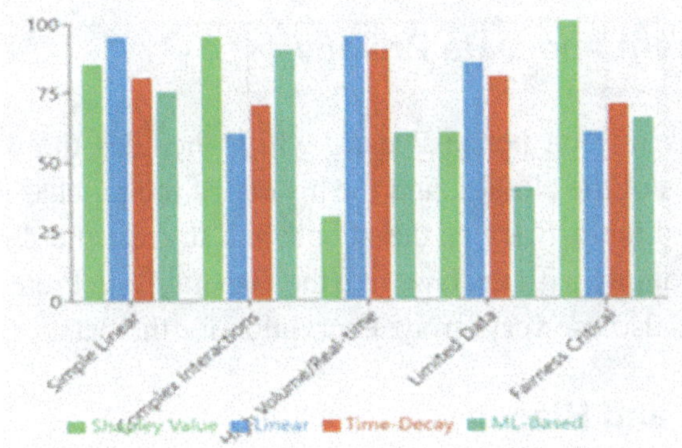

5.5 Transparency in the Supply Chain

A clear view of everything is essential for a company to go green. AI, for example, can oversee the entire supply chain of the fashion industry with the help of both identification through the blockchain and access to the images. All the fabrics getting to the market must be of the right kind, meaning they have to be picked from places that are both sustainable and recyclable. The consumer, on the other hand, gets the information certified as to where the garment is coming from thus such consumption is connected with the ethics of the brand and the responsible practices in the sector they are.

5.6 Digital Fashion and the Metaverse

Digital fashion is a perfect example of how AI could in future be applied to sustainable design. These clothes can only be worn in the digital world. By giving people something virtual to wear for their online personas and events, digital fashion helps to cut down on waste. The production of authentic and quality digital clothing requires the application of AI technologies like AR try-on filters and GAN-based texture generation. The indirect way these modern concepts help the environment is that they allow people to communicate their thoughts and feelings through digital means more than through the physical ones.

6 MORAL DILEMMAS AND COMPLICATIONS

The utilization of AI for wardrobe management has an enormous potential on the contrary, it still brings up several issues.

6.1 User Consent and Data Privacy

AI applications rely on personal data, which includes the user's body measurements, pictures of the clothes, and the history of the purchases. It is of utmost importance to keep the privacy of the people and to treat the data ethically. The developers must comply with the laws like the General Data Protection Regulation (GDPR) and must also use very strong encryption for the data.

6.2 Inclusivity and Bias

A.I models usually are tiny in the training data set, so they unbeknownst to the present age their unintentional propensity to Yang theirs and keep the members within the position quo gender, racial or size. It has been found that some of the first try-on algorithms for virtual fitting were not able to show accurately the sizes and shapes of people who did not fit the narrow standard. It is still very essential to have partnerships with minority groups and institutions that are concerned about those issues in order to create a fair exchange.

6.3 The Environmental Impact of Artificial Intelligence

AI can play an important role in making the world a more sustainable place; however, the most advanced deep learning techniques' training can be an extremely energy-consuming process. The research is on the way for the methods like model compression, federated learning, and green AI that would allow achieving performance on par with the main but much less energy-consuming approaches.

7 FUTURE DIRECTIONS

AI-driven eco-friendly design will be the future and its dependence will be on the merging of technologies like blockchain, the Internet of Things (IoT), and extended reality (XR).

AI dashboards may get instant updates on the comfort level and the entire life span of smart textiles that are connected to the Internet of Things (IoT). This will be the list that consists of how long they will last and how comfortable they will be.

The use of blockchain technology will make it very easy to tell apart sustainable materials and that is why they will always be traceable.

Virtual and physical inventories will no longer be separate as one and XR platforms will make it possible to have such "phygital" (physical + digital) fashion experiences.

The future AI studies will also look into emotional sustainability, which is the production of garments that do not only cater to the latest fashion but are also considered good for one's mental health in the long run. The fashion industry, by incorporating AI, ethics, and creativity, can transform into a really sustainable ecosystem.

8 CONCLUSION

AI technology has completely changed the way people shop for clothes. Through AI, the user has a significant amount of freedom to make better or worse decisions while working toward achieving goals such as circular fashion practice, extended apparel lives, and reduction of waste. Wardrobe monitoring systems, personalized outfit recommendations, and virtual try-ons are some of the ways in which this is achieved. These technologies not only make the process easier for consumers but also play a significant role in helping the world reach its sustainability goals by cutting down on the amount of textile waste, overproduction, and returns.

AI-assisted personal closet management will remain the pivotal connection between eco-friendliness and fashion while the industry introduces the new digital age. The future of fashion will be both sustainable and intelligent, as it will harmonize the human imagination with the machines' tech and ultimatelytake over the industry by showing its commitment without masking its diversity.

The usage of AI-operated virtual digital garments technology opens up a new area for the fashion industry to give a fresh meaning to sustainability. The focus on the production that only holds advancements is shifted to the customers being made the active stakeholders in the green movement and thus the issues of lack of visibility, accountability, and change in behaviour are solved. AI-powered inventory control, life cycle assessment, and gamified participation at the consumer level motivate people to be more careful with their buying, maintain their clothing longer, and cut down on the number of their purchases that are not really needed. Integration of powerful analytics, circular economy, and interoperability creates an ecosystem that is interconnected and facilitates the changes of use, resale, renting, and recycling on a platform level. At the same time, the industry level is getting demand forecasting, supply chain optimization, and blockchain-enabled transparency which are all very good for supporting the production models that are effective, equitable, and environmentally friendly.

The extensive framework that this research offered clearly shows that if the fashion industry were to be revolutionized by the fast fashion model being overturned and a movement towards circularity becoming the new norm, the resulting change would be based on the combination of the custom-made digital experiences and the whole industry transformation. It is true that sustainability of infrastructure, security of data, and digital access are among the major difficulties that still need to be tackled, but the new model favours practical ways to deal with these issues through joint ecosystem design, responsible AI, and distributed learning. To sum up, the digital virtual assemblies can not only help the fashion industry to cut down on its environmental impact but also to cause a cultural change that would be characterized by the values of conscious consumption, fair value distribution, and sustainability that lasts in the global fashion economy.

REFERENCES

Adanyin, A. (2024). Ethical AI in Retail: Consumer Privacy and Fairness. *European Journal of Computer Science and Information Technology, 12*(7), 21–35. DOI: 10.37745/ejcsit.2013/vol12n72135

Arantes, L. (2022). *Sustainable Digital Marketing*., DOI: 10.4018/978-1-6684-5523-4.ch004

Arantes, L., & Barbosa Costa, S. (2025). Culture and Sustainability in the Luxury Market: An Analysis of Adaptive Practices in Global Contexts. *Journal of International Consumer Marketing, 37*(4), 301–315. DOI: 10.1080/08961530.2024.2434814

Arantes, L., & Ferreira, J. J. (2025). Innovative Sustainability Strategies and the Role of Digital Transformation in Organisations. *Corporate Social Responsibility and Environmental Management, 32*(3), 3088–3121. DOI: 10.1002/csr.3123

Arantes, L., & Sousa, B. (2021). Digital Marketing and Tourism : Case Study Applied to Barcelos. *2021 16th Iberian Conference on Information Systems and Technologies (CISTI)*, 1–6. DOI: 10.23919/CISTI52073.2021.9476556

Badhwar, A., Islam, S., Tan, C. S. L., & Payne, A. (2025). A comparative review of Australia's fashion and textile industry and global climate perspectives across five decades (1970s–2020s). *Global Sustainability, 8*, e41. DOI: 10.1017/sus.2025.10030

Bang, H., & Su, J. (2022). Who Uses Virtual Wardrobes? Investigating the Role of Consumer Traits in the Intention to Adopt Virtual Wardrobes. *Sustainability (Basel), 14*(3), 1209. DOI: 10.3390/su14031209

Belen'kii, L. I., Gazieva, G. A., Evdokimenkova, Y. B., & Soboleva, N. O. (2024). *The literature of heterocyclic chemistry, Part XXI, 2021* (pp. 139–226). DOI: 10.1016/bs.aihch.2023.09.001

Copeland, L. (2024). Exploring young consumers' perceptions towards sustainable practices of fashion brands. *Fashion, Style & Popular Culture, 11*(3), 527–553. DOI: 10.1386/fspc_00125

de Amorim, L. A., Sousa, B. B., Dias, Á. L., & Santos, V. R. (2024). Exploring the outcomes of digital marketing on historic sites' visitor behaviour. *Journal of Cultural Heritage Management and Sustainable Development, 14*(6), 934–949. DOI: 10.1108/JCHMSD-11-2021-0202

Deng, Y., Shen, H., & Ji, X. (2024). Exploring Virtual Fashion Consumption through the Emotional Three-Level Theory: Reflections on Sustainable Consumer Behavior. *Sustainability (Basel), 16*(13), 5818. DOI: 10.3390/su16135818

Faludi, J. (2025). Sustainable Fashion, Circularity and Consumer Behavior – Systematic Review and a Social Marketing Research and Policy Agenda. *Social Marketing Quarterly, 31*(1), 35–59. DOI: 10.1177/15245004241309660

Glogar, M., Petrak, S., & Mahnić Naglić, M. (2025). Digital Technologies in the Sustainable Design and Development of Textiles and Clothing—A Literature Review. *Sustainability (Basel), 17*(4), 1371. DOI: 10.3390/su17041371

Hussain, W., & Waheed, A. (2025). *Digital Doppelgangers.*, DOI: 10.4018/979-8-3693-9005-4.ch008

Jiang, G., & Macintyre, L. (2025). Wardrobe Management Apps and Their Unintended Benefits for Fashion Sustainability and Well-Being: Insights from User Reviews. *Sustainability (Basel), 17*(9), 4159. DOI: 10.3390/su17094159

Liu, Z., Luo, P., Qiu, S., Wang, X., & Tang, X. (2016). DeepFashion: Powering Robust Clothes Recognition and Retrieval with Rich Annotations. *2016 IEEE Conference on Computer Vision and Pattern Recognition (CVPR)*, 1096–1104. DOI: 10.1109/CVPR.2016.124

Mohit, C. (2025). *R., Kumar, R., Nitika, & Chaudhary, K.* Global Impacts and Sustainable Practices in Fast Fashion., DOI: 10.4018/979-8-3693-7853-3.ch005

Noris, A. (2016). *Handbook of Research on Global Fashion Management and Merchandising* (Vecchi, A., & Buckley, C., Eds.). IGI Global., DOI: 10.4018/978-1-5225-0110-7

Ozuem, W. (2018). *Digital Marketing Strategies for Fashion and Luxury Brands* (W. Ozuem& Y. Azemi, Eds.). IGI Global. DOI: 10.4018/978-1-5225-2697-1

Periyasamy, A. P., & Periyasami, S. (2023). Rise of digital fashion and metaverse: Influence on sustainability. *Digital Economy and Sustainable Development, 1*(1), 16. DOI: 10.1007/s44265-023-00016-z

Ross, F. (2017). *Co-Creation via Digital Fashion Technology in New Business Models for Premium Product Innovation.*, DOI: 10.4018/978-1-5225-1865-5.ch002

Sardianou, E., & Briana, M. (2025). Platform-Driven Sustainability in E-Commerce: Consumer Behavior Toward Recycled Fashion. *Recycling, 10*(4), 161. DOI: 10.3390/recycling10040161

Tarnanidis, T. (2024). *Driving Green Marketing in Fashion and Retail* (Tarnanidis, T. K., Papachristou, E., Karypidis, M., & Ismyrlis, V., Eds.). IGI Global., DOI: 10.4018/979-8-3693-3049-4

Werdayani, D., & Widiaty, I. (2021). Virtual fitting room technology in fashion design. *IOP Conference Series. Materials Science and Engineering*, *1098*(2), 022110. DOI: 10.1088/1757-899X/1098/2/022110

Yu, M. (2021). Design of Remote Fitting Platform Based on Virtual Clothing Sales. *International Journal of Information Systems and Supply Chain Management*, *15*(3), 1–12. DOI: 10.4018/IJISSCM.290019

Zhang, Y., Zheng, Z., & Liu, L. (2024). Design Resource Deployment for Virtual Fitting Applications in the Era of Digital Fashion: An Analysis Based on Kano-QFD. *SAGE Open*, *14*(4), 21582440241296627. Advance online publication. DOI: 10.1177/21582440241296627

Chapter 10
Smart Labels and Eco-Tracking Tools for Sustainable Fashion Consumption

Sushila Sahani
http://orcid.org/0000-0002-5739-144X
Lovely Professional University, India

Vidushi Parth
http://orcid.org/0009-0004-3217-5531
Lovely Professional University, India

ABSTRACT

The integration of artificial intelligence into the fashion industry is reshaping the way consumers engage with sustainability. This chapter explores the role of smart labels and AI-enabled eco-tracking tools in promoting sustainable fashion consumption. By using smart labelling and eco-tracking technologies such as RFID, QR codes, NFC tags and provenance tracking into fashion products, brands can provide real-time access to product lifecycle data. Additionally, they can give information on ethical sourcing, and environmental impact metrics of their products. AI enhances these tools by providing personalized sustainability suggestions, usage analytics, and predictive maintenance or reuse suggestions. This approach helps in motivating consumers towards more conscious choices. Through a mix of theoretical exploration and real-world case studies, this chapter demonstrates how AI-powered intelligent systems not only increase transparency, but also drive behavior change. It helps bridge the gap between intention and action, and moves the fashion industry towards a more sustainable future.

DOI: 10.4018/979-8-3373-5525-2.ch010

INTRODUCTION

In present times, fashion industry is one of the most unsustainable sectors. It is unsustainable in terms of environmental, social as well as economic aspects. Currently the industry faces growing pressure to adopt sustainability across its supply chain. A growing global population and rapidly changing consumer tastes are driving unsustainable production and consumption. Today's fashion cycles are short and production is high. Consumption is excessive and disposal is extremely frequent. To meet demand, natural resources are being used faster than they can renew. Water, petroleum-based fibers, toxic chemicals, and energy are consumed at harmful levels. This has already caused serious environmental damage and needs urgent attention. While the industry has started to adopt sustainability strategies, new technologies can offer stronger solutions. Smart labels and eco-tracking tools which are enhanced by AI can support this production and consumption shift. These technologies possess real promise for enabling more sustainable fashion consumption. Many fashion brands still lack a clear understanding of supply chain management. Even if they do, there is often a reluctance to adopt environmentally sound practices. To achieve sustainability goals, systems need to be updated. This needs collaboration, training, and the use of digital technology at every stage of production and consumption. The fashion sector faces multiple social and environmental challenges and these hurdles make sustainable fashion production and consumption particularly difficult. To increase accountability, brands need to improve not only their own transparency but they also need to help consumers make informed decisions. Fashion companies should evaluate what information is already available to various stakeholders and identify the knowledge gaps that still exist. While it is important to raise awareness and share information, it is just as vital to apply that knowledge internally. This approach can help build stronger sustainable initiatives and reduce negative impacts across the supply chain.

As the concerns related to sustainability are rising, fashion consumers are also becoming more environmentally conscious, and communication about sustainable consumption is also increasing. Organizations are taking initiatives to provide direction and clarity, and brands are experimenting with sustainable materials and innovations. Fashion brands are also rethinking supply chains where suppliers are working to improve production processes and product quality. However, this trend is not flourishing because the fashion industry is pretty large and complex. Current efforts are insufficient to ensure a truly viable supply chain and there is an urgent need for transparency and traceability of supply chains (Aakanksha & Aravendan, 2023). Implementing traceability systems in the fashion industry is a complex process, facing many technical, economic and social barriers. The materials used in production are inexpensive and go through many stages, making it difficult to track their source.

Although data sharing tools such as barcodes, QR codes and RFID exist, challenges such as language, geographical distance, underdeveloped infrastructure and cost hinder their widespread use. Transparency requires new skills, but it is unclear who will take responsibility for this in future supply chains. Smaller brands and non-vertically integrated companies lack resources, making it difficult to perform tasks such as staffing, monitoring and data analysis. In addition, legal and environmental regulations vary by region, further adding to the complexities. Many brands are unaware of their sub-suppliers, making vertical transparency difficult. The lack of post-consumer garment storage and lifecycle data is also a major challenge. There are also questions about the accuracy, authenticity and consumer engagement of the data. Traceability is successful when leadership is clear, communication is transparent, and data privacy and intellectual property are respected. When brands works together then the costs are also reduced which results are more effective implementation of this approach (Cura et al., 2022).

The chapter aims to explain how smart labels and eco-tracking tools work in fashion, highlighting technologies such as QR codes, blockchain, and sensors that ensure traceability and transparency for garments from production conditions and material sources to ethical practices and lifecycle tracking. A key objective is to examine the enhancement provided by artificial intelligence, showing how AI streamlines data analysis, enables real-time environmental impact reporting, and facilitates predictive modeling of supply chains and resource use. This encourages brands to respond quickly to sustainability challenges and opportunities. The chapter seeks to assess the impact on consumer behavior and sustainable outcomes, discussing how transparent eco-labelling and real-time sustainability metrics increase consumer awareness, reduce misinformation, and motivate choices that favor circularity and ethical business models. In summary, the chapter's objectives are to advance knowledge of technological solutions in sustainable fashion, illuminate AI's transformative capabilities, and measure these tools' real-world effectiveness in supporting eco-conscious consumerism and industry accountability.

THE RISE OF SMART LABELS AND ECO-TRACKING IN FASHION

The shift from traditional labels to smart systems shows both technological progress and changing consumer needs. Early clothing labels in the USA focused on basic product details and durability. For example, brands such as Levi Strauss's patches, later evolving into printed tags. With the digital age, smart features like

IoT fabrics and RFID appeared. By 2020, labels started offering personalized experiences through big data. In 2024-25, innovations highlight sustainability and secure interactive systems. Fast fashion brands like Zara and H&M sped this up by moving from seasonal launches to weekly micro-seasons. Today, smart labels go beyond information. They support circular fashion with digital passports that track and update environmental impacts in real time.

In the ever-evolving landscape of the fashion industry, smart labels have emerged as a transformative technology. It helped bridge the gap between physical garments and digital ecosystems. Smart labels can be defined as advanced tags embedded or attached to clothing and accessories that store, transmit, and update digital information in real-time (Fernández-Caramés & Fraga-Lamas, 2018). Unlike traditional labels, which primarily convey static details such as size, price, or basic care instructions, smart labels integrate technologies like radio-frequency identification (RFID), quick response (QR) codes, and near-field communication (NFC) to enable interactive, data-rich experiences (Frith, 2024). These labels go beyond mere identification; they facilitate dynamic interactions, allowing consumers, retailers, and manufacturers to access and exchange information seamlessly. As the global smart labels market is projected to grow from USD 14.67 billion in 2024 to USD 42.36 billion by 2034, with a compound annual growth rate (CAGR) of 11.32%, their rise is driven by demands for sustainability, e-commerce efficiency, and enhanced consumer engagement (Precedence Research, 2025).

Smart labels encompass a variety of technologies, each tailored to specific needs within the fashion supply chain. The primary types include RFID, QR codes, and NFC tags, which collectively enhance functionality from production to post-purchase.

RFID (Radio-Frequency Identification)

RFID technology enables real-time tracking and inventory visibility without requiring line-of-sight scanning. RFID tags consist of a microchip and antenna that communicate via radio waves, storing unique identifiers that can be read from distances up to several meters (Dymkov, 2024).

Figure 1. A diagram illustrating how RFID Works

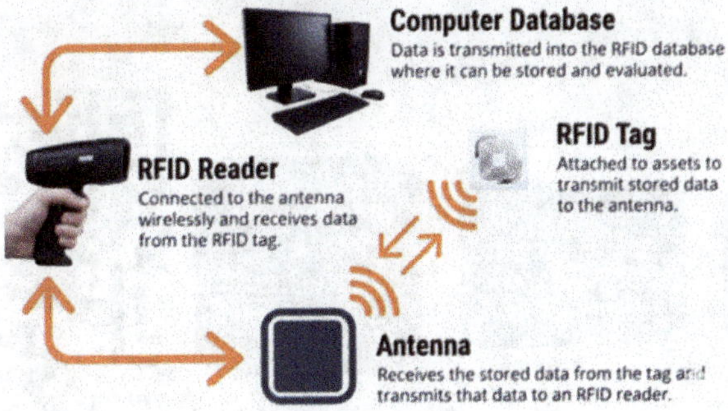

In the fashion sector, brands like Nike, Levi's, Macy's, Lululemon, Uniqlo, and Victoria's Secret have adopted RFID for comprehensive inventory management. RFID's evolution has driven efficiency, with the global market for RFID in apparel growing significantly, as evidenced by Avery Dennison's 9% rise in smart label business in 2020, primarily in clothing (McDowell, 2021). This technology not only tracks items through the supply chain but also supports features like no-scan self-checkout, as implemented by Uniqlo, where cheap $0.15 chips enable rapid transactions (Das, 2024). In inventory management, RFID provides unparalleled visibility, allowing brands to track items from manufacturing to retail with significant accuracy. This real-time data reduces stockouts and overstock, as seen in Uniqlo's system where RFID enables faster checkouts and better supply chain control (Yong, Rana, & Shanmugam, 2022)s.

QR Codes (Quick Response Codes)

QR codes are the most accessible and cost-effective smart label technology. It consists of black-and-white matrix patterns that, when scanned via a smartphone, link to digital content such as product lifecycle data. In fashion, QR codes provide consumers with immediate access to information on origins, sustainability metrics, and care instructions, fostering transparency (Ozturkcan & Kitapci, 2025). Their versatility allows for integration into labels, hang tags, or even printed directly on fabrics.

Figure 2. definition of QR Codes

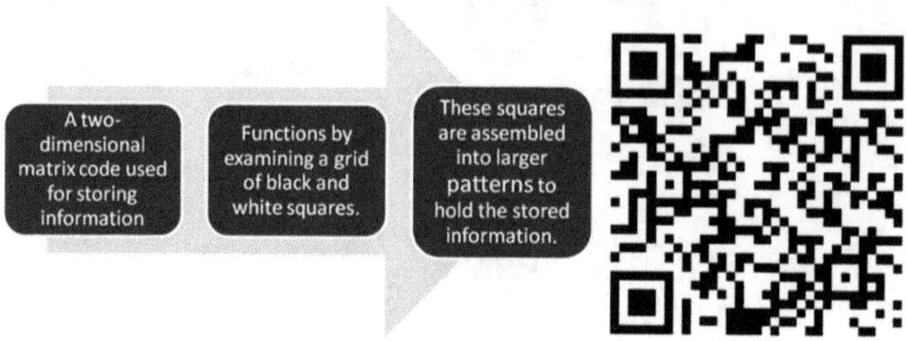

As part of the broader shift toward digital labeling, QR codes have been pivotal in enabling hyper-personalization and traceability, with brands using them to combat greenwashing by linking to verifiable data. The rise of QR codes aligns with consumer demands for ethical insights, as they can reveal supply chain details, reducing misinformation in the textile sector (James & Dutta, 2025).

NFC (Near Field Communication) Tags

NFC tags operate through short-range wireless communication (Vidakis et al., 2020), requiring a simple tap from a compatible device like a smartphone to access information. These tags excel in touch-based product authentication and interactive experiences, such as linking to brand stories or verifying authenticity. In garments, NFC enhances personalization by adding digital interactivity, combating counterfeiting, and promoting sustainability (Subramaniam et al., n.d.; Blibech & Fezzani, 2024). Luxury brands, including those partnering with blockchain platforms like LVMH's Aura, use NFC for digital certificates that prove ethical sourcing (Buckulcikova et al., 2022) and help reduce the counterfeit problem. Similarly, the KOLAB Collection has introduced its Fall/Winter 2024 line integrating Near Field Communication (NFC) technology within sustainable outerwear to enhance authentication, traceability, and lifecycle management. Each garment incorporates a durable NFC-enabled tag, facilitating provenance tracking, resale management, and extended product usability (Textile World, 2024).

Figure 3. NFC Tag

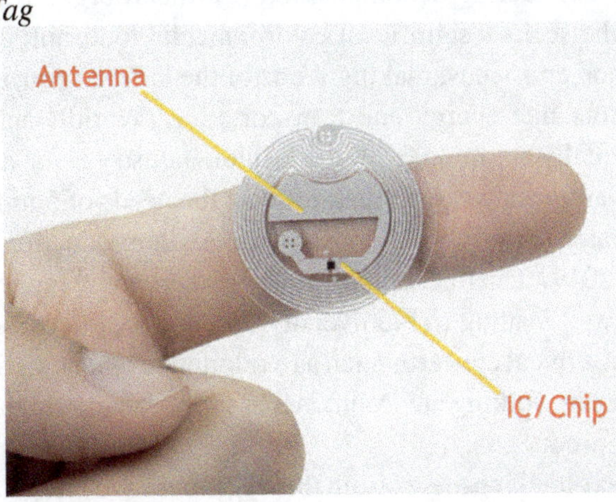

NFC's integration into smart packaging and apparel allows for real-time updates, such as monitoring product conditions, and supports fan engagement in tagged merchandise.

Such Smart labels play multifaceted roles in the fashion industry, reforming operational efficiency and consumer trust. For authentication, smart labels combat fraud by embedding unique digital identities. NFC and RFID tags allow instant verification, protecting brands like luxury houses from counterfeits. Blockchain-integrated smart labels, such as those in sustainable fashion, enhance credibility through expert verification (Lanzer, 2025).Transparency is amplified as smart labels disclose supply chain details, from fiber sourcing to production ethics. Smart labels mark a major shift in fashion, transforming passive tags into dynamic tools that enhance efficiency, authenticity, and sustainability. With evolving technologies like RFID, QR codes, and NFC, they are shaping a more transparent, interactive, and ethical industrybenefiting both consumers and the planet.

ECO-TRACKING AND ITS METRICS

The fashion industry, a global powerhouse valued at trillions of dollars, has long been synonymous with creativity, trends, and consumerism. However, its rapid growth and fast-paced production cycles have come at a steep environmental and social cost. Fast fashion, in particular, exacerbates these issues by promoting disposable clothing, leading to massive waste, pollution, and resource depletion. According to estimates, the industry produces over 100 billion garments annually, with approximately 87% or 40 million tons ending up in landfills where they contribute to air pollution through smoldering decomposition (EarthDay.org, 2025). This waste is compounded by the sector's significant environmental footprint: it accounts for 2-8% of global carbon emissions, making it one of the largest contributors to climate change after sectors like energy and transportation (World Bank, 2019). Water consumption is equally alarming, with the fashion industry using around 93 billion cubic meters of water each year, enough to meet the needs of 5 million people and contributing to water scarcity in regions where textile production is concentrated (United Nations, 2019). Chemical pollution from dyes and treatments further contaminates waterways, leading to biodiversity loss and long-term soil degradation. On the social front, ethical concerns such as exploitative labor conditions, including low wages and unsafe working environments in supply chains, highlight the human toll of unchecked production.

The need for eco-tracking arises from this urgent need to mitigate these impacts. Regulatory pressures are mounting; for instance, the European Union's proposed Digital Product Passport (DPP) mandates traceability for textiles by 2030 (Legardeur & Ospital, 2024), pushing brands toward verifiable data. Moreover, consumer demand for ethical and sustainable products is surging, with surveys indicating that 71% of shoppers prioritize eco-friendly options, driving brands to adopt tracking tools to build trust and loyalty (Horvath, 2024). By making sustainability visible, eco-tracking not only reduces environmental harm but also unlocks economic benefits, such as optimized resource use, reduced waste, and new revenue streams from circular models like resale and recycling. In essence, eco-tracking is not just a tool but a transformative approach to reimagining fashion as a force for good, aligning profitability with planetary health.

What is Eco-Tracking?

Eco-tracking refers to the systematic monitoring and transparency of a product's environmental and social footprint throughout its lifecycle, from raw material extraction to end-of-life disposal or recycling (Uluer et al., 2012). It helps address the lack of transparency in fashion supply chains, where global networks often hide production processes and limit accountability. Without tracking, brands risk greenwashing, making unsubstantiated sustainability claims while consumers remain uninformed about the true cost of their purchases. At its core, it involves integrating technologies like blockchain, Internet of Things (IoT) sensors, and artificial intelligence (AI) to create immutable records of a garment's journey from farm or factory to consumer and beyond. These systems go beyond basic labeling; they provide granular, verifiable insights into impacts, enabling stakeholders to make data-driven decisions. For example, eco-tracking platforms use Life Cycle Assessment (LCA) methodologies to quantify emissions and resource use at each stage, including raw material sourcing, manufacturing, transportation, usage, and disposal.

Figure 4. Role of Eco-tracking

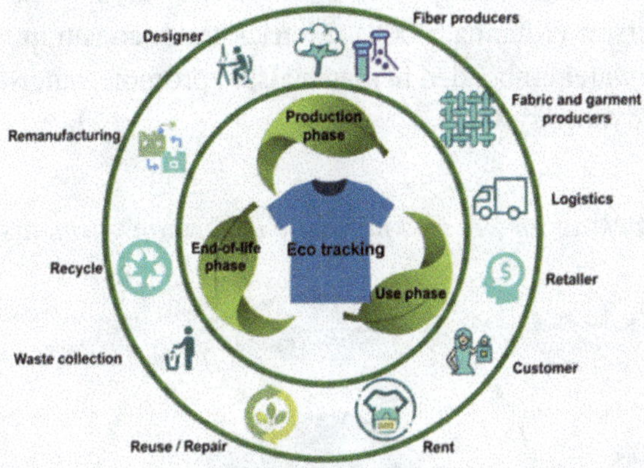

In practice, eco-tracking begins with data collection via digital tags, such as QR codes or RFID chips embedded in garments, which link to cloud-based databases. This data is then analyzed to generate reports on sustainability metrics, often visualized through dashboards for easy interpretation. The goal is transparency: brands can audit suppliers, regulators can enforce compliance, and consumers can scan items to learn about their origins. Advanced implementations incorporate blockchain for tamper-proof records, ensuring that claims of sustainability are credible and not subject to manipulation. Overall, eco-tracking shifts fashion from a linear "take-make-waste" model to a circular one, where products are designed for longevity, repair, and recycling, ultimately reducing the industry's ecological footprint.

Sustainability Metrics Monitored Through Eco-Tracking

Eco-tracking tools focus on a set of core metrics that capture the multifaceted impacts of fashion production. These metrics are derived from standardized frameworks like the Higg Index or ISO 14040/44 for LCA, ensuring comparability and reliability (Schmidt Rivera et al., 2021; Alhainen & Järvinen, 2015). These metrics are as follows:

Carbon footprint: This measures greenhouse gas emissions (GHG) across the supply chain, expressed in CO_2 equivalents (Montoya-Torres et al., 2015). Fashion contributes up to 10% of global emissions (Muthukumarana et al., 2018), primarily from energy-intensive processes like dyeing and transportation. Tracking involves calculating emissions from raw materials (e.g., cotton farming releases methane (Khabbaz, 2010)) to end-use, helping brands identify hotspots for reduction, such as switching to renewable energy sources.

Water Usage: The industry is the second-largest consumer of water, with a single cotton T-shirt requiring up to 2,700 liters equivalent to 2.5 years of drinking water for one person (Khanna, 2008). Metrics track consumption and pollution, including virtual water embedded in materials, to promote water-efficient practices like closed-loop dyeing systems.

Figure 5. Eco-Tracking for pre and post sale of fashion garments

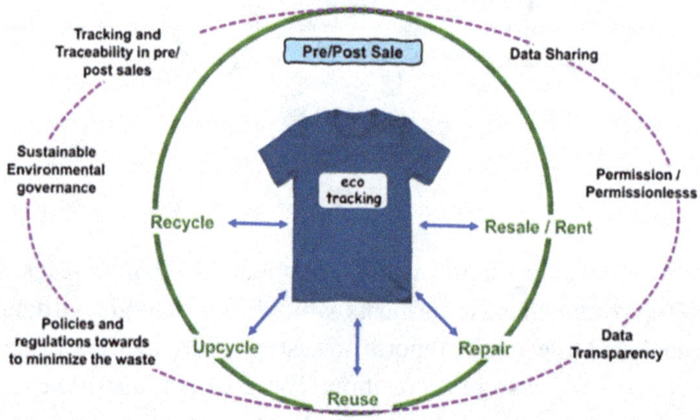

Chemical Use and Toxicity: The application of toxic chemicals in textile dyes, finishes, and processing agents is a major contributor to water pollution, soil contamination, and occupational health hazards. Eco-tracking metrics evaluate the *chemical footprint* of production by assessing not only the volume of chemicals used but also their inherent toxicity, persistence in the environment, and potential for bioaccumulation in living organisms (Sala & Goralczyk, 2013) . These indicators help identify substances of concern, measure compliance with regulations such as REACH (Registration, Evaluation, Authorisation and Restriction of Chemicals) and ZDHC (Zero Discharge of Hazardous Chemicals), and promote the substitution of hazardous inputs with safer, more sustainable alternatives (Amutha, 2017). In addition, tracking chemical use provides transparency across the supply chain, enabling brands, regulators, and consumers to hold producers accountable for chemical safety and environmental preservation.

Labor Conditions and Ethical Sourcing: Beyond environmental metrics, eco-tracking includes social indicators like fair wages, safe working conditions, and absence of child labor. This involves auditing supply chains for compliance with standards like Fair Trade or SA8000 (Social Accountability Standard), ensuring ethical sourcing from raw materials to assembly (Robinson, 2009).

Additional metrics often include recyclability (e.g., percentage of biodegradable materials) and waste generation, providing a holistic view. By monitoring these, brands can benchmark progress and report under frameworks like the Global Reporting Initiative (GRI).

STANDARDIZED TOOLS AND FRAMEWORKS FOR ECO-TRACKING

Standardized tools and frameworks for eco-tracking provide the apparel and footwear industry with consistent methods to evaluate and report on environmental and social performance across the value chain. These instruments establish common metrics and benchmarks, enabling comparability, transparency, and accountability among brands, suppliers, and consumers. Collectively, these tools form the backbone of eco-tracking, providing data-driven insights that allow stakeholders to reduce risks, validate sustainability claims, and advance industry-wide goals of transparency, responsibility, and circularity.

Environmental & Social Assessment Tools

These tools measure impacts such as greenhouse gas emissions, water consumption, chemical use, and waste generation, enabling companies to identify hotspots and implement resource-efficient practices. They also assess labor conditions, workplace safety, wages, and ethical compliance, ensuring fair treatment of workers and alignment with international labor standards. By providing reliable and comparable data, these tools promote transparency, reduce the risk of greenwashing, and support informed decision-making for brands, regulators, and consumers alike.

Higg Index (Sustainable Apparel Coalition -SAC)

In response to these challenges, particularly following high-profile incidents like the 2013 Rana Plaza collapse, a suite of sustainability tools has emerged to measure, mitigate, and improve environmental and social impacts (Chowdhury, 2017). At the forefront is the Higg Index, developed by the Sustainable Apparel Coalition (SAC), which serves as a foundational framework for holistic assessments (Chong, 2022). Key modules include the Higg Materials Sustainability Index (MSI), which evaluates material impacts on water, energy, and chemistry; the Facility Environmental Module (FEM), focusing on factory-level assessments; the Brand & Retail Module (BRM), for corporate strategy evaluation; and the Product Module, for item-specific footprints (Svensson, 2020; Shamsuzzaman et al., 2023; (Palomo-Lovinski, 2024). In Higg FEM, Seven impact areas are assessed (energy, water, wastewater, air emissions, chemicals, waste, EMS). Each section contributes equally (14.3%) to the overall score. If a section does not apply, its weight is redistributed across others. The Higg FEM scoring system is designed to drive behavior change within apparel and footwear facilities. Points are awarded only for "Yes" or "Partial Yes" responses to questions that reflect actions, decisions, and practices leading to improved environmental sustainability outcomes. In other words, to earn points, facilities must demonstrate that they are actively engaging in measurable practices rather than simply acknowledging intent. In the Higg FEM framework, progression follows a tiered structure. If a facility has not implemented Level 1 practices, meaning it cannot answer "Yes" or "Partial Yes" to all scored Level 1 questions, it is not permitted to advance to Level 2 or Level 3 practices. This design ensures that facilities first demonstrate compliance with fundamental sustainability requirements before adopting more advanced or leading practices. In doing so, the system promotes a step-by-step improvement process, ensuring consistency and credibility in sustainability performance (Cascale Inc. 2024).

However, limitations persist, such as reliance on self-reporting, which can introduce inconsistencies, and the need for third-party verification to combat greenwashing. Recent developments in 2025 include expanded data analytics features, enabling predictive modeling for sustainability risks, making it a pivotal tool for aligning with global regulations like the EU's Corporate Sustainability Reporting Directive.

Life Cycle Assessment (LCA) Tools

Life Cycle Assessment (LCA) tools are essential for quantifying the environmental impacts of apparel from cradle-to-grave, encompassing raw material extraction, production, use, and disposal. These methodologies help measure metrics like carbon footprint, water consumption, and resource depletion, providing data-driven insights for sustainable design (Roy Choudhury, 2014).

a) **GaBi,** developed by Sphera, is a proprietary LCA software built on over 20,000 annually updated datasets from its Managed LCA Content database. It enables detailed modeling of impacts such as carbon emissions and water use in apparel supply chains, with flexible simulations for scenario analysis (Murphy, 2025). In fashion, GaBi integrates with tools like the Higg Index for comprehensive evaluations (Varon, 2025). Benefits include high reliability for regulatory compliance, though its cost can limit accessibility for smaller brands.

b) **SimaPro,** available in versions like Craft (for individuals) and Synergy (for enterprises), offers good LCA capabilities with integration of databases such as ecoinvent v3.11 (Li et al., 2025). It supports multi-impact assessments, including eutrophication and toxicity relevant to textile dyeing processes (Costa et al., 2021). Benefits includes scientific accuracy and versatility, aiding strategic sustainability transitions, while limitations involve a learning curve for beginners.

c) **OpenLCA,** a free open-source tool from GreenDelta, facilitates professional modeling with a broad range of impact categories and databases (Gonçalves et al., 2024). Its modular design allows customization for apparel assessments, such as evaluating recycled polyester versus virgin materials. It promotes transparency through shareable models and low ownership costs, which makes it ideal for small-to-medium enterprises in fashion, though it requires technical expertise for complex analyses.

Chemical Management Tools

Chemical management tools address the apparel industry's heavy reliance on hazardous substances, promoting safer alternatives and reducing pollution from processes like dyeing and finishing.

a) **The Bluesign System** focuses on eliminating harmful chemicals while enhancing resource efficiency and production safety. The certification process involves supply chain audits, benefiting worker health and ecosystem protection, though high implementation barriers exist for smaller suppliers (Pant & Kanchi, 2024).

b) **OEKO-TEX Standard 100 tests** final products for harmful substances, ensuring chemical safety with globally standardized criteria, while STeP certifies sustainable production processes (Popescu, 2024). These tools cover over 100 parameters, including banned azo dyes and heavy metals common in apparel (Rovira et al., 2025). Benefits include consumer trust and regulatory compliance.

c) **ZDHC Gateway Tools,** part of the Roadmap to Zero Programme, include the Manufacturing Restricted Substances List (MRSL), Wastewater Guidelines, and Chemical Gateway (Pant & Kanchi, 2024). Limitations include dependency on supplier participation.

Carbon, Climate & Energy Tools

These tools standardize greenhouse gas (GHG) accounting and target-setting to combat climate change in apparel's emission-heavy supply chains.

a) **The Science Based Targets initiative (SBTi)** for Fashion guides brands in setting emissions reductions aligned with the Paris Agreement's 1.5C pathway (Negro, 2025). As per one study, over 8,600 companies have committed globally, including apparel firms benefiting from innovation and reputation gains (Marini et al., 2024). As of 2025, expansions include sector-specific guidance, though fashion-specific committed lists are not detailed.
b) **CDP** (Carbon Disclosure Project) serves as a reporting platform for carbon, water, and supply chain risks, scoring over 22,700 companies in 2024 on an D- to A scale (Sultanoğlu, 2025; Net0, 2024).
c) **The GHG (Greenhouse Gas) Protocol** provides internationally recognized standards for measuring and reporting greenhouse gas emissions across businesses, including detailed methods for value chain analysis through its Scope 3 standard. Scope 3 covers indirect emissions that occur across a company's value chain but are not owned or controlled by the company itself, such as those from the production of purchased goods, transportation, and waste disposal (Majamäki, 2022).

Social & Labor Assessment Tools

Social tools ensure fair labor practices, addressing issues like wages and safety in garment factories.

a) **Fair Wear Foundation (FWF)** tools focus on labor rights through audits and Brand Performance Checks, promoting living wages and safe conditions (Dreismann, 2020).
b) **The Social & Labor Convergence Program (SLCP)** uses the Converged Assessment Framework (CAF) for standardized data collection, reducing audit duplication. This is a detailed questionnaire used by facilities to self-assess or jointly assess social and labor conditions, covering areas such as wages, working hours, health and safety, freedom of association, and nondiscrimination. SLCP does not replace certification or existing codes but provides compatible data that brands can score or align with their own codes of conduct, facilitating integration into varied compliance frameworks (Alam et al., 2021).
c) **Sedex/SMETA audits** cover labor, health/safety, environment, and ethics, used by many companies. Companies engage collaboratively in working groups that address a range of social compliance topics, including audit non-conformances, wages and working hours, joint remediation efforts, worker feedback mechanisms, and issues related to forced labor (Bayer et al., 2018).
d) **SA8000** certifies against child labor, discrimination, and excessive hours. Documentation such as timecards and payroll records are reviewed to verify

adherence, especially during peak production periods when overtime tends to increase (Sarna, 2023).

Circularity & Transparency Tools

These tools promote closed-loop systems and verifiable claims in apparel.

Global Recycled Standard (GRS) and Recycled Claim Standard (RCS) track recycled content with chain-of-custody verification, essential for sustainable textiles. GRS is an international, voluntary, product-specific standard that requires at least 50% recycled content in a product to qualify for certification. It also includes additional social and environmental criteria related to chemical use, water management, energy consumption, and workers' rights during production. RCS focuses solely on tracking recycled material content and claims but lacks the social and environmental process requirements embedded in GRS. It typically certifies products with lower thresholds or mix blends of recycled and virgin materials (Amutha, 2016; Athalye, 2022).

Cradle to Cradle Certified assesses products on safety, circularity, and impact, with levels from Basic to Platinum. Products must be recertified every three years with evidence of measurable progress toward higher certification levels, ensuring ongoing commitment to sustainability (Bach et al., 2018; Minkov et al., 2018).

Textile Exchange Standards are globally recognized certifications that focus on ensuring the sustainability and responsible sourcing of raw materials in the textile and apparel industry. Three key standards administered by Textile Exchange include the Organic Content Standard (OCS), Responsible Wool Standard (RWS), and Responsible Down Standard (RDS), all designed to certify sustainable raw materials with verified traceability and environmental and social best practices. They improve consumer confidence by allowing brands to demonstrate genuine sustainability commitment (Blum, 2021; Naikwadi, 2024).

ISO 14040-44 guides LCA principles, ensuring credible assessments, with applications in apparel for standardized impact evaluations. Applying ISO 14040-44 standards allows companies to perform standardized and comparable LCAs of apparel products, assessing impacts such as water use, carbon emissions, chemical use, and end-of-life footprint (Manzardo & Cavalli, 2024).

ECO-TRACKING PLATFORMS AND SOFTWARE SOLUTIONS

In today's context of growing environmental accountability, eco-tracking platforms have become essential for industries aiming to reduce their ecological footprint. In the fashion sector, known for resource-heavy supply chains, high water use, and carbon emissions, these tools help brands track and improve sustainability across product lifecycles. Using technologies such as artificial intelligence (AI), blockchain, and data analytics, they enhance transparency, efficiency, and compliance with global regulations like the EU Green Deal and the Corporate Sustainability Reporting Directive (CSRD).

AI algorithms analyze large datasets to predict and reduce environmental risks, while blockchain provides secure, transparent records that prevent greenwashing and build stakeholder trust. Data analytics combines information from multiple sources to generate insights, such as identifying areas with high carbon emissions or water use. These tools often connect with Life Cycle Assessment (LCA) software, automating processes that were previously time-consuming. This integration minimizes errors, speeds up assessments, and improves accuracy by using real-time data from IoT devices and supply chain partners.

Key Eco-Tracking Platforms

Various platforms support eco-tracking by offering complete visibility across supply chains. These solutions track environmental metrics while also supporting circular practices, ethical compliance, and real-time decision-making. The following are three notable examples:

Eon CircularID™

Eon CircularID™ is a blockchain-based system designed for the fashion and retail industries, giving products unique digital identities to support lifecycle tracking and circular economy practices. Created by EON, a leader in product digitization, it provides "Digital IDs" that serve as detailed passports for garments, containing information on materials, authenticity, production history, and post-consumer options like resale, repair, or recycling. By standardizing data through the Circular Product ID Data Protocol, Eon enables smooth communication among brands, consumers, and recyclers (Ying & Mok, 2023; Iseal, 2025).

Key features include blockchain-secured data immutability, which prevents tampering and ensures verifiable sustainability claims. For instance, brands can embed QR codes or NFC tags on products, allowing customers to scan and access detailed environmental impact histories, such as carbon footprint or ethical sourcing details (Berg et al., 2022; Iseal, 2025). This fosters transparency and boosts resale value in secondary markets, aligning with circular services. In practice, clients like H&M have used Eon to digitize thousands of products, reducing waste by enabling efficient sorting for recycling and extending product lifespans (Alatalo & Ekelund, 2021). The platform's integration with IoT and AI further allows real-time tracking of logistics, minimizing emissions from transportation. However, challenges such as initial implementation costs and the need for supply chain partner buy-in persist, though Eon's scalable model mitigates these through phased rollouts (Iseal, 2025). Luxury labels like Gabriela Hearst and Yoox Net-a-Porter have also adopted this technology, reporting an increase in resale value through enhanced product traceability (Chrimes, 2024). By digitizing garments, Eon helps brands unlock new post-purchase revenue streams and supports consumers in making informed, eco-conscious choices.

Provenance

Provenance uses blockchain technology to build transparent supply chain maps, helping brands verify claims about materials, ethics, and sustainability (Azevedo et al., 2023). Focused on consumer-packaged goods (CPG) and retail, including fashion, it provides digital passports that confirm product authenticity and origin. Unlike traditional tracking systems, Provenance prioritizes validating sustainability claims throughout the customer journey, using blockchain to securely record data from farm to shelf (Provenance Team, 2023).

Core features include supply chain visualization tools that allow brands to showcase ethical sourcing, such as fair labor practices or organic materials, via scannable codes on product labels. Provenance's platform reduces administrative burdens by automating audits and reporting, enabling brands to build consumer trust through verifiable narratives. For fashion brands, this means tracing textiles back to sustainable farms or recycled sources, combating issues like counterfeit eco-labels. Despite its strengths, scalability in complex global supply chains remains a hurdle which can be addressed by Provenance's modular design that allows incremental adoption. Designers like Martina Spetlova use Provenance to give consumers direct access to verified supply chain data via scannable labels (Buck, 2022).

Blockchain for Supply Chain

Blockchain for Supply Chain combines blockchain, IoT, and AI to deliver end-to-end traceability with real-time sustainability data across industries, including fashion. As a permissioned blockchain, it enables secure data sharing, giving access only to authorized partners while maintaining a tamper-proof record of transactions (Aditya et al., 2024). Additional benefits include cost savings through streamlined operations and greater resilience against disruptions, demonstrated in IBM's work with Walmart to improve supply chain visibility (Pham, 2018).

INTERACTIVE CONSUMER INTERFACES FOR PROMOTING SUSTAINABLE FASHION

Interactive consumer interfaces can play a crucial role in connecting backend eco-tracking systems with end-users, promoting sustainable fashion. They will allow consumers to access and engage with sustainability data, supporting informed choices and ethical consumption. By linking with platforms like Eon CircularID™ and Provenance, these interfaces convert complex data into intuitive, user-friendly experiences. Common forms can include web dashboards and mobile apps, each offering distinct ways to visualize and interact with eco-metrics such as carbon footprints, material origins, and product lifecycle impacts. Leading examples include:

Good On You, an app that evaluates thousands of fashion brands on environmental, labor, and animal welfare criteria, assigning scores and alternatives to encourage ethical shopping. Users can access detailed reports on various brand's sustainability ratings.

Depop is another example. It is a resale app which promotes circular fashion by tracking second-hand purchases' carbon savings.

Wardrobe-tracking apps like Whering and 30Wears allow users to digitize closets, monitor wear counts, and calculate cost-per-wear, discouraging fast fashion by highlighting underutilized items.

SPECIALIZED LCA SOFTWARE FOR FASHION

The real strength of eco-tracking platforms lies in their integration with LCA software, which measures environmental impacts throughout a product's lifecycle. This connection automates data collection from blockchain records or AI analytics, feeding LCA models to produce detailed reports on metrics such as greenhouse gas emissions, water use, and biodiversity impacts. By minimizing manual input, these integrations improve accuracy, reduce human error, and allow assessments at portfolio scale, enabling brands to compare variants by color, size, or supplier. For example, data from platforms like Eon or Provenance can directly update LCA tools in real time as supply chains change.

Ecochain

Ecochain offers LCA automation software for product and portfolio footprinting, specializing in manufacturing sectors like fashion. Its tools, including Mobius for single-product assessments and Helix for bulk analyses, calculate impacts from cradle-to-grave using verifiable methodologies. Features like ecodesign modules identify hotspots in materials or processes, while user-friendly interfaces democratize LCA for non-experts (Ecochain, n.d.) .

Carbonfact

Carbonfact is a fashion-specific platform for carbon accounting and LCA, automating cradle-to-grave assessments for entire catalogs Real-time dashboards, product analytics, and scenario analysis enable companies to systematically monitor progress toward carbon reduction targets, model the potential outcomes of product-level modifications, and examine detailed environmental performance data. Incorporating carbon accounting for Scope 1, 2, and 3 emissions offers a comprehensive assessment of an organization's total carbon footprint, thereby facilitating data-driven decision-making and the development of more effective sustainability strategies (Carbonfact, n.d.).

GreenStitch

GreenStitch provides AI-powered LCA for apparel and textiles, tracking full lifecycles from raw materials to disposal. The platform enables granular tracking of Scope 1, 2, and 3 emissions, modeling of product-level LCAs, generation of ESG reports, and strategic decarbonization planning. It also supports the creation of Digital Product Passports and performance benchmarking, ensuring full alignment with regulatory and reporting frameworks such as Business Responsibility and Sustainability Reporting (BRSR), Corporate Sustainability Reporting Directive (CSRD), Ecodesign for Sustainable Products Regulation (ESPR), and the Science Based Targets initiative (SBTi) (GreenStitch, n.d.).

Glimpact

Glimpact uses the Product Environmental Footprint (PEF) method, developed under the European Commission, to assess products across 16 environmental impact categories, including climate change, water and resource depletion, land use, pollution, and toxicity. This method evaluates every stage of a product's lifecycle from raw materials to end-of-life and consolidates the results into a single, clear environmental score for objective comparison (Glimpact, n.d.).

These platforms help reduce environmental impacts by optimizing processes, while challenges such as data inter-operability are being tackled through standards like the Circular Product Data Protocol. As more brands adopt these solutions, the fashion industry moves closer to a circular model that supports both environmental sustainability and economic rowth.

AI INTEGRATION IN SMART LABELS: ECO-TRACKING AND IMPACT ON CONSUMER BEHAVIOUR

AI enhances sustainability in fashion by converting data from smart labels such as RFID or IoT-enabled tags into actionable insights. These labels track key factors like material composition, transportation routes, energy consumption, and end-of-life disposal. Hyperspectral imaging with AI enhances fabric identification, allowing precise calculations of carbon emissions, water usage, and waste generation (Li et al., 2019). Machine learning models analyze variables such as raw material sourcing, dyeing, and logistics to estimate environmental impacts and suggest interventions for greater efficiency (Yılmaz et al., 2024). Smart labels transmit this data through protocols like Sigfox or Wirepas for real-time monitoring (Figueiredo e Silva et al., 2018). Cloud-based AI platforms then process the information, generating instant dashboards for stakeholders (Neupane, 2024). This enables faster decision-making on emissions, water management, and recyclability while enhancing compliance and reporting accuracy.

Personalized Consumer Engagement

AI can personalize sustainability by offering usage analytics, predictive maintenance, and reuse recommendations. AI can track wear patterns and purchase history to calculate metrics like cost-per-wear and cumulative carbon footprint, promoting mindful consumption. Machine learning forecasts repair needs by analyzing material durability and usage, helping extend garment lifecycles (Priyadarshanie, 2024). Algorithms can suggest resale or upcycling options, supporting circular practices and reducing waste. These features, integrated into mobile apps and wearables can make sustainability interactive through notifications, AR try-ons, and real-time impact tracking. This seamless integration can create a connected ecosystem, enhancing consumer awareness and sustainable decision-making. Examples of AI applications include:

a) Chatbots for answering sustainability-related questions (Swanberg & Narmashiri, 2025).
b) Image recognition for sorting textiles during recycling (Karmali & Valilai, 2025).
c) Smart wardrobes suggesting eco-friendly outfit combinations (Vaidya et al., 2023).

Consumer Behavior and Psychological Impact

Despite growing interest in sustainable fashion, a gap remains between consumer intentions and actions due to habits, limited knowledge, and psychological distance from environmental impacts. AI and smart labels can help bridge this gap by providing personalized education, verifiable sourcing data, and real-time environmental tracking (Omisola et al., 2023). Gamified eco-tracking tools engage consumers with rewards and milestones, encouraging consistent sustainable behaviors (Heidari & Hosseinalibeiki, 2025). By combining psychological strategies with AI-driven interventions, brands can foster loyalty while advancing circular fashion systems.

INDUSTRY INTEGRATION: CASE STUDIES

Leading brands and startups are pioneering innovative solutions that bridge the gap between sustainability commitments and tangible action, demonstrating how technology can drive circularity and responsible consumption.

Stella McCartney x Google Cloud: Environmental Impact Mapping

In 2019, Stella McCartney partnered with Google Cloud to pilot a machine learning tool that maps the environmental impact of raw materials such as cotton and viscose. The system analyzes complex data sets on water scarcity, air pollution, and biodiversity, providing actionable insights for sustainable sourcing decisions. This collaboration exemplifies how data-driven mapping and AI-powered analytics can standardize risk assessments, ultimately guiding the entire fashion industry toward smarter, more sustainable sourcing practices (Candeloro, 2020).

H&M Conscious Line: Digital Care Labels and Product Passports

H&M has embedded QR-enabled digital care labels into its Conscious Collection, transforming garments into interactive product passports. These labels provide detailed information about sustainable materials, recycling options, and garment care tips designed to extend product lifespans (Jæger & Myrold, 2023). The initiative aligns with emerging regulatory requirements, such as France's AGEC law, and has expanded to include men's essentials. When scanned, consumers can access transparent supply chain stories and circular services. This model demonstrates how smart labeling can both educate consumers and encourage sustainable behavior at scale (EON, n.d.).

Nike: RFID for Authentication and Recycling Take-Back Programs

Nike integrates RFID technology into its footwear and apparel to authenticate products and combat counterfeiting while powering circular initiatives. Through its Reuse-A-Shoe program, RFID tags ensure full traceability, tracking products from drop-off to recycling or repurposing into Nike Grind material (Emon & Khan, 2025). Pilot programs in select stores have successfully diverted millions of pounds of waste from landfills. Moreover, RFID's unique identifiers (UIDs) have reduced supply chain losses, demonstrating how authentication technologies can be seamlessly integrated with take-back and refurbishment systems, creating a closed-loop model that supports both sustainability and operational efficiency. However, Nike currently focuses primarily on downcycling and operates within linear production chains. As a result, significant opportunities to reduce environmental impacts remain unaddressed. To unlock this potential, the company must adopt a more comprehensive closed-loop production model, emphasizing recycling, reuse, and circular design principles (Curtis & Hansson, 2019).

ADVANTAGES OF AI ADOPTION FOR ECO-TRACKING

The adoption of AI-driven tools, smart labels, and eco-tracking systems benefits both retailers and consumers by fostering a more transparent and circular fashion ecosystem.

Enhanced Traceability

Smart labels offer end-to-end visibility, enabling retailers to accurately manage inventory and reduce shrinkage through RFID tracking. For consumers, these labels provide clear insights into ethical sourcing, leading to greater confidence and loyalty.

Circular Economy Participation

Consumers can access care guides, recycling information, and repair services directly through digital tags, helping to extend garment lifespans. This approach democratizes participation in the circular economy while creating new revenue opportunities for retailers.

Stronger Post-Purchase Engagement

Digital product passports open the door to personalized interactions, such as care reminders, resale prompts, and sustainability updates. This drives an increase in customer engagement, giving retailers valuable data-driven insights while empowering consumers to make informed, eco-friendly decisions throughout the garment's lifecycle.

CHALLENGES AND LIMITATIONS OF AI ADOPTION FOR ECO-TRACKING

Privacy and Data Security

Handling large volumes of user and operational data raises risks of breaches, unauthorized access, and compromised trust.AI models need strong encryption and regulatory compliance, especially when using sensitive personal or supply chain data. Poorly designed or governed AI systems can accidentally leak information or perpetuate algorithmic bias.

Standardization and Interoperability

Lack of industry-wide standards prevents seamless integration of AI systems across brands and platforms. Proprietary formats and divergent data protocols make cross-system communication difficult and increase development costs. Additionally, current absence of global regulatory frameworks leads to further fragmentation and reduced effectiveness.

Economic and Technological Barriers for Small Business

High costs of AI software, hardware, skilled labor, and ongoing maintenance put small businesses at a disadvantage. Integrating AI with outdated legacy systems is complex and expensive, leading to inefficiencies. Additionally, small businesses often lack in-house AI expertise and face challenges in recruiting or training specialized talent.

Data Quality, Management, and Bias

Effective AI requires high-quality, diverse, and unbiased data, which many fashion brands struggle to obtain and maintain. When training data is skewed, it can lead to algorithmic bias, resulting in discriminatory outcomes and harm to a brand's reputation. Data collection is particularly challenging in the fashion industry due to fragmented supply chains and limited digital infrastructure.

Greenwashing and Consumer Skepticism

AI-generated sustainability claims may sometimes be exaggerated or difficult to verify, which can lead to "greenwashing" and a loss of consumer trust. More than 55% of global consumers are skeptical of such claims and increasingly demand transparency and third-party audits. Brands face significant reputational risks if their AI-based statements about environmental impact or supply chain ethics cannot be fully proven.

Skills, Creativity, and Workforce Impact

There is a shortage of AI-trained professionals who also understand the specific needs of the fashion industry, creating a significant talent gap. Resistance to change among traditional designers and business leaders further slows digital transformation. Additionally, there are concerns that AI could undermine creativity or lead to homogenized styles, resulting in a loss of human touch and design diversity.

Operational and Technical Barriers

Implementation often requires comprehensive and costly upgrades to infrastructure, including cloud systems, connectivity, and cybersecurity. Integrating AI with supply chain systems is especially challenging because of data silos and complex stakeholder networks. Furthermore, the rapid evolution of AI technology demands continuous investment to keep solutions up to date and competitive.

Transparency, Accountability, and Legal Issues

Many AI algorithms operate as "black boxes," making it difficult to ensure accountability and to detect or correct biases. AI-generated creative work also raises ambiguities in intellectual property, copyright, and trademark laws. Additionally, the absence of clear regulatory guidelines and transparency standards limits responsible innovation and makes compliance more challenging.

Societal and Cultural Concerns

Automation through AI can disproportionately impact low-skilled workers and marginalized groups, potentially widening the digital divide. The globalization of AI-driven fashion may also threaten cultural uniqueness and heritage, raising concerns about diversity and representation. Addressing these interconnected challenges requires coordinated action from industry leaders, policymakers, and technologists to ensure that AI is integrated into fashion and sustainability in an ethical, equitable, and effective way.

FUTURE OUTLOOK AND INNOVATIONS

The fashion industry stands at a pivotal crossroads, where technological advancements and Regulatory policies like the EU's Digital Product Passport (DPP) initiative, combined with innovations in AI, blockchain, and digital standards, are reshaping fashion through mandatory transparency, traceability, and circularity.

Policy and Regulations

The EU's DPP initiative, part of the Ecodesign for Sustainable Products Regulation, will require all apparel and footwear sold in the EU to have a digital record by 2030. This record must include details about materials, manufacturing, carbon footprint, repairability, and recyclability, accessible through QR codes, RFID, or NFC tags. Brands like H&M and Zara are piloting DPPs, often using blockchain to secure and verify data, making sustainability claims tamper-proof and ensuring compliance. Standards like GS1 and ISO can enable seamless global integration of these systems across supply chains.

AI and Blockchain Integration and Circular Fashion

Blockchain ensures accurate, unalterable data about sourcing, water use, and carbon emissions. AI can analyze this data to detect problems, prevent fraud, and optimize processes. Together, AI and blockchain support automated recycling and take-back systems, with sorting robots and predictive logistics enabling closed-loop recycling. Thanks to DPPs every garment will have a digital twin powered by AI and blockchain, tracking its entire journey from production to renewal. DPPs centralize data across a garment's life cycle, making it easier to meet regulations and support recycling, repair, and resale. However, implementing these systems will require overcoming challenges such as high costs, data accuracy, staff training, and managing compliance across different regions. AI-driven marketplaces will match pre-loved clothing with buyers, creating efficient circular systems.Continuous data feedback will guide production based on consumption trends and sustainability results, leading to zero-waste, adaptive fashion models.

CONCLUSION

The fashion industry is changing rapidly to address its environmental, social, and economic challenges. Smart labels and eco-tracking tools, powered by AI, are creating new ways to improve transparency, accountability, and circularity in global supply chains. These technologies go beyond traditional labels by giving garments digital records of their origin, production methods, and environmental impact. By using RFID, NFC, QR codes, blockchain, and AI, brands can track products from raw materials to end-of-life. This helps ensure authenticity, reduce greenwashing, and give consumers reliable information to make ethical choices. Leading brands like Stella McCartney, Nike, and H&M are already using these tools to connect sustainability goals with real action. However, many challenges still remain, including cost, standardization, privacy, and data sharing. Solving these issues will require cooperation between policymakers, industry leaders, and tech innovators to create fair and consistent systems for all, including smaller brands and developing regions. In the future, AI and blockchain, supported by initiatives like the EU's Digital Product Passport, will transform how fashion works. Each garment could have a digital twin, enabling authenticated resale, recycling, and better resource management. Ultimately, smart labels and eco-tracking are not just tech upgrades; they are dri vers of systemic change. By adopting them, the fashion industry can reduce its environmental impact, encourage responsible production, and promote conscious consumer behavior, moving toward a more sustainable and transparent future.

REFERENCES

Aakanksha, L., & Aravendan, M. (2023). Impacts of transparency and traceability on fashion supply chain system. *Intelligent Information Management, 15*(3), 100–119. DOI: 10.4236/iim.2023.153006

Aditya, K., Chakraborty, S., Dahire, A., Kumari, A., & Milanova, M. (2024). Integrating Blockchain, IoT, and AI in Supply Chain Management. In *Blockchain, IoT, and AI Technologies for Supply Chain Management: Apply Emerging Technologies to Address and Improve Supply Chain Management* (pp. 237–264). Apress. DOI: 10.1007/979-8-8688-0315-4_9

Alam, A. M. U., Öhler, W., Bundgaard, J., Faruquee, M., Vang, J., & Hasle, P. (2021). The Market for social compliance audits in Bangladesh: On the edge of a paradigm shift?.

Alatalo, A., & Ekelund, E. (2021). Industry 4.0 as an Enabler of Circular Business Models: Within the clothing industry.

Alhainen, N., & Järvinen, J. (2015). Measuring sustainability: Balanced scorecard approach to Higg Index.

Amutha, K. (2016). Sustainable practices in textile industry: standards and certificates. In *Sustainability in the textile industry* (pp. 79–107). Springer Singapore.

Amutha, K. (2017). Sustainable chemical management and zero discharges. In *Sustainable fibres and textiles* (pp. 347–366). Woodhead Publishing. DOI: 10.1016/B978-0-08-102041-8.00012-3

Athalye, A. (2022). Evolutions in Green Chemistry and Sustainable Economy. Textile Dyes and Pigments: A Green Chemistry Approach, 421-441.

Azevedo, P., Gomes, J., & Romão, M. (2023). Supply chain traceability using blockchain. *Operations Management Research : Advancing Practice Through Research, 16*(3), 1359–1381. DOI: 10.1007/s12063-023-00359-y

Bach, V., Minkov, N., & Finkbeiner, M. (2018). Assessing the ability of the Cradle to Cradle Certified™ Products Program to reliably determine the environmental performance of products. *Sustainability (Basel), 10*(5), 1562. DOI: 10.3390/su10051562

Bayer, C. N., Margherita, M., Vogel, G., & Xu, J. (2018). GLOBAL GOVERNANCE–Compliance and Conformance with UK MSA and Good Practice in Human Rights: FTSE 100 and Real Estate 100.

Berg, H., Kulinna, R., Stöcker, C., Guth-Orlowski, S., Thiermann, R., & Porepp, N. (2022). *Overcoming information asymmetry in the plastics value chain with digital product passports: how decentralised identifiers and verifiable credentials can enable a circular economy for plastics* (Vol. 197). Wuppertal Institut für Klima, Umwelt, Energie.

Blibech, O., & Fezzani, W. E. (2024). NFC Cards Technology for a Non-print Campus Project: Prototyping a Transition Towards Environmental Sustainability. In *Business Sustainability with Artificial Intelligence (AI): Challenges and Opportunities* (Vol. 2, pp. 139–152). Springer Nature Switzerland.

Blum, P. (2021). Circular fashion: Making the fashion industry sustainable. Hachette UK.

Buck, L. (2022). *Products with Provenance: Developing a sense of place in product design education.* The Design Society.

Buckulcikova, D., Motta, D., Cornuz, A., & Brasser, S. (2022). The future of fashion. ROBECO The Investment Engineers, 2-46.

Candeloro, D. (2020). Towards sustainable fashion: the role of artificial intelligence---H&M, Stella McCartney, Farfetch, Moosejaw: A multiple case study. *ZoneModa Journal, 10*(2), 91–105.

Carbonfact. (n.d.). Carbon Management Platform built for fashion and footwear brands. Retrieved from https://www.carbonfact.com/carbon-management-platform

Cascale Inc. (2024). Higg Facility Environmental Module (Higg FEM): How to Higg Guide 2024 – January 15, 2025 [PDF]. Retrieved from HowToHigg: Higg FEM Guide website

Chong, C. S. (2022). An investigation of Higg Index evaluation towards the sustainable development of apparel industry in Bangladesh/Chong Chen Seng (Doctoral dissertation, Universiti Malaya).

Chowdhury, R. (2017). The Rana Plaza disaster and the complicit behavior of elite NGOs. *Organization, 24*(6), 938–949. DOI: 10.1177/1350508417699023

Chrimes, C. (2024). The Role of Blockchain in Facilitating the Transition to a Circular Economy: A Critical Review of Current Applications in the Fashion Industry. The Palgrave Handbook of Sustainability in Fashion, 347-369.

Costa, A. F., Aragao, J. V., Duarte, A. D., Macedo, J. S., Galdino, C. J.Jr, Milanez, V. F., & Sarubbo, L. A. (2021). Analysis of the environmental life cycle of dyeing in textiles. *Chemical Engineering Transactions, 86*, 727–732.

Cura, K., Sheenam, J., & Niinimäki, K. (2022). Transparency and traceability in the textile value chain.

Curtis, A., & Hansson, A. (2019). Examining the viability of corporate recycling initiatives and their overall environmental impact: The case of nike grind and the reuse-a-shoe program. *Case Studies in the Environment, 3*(1), 1–7. DOI: 10.1525/cse.2019.001974

Das, D. (2024, September). RFID is crazy underrated tech [Post]. LinkedIn. Retrieved from https://www.linkedin.com

Dreismann, J. K. (2020). Employment quality in supply chains of circular fashion-a comparison of standards and practices of circular fashion enterprises & social sustainability targeting apparel players (Master's thesis).

Dymkov, A. (2024). RFID technologies: Analysis of current status and development. *Synchroinfo Journal, 10*(5), 33–41. DOI: 10.36724/2664-066X-2024-10-5-33-41

EarthDay.org. (2025, January 22). Broken Threads & Twisted Yarns: Legislating the reform of fashion. EarthDay.org. Retrieved from https://www.earthday.org/press-release/earth-day-org-releases-first-of-its-kind-fast-fashion-legislation-report/

Ecochain. (n.d.). Mobius – product footprint software. Ecochain. Retrieved from https://ecochain.com/mobius/

Emon, M. M. H., & Khan, T. (2025). The Rise of Circular Supply Chains: Recycling and Closed-Loop Systems Could Mitigate Inflationary Pressures. In Supply Chain Disruptions and Impact on Global Inflation (pp. 195-226). IGI Global Scientific Publishing.

EON. (n.d.). H&M | Case study: Digital IDs powered by EON. EON. Retrieved [access date], from https://www.eon.xyz/clients/h-m

Fernández-Caramés, T. M., & Fraga-Lamas, P. (2018). A review on human-centered IoT-connected smart labels for the industry 4.0. *IEEE Access : Practical Innovations, Open Solutions, 6*, 25939–25957. DOI: 10.1109/ACCESS.2018.2833501

Figueiredo e Silva, P., Kaseva, V., & Lohan, E. S. (2018). Wireless positioning in IoT: A look at current and future trends. *Sensors (Basel), 18*(8), 2470. DOI: 10.3390/s18082470 PMID: 30061535

Frith, J. (2024). *A billion little pieces: RFID and infrastructures of identification.* Mit Press.

Glimpact. (n.d.). Glimpact: Measure your global environmental footprint. Retrieved from https://www.glimpact.com/

Gonçalves, A., Baêta, M., Nagy, M., & Silva, C. (2024). Looking for environmental scoring: A case study of a Portuguese cotton white T-shirt made with recycled Fiber. *Sustainability (Basel)*, *16*(14), 5896. DOI: 10.3390/su16145896

GreenStitch. (n.d.). Why GreenStitch- Your partner in fashion sustainability. Retrieved from https://greenstitch.io/why-greenstitch/

Heidari, M., & Hosseinalibeiki, H. (2025). Tokenized Incentives and Loyalty: Leveraging Blockchain-Based Smart Contracts for Enhancing Eco-Tourism Behavioral Engagement.

Horvath, M. (2024, January 9). Global surge: 71% increase in online searches for sustainable goods reflects growing consumer commitment to eco-friendly choices. More Gratitude. https://more-gratitude.com/blog/global-surge-increase-in-online-searches-for-sustaible-goods/

Iseal, S. (2025). Leveraging AI for Life Cycle Assessment in Fashion: A Sustainable Future.

Jæger, B., & Myrold, S. (2023, September). Textile industry circular supply chains and digital product passports. Two case studies. In IFIP International Conference on Advances in Production Management Systems (pp. 350-363). Cham: Springer Nature Switzerland.

James, P. A. K., & Dutta, S. (2025). Luxury without limits: The rise of demi-fine jewellery through social media technology. Journal of Information Technology Teaching Cases, 20438869251360356.

Karmali, I. M., & Valilai, O. F. (2025). Exploring the Role of Artificial Intelligence for Pattern Recognition of Textile Sorting and Recycling for Circular Economy. *Procedia Computer Science*, *253*, 346–356. DOI: 10.1016/j.procs.2025.01.097

Khabbaz, B. G. (2010). Life cycle energy use and greenhouse gas emissions of Australian cotton: Impact of farming systems (Doctoral dissertation, University of Southern Queensland).

Khanna, G. B. (2008). Textile Industry Polluting Sector in Varied Forms.

Lanzer, L. (2025). The future of sustainable supply chain management: blockchain and smart contracts in the fashion industry-a case study of a european denim brand.

Legardeur, J., & Ospital, P. (2024). Digital product passport for the textile sector (Doctoral dissertation, Parlement Européen).

Li, J., Meng, X., Wang, W., & Xin, B. (2019). A novel hyperspectral imaging and modeling method for the component identification of woven fabrics. *Textile Research Journal, 89*(18), 3752–3767. DOI: 10.1177/0040517518821907

Li, J. L., Minds, S., & Hammer, K. (2025). Life cycle assessment (lca) of isolatek international passive fire protection products.

Majamäki, T. (2022). Understanding the importance of Scope 3 Upstream emissions in the textile industry value chain: a case study of a Finnish textile company.

Manzardo, A., & Cavalli, M. (2024) Development and Application of an Integrated Life Cycle Assessment and Multi-Criteria Decision-Making Model to Support Sustainable Solutions in the Fashion Industry: The Case of Fashion Art.

Marini, M., Pigosso, D. C., Pieroni, M., & McAloone, T. C. (2024). To what extent are circular economy strategies accounted in science-based targets for carbon emission reduction? *Computers & Industrial Engineering, 197*, 110594. DOI: 10.1016/j.cie.2024.110594

McDowell, M. (2021, June 29). The tech shaking up fashion's inventory load. Vogue Business. Retrieved from https://www.voguebusiness.com/technology/the-tech-shaking-up-fashions-inventory-load

Montoya-Torres, J. R., Gutierrez-Franco, E., & Blanco, E. E. (2015). Conceptual framework for measuring carbon footprint in supply chains. *Production Planning and Control, 26*(4), 265–279. DOI: 10.1080/09537287.2014.894215

Murphy, G. (2025). Transforming green waste into black gold: a life cycle assessment of biochar production from municipal waste.

Muthukumarana, T. T., Karunathilake, H. P., Punchihewa, H. K. G., Manthilake, M. M. I. D., & Hewage, K. N. (2018). Life cycle environmental impacts of the apparel industry in Sri Lanka: Analysis of the energy sources. *Journal of Cleaner Production, 172*, 1346–1357. DOI: 10.1016/j.jclepro.2017.10.261

Naikwadi, S. (2024). Role of Governments and Consumers. In *Climate Action Through Eco-Friendly Textiles* (pp. 163–178). Springer Nature Singapore. DOI: 10.1007/978-981-99-9856-2_11

Net0. (2024, February 28). Carbon Disclosure Project (CDP) reporting: Facts to get you started. Net0. Retrieved from https://net0.com/blog/cdp-reporting/

Negro, G. D. (2025). Bridging Methodologies for Sustainability: A Review of Environmental Assessment Frameworks.

Neupane, B. (2024). Artificial Intelligence and Big Data Technologies to Optimize Government Decision-Making Processes in Cloud-Based Environments. *Journal of Artificial Intelligence and Machine Learning in Cloud Computing Systems*, *8*(11), 1–12.

Omisola, J. O., Bihani, D., Daraojimba, A. I., Osho, G. O., Ubamadu, B. C., & Etukudoh, E. A. (2023). Blockchain in supply chain transparency: A conceptual framework for real-time data tracking and reporting using blockchain and AI. International Journal of Multidisciplinary Research and Growth Evaluation, 4.

Ozturkcan, S., & Kitapci, O. (2025). A sustainable solution for the hospitality industry: The QR code menus. *Journal of Information Technology Teaching Cases*, *15*(1), 2–7. DOI: 10.1177/20438869231181599

Palomo-Lovinski, N. (2024). Missed opportunities: Fashion fabric sourcing professionals' use of the MSI in the Higg Index. *Fashion Practice*, *16*(3), 373–390. DOI: 10.1080/17569370.2024.2312925

Pant, P., & Kanchi, G. (2024). Sustainability standards for textile processing. In *Sustainable Textile Chemical Processing* (pp. 415–464). CRC Press.

Pham, H. (2018). The impact of Blockchain Technology on the improvement of Food Supply Chain Management: Transparency and Traceability: A case study of Walmart and Atria.

Popescu, A. (2024). Enhancing environmental standards in textiles: The role of OEKO-TEX® standard 100. *Bulletin of the Transilvania University of Brasov. Series V, Economic Sciences*, •••, 59–68. DOI: 10.31926/but.es.2024.17.66.1.6

Precedence Research. (2025, July 16). Smart labels market accelerates in 2025: Sustainability and e-commerce drive demand globally [Press release]. GlobeNewswire. Retrieved from https://www.globenewswire.com/news-release/2025/07/16/3116563/0/en/Smart-Labels-Market-Accelerates-in-2025-Sustainability-and-E-Commerce-Drive-Demand-Globally.html

Priyadarshanie, E. A. A. (2024). Predicting garment quality based on fabric characteristics via machine learning.

Provenance Team. (2015, September 21; updated 2023, December 19). Blockchain: the solution for transparency in product supply chains. Provenance. Retrieved from https://www.provenance.org/news-insights/blockchain-the-solution-for-transparency-in-product-supply-chains

Robinson, P. K. (2009). Responsible retailing: Regulating fair and ethical trade. Journal of International Development. *The Journal of the Development Studies Association, 21*(7), 1015–1026.

Rovira, J., Souza, M. C. O., Nadal, M., & Domingo, J. L. (2025). Human health risks from textile chemicals: A critical review of recent evidence (2019–2025). *Journal of Environmental Science and Health. Part A, Toxic/Hazardous Substances & Environmental Engineering, 60*(2), 1–13. DOI: 10.1080/10934529.2025.2514406 PMID: 40482050

Roy Choudhury, A. K. (2014). Environmental impacts of the textile industry and its assessment through life cycle assessment. In *Roadmap to sustainable textiles and clothing: environmental and social aspects of textiles and clothing supply chain* (pp. 1–39). Springer Singapore. DOI: 10.1007/978-981-287-110-7_1

Sala, S., & Goralczyk, M. (2013). Chemical footprint: A methodological framework for bridging life cycle assessment and planetary boundaries for chemical pollution. *Integrated Environmental Assessment and Management, 9*(4), 623–632. DOI: 10.1002/ieam.1471 PMID: 23907984

Sarna, N. H. (2023). Building Seats at the Table: The Use of Worker-Driven Social Responsibility Agreements to Address Forced Labor in the Global Value Chain. *J. Int'l Bus. & L., 23*, 62.

Schmidt Rivera, X. C., Balcombe, P., & Niero, M. (2021). Life cycle assessment as a metric for circular economy.

Shamsuzzaman, M., Islam, M. M., Hasan, H. R. U., Khan, A. M., & Sayem, A. S. M. (2023). Mapping environmental sustainability of knitted textile production facilities. *Journal of Cleaner Production, 405*, 136900. DOI: 10.1016/j.jclepro.2023.136900

Subramaniam, R., Azzuhri, D. S. R., & Wah, D. T. Y. A Review on Combating Counterfeiting by Empowering Consumers Via Nfc Enabled Mobile Computing Leveraging on Blockchain Technology. Available at *SSRN* 5012178. DOI: 10.2139/ssrn.5012178

Sultanoğlu, B. (2025) global and local developments in sustainability reporting: key changes and trends. In viii. International symposium on accounting and finance symposuim proceeding book (p. 1).

Svensson, V. (2020). The apparel industry's environmental impact, mitigation and adaptation to climate change: A case study of three Swedish companies.

Swanberg, E., & Narmashiri, M. (2025). A Factual Sustainability Chatbot: Leveraging Natural Language Understanding and Embedding Models for Reliable Q&A.

Textile World. (2024, November 18). KOLAB Collection launches NFC (Near Field Communication)-tagged sustainable clothing line. Textile World. Retrieved from https://www.textileworld.com/textile-world/knitting-apparel/2024/11/kolab-collection-launches-nfc-near-field-communication-tagged-sustainable-clothing-line/

Uluer, M. U., Gök, G., Ünver, H. Ö., & Kılıç, S. E. (2012). Towards a Decision Support Framework for Sustainable Manufacturing. In *Sustainable Manufacturing: Shaping Global Value Creation* (pp. 83–88). Springer Berlin Heidelberg. DOI: 10.1007/978-3-642-27290-5_12

United Nations. (2019, March 25). UN launches drive to highlight environmental cost of staying fashionable. UN News. Retrieved from https://news.un.org/en/story/2019/03/1035161

Vaidya, C. P., Kulkarni, N., Kulkarni, R., Singh, P., & Singh, A. P. (2023, April). Smart wardrobe: A deep learning model. In 2023 1st International Conference on Cognitive Computing and Engineering Education (ICCCEE) (pp. 1-4). IEEE. DOI: 10.1109/ICCCEE55951.2023.10424541

Varon, L. M. S. (2025). Longevity extension of textile apparel based on strategies of ecodesign, circular economy and value chain traceability (Doctoral dissertation, Kauno technologijos universitetas.).

Vidakis, K., Mavrogiorgou, A., Kiourtis, A., & Kyriazis, D. (2020, June). A comparative study of short-range wireless communication technologies for health information exchange. In 2020 International conference on electrical, communication, and computer engineering (ICECCE) (pp. 1-6). IEEE. DOI: 10.1109/ICECCE49384.2020.9179478

World Bank. (2019, September 23). How much do our wardrobes cost to the environment? World Bank. Retrieved from World Bank website World Bank

Yılmaz, K., Aksu, İ. Ö., Göçken, M., & Demirdelen, T. (2024). Sustainable textile manufacturing with revolutionizing textile dyeing: Deep learning-based, for energy efficiency and environmental-impact reduction, pioneering green practices for a sustainable future. *Sustainability (Basel)*, *16*(18), 8152. DOI: 10.3390/su16188152

Ying, N. S., & Mok, P. Y. (2023). A Review of Blockchain Technology for Sustainable Fashion. Digital Fashion Innovations, 179-204.

Yong, A., Rana, M. E., & Shanmugam, K. (2022, March). Improved shopping experience through RFID based smart shopping system. In *2022 International Conference on Decision Aid Sciences and Applications (DASA)* (pp. 635-644). IEEE. DOI: 10.1109/DASA54658.2022.9765064

Compilation of References

Aakanksha, L., & Aravendan, M. (2023). Impacts of transparency and traceability on fashion supply chain system. *Intelligent Information Management*, *15*(3), 100–119. DOI: 10.4236/iim.2023.153006

Aakash, V. B., Akmal, A., Chandrababu, A., & Vijay, A. (2024). A Comprehensive Survey on AI-Driven Fashion Technologies: Clothing Detection, Recommendation Systems, and Virtual Try-On Solutions. *International Journal of Advances in Engineering and Management*, *2024*(11), 6. DOI: 10.35629/5252-0611247252

Abd Ali, H. N. (2024). Advancements in Natural Language Processing: Towards Human-Like Understanding and Generation of Text by AI. *BIOS: Jurnal Informatika dan Sains, 2*(02), 129-139.

Abrardi, L., Cambini, C., & Rondi, L. (2022). Artificial intelligence, firms and consumer behavior: A survey. *Journal of Economic Surveys*, *36*(4), 969–991. DOI: 10.1111/joes.12455

Accenture. (2025). *Technology Vision 2025: Reinventing retail with AI.* Accenture Research. https://www.accenture.com

Acciai, E., & Perez-Bou, S. (2025). Exploring the role of digital product passports for supply chain traceability in the "Made in Italy" textile sector. *Asia Pacific Journal of Marketing and Logistics*, 1–17. Advance online publication. DOI: 10.1108/APJML-03-2025-0371

Acquisti, A., Taylor, C., & Wagman, L. (2020). The Economics of Privacy. *Journal of Economic Literature*, *54*(2), 442–492. https://www.aeaweb.org/articles?id=10.1257/jel.54.2.442. DOI: 10.1257/jel.54.2.442

Adamkiewicz, J., Kochańska, E., Adamkiewicz, I., & Łukasik, R. M. (2022a). Greenwashing and sustainable fashion industry. *Current Opinion in Green and Sustainable Chemistry*, *38*, 100710. DOI: 10.1016/j.cogsc.2022.100710

Adam, M., Diebel, C., Goutier, M., & Benlian, A. (2024). Navigating autonomy and control in human-AI delegation: User responses to technology- versus user-invoked task allocation. *Decision Support Systems, 180*, 114193. DOI: 10.1016/j.dss.2024.114193

Adanyin, A. (2024). Ethical AI in Retail: Consumer Privacy and Fairness. *European Journal of Computer Science and Information Technology, 12*(7), 21–35. DOI: 10.37745/ejcsit.2013/vol12n72135

Aditya, K., Chakraborty, S., Dahire, A., Kumari, A., & Milanova, M. (2024). Integrating Blockchain, IoT, and AI in Supply Chain Management. In *Blockchain, IoT, and AI Technologies for Supply Chain Management: Apply Emerging Technologies to Address and Improve Supply Chain Management* (pp. 237–264). Apress. DOI: 10.1007/979-8-8688-0315-4_9

Agapiou, A. (2024). A systematic review of the socio-legal dimensions of responsible AI and its role in improving health and safety in construction. *Buildings (Basel, Switzerland), 14*(5), 1469. DOI: 10.3390/buildings14051469

Aghbari, A. I. (2025, October 03). S., Mohammed, A., Zubairu, N., & Rahman, N. S. F. A. (2025). Exploring the social and environmental performance in fast-fashion supply chains: A comparative analysis between MNCs and SMEs. *International Journal of Productivity and Performance Management, 74*(8), 2932–2958. Advance online publication. DOI: 10.1108/IJPPM-05-2024-0342

Agrawal, G. (2024). Accountability, trust, and transparency in AI systems from the public policy perspective: Elevating ethical standards. In *AI healthcare applications and security, ethical, and legal considerations* (pp. 148–162). IGI Global. DOI: 10.4018/979-8-3693-7452-8.ch009

Ajzen, I. (1991). The theory of planned behavior. *Organizational Behavior and Human Decision Processes, 50*(2), 179–211. DOI: 10.1016/0749-5978(91)90020-T

Akbar, Z., & Tohar, K. (2021). Fundamental movement skills and sensory movement strategies to support online learning in early childhood. *Journal of Physical Education and Sport, 21*, 2364–2371.

Akpobome, O. (2024). The impact of emerging technologies on legal frameworks: A model for adaptive regulation. *International Journal of Research Publication and Reviews, 5*(10), 5046–5060. DOI: 10.55248/gengpi.5.1024.3012

Akram, S. V., Malik, P. K., Singh, R., Gehlot, A., Juyal, A., Ghafoor, K. Z., & Shrestha, S. (2022). Implementation of Digitalized Technologies for Fashion Industry 4.0: Opportunities and Challenges. *Scientific Programming*, *2022*, 1–17. DOI: 10.1155/2022/7523246

Alabaddi, Z., Obidat, A., & Alziyadat, Z. (2023). Exploring the effect of blockchain technology on supply chain resilience and transparency: Evidence from the healthcare industry. *Uncertain Supply Chain Management*, *11*(2), 787–798. DOI: 10.5267/j.uscm.2023.1.001

Alam, A. M. U., Öhler, W., Bundgaard, J., Faruquee, M., Vang, J., & Hasle, P. (2021). The Market for social compliance audits in Bangladesh: On the edge of a paradigm shift?.

Alatalo, A., & Ekelund, E. (2021). Industry 4.0 as an Enabler of Circular Business Models: Within the clothing industry.

Albustanji, R. N., Alkhatib, A., & Shaheen, A. (2025, May). Technical and Ethical Strategies to Prevent Machine Learning Models from Exploiting Personally Identifiable Information (PII). In *2025, the 12th International Conference on Information Technology (ICIT)* (pp. 253-257). IEEE.

Alhainen, N., & Järvinen, J. (2015). Measuring sustainability: Balanced scorecard approach to Higg Index.

Ali, A. (2025). *Influence of Perceived Uniqueness on Purchase Intention in a Virtual Try-on Store* (Master's thesis, Itä-Suomen yliopisto).

Alkaoud, M. (2024). A bilingual benchmark for evaluating large language models. *PeerJ. Computer Science*, *10*, e1893. DOI: 10.7717/peerj-cs.1893

Allahverdiyev, K. (2025). Leveraging AI for Enhancing Sustainable Marketing and Consumer Experience in E-Commerce. *Journal of Emerging Trends in Marketing and Management*, *1*(1), 49–59.

Allcott, H. (2011). Social norms and energy conservation. *Journal of Public Economics*, *95*(9–10), 1082–1095. DOI: 10.1016/j.jpubeco.2011.03.003

Allioui, H., & Mourdi, Y. (2023). Exploring the full potential of IoT for better financial growth and stability: A comprehensive survey. *Sensors (Basel)*, *23*(19), 8015. DOI: 10.3390/s23198015

Al-Olfi, S. A. A., Song, Y., & Al-Hajj, Y. M. (2025). The Impact of Sustainable Supply Chain Strategies on E-Commerce Consumer Purchasing Behavior: Considering the Moderating Effect of Big Data Analytics. *Journal of the Knowledge Economy*, •••, 1–36. DOI: 10.1007/s13132-025-02671-3

Alves, G., Jannach, D., de Souza, R. F., Damian, D., & Manzato, M. G. (2024). Digitally nudging users to explore off-profile recommendations: Here be dragons. *User Modeling and User-Adapted Interaction*, *34*(2), 441–481. DOI: 10.1007/s11257-023-09378-7

Amutha, K. (2016). Sustainable practices in textile industry: standards and certificates. In *Sustainability in the textile industry* (pp. 79–107). Springer Singapore.

Amutha, K. (2017). Sustainable chemical management and zero discharges. In *Sustainable fibres and textiles* (pp. 347–366). Woodhead Publishing. DOI: 10.1016/B978-0-08-102041-8.00012-3

Ananny, M., & Crawford, K. (2018). Seeing Without Knowing: Limitations of the Transparency Ideal and Its Application to Algorithmic Accountability. *New Media & Society*, *20*(3), 973–989. DOI: 10.1177/1461444816676645

André, J. A. (2024). *Ai-Driven Personalization in Fast Fashion and Its Implications for Consumer Behavior and Sustainability* (Master's thesis, ISCTE-Instituto Universitario de Lisboa (Portugal)).

Antil, H., Löhner, R., & Price, R. (2022). *NINNs: Nudging induced neural networks* (arXiv:2203.07947). arXiv. https://arxiv.org/abs/2203.07947

Apriliani, L. (2025). Hypernudging in the digital era: Exploring the impact and ethical considerations of advanced behavioral interventions. *UPY Business and Management Journal*, *4*(2), 200–215. Advance online publication. DOI: 10.31316/ubmj.v4i2.7947

Arantes, L., & Sousa, B. (2021). Digital Marketing and Tourism : Case Study Applied to Barcelos. *2021 16th Iberian Conference on Information Systems and Technologies (CISTI)*, 1–6. DOI: 10.23919/CISTI52073.2021.9476556

Arantes, L. (2022). *Sustainable Digital Marketing*., DOI: 10.4018/978-1-6684-5523-4.ch004

Arantes, L., & Barbosa Costa, S. (2025). Culture and Sustainability in the Luxury Market: An Analysis of Adaptive Practices in Global Contexts. *Journal of International Consumer Marketing*, *37*(4), 301–315. DOI: 10.1080/08961530.2024.2434814

Arantes, L., & Ferreira, J. J. (2025). Innovative Sustainability Strategies and the Role of Digital Transformation in Organisations. *Corporate Social Responsibility and Environmental Management*, *32*(3), 3088–3121. DOI: 10.1002/csr.3123

Ariely, D., & Wertenbroch, K. (2002). Procrastination, deadlines, and performance: Self-control by precommitment. *Psychological Science*, *13*(3), 219–224. DOI: 10.1111/1467-9280.00441 PMID: 12009041

Armstrong, C. M. J., & Park, H. (2020). Online clothing resale: A practice theory approach to evaluate sustainable consumption gains. *Journal of Sustainability Research*, *2*(1), 17. Advance online publication. DOI: 10.20900/jsr20200017

Asghar, M. (2023). Consumer perception of Nike green business strategy and implementation of profitable and sustainable products.

Ashuro, T., Kant, S., & Adula, M. (2025). Multi-Stakeholder Collaboration Effect on Sustainable Supply Chain Optimization by Mediation of Vendor Managed Inventory in the Horn of Africa. In *Multi-Stakeholder Collaboration for Sustainable Supply Chain* (pp. 203–224). IGI Global Scientific Publishing. DOI: 10.4018/979-8-3693-8925-6.ch009

Assaker, G., & O'Connor, P. (2023). The importance of green certification labels/badges in online hotel booking choice: A conjoint investigation of consumers' preferences pre- and post-COVID-19. *Cornell Hospitality Quarterly*, *64*(4), 401–414. DOI: 10.1177/19389655231184474

Ates, G. C., Mohan, P., & Celik, E. (2023). Dual cross-attention for medical image segmentation. *Engineering Applications of Artificial Intelligence*, *126*, 107139. DOI: 10.1016/j.engappai.2023.107139

Athalye, A. (2022). Evolutions in Green Chemistry and Sustainable Economy. Textile Dyes and Pigments: A Green Chemistry Approach, 421-441.

Ayabe, S., Otomo, T., Kera, H., & Kawamoto, K. (2025). Robustness evaluation of offline reinforcement learning for robot control against action perturbations. *International Journal of Advanced Robotic Systems*, *22*(4), 17298806251360454. Advance online publication. DOI: 10.1177/17298806251360454

Aydin, G. (2025). Status or sustainability, can we have both, please? Decoding the factors shaping eco-friendly fashion buying. *Journal of Fashion Marketing and Management*, *29*(3), 434–458. DOI: 10.1108/JFMM-02-2024-0061

Azevedo, P., Gomes, J., & Romão, M. (2023). Supply chain traceability using blockchain. *Operations Management Research : Advancing Practice Through Research*, *16*(3), 1359–1381. DOI: 10.1007/s12063-023-00359-y

Bach, V., Minkov, N., & Finkbeiner, M. (2018). Assessing the ability of the Cradle to Cradle Certified™ Products Program to reliably determine the environmental performance of products. *Sustainability (Basel), 10*(5), 1562. DOI: 10.3390/su10051562

Badhwar, A., Islam, S., Tan, C. S. L., & Payne, A. (2025). A comparative review of Australia's fashion and textile industry and global climate perspectives across five decades (1970s–2020s). *Global Sustainability, 8*, e41. DOI: 10.1017/sus.2025.10030

Bai, Y., Jones, A., Ndousse, K., Askell, A., Chen, A., DasSarma, N., . . . Kaplan, J. (2022). Training a helpful and harmless assistant with reinforcement learning from human feedback. *arXiv preprint arXiv:2204.05862.*

Bailey, K., Basu, A., & Sharma, S. (2022a). The Environmental Impacts of Fast Fashion on Water Quality: A Systematic Review. *Water (Basel), 14*(7), 1073. DOI: 10.3390/w14071073

Baker, C. (2024). *Obsolete: How change brands are changing the world.* Bloomsbury Publishing. DOI: 10.5040/9781399416634

Bamberg, S., & Möser, G. (2007). Twenty years after Hines, Hungerford and Tomera: A new meta-analysis of psycho-social determinants of pro-environmental behaviour. *Journal of Environmental Psychology, 27*(1), 14–25. DOI: 10.1016/j.jenvp.2006.12.002

Banerjee, S., Agarwal, A., & Singh, E. (2024). The Vulnerability of Language Model Benchmarks: Do They Accurately Reflect True LLM Performance? *arXiv preprint arXiv:2412.03597.*

Bang, H., & Su, J. (2022). Who uses virtual wardrobes? Investigating the role of consumer traits in the intention to adopt virtual wardrobes. *Sustainability (Basel), 14*(3), 1209. DOI: 10.3390/su14031209

Bankins, S., & Formosa, P. (2023). The Ethical Implications of Artificial Intelligence (AI) For Meaningful Work. *Journal of Business Ethics, 185*(4), 725–740. DOI: 10.1007/s10551-023-05339-7

BARBOSA, B. K. D. S. (2024). LLMs as tools for evaluating textual coherence: a comparative analysis.

Bashynska, I. (2023). AI-driven personalization in advertising: Transforming consumer engagement through sustainability and circular economy. *Scientific Journal of Bielsko-Biala School of Finance and Law, 27*(4), 106–112.

Basirulla, M. D., & Tasnim, F. (2023). Nature of Human Rights Violation on Female Garments Workers in Bangladesh. *Khazanah Hukum*, *5*(1), 1–17. DOI: 10.15575/kh.v5i1.22713

Bayer, C. N., Margherita, M., Vogel, G., & Xu, J. (2018). GLOBAL GOVERNANCE–Compliance and Conformance with UK MSA and Good Practice in Human Rights: FTSE 100 and Real Estate 100.

Baylor, D.. (2017). TFX: A TensorFlow-based production-scale machine learning platform. In *Proceedings of the 23rd ACM SIGKDD International Conference on Knowledge Discovery and Data Mining* (pp. 1387–1395). DOI: 10.1145/3097983.3098021

Bebis, G., & Georgiopoulos, M. (1994). Feed-forward neural networks. *IEEE Potentials*, *13*(4), 27–31. DOI: 10.1109/45.329294

Belen'kii, L. I., Gazieva, G. A., Evdokimenkova, Y. B., & Soboleva, N. O. (2024). *The literature of heterocyclic chemistry, Part XXI, 2021* (pp. 139–226). DOI: 10.1016/bs.aihch.2023.09.001

Bengio, Y., Ducharme, R., Vincent, P., & Jauvin, C. (2003). A neural probabilistic language model. *Journal of Machine Learning Research*, *3*(Feb), 1137–1155.

Berestova, A., Kim, D.-Y., & Kim, S.-Y. (2022). Consumers' Active Reaction to Brands Taking Stands on Public Issues on Twitter. *Sustainability (Basel)*, *14*(1), 567. DOI: 10.3390/su14010567

Berg, H., Kulinna, R., Stöcker, C., Guth-Orlowski, S., Thiermann, R., & Porepp, N. (2022). *Overcoming information asymmetry in the plastics value chain with digital product passports: how decentralised identifiers and verifiable credentials can enable a circular economy for plastics* (Vol. 197). Wuppertal Institut für Klima, Umwelt, Energie.

Bhagat, C. (2024). Greenwashing vs. genuine efforts: The role of transparent communication in building corporate credibility. *Journal of Jurivox*, *1*(2), 51–62.

Bhattacharya, P., Prasad, V. K., Verma, A., Gupta, D., Sapsomboon, A., Viriyasitavat, W., & Dhiman, G. (2024). Demystifying ChatGPT: An in-depth survey of OpenAI's robust large language models. *Archives of Computational Methods in Engineering*, *31*(8), 4557–4600. DOI: 10.1007/s11831-024-10115-5

Bicchieri, C., & Dimant, E. (2022). Nudging with care: The risks and benefits of social information. *Public Choice*, *191*(3-4), 443–464. DOI: 10.1007/s11127-019-00684-6

Biega, A. J., Gummadi, K. P., & Weikum, G. (2018). Equity of attention: Amortizing individual fairness in rankings. In *Proceedings of the 41st International ACM SIGIR Conference on Research & Development in Information Retrieval* (SIGIR '18) (pp. 405–414). Association for Computing Machinery. https://doi.org/DOI: 10.1145/3209978.3210063

Blair, D. C., & Maron, M. E. (1985). An evaluation of retrieval effectiveness for a full-text document-retrieval system. *Communications of the ACM, 28*(3), 289–299. DOI: 10.1145/3166.3197

Blazquez, M. (2024). The Metaverse and its potential for digital sustainability in fashion. *Journal of Global Fashion Marketing, 15*(3), 303–319. DOI: 10.1080/20932685.2024.2339236

Blibech, O., & Fezzani, W. E. (2024). NFC Cards Technology for a Non-print Campus Project: Prototyping a Transition Towards Environmental Sustainability. In *Business Sustainability with Artificial Intelligence (AI): Challenges and Opportunities* (Vol. 2, pp. 139–152). Springer Nature Switzerland.

Blum, P. (2021). Circular fashion: Making the fashion industry sustainable. Hachette UK.

Bollinger, B., Gillingham, K. T., & Wight, K. G. (2023). Making prosocial social: The effectiveness of social proof for energy conservation using social media. *Journal of the Association for Consumer Research, 8*(3), 290–300. DOI: 10.1086/725031

Boussen, S., Denis, J. B., Simeone, P., Lagier, D., Bruder, N., & Velly, L. (2023). ChatGPT and the stochastic parrot: Artificial intelligence in medical research. *British Journal of Anaesthesia, 131*(4), e120–e121. DOI: 10.1016/j.bja.2023.06.065

Brolin, S., & Lundgren, I. (2024). Return handling practices and strategies: Towards sustainable e-commerce in the fashion and electronics industries.

Brown, P. F., Cocke, J., Della Pietra, S. A., Della Pietra, V. J., Jelinek, F., Mercer, R. L., & Roossin, P. (1988). A statistical approach to language translation. In *Coling Budapest 1988* Volume 1*: International Conference on Computational Linguistics.*

Buck, L. (2022). *Products with Provenance: Developing a sense of place in product design education.* The Design Society.

Buckulcikova, D., Motta, D., Cornuz, A., & Brasser, S. (2022). The future of fashion. ROBECO The Investment Engineers, 2-46.

Bulchand-Gidumal, J., William Secin, E., O'Connor, P., & Buhalis, D. (2024). Artificial intelligence's impact on hospitality and tourism marketing: Exploring key themes and addressing challenges. *Current Issues in Tourism*, *27*(14), 2345–2362. DOI: 10.1080/13683500.2023.2229480

Burnstine, A. (2025). The Role of Artificial Intelligence in Transforming Physical and Online Fashion Retail: Enhancing Experiences, Driving Sustainability, and Fostering Innovation. *International Journal of Business and Management*, *20*(2), 144. DOI: 10.5539/ijbm.v20n2p144

Candeloro, D. (2020). Towards sustainable fashion: the role of artificial intelligence--H&M, Stella McCartney, Farfetch, Moosejaw: A multiple case study. *ZoneModa Journal*, *10*(2), 91–105.

Canhoto, A. I., Keegan, B. J., & Ryzhikh, M. (2024a). Snakes and Ladders: Unpacking the Personalisation-Privacy Paradox in the Context of AI-Enabled Personalisation in the Physical Retail Environment. *Information Systems Frontiers*, *26*(3), 1005–1024. DOI: 10.1007/s10796-023-10369-7 PMID: 36684411

Canlas, I. P., Plecerda, L. P., Panit, N. M., Sereno, R. M., & Gamez, A. L. (2025). Differential effect of environmental sustainability beliefs and norms on green consumption and energy conservation behaviors among pre-service teachers. *Human Ecology: an Interdisciplinary Journal*, *53*(3), 581–596. Advance online publication. DOI: 10.1007/s10745-025-00608-7

Cao, Y. S., Wang, W. Z., Zhang, Y. J., Deveci, M., Kadry, S., & Wang, L. M. (2025). Analyzing adoption factors of data-driven nudging for e-commerce platforms using an integrated decision model. *Electronic Commerce Research and Applications*, *71*, 101500. DOI: 10.1016/j.elerap.2025.101500

Capasso, M., Guidetti, M., Bianchi, M., Cavazza, N., & Caso, D. (2025). Enhancing intentions to reduce meat consumption: An experiment comparing the role of self- and social pro-environmental identities. *Journal of Environmental Psychology*, *101*, 102494. DOI: 10.1016/j.jenvp.2024.102494

Caraban, A., Karapanos, E., Gonçalves, D., & Campos, P. F. (2019). 23 ways to nudge: A review of technology-mediated nudging in human–computer interaction. In *Proceedings of the 2019 CHI Conference on Human Factors in Computing Systems* (Paper No. 373). Association for Computing Machinery. https://doi.org/DOI: 10.1145/3290605.3300733

Carbonfact. (n.d.). Carbon Management Platform built for fashion and footwear brands. Retrieved from https://www.carbonfact.com/carbon-management-platform

Carlson, E., Farhat, A., Martinez, V. R., & Victor, C. (2024). *On the infinite-nudging limit of the nudging filter for continuous data assimilation* (arXiv preprint). https://arxiv.org/abs/2408.02646

Carrera-Rivera, A., Larrinaga, F., & Lasa, G. (2022). Context-awareness for the design of Smart-product service systems: Literature review. *Computers in Industry, 142*, 103730. DOI: 10.1016/j.compind.2022.103730

Cascale Inc. (2024). Higg Facility Environmental Module (Higg FEM): How to Higg Guide 2024 – January 15, 2025 [PDF]. Retrieved from HowToHigg: Higg FEM Guide website

Casciani, D., Chkanikova, O., & Pal, R. (2022). Exploring the nature of digital transformation in the fashion industry: opportunities for supply chains, business models, and sustainability-oriented innovations. Sustainability: Science. *Sustainability, 18*(1), 773–795. DOI: 10.1080/15487733.2022.2125640

Casper, S., Davies, X., Shi, C., Gilbert, T. K., Scheurer, J., Rando, J., . . . Hadfield-Menell, D. (2023). Open problems and fundamental limitations of reinforcement learning from human feedback. *arXiv preprint arXiv:2307.15217.*

Chang, K., Gidwani, M., Patel, J. B., Li, M. D., & Kalpathy-Cramer, J. (2021). Data Curation Challenges for Artificial Intelligence. In *Auto-Segmentation for Radiation Oncology* (pp. 201–216). CRC Press. DOI: 10.1201/9780429323782-17

Chang, Y. W., & Hsu, Y. (2022). The factors that affect members' use of a beauty industry matchmaking platform: Validation of the COM-B extended model. *Frontiers in Psychology, 13*, 976109. DOI: 10.3389/fpsyg.2022.976109 PMID: 36300047

Chang, Y., Wang, X., Wang, J., Wu, Y., Yang, L., Zhu, K., Chen, H., Yi, X., Wang, C., Wang, Y., Ye, W., Zhang, Y., Chang, Y., Yu, P. S., Yang, Q., & Xie, X. (2024). A survey on evaluation of large language models. *ACM Transactions on Intelligent Systems and Technology, 15*(3), 1–45. DOI: 10.1145/3641289

Che, F., Zhou, Y., & Liu, Y. (2022). Social quality, knowledge hiding, and community capacity: A study on multi-ethnic communities in Chinese cities. *Journal of Business Research, 144*, 1024–1038. DOI: 10.1016/j.jbusres.2022.02.041

Chen, L., Wang, Z., Ren, S., Li, L., Zhao, H., Li, Y., . . . Chang, B. (2024). Next token prediction towards multimodal intelligence: A comprehensive survey. *arXiv preprint arXiv:2412.18619.*

Chen, H., Liu, X., Yin, D., & Tang, J. (2017). A survey on dialogue systems: Recent advances and new frontiers. *SIGKDD Explorations, 19*(2), 25–35. DOI: 10.1145/3166054.3166058

Chen, L., Chen, P., & Lin, Z. (2020). Artificial Intelligence in Education: A Review. *IEEE Access : Practical Innovations, Open Solutions, 8*, 75264–75278. DOI: 10.1109/ACCESS.2020.2988510

Chen, X., Wang, X., & Qu, Y. (2023). Constructing Ethical AI Based on the "Human-in-the-Loop" System. *Systems, 11*(11), 548. DOI: 10.3390/systems11110548

Chen, Z., Xu, L., Zheng, H., Chen, L., Tolba, A., Zhao, L., Yu, K., & Feng, H. (2024). Evolution and Prospects of Foundation Models: From Large Language Models to Large Multimodal Models. *Computers, Materials & Continua, 80*(2), 1753–1808. DOI: 10.32604/cmc.2024.052618

Chkirbene, Z., Hamila, R., Gouissem, A., & Devrim, U. (2024, December). Large language models (llm) in industry: A survey of applications, challenges, and trends. In *2024 IEEE 21st International Conference on Smart Communities: Improving Quality of Life using AI, Robotics and IoT (HONET)* (pp. 229-234). IEEE.

Choi, K. H. (2022). 3D dynamic fashion design development using digital technology and its potential in online platforms. *Fashion and Textiles, 9*(1), 9. DOI: 10.1186/s40691-021-00286-1

Chong, C. S. (2022). An investigation of Higg Index evaluation towards the sustainable development of apparel industry in Bangladesh/Chong Chen Seng (Doctoral dissertation, Universiti Malaya).

Choufan, L. (2022). Fashion you do not own, fashion you cannot feel: Toward a new paradigm of sharing fashion in the digital age. *Fashion Theory, 26*(3), 307–328. DOI: 10.1080/1362704X.2021.1912954

Chowdhury, R. (2017). The Rana Plaza disaster and the complicit behavior of elite NGOs. *Organization, 24*(6), 938–949. DOI: 10.1177/1350508417699023

Chrimes, C. (2024). The Role of Blockchain in Facilitating the Transition to a Circular Economy: A Critical Review of Current Applications in the Fashion Industry. The Palgrave Handbook of Sustainability in Fashion, 347-369.

Cialdini, R. B. (2003). Crafting normative messages to protect the environment. *Current Directions in Psychological Science, 12*(4), 105–109. DOI: 10.1111/1467-8721.01242

Cialdini, R. B., Demaine, L. J., Sagarin, B. J., Barrett, D. W., Rhoads, K., & Winter, P. L. (2006). Managing social norms for persuasive impact. *Social Influence, 1*(1), 3–15. DOI: 10.1080/15534510500181459

Clune, J. (2019). AI-GAs: AI-generating algorithms, an alternate paradigm for producing general artificial intelligence. *arXiv preprint arXiv:1905.10985*.

Coeckelbergh, M. (2025). LLMs, truth, and democracy: An overview of risks. *Science and Engineering Ethics, 31*(1), 4. DOI: 10.1007/s11948-025-00529-0

Copeland, L. (2024). Exploring young consumers' perceptions towards sustainable practices of fashion brands. *Fashion, Style & Popular Culture, 11*(3), 527–553. DOI: 10.1386/fspc_00125

Corea, F. (2017). *Artificial intelligence and exponential technologies: Business models evolution and new investment opportunities*. Springer.

Cortazar, L. O., Cachón-Rodríguez, G., Nebreda, L. P., & Medrano, M. L. (2025). Motivational dimensions of slow fashion to promote environmentally and socially sustainable consumption in the fashion industry. *Journal of Fashion Marketing and Management, 29*(5), 761–780. DOI: 10.1108/JFMM-07-2023-0184

Cossatin, A. G., Mauro, N., & Ardissono, L. (2024). Promoting green fashion consumption through digital nudges in recommender systems. *IEEE Access : Practical Innovations, Open Solutions, 12*, 6812–6829. DOI: 10.1109/ACCESS.2024.3349710

Costa, A. F., Aragao, J. V., Duarte, A. D., Macedo, J. S., Galdino, C. J.Jr, Milanez, V. F., & Sarubbo, L. A. (2021). Analysis of the environmental life cycle of dyeing in textiles. *Chemical Engineering Transactions, 86*, 727–732.

Course, L. L. M. (2021). Algorithms and Legal Challenges: An Analysis of Specific Issues from the Viewpoint of Law and Economics.

Covington, P., Adams, J., & Sargin, E. (2016). Deep neural networks for YouTube recommendations. In *Proceedings of the 10th ACM Conference on Recommender Systems* (pp. 191–198). https://doi.org/DOI: 10.1145/2959100.2959190

Cunha, M. N. (2025). Transforming Online Retail: The impact of augmented and virtual reality on consumer engagement and experience in e-commerce in the context of the Sustainable Development Goals (SDG). *Journal of Lifestyle and SDGs Review, 5*(3), e4816–e4816. DOI: 10.47172/2965-730X.SDGsReview.v5.n03.pe04816

Cura, K., Sheenam, J., & Niinimäki, K. (2022). Transparency and traceability in the textile value chain.

Curtis, A., & Hansson, A. (2019). Examining the viability of corporate recycling initiatives and their overall environmental impact: The case of nike grind and the reuse-a-shoe program. *Case Studies in the Environment, 3*(1), 1–7. DOI: 10.1525/cse.2019.001974

Cutinha, Z. P., & Mokshagundam, D. S. (2024). Sustainability practices in E-commerce: Opportunities and challenges for digital marketers. *International Journal of Research Publication and Reviews*, *5*(2), 1068–1075. DOI: 10.55248/gengpi.5.0224.0435

Dahiya, V. K., Dahiya, R., Dev, R., Sharma, A., Sharma, A., Kiran, P. B. N., Yadav, P. S., & Yadav, S. (2024). Exploring the Role of Artificial Intelligence in Predictive Analytics for Financial Markets. In 2024 International Conference on Computing, Sciences and Communications (ICCSC) (pp. 1–5). 2024 International Conference on Computing, Sciences and Communications (ICCSC). IEEE. https://doi.org/DOI: 10.1109/ICCSC62048.2024.10830442

Das, D. (2024, September). RFID is crazy underrated tech [Post]. LinkedIn. Retrieved from https://www.linkedin.com

Das, S., Barve, A., Sahu, N. C., & Muduli, K. (2023). Enabling artificial intelligence for sustainable food grain supply chains: An agri 5.0 and circular economy perspective. *Operations Management Research : Advancing Practice Through Research*, *16*(4), 2104–2124. DOI: 10.1007/s12063-023-00390-z

Datta, J., Rabbi, R., Saha, P., Zereen, A. N., Abdullah-Al-Wadud, M., & Uddin, J. (2025). Deep representation learning using layer-wise VICReg losses. *Scientific Reports*, *15*(1), 27049. DOI: 10.1038/s41598-025-08504-2 PMID: 40715190

Daugherty, P. R., & Wilson, H. J. (2024). *Human+ Machine, Updated and Expanded: Reimagining Work in the Age of AI*. Harvard Business Press.

Davenport, T., Guha, A., Grewal, D., & Bressgott, T. (2020). How artificial intelligence will change the future of marketing. *Journal of the Academy of Marketing Science*, *48*(1), 24–42. DOI: 10.1007/s11747-019-00696-0

De Almeida, P. G. R., Dos Santos, C. D., & Farias, J. S. (2021). Artificial intelligence regulation: A framework for governance. *Ethics and Information Technology*, *23*(3), 505–525. DOI: 10.1007/s10676-021-09593-z

de Amorim, L. A., Sousa, B. B., Dias, Á. L., & Santos, V. R. (2024). Exploring the outcomes of digital marketing on historic sites' visitor behaviour. *Journal of Cultural Heritage Management and Sustainable Development*, *14*(6), 934–949. DOI: 10.1108/JCHMSD-11-2021-0202

de Freitas Netto, S. V., Sobral, M. F. F., Ribeiro, A. R. B., & Soares, G. R. (2020). Concepts and forms of greenwashing: A systematic review. *Environmental Sciences Europe*, *32*(1), 19. DOI: 10.1186/s12302-020-0300-3

De Manuel, A., Delgado, J., Parra Jounou, I., Ausín, T., Casacuberta, D., Cruz, M., Guersenzvaig, A., Moyano, C., Rodríguez-Arias, D., Rueda, J., & Puyol, A. (2023). Ethical assessments and mitigation strategies for biases in AI-systems used during the COVID-19 pandemic. *Big Data & Society*, *10*(1), 20539517231179199. DOI: 10.1177/20539517231179199

De Silva, D., & Alahakoon, D. (2022). An artificial intelligence life cycle: From conception to production. *Patterns (New York, N.Y.)*, *3*(6), 100489. DOI: 10.1016/j.patter.2022.100489

de Wagenaar, D., Galama, J., & Sijtsema, S. J. (2022). Exploring Worldwide Wardrobes to Support Reuse in Consumers' Clothing Systems. *Sustainability (Basel)*, *14*(1), 487. DOI: 10.3390/su14010487

Deci, E. L., & Ryan, R. M. (2000). The "what" and "why" of goal pursuits: Human needs and the self-determination of behavior. *Psychological Inquiry*, *11*(4), 227–268. DOI: 10.1207/S15327965PLI1104_01

Dehghani, N., & Levin, M. (2024). Bio-inspired ai: Integrating biological complexity into artificial intelligence. *arXiv preprint arXiv:2411.15243.*

Deng, M., Liu, Y., & Chen, L. (2023). AI-driven innovation in ethnic clothing design: An intersection of machine learning and cultural heritage. *Electronic Research Archive*, *31*(9), 5793–5814. DOI: 10.3934/era.2023295

Deng, Y., Shen, H., & Ji, X. (2024). Exploring virtual fashion consumption through the emotional three-level theory: Reflections on sustainable consumer behavior. *Sustainability (Basel)*, *16*(13), 5818. DOI: 10.3390/su16135818

Devakunchari, R., & Valliyammai, C. (2016). Big Social Data Analytics: Opportunities, Challenges and Implications on Society. Online Journal of Communication and Media Technologies, 6(September 2016-Special Issue), 17–32. DOI: 10.30935/ojcmt/5659

Dhama, A., Kaur, A., Döngül, E. S., & Singh, N. (2024). Artificial intelligence and sustainable green fashion industry. In *Handbook of Artificial Intelligence Applications for Industrial Sustainability* (pp. 74–91). CRC Press. DOI: 10.1201/9781003348351-6

Dhiwar, K. (2024, January). Artificial intelligence and machine learning in fashion: reshaping design, production, consumer experience and sustainability. In *2024 ASU International Conference in Emerging Technologies for Sustainability and Intelligent Systems (ICETSIS)* (pp. 1766-1775). IEEE. DOI: 10.1109/ICETSIS61505.2024.10459436

Dillard, J. P., & Shen, L. (2005). On the nature of reactance and its role in persuasive health communication. *Communication Monographs*, *72*(2), 144–168. DOI: 10.1080/03637750500111815

Dogruel, L., Facciorusso, D., & Stark, B. (2022). 'I'm still the master of the machine.' Internet users' awareness of algorithmic decision-making and their perception of its effect on their autonomy. *Information Communication and Society*, *25*(9), 1311–1332. DOI: 10.1080/1369118X.2020.1863999

Dong, Y. J., Li, W., & Chen, M. (2023). Personalization reactance in online medical consultations: Effects of two-sided personalization and health topic sensitivity on reactance. *Human Communication Research*, *50*(1), 66–78. DOI: 10.1093/hcr/hqad039

Dourado, P., Llovet-Rodríguez, C., & Gallego-Gómez, C. (2024). Social responsibility of designer fashion brands in Spain: Analysis of websites based on sustainability and transparency. *Revista Internacional de Relaciones Públicas*, *14*(28), 67–86. DOI: 10.5783/revrrpp.v14i28.871

Dreismann, J. K. (2020). Employment quality in supply chains of circular fashion-a comparison of standards and practices of circular fashion enterprises & social sustainability targeting apparel players (Master's thesis).

D'Souza, J., Al Mustafa, T., Auer, D. F., Bachinger, S. T., Brinner, M., Daniel, C., ... & Heger, T. (2025). Reflections from the 2025 EcoHack: AI & LLM Hackathon for Applications in Evidence-based Ecological Research & Practice.

Dudík, M., Erhan, D., Langford, J., & Li, L. (2014). Doubly robust policy evaluation and optimization. *Statistical Science*, *29*(4), 485–511. DOI: 10.1214/14-STS500

Dwivedi, Y. K., Sharma, A., Rana, N. P., Giannakis, M., Goel, P., & Dutot, V. (2023). Evolution of artificial intelligence research in Technological Forecasting and Social Change: Research topics, trends, and future directions. *Technological Forecasting and Social Change*, *192*, 122579. DOI: 10.1016/j.techfore.2023.122579

Dymkov, A. (2024). RFID technologies: Analysis of current status and development. *Synchroinfo Journal*, *10*(5), 33–41. DOI: 10.36724/2664-066X-2024-10-5-33-41

EarthDay.org. (2025, January 22). Broken Threads & Twisted Yarns: Legislating the reform of fashion. EarthDay.org. Retrieved from https://www.earthday.org/press-release/earth-day-org-releases-first-of-its-kind-fast-fashion-legislation-report/

Ebeling, F., & Lotz, S. (2015). Domestic uptake of green energy promoted by opt-out tariffs. *Nature Climate Change*, *5*(9), 868–871. DOI: 10.1038/nclimate2681

Ecochain. (n.d.). Mobius – product footprint software. Ecochain. Retrieved from https://ecochain.com/mobius/

Edizel, B., Bonchi, F., Hajian, S., Panisson, A., & Tassa, T. (2020). FaiRecSys: Mitigating algorithmic bias in recommender systems. *International Journal of Data Science and Analytics*, *9*(2), 197–213. DOI: 10.1007/s41060-019-00181-5

Eitel-Porter, R. (2021). Beyond the promise: Implementing ethical AI. *AI and Ethics*, *1*(1), 73–80. DOI: 10.1007/s43681-020-00011-6

Ekstrand, M. D., Das, A., Burke, R., & Diaz, F. (2022). *Fairness in information access systems. Foundations and Trends® in Information Retrieval, 16*(1–2), 1–177. https://doi.org/DOI: 10.1561/1500000079

El-Kassas, W. S., Salama, C. R., Rafea, A. A., & Mohamed, H. K. (2021). Automatic text summarization: A comprehensive survey. *Expert Systems with Applications*, *165*, 113679. DOI: 10.1016/j.eswa.2020.113679

Ellen MacArthur Foundation. (2017) A New Textiles Economy: Redesigning Fashion's Future. https://www.ellenmacarthurfoundation.org/assets/downloads/publications/A-New-Textiles-Economy_Full-Report.pdf

Ellen, P. S., Wiener, J. L., & Cobb-Walgren, C. (1991). The role of perceived consumer effectiveness in motivating environmentally conscious behaviors. *Journal of Public Policy & Marketing*, *10*(2), 102–117. DOI: 10.1177/074391569101000206

Emon, M. M. H., & Khan, T. (2025). The Rise of Circular Supply Chains: Recycling and Closed-Loop Systems Could Mitigate Inflationary Pressures. In Supply Chain Disruptions and Impact on Global Inflation (pp. 195-226). IGI Global Scientific Publishing.

Eom, K., & Choy, B. K. C. (2025). Is common behavior considered moral? The role of perceived others' motives in moral norm inferences and motivation about environmental behavior. *Journal of Experimental Social Psychology*, *116*, 104684. DOI: 10.1016/j.jesp.2024.104684

EON. (n.d.). H&M | Case study: Digital IDs powered by EON. EON. Retrieved [access date], from https://www.eon.xyz/clients/h-m

Escandón, P. A., & Mejía, G. M. (2022). Decision-making using heuristic evaluation in design for behaviour change. *Journal of Desert Research*, *20*(3), 209–229.

European Data Protection Board. (2023). *Guidelines 3/2022 on deceptive design patterns in social media platform interfaces.* Retrieved from, https://www.edpb.europa.eu/our-work-tools/our-documents/guidelines/guidelines-032022-deceptive-design-patterns-social-media_en

Fahad, M., Basri, T., Hamza, M. A., Faisal, S., Akbar, A., Haider, U., & Hajjami, S. E. (2024). The benefits and risks of artificial general intelligence (AGI). In *Artificial general intelligence (AGI) security: Smart applications and sustainable technologies* (pp. 27–52). Springer Nature Singapore.

Faludi, J. (2025). Sustainable Fashion, Circularity and Consumer Behavior – Systematic Review and a Social Marketing Research and Policy Agenda. *Social Marketing Quarterly*, *31*(1), 35–59. DOI: 10.1177/15245004241309660

Farzin, M., Shababi, H., Shirchi Sasi, G., Sadeghi, M., & Makvandi, R. (2023). The determinants of eco-fashion purchase intention and willingness to pay. *Spanish Journal of Marketing - ESIC*, *27*(3), 348–366. DOI: 10.1108/SJME-07-2022-0158

Faulhaber, M. E. (2023). *A nudge-based social media intervention to improve impulse buying, problematic social media usage, and self-regulation*. Iowa State University. DOI: 10.31274/td-20240617-356

Fazil, A. W., Hakimi, M., & Shahidzay, A. K. (2023). A comprehensive review of bias in AI algorithms. *Nusantara Hasana Journal*, *3*(8), 1–11. DOI: 10.59003/nhj.v3i8.1052

Federal Trade Commission. (2022a, September). *Bringing dark patterns to light* (Staff Report). Retrieved from, https://www.ftc.gov/reports/bringing-dark-patterns-light

Federal Trade Commission. (2022b, November 28). *FTC, states sue Google and iHeartMedia for deceptive ads promoting the Pixel 4 smartphone* [Press release]. Retrieved from, https://www.ftc.gov/news-events/news/press-releases/2022/11/ftc-states-sue-google-iheartmedia-deceptive-ads-promoting-pixel-4-smartphone

Feldman, M., Friedler, S. A., Moeller, J., Scheidegger, C., & Venkatasubramanian, S. (2015). Certifying and removing disparate impact. In *Proceedings of the 21st ACM SIGKDD International Conference on Knowledge Discovery and Data Mining* (pp. 259–268).

Felfernig, A., Jeran, M., Ninaus, G., Reinfrank, F., & Reiterer, S. (2013). Toward the Next Generation of Recommender Systems: Applications and Research Challenges. In Tsihrintzis, G., Virvou, M., & Jain, L. (Eds.), *Multimedia Services in Intelligent Environments. Smart Innovation, Systems and Technologies* (Vol. 24). Springer., DOI: 10.1007/978-3-319-00372-6_5

Feng, C. Y., Martinez-Lopez, F. J., Li, Y. C., & Campo-Fernandez, J. (2025). Personalize it, no return: Nudging online consumers towards product personalization that makes the product non-returnable with herd instinct and regret nudges. *Electronic Commerce Research and Applications*, *73*, 101525. DOI: 10.1016/j.elerap.2025.101525

Ferdaus, M. M., Abdelguerfi, M., Ioup, E., Niles, K. N., Pathak, K., & Sloan, S. (2024). Towards trustworthy ai: A review of ethical and robust large language models. *arXiv preprint arXiv:2407.13934*.

Fernández-Caramés, T. M., & Fraga-Lamas, P. (2018). A review on human-centered IoT-connected smart labels for the industry 4.0. *IEEE Access : Practical Innovations, Open Solutions*, *6*, 25939–25957. DOI: 10.1109/ACCESS.2018.2833501

Fernández, J. D., Willburger, L., Wiethe, C., Wenninger, S., & Fridgen, G. (2025). Scaling smart cities with federated learning. *Business & Information Systems Engineering*. Advance online publication. DOI: 10.1007/s12599-025-00957-z

Figueiredo e Silva, P., Kaseva, V., & Lohan, E. S. (2018). Wireless positioning in IoT: A look at current and future trends. *Sensors (Basel)*, *18*(8), 2470. DOI: 10.3390/s18082470 PMID: 30061535

Finkbeiner, M., Inaba, A., Tan, R. B. H., Christiansen, K., & Klüppel, H.-J. (2006). The new international standards for life cycle assessment: ISO 14040 and ISO 14044. *The International Journal of Life Cycle Assessment*, *11*(2), 80–85. DOI: 10.1065/lca2006.02.002

Fink, G. A. (2014). N-gram models. In *Markov Models for Pattern Recognition: From Theory to Applications* (pp. 107–127). Springer London. DOI: 10.1007/978-1-4471-6308-4_6

Fitria, T. N. (2021). QuillBot as an online tool: Students' alternative in paraphrasing and rewriting of English writing. *Englisia: Journal of Language, Education, and Humanities*, *9*(1), 183–196. DOI: 10.22373/ej.v9i1.10233

Floridi, L., & Cowls, J. (2019). A Unified Framework of Five Principles for AI in Society. *Harvard Data Science Review*, *1*, 2–15. DOI: 10.1162/99608f92.8cd550d1

Friedman, B., & Hendry, D. G. (2019). *Value sensitive design: Shaping technology with moral imagination*. The MIT Press., DOI: 10.7551/mitpress/7585.001.0001

Frith, J. (2024). *A billion little pieces: RFID and infrastructures of identification*. Mit Press.

Fruttaldo, S. (2024). *Design for behavioural change: study of a concept and recommendations for information systems supporting eco-driving* (Doctoral dissertation, Loughborough University).

Fu, C., Dai, Y., Luo, Y., Li, L., Ren, S., Zhang, R., & Sun, X. (2025). Video-mme: The first-ever comprehensive evaluation benchmark of multi-modal llms in video analysis. In *Proceedings of the Computer Vision and Pattern Recognition Conference* (pp. 24108-24118). DOI: 10.1109/CVPR52734.2025.02245

Gallotta, R., Todd, G., Zammit, M., Earle, S., Liapis, A., Togelius, J., & Yannakakis, G. N. (2024). Large language models and games: A survey and roadmap. *IEEE Transactions on Games*, 1–18. DOI: 10.1109/TG.2024.3461510

Gao, B., Wang, Y., Xie, H., Hu, Y., & Hu, Y. (2023). Artificial Intelligence in Advertising: Advancements, Challenges, and Ethical Considerations in Targeting, Personalization, Content Creation, and Ad Optimization. *SAGE Open*, *13*(4), 21582440231210759. Advance online publication. DOI: 10.1177/21582440231210759

Gao, Y., & Liang, J. (2025). The Impact of AI-Powered Try-On Technology on Online Consumers' Impulsive Buying Intention: The Moderating Role of Brand Trust. *Sustainability (Basel)*, *17*(7), 2789. DOI: 10.3390/su17072789

Garcia, C. C. (2022). Fashion forecasting: An overview from material culture to industry. *Journal of Fashion Marketing and Management*, *26*(3), 436–451. DOI: 10.1108/JFMM-11-2020-0241

Gautam, P., Maheshwari, S., Kausar, A., & Jaggi, C. K. (2023). Sustainable retail model with preservation technology investment to moderate deterioration with environmental deliberations. *Journal of Cleaner Production*, *390*, 136128. DOI: 10.1016/j.jclepro.2023.136128

Gebru, T., Morgenstern, J., Vecchione, B., Vaughan, J. W., Wallach, H., Iii, H. D., & Crawford, K. (2021). Datasheets for datasets. *Communications of the ACM*, *64*(12), 86–92. DOI: 10.1145/3458723

George, A. S. (2024). The Hidden Cost: Understanding the Environmental Impact of Online Purchase Returns. *Partners Universal Innovative Research Publication*, 2(1), 132–149.

Ghosal, S. (2025). Transforming Retail. *Sustainable Practices in the Fashion and Retail Industry*, 1.

Glimpact. (n.d.). Glimpact: Measure your global environmental footprint. Retrieved from https://www.glimpact.com/

Global Fashion Agenda. (2024). *Fashion CEO agenda 2024: Scaling sustainability in fashion.* Global Fashion Agenda. https://globalfashionagenda.org

Glogar, M., Petrak, S., & Mahnić Naglić, M. (2025). Digital technologies in the sustainable design and development of textiles and clothing—A literature review. *Sustainability (Basel), 17*(4), 1371. DOI: 10.3390/su17041371

Gökbunar, H. B., & Soylu, B. (2024). *Blockchain Enabled Lateral Transshipment System for the Redistribution of Unsold Textile Products in a Circular Economy.*, DOI: 10.1007/978-981-99-6062-0_58

Goldstein, N. J., Cialdini, R. B., & Griskevicius, V. (2008). A room with a viewpoint: Using social norms to motivate environmental conservation. *The Journal of Consumer Research, 35*(3), 472–482. DOI: 10.1086/586910

Gomes de Oliveira, L., Miranda, F. G., & de Paula Dias, M. A. (2022). Sustainable practices in slow and fast fashion stores: What does the customer perceive? *Cleaner Engineering and Technology, 6*, 100413. DOI: 10.1016/j.clet.2022.100413

Gonçalves, A., Baêta, M., Nagy, M., & Silva, C. (2024). Looking for environmental scoring: A case study of a Portuguese cotton white T-shirt made with recycled Fiber. *Sustainability (Basel), 16*(14), 5896. DOI: 10.3390/su16145896

González–Cebrián, A., Bradford, M., Chis, A. E., & González-Vélez, H. (2024). Standardised versioning of datasets: A FAIR-compliant proposal. *Scientific Data, 11*(1), 358. DOI: 10.1038/s41597-024-03153-y PMID: 38594314

Gossen, M., Jäger, S., Hoffmann, M. L., Bießmann, F., Korenke, R., & Santarius, T. (2022). Nudging sustainable consumption: A large-scale data analysis of sustainability labels for fashion in German online retail. *Frontiers in Sustainability, 3*, 922984. DOI: 10.3389/frsus.2022.922984

GreenStitch. (n.d.). Why GreenStitch- Your partner in fashion sustainability. Retrieved from https://greenstitch.io/why-greenstitch/

Guan, Z., Wu, L., Zhao, H., He, M., & Fan, J. (2025). Attention Mechanisms Perspective: Exploring LLM Processing of Graph-Structured Data. *arXiv preprint arXiv:2505.02130.*

Guliyev, E., Ramirez, J. S., De Caigny, A., & Coussement, K. (2025). Improving B2B customer churn through action rule mining. *Industrial Marketing Management, 125*, 1–11. DOI: 10.1016/j.indmarman.2024.12.005

Guo, Y., Morris, K. E., Sumner, M., & Taylor, M. (2025). A framework for measuring physical garment durability. *Cleaner and Responsible Consumption*, *16*, 100245. DOI: 10.1016/j.clrc.2024.100245

Guo, Y., Shi, H., Kumar, A., Grauman, K., Rosing, T., & Feris, R. (2019). Spottune: transfer learning through adaptive fine-tuning. In *Proceedings of the IEEE/CVF conference on computer vision and pattern recognition* (pp. 4805-4814).

Gutiérrez, P., & Gérardy, J.-Y. (2017). Causal inference and uplift modelling: A review of the literature. In *Proceedings of the 3rd International Conference on Predictive Applications and APIs* (pp. 1–13). PMLR.

Gwa, J. M., Shirazi, F., Nisar, T. M., & Hajli, N. (2025). Promoting circular practices in fashion: Strategies for sustainable business growth. *Strategy and Leadership*, •••, 1–25. DOI: 10.1108/SL-06-2025-0149

Hadi, M. U., Qureshi, R., Shah, A., Irfan, M., Zafar, A., Shaikh, M. B., & Mirjalili, S. (2023). Large language models: a comprehensive survey of its applications, challenges, limitations, and future prospects. *Authorea preprints, 1*(3), 1-26.

Hadizadeh Hafshejani, E., TaheriNejad, N., Rabbani, R., Azizi, Z., Mohin, S., Fotowat-Ahmady, A., & Mirabbasi, S. (2022). Self-Aware Data Processing for Power Saving in Resource-Constrained IoT Cyber-Physical Systems. *IEEE Sensors Journal*, *22*(4), 3648–3659. DOI: 10.1109/JSEN.2021.3133405

Hamernik, R. P., & Qiu, W. (2001). Energy-independent factors influencing noise-induced hearing loss in the chinchilla model. *The Journal of the Acoustical Society of America*, *110*(6), 3163–3168. DOI: 10.1121/1.1414707

Han, H., Shiwakoti, R. K., Jarvis, R., Mordi, C., & Botchie, D. (2023). Accounting and auditing with blockchain technology and artificial Intelligence: A literature review. *International Journal of Accounting Information Systems*, *48*, 100598. DOI: 10.1016/j.accinf.2022.100598

Han, S., Wang, M., Zhang, J., Li, D., & Duan, J. (2024). A review of large language models: Fundamental architectures, key technological evolutions, interdisciplinary technologies integration, optimization and compression techniques, applications, and challenges. *Electronics (Basel)*, *13*(24), 5040. DOI: 10.3390/electronics13245040

Hansen, P. G., & Jespersen, A. M. (2013). Nudge and the manipulation of choice: A framework for the responsible use of the nudge approach to behaviour change in public policy. *European Journal of Risk Regulation*, *4*(1), 3–28. DOI: 10.1017/S1867299X00002762

Hardadi, G., Buchholz, A., & Pauliuk, S. (2021). Implications of the distribution of German household environmental footprints across income groups for integrating environmental and social policy design. *Journal of Industrial Ecology*, *25*(1), 95–113. DOI: 10.1111/jiec.13045

Hari, A., & Abdulla, M. S. (2023). *Ai safety: where do we stand presently* (No. 584).

Hassija, V., Chamola, V., Mahapatra, A., Singal, A., Goel, D., Huang, K., Scardapane, S., Spinelli, I., Mahmud, M., & Hussain, A. (2024). Interpreting black-box models: A review on explainable artificial intelligence. *Cognitive Computation*, *16*(1), 45–74. DOI: 10.1007/s12559-023-10179-8

Hawken, P. (2021). *Regeneration: Ending the climate crisis in one generation.* Penguin Books.

Heidari, M., & Hosseinalibeiki, H. (2025). Tokenized Incentives and Loyalty: Leveraging Blockchain-Based Smart Contracts for Enhancing Eco-Tourism Behavioral Engagement.

Heilinger, J.-C. (2022). The Ethics of AI Ethics. A Constructive Critique. *Philosophy & Technology*, *35*(3), 61. DOI: 10.1007/s13347-022-00557-9

Helberger, N., Pierson, J., & Poell, T. (2018). Governing online platforms: From contested to cooperative responsibility. *The Information Society*, *34*(1), 1–14. DOI: 10.1080/01972243.2017.1391913

Hertwig, R., & Grüne-Yanoff, T. (2017). Nudging and boosting: Steering or empowering good decisions. *Perspectives on Psychological Science*, *12*(6), 973–986. DOI: 10.1177/1745691617702496 PMID: 28792862

Hoffmann, J., Borgeaud, S., Mensch, A., Buchatskaya, E., Cai, T., Rutherford, E., . . . Sifre, L. (2022). Training compute-optimal large language models. *arXiv preprint arXiv:2203.15556.*

Hogh, N., Braun, J., Watermann, L., & Kubowitsch, S. (2025). I Don't Buy It! A Critical Review of the Research on Factors Influencing Sustainable Fashion Buying Behavior. *Sustainability (Basel)*, *17*(9), 4015. DOI: 10.3390/su17094015

Horvath, M. (2024, January 9). Global surge: 71% increase in online searches for sustainable goods reflects growing consumer commitment to eco-friendly choices. More Gratitude. https://more-gratitude.com/blog/global-surge-increase-in-online-searches-for-sustaible-goods/

Houf, L., Szymkowiak, A., & Shepherd, L. A. (2024). Promotion of sustainable products: Can sustainability labels promote user selection of environmentally friendly products? *Sustainability (Basel)*, *16*(13), 5390. DOI: 10.3390/su16135390

Hou, Y. M., Song, Y. Q., & Wang, Z. J. (2025). Transfer learning for linear regression with differential privacy. *Complex & Intelligent Systems*, *11*(1), 100. Advance online publication. DOI: 10.1007/s40747-024-01759-8

Hu, T., & Zhou, X. H. (2024). Unveiling LLM evaluation focused on metrics: Challenges and solutions. *arXiv preprint arXiv:2404.09135*.

Huang, J., Xu, Y., Wang, Q., Wang, Q. C., Liang, X., Wang, F., Zhang, Z., Wei, W., Zhang, B., Huang, L., Chang, J., Ma, L., Ma, T., Liang, Y., Zhang, J., Guo, J., Jiang, X., Fan, X., An, Z., & Fei, A. (2025). Foundation models and intelligent decision-making: Progress, challenges, and perspectives. *Innovation (Cambridge (Mass.))*, *6*(6), 100948. DOI: 10.1016/j.xinn.2025.100948

Huang, L., Yu, W., Ma, W., Zhong, W., Feng, Z., Wang, H., Chen, Q., Peng, W., Feng, X., Qin, B., & Liu, T. (2025). A survey on hallucination in large language models: Principles, taxonomy, challenges, and open questions. *ACM Transactions on Information Systems*, *43*(2), 1–55. DOI: 10.1145/3703155

Huang, M., & Fang, S. (2024). Mechanisms of self-control in the influence of moral elevation on pro-social behavior: A study based on an experimental paradigm. *Psychology Research and Behavior Management*, *17*, 537–552. DOI: 10.2147/PRBM.S446186 PMID: 38374937

Huang, M.-H., & Rust, R. T. (2021). A strategic framework for artificial intelligence in marketing. *Journal of the Academy of Marketing Science*, *49*(1), 30–50. DOI: 10.1007/s11747-020-00749-9

Hu, J., Dong, T., Gang, L., Ma, H., Zou, P., Sun, X., & Wang, M. (2024). Psychology: Enhancing LLM for psychological understanding and evaluation. *IEEE Transactions on Computational Social Systems*.

Hu, L., Liu, Z., Zhao, Z., Hou, L., Nie, L., & Li, J. (2023). A survey of knowledge-enhanced pre-trained language models. *IEEE Transactions on Knowledge and Data Engineering*, *36*(4), 1413–1430. DOI: 10.1109/TKDE.2023.3310002

Hussain, W., & Waheed, A. (2025). *Digital Doppelgangers.*, DOI: 10.4018/979-8-3693-9005-4.ch008

Hwang, T. (2018). Computational power and the social impact of artificial intelligence. *arXiv preprint arXiv:1803.08971*.

Hyun, J., Lee, K., & Kim-Vick, J. (2021). Consumer responses to trade-offs in eco-friendly clothing: The moderating effects of fashion leadership and regulatory focus. *Journal of Retailing and Consumer Services*, *59*, 102365. DOI: 10.1016/j.jretconser.2020.102365

Ikram, M. (2022). Transition toward green economy: Technological Innovation's role in the fashion industry. *Current Opinion in Green and Sustainable Chemistry*, *37*, 100657. DOI: 10.1016/j.cogsc.2022.100657

Iranmanesh, M., Maroufkhani, P., Asadi, S., Ghobakhloo, M., Dwivedi, Y. K., & Tseng, M.-L. (2023). Effects of supply chain transparency, alignment, adaptability, and agility on blockchain adoption in supply chain among SMEs. *Computers & Industrial Engineering*, *176*, 108931. DOI: 10.1016/j.cie.2022.108931

Iseal, S. (2025). Leveraging AI for Life Cycle Assessment in Fashion: A Sustainable Future.

ISO. (2006). *ISO 14040: Life cycle assessment—Principles and framework*. International Organization for Standardization. Retrieved from, https://www.iso.org/standard/37456.html

ISO. (2014). *ISO 14046: Water footprint—Principles, requirements and guidelines*. International Organization for Standardization. Retrieved from, https://www.iso.org/standard/43263.html

Itani, O. S., Loureiro, S. M. C., & Ramadan, Z. (2023). Engaging with omnichannel brands: The role of consumer empowerment. *International Journal of Retail & Distribution Management*, *51*(2), 238–261. DOI: 10.1108/IJRDM-02-2022-0044

Ivanov, T., & Penchev, V. (2024). AI Benchmarks and Datasets for LLM Evaluation. *arXiv preprint arXiv:2412.01020*.

Jachimowicz, J. M., Duncan, S., Weber, E. U., & Johnson, E. J. (2019). When and why defaults influence decisions: A meta-analysis of default effects. *Behavioural Public Policy*, *3*(2), 159–186. DOI: 10.1017/bpp.2018.43

Jæger, B., & Myrold, S. (2023, September). Textile industry circular supply chains and digital product passports. Two case studies. In IFIP International Conference on Advances in Production Management Systems (pp. 350-363). Cham: Springer Nature Switzerland.

James, P. A. K., & Dutta, S. (2025). Luxury without limits: The rise of demi-fine jewellery through social media technology. Journal of Information Technology Teaching Cases, 20438869251360356.

Jannach, D. (2022). Massimo Quadrana, Paolo Cremonesi: Session-based Recommender Systems. In Ricci, (Eds.), *Recommender Systems Handbook* (3rd ed., pp. 301–333). Springer. DOI: 10.1007/978-1-0716-2197-4_8

Janson, A., & Barev, T. J. (2024). Making the default more legitimate: The role of autonomy and transparency for digital privacy nudges. *Information Technology & People, 2024*. Advance online publication. DOI: 10.1108/ITP-04-2023-0334

Jestratijevic, I., Uanhoro, J. O., & Creighton, R. (2022). To disclose or not to disclose? Fashion brands' strategies for transparency in sustainability reporting. *Journal of Fashion Marketing and Management, 26*(1), 36–50. DOI: 10.1108/JFMM-09-2020-0182

Ji, W., Yuan, W., Getzen, E., Cho, K., Jordan, M. I., Mei, S., . . . Zhang, L. (2025). An overview of large language models for statisticians. *arXiv preprint arXiv:2502.17814*.

Jiang, G., & Macintyre, L. (2025). Wardrobe Management Apps and Their Unintended Benefits for Fashion Sustainability and Well-Being: Insights from User Reviews. *Sustainability (Basel), 17*(9), 4159. DOI: 10.3390/su17094159

Jin, P., Zhu, B., Yuan, L., & Yan, S. (2024). Moh: Multi-head attention as mixture-of-head attention. *arXiv preprint arXiv:2410.11842*.

Jio, W., Kant, S., & Lemi, K. (2025). Ethical Leadership: Effect on Future of Organizational Citizenship Behavior by Mediation of Organizational Culture in Ethiopia. In *Generation Alpha and Next Generation Leadership for Greener Futures* (pp. 41-62). IGI Global Scientific Publishing.

Jöhnk, J., Weißert, M., & Wyrtki, K. (2021). Ready or Not, AI Comes— An Interview Study of Organizational AI Readiness Factors. *Business & Information Systems Engineering, 63*(1), 5–20. DOI: 10.1007/s12599-020-00676-7

Johnsen, E. B., Kobialka, P., Pferscher, A., & Tapia Tarifa, S. L. (2024). Nudging strategies for user journeys: Take a path on the wild side. In *Lecture Notes in Computer Science* (Vol. 15230). Springer. https://doi.org/DOI: 10.1007/978-3-031-73751-0_6

Joshi, S. (2025). Evaluation of Large Language Models: Review of Metrics, Applications, and Methodologies.

Juneja, P., & Mitra, T. (2022). *Algorithmic nudge to make better choices: Evaluating effectiveness of XAI frameworks to reveal biases in algorithmic decision making to users* (arXiv:2202.02479). arXiv. https://arxiv.org/abs/2202.02479

Jung, K. H. (2023). Uncover this tech term: Foundation model—Korean. *Journal de Radiologie, 24*(10), 1038.

Kahneman, D. (2011). *Thinking, fast and slow.* Farrar, Straus and Giroux.

Kaliszewicz, A., Panteleeva, N., Karaban, K., Runka, T., Winczek, M., Beck, E., Poniatowska, A., Olejniczak, I., Boniecki, P., Golovanova, E. V., & Romanowski, J. (2023). First Evidence of Microplastic Occurrence in the Marine and Freshwater Environments in a Remote Polar Region of the Kola Peninsula and a Correlation with Human Presence. *Biology (Basel), 12*(2), 259. DOI: 10.3390/biology12020259 PMID: 36829537

Kalpokas, I. (2019). Personalisation, emotion, and nudging. In *Algorithmic governance: Politics and law in the post-human era* (pp. 49–65). Palgrave Pivot., DOI: 10.1007/978-3-030-31922-9_4

Kang, H., Park, S., Lee, B., Ahn, J., & Kim, S. (2021). Impact of Chitosan Pretreatment to Reduce Microfibers Released from Synthetic Garments during Laundering. *Water (Basel), 13*(18), 2480. DOI: 10.3390/w13182480

Kant, S., Adula, M., & Badi, S. (2025). Digital Transition Effect on Green Jobs by Mediation of Knowledge Management in Circular Economy. In Insights Into Digital Business, Human Resource Management, and Competitiveness (pp. 171-190). IGI Global Scientific Publishing. DOI: 10.4018/979-8-3693-9440-3.ch007

Kant, S., Adula, M., Nimbrain, N., & Kumari, M. (2025). Optimizing Resource Allocation for Green IT Future by Mediation of AI in the Horn of Africa. In Sustainable Information Security in the Age of AI and Green Computing (pp. 503-522). IGI Global Scientific Publishing. DOI: 10.4018/979-8-3693-8034-5.ch025

Kant, S., Adula, M., & Jio, W. (2025). Consumer Neuroscience in the Perception of AI and Market Orientation. In *Advancing Medical Research Through Neuroscience* (pp. 21–46). IGI Global Scientific Publishing. DOI: 10.4018/979-8-3693-5464-3.ch002

Kant, S., Niguse, T., Olubiyi, T. O., Adula, M., & Kebede, K. (2025). Sustainable Fashion-Based Innovations and Consumer Behavior in Ethiopia. In *Global Impacts and Sustainable Practices in Fast Fashion* (pp. 167–196). IGI Global Scientific Publishing. DOI: 10.4018/979-8-3693-7853-3.ch007

Kant, S., Toma, F., Niguse, T., & Adula, M. (2025). Eco-Friendly Packaging Effect on the Future of Consumer Shopping Habits by Mediation of Consumer Awareness in Retail Industries in the Horn of Africa. In *Sustainable Practices in the Fashion and Retail Industry* (pp. 179–202). IGI Global Scientific Publishing. DOI: 10.4018/979-8-3693-9959-0.ch008

Kaplan, J., McCandlish, S., Henighan, T., Brown, T. B., Chess, B., Child, R., . . . Amodei, D. (2020). Scaling laws for neural language models. *arXiv preprint arXiv:2001.08361*.

Kapoor, P. S., Maggon, M., & Gangwani, K. K. (2025). Inform me or make me laugh: Influencer marketing and the role of emotional contagion and information value. *International Journal of Consumer Studies*, *49*(1), e70005. DOI: 10.1111/ijcs.70005

Karadayi-Usta, S. (2024). Role of artificial intelligence and augmented reality in fashion industry from consumer perspective: Sustainability through waste and return mitigation. *Engineering Applications of Artificial Intelligence*, *133*, 108114. DOI: 10.1016/j.engappai.2024.108114

Karmali, I. M., & Valilai, O. F. (2025). Exploring the Role of Artificial Intelligence for Pattern Recognition of Textile Sorting and Recycling for Circular Economy. *Procedia Computer Science*, *253*, 346–356. DOI: 10.1016/j.procs.2025.01.097

Kathuria, A., & Bakshi, A. (2024). Influence of promotional factors on online impulse buying: Exploring the mediating role of impulse buying tendency. *Current Psychology (New Brunswick, N.J.)*, *43*(44), 34035–34051. DOI: 10.1007/s12144-024-06911-8

Ke, L., Tong, S., Cheng, P., & Peng, K. (2024). Exploring the frontiers of LMS in psychological applications: A comprehensive review. *arXiv preprint arXiv:2401.01519*.

Kemi, A. P., & Zilahy, G. (2025). Sustainable post-purchase behaviour of consumers of fashion textile products. *Discover Sustainability*, *6*(1), 94. DOI: 10.1007/s43621-025-00888-5

Khabbaz, B. G. (2010). Life cycle energy use and greenhouse gas emissions of Australian cotton: Impact of farming systems (Doctoral dissertation, University of Southern Queensland).

Khagokpam, D., Sharma, A., Sharma, R. S., & Mishra, V. (2025). Corporate Social Responsibility: A Pathway to Sustainability in the Fashion Industry. In *Circular Economy and Environmental Resilience: Solutions for a Sustainable Tomorrow* (Vol. 1, pp. 343–369). Springer Nature Switzerland. DOI: 10.1007/978-3-031-93091-1_14

Khalifa, M., & Albadawy, M. (2024). Using artificial intelligence in academic writing and research: An essential productivity tool. *Computer Methods and Programs in Biomedicine Update*, *5*, 100145. DOI: 10.1016/j.cmpbup.2024.100145

Khanh Linh, C., Tung Lam, N., & Tram Anh, N. (2025). Motivating Gen Z to Adopt AI Chatbots for Sustainable Consumption on Fashion E-Commerce Platforms: An Integrated Model.

Khanna, G. B. (2008). Textile Industry Polluting Sector in Varied Forms.

Khosravy, M., Nakamura, K., Pasquali, A., Witkowski, O., Nitta, N., & Babaguchi, N. (2022, December). When AI facilitates trust violation: an ethical report on deep model inversion privacy attack. In the *2022 International Conference on Computational Science and Computational Intelligence (CSCI)* (pp. 929–935). IEEE. DOI: 10.1109/CSCI58124.2022.00166

Kim, B., & Seo, S. (2023). EfficientNetV2-based dynamic gesture recognition using transformed scalogram from triaxial acceleration signal. *Journal of Computational Design and Engineering*, *10*(4), 1694–1706. DOI: 10.1093/jcde/qwad068

Kim, J., Kang, S., & Bae, J. (2022). The effects of customer consumption goals on artificial intelligence driven recommendation agents: Evidence from Stitch Fix. *International Journal of Advertising*, *41*(6), 997–1016. DOI: 10.1080/02650487.2021.1963098

Kohavi, R., & Longbotham, R. (2023). Online controlled experiments and A/B tests. In Phung, D., Webb, G. I., & Sammut, C. (Eds.), *Encyclopedia of Machine Learning and Data Science*. Springer., DOI: 10.1007/978-1-4899-7502-7_891-2

Kohavi, R., Tang, D., & Xu, Y. (2020). *Trustworthy online controlled experiments: A practical guide to A/B testing*. Cambridge University Press. DOI: 10.1017/9781108653985

Kosar, T., Mernik, M., & Carver, J. C. (2012). Program comprehension of domain-specific and general-purpose languages: Comparison using a family of experiments. *Empirical Software Engineering*, *17*(3), 276–304. DOI: 10.1007/s10664-011-9172-x

Kosiba, J. P., Acheampong, A., Adeola, O., & Hinson, R. E. (2020). The moderating role of demographic variables on customer expectations in airport retail patronage intentions of travellers. *Journal of Retailing and Consumer Services*, *54*, 102033. DOI: 10.1016/j.jretconser.2020.102033

Koul, S., & Jasrotia, S. S. (2025). How much is too much? Journey from compulsive buying to addiction of fashion products. *Social Responsibility Journal*, *21*(8), 1686–1703. DOI: 10.1108/SRJ-02-2025-0122

Kozyreva, A., Lorenz-Spreen, P., Hertwig, R., Lewandowsky, S., & Herzog, S. M. (2021). Public attitudes towards algorithmic personalization and use of personal data online: Evidence from Germany, Great Britain, and the United States. *Humanities & Social Sciences Communications*, *8*(1), 117. DOI: 10.1057/s41599-021-00787-w

Kublik, S., & Saboo, S. (2022). *GPT-3* (pp. 1-150). Sebastopol, CA, USA: O'Reilly Media, Incorporated.

Kulkarni, C. (2023). The evolution of large language models in natural language understanding. *J. Artif. Intell. Mach. Learn. Data Sci, 1*(4), 49–53. DOI: 10.51219/JAIMLD/chinmay-shripad-kulkarni/28

Kumar, A., Lu, C., Kirsch, L., Tang, Y., Stanley, K. O., Isola, P., & Ha, D. (2024). Automating the search for artificial life with foundation models. *arXiv preprint arXiv:2412.17799.*

Kumar, P. (2024). Large language models (LLMs): Survey, technical frameworks, and future challenges. *Artificial Intelligence Review, 57*(10), 260. DOI: 10.1007/s10462-024-10888-y

Kumar, R., Singh, R., & Dwivedi, Y. K. (2020). Application of industry 4.0 technologies in SMEs for ethical and sustainable operations: Analysis of challenges. *Journal of Cleaner Production, 275*, 124063. DOI: 10.1016/j.jclepro.2020.124063 PMID: 32921931

Kumar, S., & Taneja, N. (2025). Flow-induced impulse buying and return intentions: Strategic implications for live streaming entrepreneurs. *Journal of Small Business and Enterprise Development, 32*(6), 1–27. DOI: 10.1108/JSBED-12-2023-0592

Kumar, V., Dixit, A., Javalgi, R. G., & Dass, M. (2021). Digital Transformation and AI Adoption in Marketing and Sales: Opportunities and Challenges. *Industrial Marketing Management, 95*, 48–60. DOI: 10.1016/j.indmarman.2021.03.008

Langåsdalen, I. L. (2024). *Bracketing in Online Shopping: An Investigation of the Underlying Psychological and Contextual Factors* (Master's thesis, University of South-Eastern Norway).

Lanzer, L. (2025). The future of sustainable supply chain management: blockchain and smart contracts in the fashion industry-a case study of a european denim brand.

Lata, S., & Rana, K. (2025). AI's influence on young consumer behavior: Fostering sustainable consumption. *Young Consumers, 26*(5), 848–864. DOI: 10.1108/YC-05-2024-2081

Leal Filho, W., Perry, P., Heim, H., Dinis, M. A. P., Moda, H., Ebhuoma, E., & Paço, A. (2022). An overview of the contribution of the textiles sector to climate change. *Frontiers in Environmental Science, 10*, 973102. Advance online publication. DOI: 10.3389/fenvs.2022.973102

Lee, S. H. N., Kim, H., & Yang, K. (2015). Impacts of sustainable value and business stewardship on lifestyle practices in clothing consumption. *Fashion and Textiles, 2*(1), 17. DOI: 10.1186/s40691-015-0043-8

Legardeur, J., & Ospital, P. (2024). Digital product passport for the textile sector (Doctoral dissertation, Parlement Européen).

Lemi, K., Kant, S., & Jio, W. (2025). Greener Hospital Future in the Horn of Africa by Transactional Leadership: Outcome on Altruism Through Adaptability. In *Generation Alpha and Next Generation Leadership for Greener Futures* (pp. 1-22). IGI Global Scientific Publishing.

Li, H., Dong, Q., Chen, J., Su, H., Zhou, Y., Ai, Q., . . . Liu, Y. (2024). Llms-as-judges: a comprehensive survey on llm-based evaluation methods. *arXiv preprint arXiv:2412.05579.*

Li, J. L., Minds, S., & Hammer, K. (2025). Life cycle assessment (lca) of isolatek international passive fire protection products.

Li, L., Chen, G., Shi, H., Xiao, J., & Chen, L. (2024). A survey on multimodal benchmarks: In the era of large AI models. *arXiv preprint arXiv:2409.18142.*

Liang, W., Zhang, Y., Wu, Z., Lepp, H., Ji, W., Zhao, X., . . . Zou, J. Y. (2024). Mapping the increasing use of LLMs in scientific papers. *arXiv preprint arXiv:2404.01268.*

Lianos, I. (2024). *Synthetic Futures and Competition Law: Towards the Emergence of Precautionary Principle-Minded Approaches*. Forthcoming Theoretical Inquiries in Law.

Liao, J., Shi, Y., Gong, M., Shou, L., Eskimez, S., Lu, L., . . . Zeng, M. (2021, June). Generating a human-readable transcript for automatic speech recognition with a pre-trained language model. In *ICASSP 2021-2021 IEEE International Conference on Acoustics, Speech and Signal Processing (ICASSP)* (pp. 7578–7582). IEEE. DOI: 10.1109/ICASSP39728.2021.9414626

Liao, Q. V., & Vaughan, J. W. (2023). Ai transparency in the age of llms: A human-centered research roadmap. *arXiv preprint arXiv:2306.01941, 10.*

Li, B., Ge, Y., Ge, Y., Wang, G., Wang, R., Zhang, R., & Shan, Y. (2024). Seed-bench: Benchmarking multimodal large language models. In *Proceedings of the IEEE/CVF Conference on Computer Vision and Pattern Recognition* (pp. 13299-13308).

Li, J., Meng, X., Wang, W., & Xin, B. (2019). A novel hyperspectral imaging and modeling method for the component identification of woven fabrics. *Textile Research Journal, 89*(18), 3752–3767. DOI: 10.1177/0040517518821907

Li, L., & Lorenzo, L. C. (2025). Case Project Paper on the Promoting Brand Transparency, Consumer Trust, and Purchase Decisions in an Apparel Business in Fujian Province, China. *European Journal of Business. Economics & Management, 1*(2), 97–119.

Li, M., Tan, M., Wang, S., Li, J., Zhang, G., & Zhong, Y. (2021). The effect of preceding self-control on green consumption behavior: The moderating role of moral elevation. *Psychology Research and Behavior Management, 14*, 2169–2180. DOI: 10.2147/PRBM.S341786 PMID: 34992478

Lin, L., Wang, L., Guo, J., & Wong, K. F. (2024). Investigating bias in LLM-based bias detection: Disparities between LLMs and human perception. *arXiv preprint arXiv:2403.14896*.

Lingling, L., & Ye, L. (2023). The impact of digital empowerment on open innovation performance of enterprises from the perspective of SOR. *Frontiers in Psychology, 14*, 1109149. Advance online publication. DOI: 10.3389/fpsyg.2023.1109149 PMID: 36844287

Lin, Z., Guan, S., Zhang, W., Zhang, H., Li, Y., & Zhang, H. (2024). Towards trustworthy LLMs: A review on debiasing and dehallucinating in large language models. *Artificial Intelligence Review, 57*(9), 243. DOI: 10.1007/s10462-024-10896-y

Li, P., Wu, C., & Spence, C. (2023). Comparing the influence of visual information and the perceived intelligence of voice assistants when shopping for sustainable clothing online. *Humanities & Social Sciences Communications, 10*(1), 727. DOI: 10.1057/s41599-023-02244-2

Liu, S., & Liu, C. (2025). Mapping the digital transformation in the fashion industry: The past, present and future. *Journal of Fashion Marketing and Management, 29*(7), 1292–1319. DOI: 10.1108/JFMM-09-2024-0380

Liu, X., & Croft, W. B. (2005). Statistical language modeling for information retrieval. *Annual Review of Information Science & Technology, 39*(1), 1–31. DOI: 10.1002/aris.1440390108

Liu, Z., Luo, P., Qiu, S., Wang, X., & Tang, X. (2016). DeepFashion: Powering Robust Clothes Recognition and Retrieval with Rich Annotations. *2016 IEEE Conference on Computer Vision and Pattern Recognition (CVPR)*, 1096–1104. DOI: 10.1109/CVPR.2016.124

Li, Z., Li, H., & Wang, S. (2022). How Multidimensional Digital Empowerment Affects Technology Innovation Performance: The Moderating Effect of Adaptability to Technology Embedding. *Sustainability (Basel), 14*(23), 15916. DOI: 10.3390/su142315916

Lo, C. H., & Lin, L. F. (2024, July). Personalized E-Shopping Recommendations for Sustainable Consumption. In *2024 16th IIAI International Congress on Advanced Applied Informatics (IIAI-AAI)* (pp. 585-588). IEEE. DOI: 10.1109/IIAI-AAI63651.2024.00111

Lohn, A. (2023). *Scaling AI.* Technical report, Center for Security and Emerging Technology.

Long, X., & Nasiry, J. (2022). Sustainability in the Fast Fashion Industry. *Manufacturing & Service Operations Management, 24*(3), 1276–1293. DOI: 10.1287/msom.2021.1054

Lou, X. Q., & Xu, Y. J. (2024). Consumption of sustainable denim products: The contribution of blockchain certified eco-labels. *Journal of Theoretical and Applied Electronic Commerce Research, 19*(1), 396–411. DOI: 10.3390/jtaer19010021

Lu, S., Wang, M., Liang, S., Lin, J., & Wang, Z. (2020, September). Hardware accelerator for multi-head attention and position-wise feed-forward in the transformer. In *2020, IEEE 33rd International System-on-Chip Conference (SOCC)* (pp. 84–89). IEEE. DOI: 10.1109/SOCC49529.2020.9524802

Lukin, A., & Gülseren, O. (2024). *Unlocking the Hidden Potential of the Data-Driven Nanocarbon Genome: Unleashing Novel Neural Pathways.* Elucidating Growth-Property Relationships, and Enabling Inverse Design.

Luo, Q., Su, J., Yang, C., Gui, W., Silven, O., & Liu, L. (2022). CAT-EDNet: Cross-attention transformer-based encoder–decoder network for salient defect detection of strip steel surface. *IEEE Transactions on Instrumentation and Measurement, 71*, 1–13. DOI: 10.1109/TIM.2022.3165270

MacArthur, E. (2017). Beyond plastic waste. *Science, 358*(6365), 843–843. DOI: 10.1126/science.aao6749 PMID: 29146782

Mądra-Sawicka, M., Nord, J. H., Paliszkiewicz, J., & Lee, T.-R. (2020). Digital Media: Empowerment and Equality. *Information (Basel), 11*(4), 225. DOI: 10.3390/info11040225

Mahajan, A., Sharma, S., Agrawal, V., & Nikalje, V. (2025). Influence of artificial intelligence on consumers' lifestyle product choices and the key to driving sustainable behaviour. *Young Consumers, 26*(5), 808–830. DOI: 10.1108/YC-10-2024-2307

Mahmoodi, J., Patel, M. K., & Brosch, T. (2021). Pay now, save later: Using insights from behavioural economics to commit consumers to environmental sustainability. *Journal of Environmental Psychology*, *76*, 101625. DOI: 10.1016/j.jenvp.2021.101625

Mahmood, M. S., Ruma, N. H., Ahmed, T., & Nagai, Y. (2021). Exploring Suppliers' Approaches toward Workplace Safety Compliance in the Global Garment Sector: From Bangladesh Perspective. *Social Sciences (Basel, Switzerland)*, *10*(3), 90. DOI: 10.3390/socsci10030090

Mahmoud, A. B., Hack-Polay, D., Grigoriou, N., Mohr, I., & Fuxman, L. (2021). A generational investigation and sentiment and emotion analyses of female fashion brand users on Instagram in Sub-Saharan Africa. *Journal of Brand Management*, *28*(5), 526–544. DOI: 10.1057/s41262-021-00244-8

Mai, G., Huang, W., Sun, J., Song, S., Mishra, D., Liu, N., . . . Lao, N. (2023). On the opportunities and challenges of foundation models for geospatial artificial intelligence. *arXiv preprint arXiv:2304.06798.*

Maity, S. (2019). Identifying opportunities for artificial intelligence in the evolution of training and development practices. *Journal of Management Development*, *38*(8), 651–663. DOI: 10.1108/JMD-03-2019-0069

Majamäki, T. (2022). Understanding the importance of Scope 3 Upstream emissions in the textile industry value chain: a case study of a Finnish textile company.

Maki, A., Carrico, A. R., Raimi, K. T., Truelove, H. B., Araujo, B., & Yeung, K. L. (2019). Meta-analysis of pro-environmental behaviour spillover. *Nature Sustainability*, *2*(4), 307–315. DOI: 10.1038/s41893-019-0263-9

Mallon, S. (2024). Digital Clothes and the Future of Fashion. In Technology, Sustainability and the Fashion Industry (pp. 1-15). Routledge. DOI: 10.4324/9781032658506-1

Manfredi, R., Prontera, C. T., Mariano, F., Pugliese, M., Maggiore, A., Zizzari, A., Cinquino, M., Tarantini, I., Gigli, G., & Maiorano, V. (2025). Optimization of electron transport layer inkjet printing towards fully solution-processable OLEDs. *Materials (Basel)*, *18*(14), 3231. DOI: 10.3390/ma18143231 PMID: 40731441

Mangan, S., & Alon, U. (2003). Structure and function of the feed-forward loop network motif. *Proceedings of the National Academy of Sciences of the United States of America*, *100*(21), 11980–11985. DOI: 10.1073/pnas.2133841100

Mangudhla, T. (2025). Sustainable E-Commerce Platforms: Integrating Green Marketing Strategies in Digital Marketplaces. In *Regulatory Frameworks and Digital Compliance in Green Marketing* (pp. 259-290). IGI Global Scientific Publishing.

Mansurova, A., Mansurova, A., & Nugumanova, A. (2024). QA-RAG: Exploring LLM reliance on external knowledge. *Big Data and Cognitive Computing*, *8*(9), 115. DOI: 10.3390/bdcc8090115

Manzardo, A., & Cavalli, M. (2024) Development and Application of an Integrated Life Cycle Assessment and Multi-Criteria Decision-Making Model to Support Sustainable Solutions in the Fashion Industry: The Case of Fashion Art.

Manzo, D. S. H., Jiang, Y., Elyan, E., & Isaacs, J. (2025). Artificial intelligence-based conversational agents used for sustainable fashion: Systematic literature review. *International Journal of Human-Computer Interaction*, *41*(8), 4640–4652. DOI: 10.1080/10447318.2024.2352920

Mao, Y., Yu, X., Huang, K., Zhang, Y. J. A., & Zhang, J. (2024). Green edge AI: A contemporary survey. *Proceedings of the IEEE*.

Mari, A., Mandelli, A., & Algesheimer, R. (2020). *The Evolution of Marketing in the Context of Voice Commerce: A Managerial Perspective*., DOI: 10.1007/978-3-030-50341-3_32

Marini, M., Pigosso, D. C., Pieroni, M., & McAloone, T. C. (2024). To what extent are circular economy strategies accounted in science-based targets for carbon emission reduction? *Computers & Industrial Engineering*, *197*, 110594. DOI: 10.1016/j.cie.2024.110594

Marti, P. (2024). WEAVING FASHION WITH A.I. *Fashion Highlight*, *2*(2), 52–58. DOI: 10.36253/fh-2500

Matarazzo, A., & Torlone, R. (2025). A survey on large language models with insights into their capabilities and limitations. *arXiv preprint arXiv:2501.04040*.

Mattis, N., Masur, P., Möller, J., & van Atteveldt, W. (2024a). Nudging towards news diversity: A theoretical framework for facilitating diverse news consumption through recommender design. *New Media & Society*, *26*(7), 3681–3706. DOI: 10.1177/14614448221104413

McDowell, M. (2021, June 29). The tech shaking up fashion's inventory load. Vogue Business. Retrieved from https://www.voguebusiness.com/technology/the-tech-shaking-up-fashions-inventory-load

Mehrabi, N., Morstatter, F., Saxena, N., Lerman, K., & Galstyan, A. (2021). A survey on bias and fairness in machine learning. *ACM Computing Surveys, 54*(6), 1–35.

Mekkaoui, S. (2022). *The Role and Impact of the Influencer Marketing Strategy in Fashion Companies: Farfetch Case Study* (Master's thesis, ISCTE-Instituto Universitario de Lisboa (Portugal)).

Mesjar, L., Cross, K., Jiang, Y., & Steed, J. (2023). The intersection of fashion, immersive technology, and sustainability: A literature review. *Sustainability (Basel), 15*(4), 3761. DOI: 10.3390/su15043761

Methnani, L., Aler Tubella, A., Dignum, V., & Theodorou, A. (2021). Let Me Take Over: Variable Autonomy for Meaningful Human Control. *Frontiers in Artificial Intelligence, 4*, 737072. Advance online publication. DOI: 10.3389/frai.2021.737072 PMID: 34595471

Michels, L., Ochmann, J., Schmitt, K., Laumer, S., & Tiefenbeck, V. (2024). Salience, transparency, and self-nudging: A digital nudge to promote healthier food product choices. *European Journal of Information Systems, 33*(5), 717–747. DOI: 10.1080/0960085X.2023.2229787

Milano, S., Taddeo, M., & Floridi, L. (2020). Recommender systems and their ethical challenges. *AI & Society, 35*(4), 957–967. DOI: 10.1007/s00146-020-00950-y

Miller, T. (2019). Explanation in artificial intelligence: Insights from the social sciences. *Artificial Intelligence, 267*, 1–38. DOI: 10.1016/j.artint.2018.07.007

Mills, S. (2022). Personalised nudging. *Behavioural Public Policy, 6*(1), 150–159. DOI: 10.1017/bpp.2020.7

Minaee, S., Mikolov, T., Nikzad, N., Chenaghlu, M., Socher, R., Amatriain, X., & Gao, J. (2024). Large language models: A survey. *arXiv preprint arXiv:2402.06196.*

Min, B., Ross, H., Sulem, E., Veyseh, A. P. B., Nguyen, T. H., Sainz, O., Agirre, E., Heintz, I., & Roth, D. (2023). Recent advances in natural language processing via large pre-trained language models: A survey. *ACM Computing Surveys, 56*(2), 1–40. DOI: 10.1145/3605943

Mirchandani, S., Xia, F., Florence, P., Ichter, B., Driess, D., Arenas, M. G., . . . Zeng, A. (2023). Large language models as general pattern machines. *arXiv preprint arXiv:2307.04721.*

MIT Sloan Management Review. (2024). *Generative AI in business: Balancing opportunity and responsibility*. MIT Sloan Management Review. https://sloanreview.mit.edu

Mitchell, J. R., Mitchell, R. K., Hunt, R. A., Townsend, D. M., & Lee, J. H. (2022). Stakeholder Engagement, Knowledge Problems and Ethical Challenges. *Journal of Business Ethics*, *175*(1), 75–94. DOI: 10.1007/s10551-020-04550-0

Mitchell, M., Wu, S., Zaldivar, A., Barnes, P., Hutchinson, B., Spitzer, E., Raji, I. D., & Gebru, T. (2019). Model cards for model reporting. In *Proceedings of the 2019 Conference on Fairness, Accountability, and Transparency* (pp. 220–229). https://doi.org/DOI: 10.1145/3287560.3287596

Mohamed, Y. A., Khanan, A., Bashir, M., Mohamed, A. H. H., Adiel, M. A., & Elsadig, M. A. (2024). The impact of artificial intelligence on language translation: A review. *IEEE Access : Practical Innovations, Open Solutions*, *12*, 25553–25579. DOI: 10.1109/ACCESS.2024.3366802

Mohammadian, B. (2024). Smart Nudge Marketing: Ai-Driven Behavioural Interventions For Sustainable Tourism. In *Proceedings of the International Management Conference* (Vol. 18, No. 1, pp. 529-539). Faculty of Management, Academy of Economic Studies, Bucharest, Romania.

Mohit, C. (2025). *R., Kumar, R., Nitika, & Chaudhary, K.* Global Impacts and Sustainable Practices in Fast Fashion., DOI: 10.4018/979-8-3693-7853-3.ch005

Mohiuddin Babu, M., Akter, S., Rahman, M., Billah, M. M., & Hack-Polay, D. (2024). The role of artificial intelligence in shaping the future of Agile fashion industry. *Production Planning and Control*, *35*(15), 2084–2098. DOI: 10.1080/09537287.2022.2060858

Moncayo, Á., & Silveira, A. C. (2017). Current epidemiological trends of Chagas disease in Latin America and future challenges: Epidemiology, surveillance, and health policies. *American Trypanosomiasis Chagas Disease*, 59-88.

Montoya-Torres, J. R., Gutierrez-Franco, E., & Blanco, E. E. (2015). Conceptual framework for measuring carbon footprint in supply chains. *Production Planning and Control*, *26*(4), 265–279. DOI: 10.1080/09537287.2014.894215

Morandi, A., & Tonelli, C. (2023). The impact of 3D technology on sustainability in fashion luxury product design: evidences from an exploratory analysis (Doctoral dissertation, Master's Thesis, Scuola di Ingegneria Industriale e dell'Informazione, Milano).

Morley, J., Kinsey, L., Elhalal, A., Garcia, F., Ziosi, M., & Floridi, L. (2023). Operationalising AI ethics: Barriers, enablers and next steps. *AI & Society*, *38*(1), 411–423. DOI: 10.1007/s00146-021-01308-8

Mukherjee, S., Thapliyal, K., Manchanda, M., & Jha, S. (2024, November). Sustainable E-Commerce Through Customer Emotion Recognition with Machine Learning. In *2024 3rd Edition of IEEE Delhi Section Flagship Conference (DELCON)* (pp. 1-7). IEEE. DOI: 10.1109/DELCON64804.2024.10866879

Mukherjee, A., & Bharti, L. (2025). Present Challenges and Future Opportunities of Sustainable Retailing in the Apparel Industry. In *Sustainable Apparel Retailing* (pp. 59–95). Springer Nature Switzerland. DOI: 10.1007/978-3-031-83875-0_4

Mumuni, A., & Mumuni, F. (2025). Large language models for artificial general intelligence (AGI): A survey of foundational principles and approaches. *arXiv preprint arXiv:2501.03151.*

Murphy, G. (2025). Transforming green waste into black gold: a life cycle assessment of biochar production from municipal waste.

Murugadoss, B., Poelitz, C., Drosos, I., Le, V., McKenna, N., Negreanu, C. S., Parnin, C., & Sarkar, A. (2025, April). Evaluating the evaluator: Measuring LLMs' adherence to task evaluation instructions. *Proceedings of the AAAI Conference on Artificial Intelligence, 39*(18), 19589–19597. DOI: 10.1609/aaai.v39i18.34157

Murugesan, B., Jayanthi, K. B., & Karthikeyan, G. (2024). Integrating Digital Twins and 3D Technologies in Fashion: Advancing Sustainability and Consumer Engagement. In *Illustrating Digital Innovations Towards Intelligent Fashion: Leveraging Information System Engineering and Digital Twins for Efficient Design of Next-Generation Fashion* (pp. 1–88). Springer Nature Switzerland. DOI: 10.1007/978-3-031-71052-0_1

Musiol, M. (2024). *Generative AI: Navigating the course to the artificial general intelligence future.* John Wiley & Sons.

Musova, Z., Musa, H., Drugdova, J., Lazaroiu, G., & Alayasa, J. (2021). Consumer attitudes towards new circular models in the fashion industry. *Journal of Competitiveness, 13*(3), 111–128. DOI: 10.7441/joc.2021.03.07

Muthukumarana, T. T., Karunathilake, H. P., Punchihewa, H. K. G., Manthilake, M. M. I. D., & Hewage, K. N. (2018). Life cycle environmental impacts of the apparel industry in Sri Lanka: Analysis of the energy sources. *Journal of Cleaner Production, 172*, 1346–1357. DOI: 10.1016/j.jclepro.2017.10.261

Mylrea, M., & Robinson, N. (2023). Artificial Intelligence (AI) Trust Framework and Maturity Model: Applying an Entropy Lens to Improve Security, Privacy, and Ethical AI. *Entropy (Basel, Switzerland), 25*(10), 1429. DOI: 10.3390/e25101429 PMID: 37895550

Nablsi, R. (2024). "Buy Now, Think Later?": The AI Product Recommendations Effect: From Impulse Buying to Post-Purchase Emotions.

Naikwadi, S. (2024). Role of Governments and Consumers. In *Climate Action Through Eco-Friendly Textiles* (pp. 163–178). Springer Nature Singapore. DOI: 10.1007/978-981-99-9856-2_11

National Academies of Sciences. Medicine, Division on Engineering, Physical Sciences, Space Studies Board, Committee on the Decadal Survey for Earth Science, & Applications from Space. (2019). *Thriving on our changing planet: A decadal strategy for Earth observation from space*. National Academies Press.

National Institute of Standards and Technology. (2023). *Artificial intelligence risk management framework (AI RMF 1.0)* (pp. 1–42). https://doi.org/DOI: 10.6028/NIST.AI.100-1

Negro, G. D. (2025). Bridging Methodologies for Sustainability: A Review of Environmental Assessment Frameworks.

Net0. (2024, February 28). Carbon Disclosure Project (CDP) reporting: Facts to get you started. Net0. Retrieved from https://net0.com/blog/cdp-reporting/

Neupane, B. (2024). Artificial Intelligence and Big Data Technologies to Optimize Government Decision-Making Processes in Cloud-Based Environments. *Journal of Artificial Intelligence and Machine Learning in Cloud Computing Systems*, *8*(11), 1–12.

Nichifor, B., Zait, L., & Timiras, L. (2025). Drivers, barriers, and innovations in sustainable food consumption: A systematic literature review. *Sustainability (Basel)*, *17*(5), 2233. DOI: 10.3390/su17052233

Nicolaï, M., & Grange, C. (2021). The digital transformation of retail during the Covid-19 pandemic: A comparative study in Canada, China, and France. In E. Mazaheri (Ed.), *The impact of Covid-19 on e-commerce* (pp. xx–xx). Proud Pen. https://doi.org/DOI: 10.51432/978-1-8381524-8-2_1

Niguse, T., Kant, S., Kebede, K., & Alemu, Z. K. (2026). The Role of Co-Marketing on the Digital Fashion Integration in Smart Product by Mediation of Cross-Cultural Marketing in Ethiopia. In *Sustainable Branding, Cultural Intelligence and Co-Marketing* (pp. 75-100). IGI Global Scientific Publishing.

Niguse, T., Kant, S., Kebede, K., & Alemu, Z. K. (2026). Effect of Green Branding on Sustainable Competitive Advantage With Mediating Role of Continuous Learning in the Case of Luxury Products, Ethiopia. In *Technology-Driven Market Transformations for Digital Fashion and Smart Luxury* (pp. 93–120). IGI Global Scientific Publishing.

Niinimäki, K., Peters, G., Dahlbo, H., Perry, P., Rissanen, T., & Gwilt, A. (2020). The environmental price of fast fashion. *Nature Reviews. Earth & Environment, 1*(4), 189–200. DOI: 10.1038/s43017-020-0039-9

Nithish, K. K., Karthikeyan, P., Dharmesh Nithil, K., Reshma, P., Vaishnavi, V., & Prakash, N. (2023, December). The Study of Ethical Aspects of Implementing Large Language Models in Business and Society. In *International Conference on Soft Computing and Pattern Recognition* (pp. 156–166). Cham: Springer Nature Switzerland.

Noris, A. (2016). *Handbook of Research on Global Fashion Management and Merchandising* (Vecchi, A., & Buckley, C., Eds.). IGI Global., DOI: 10.4018/978-1-5225-0110-7

O'Sullivan, S., Nevejans, N., Allen, C., Blyth, A., Leonard, S., Pagallo, U., Holzinger, K., Holzinger, A., Sajid, M. I., & Ashrafian, H. (2019). Legal, regulatory, and ethical frameworks for the developing standards in artificial intelligence (AI) and autonomous robotic surgery. *International Journal of Medical Robotics and Computer Assisted Surgery, 15*(1), e1968. DOI: 10.1002/rcs.1968

Oh, J., Nah, S., & Yang, Z. D. (2025). How autonomy of artificial intelligence technology and user agency influence AI perceptions and attitudes: Applying the theory of psychological reactance. *Journal of Broadcasting & Electronic Media, 69*(3), 161–182. DOI: 10.1080/08838151.2025.2485319

Okur, N., & Saricam, C. (2025). Modern Tools in Fashion Retailing and Consumer Perspective. In *Changing Textile and Apparel Consumption in Transformative Era of Sustainability and Digitalization* (pp. 163–223). Springer Nature Switzerland. DOI: 10.1007/978-3-031-97419-9_5

Omisola, J. O., Bihani, D., Daraojimba, A. I., Osho, G. O., Ubamadu, B. C., & Etukudoh, E. A. (2023). Blockchain in supply chain transparency: A conceptual framework for real-time data tracking and reporting using blockchain and AI. International Journal of Multidisciplinary Research and Growth Evaluation, 4.

Onitiu, D. (2022). Algorithmic abstractions of 'fashion identity' and the role of privacy with regard to algorithmic personalisation systems in the fashion domain. *AI & Society, 37*(4), 1749–1758. DOI: 10.1007/s00146-021-01235-8

Onwezen, M. C., Bartels, J., & Antonides, G. (2014). The self-regulatory function of anticipated pride and guilt in a sustainable and healthy consumption context. *European Journal of Social Psychology*, *44*(1), 53–68. DOI: 10.1002/ejsp.1991

Opitz, S., Sliwka, D., Vogelsang, T., & Zimmermann, T. (2023). *The algorithmic assignment of incentive schemes*. *SSRN*. https://doi.org/DOI: 10.2139/ssrn.4077778

Orisadare, E. A., Achukwu, O. E., Ogunyemi, A. A., Adedeji, D. O., Diyaolu, I. J., Ugwu, E. I., Oluwatope, A. O., Bakare, K. O., & Awoyelu, I. O. (2025). Digitalisation and green strategies: A systematic review of the textile, apparel and fashion industries. *Circular Economy and Sustainability*, *5*(4), 1–53. DOI: 10.1007/s43615-025-00555-x

Ornati, M. (2023, July). A Conceptual Model of Dress Embodiment and Technological Mediation in Digital Fashion. In International Conference on Fashion communication: between tradition and future digital developments (pp. 57-67). Cham: Springer Nature Switzerland. DOI: 10.1007/978-3-031-38541-4_6

Owusu, P., Li, Z., & Omari-Sasu, A. Y. (2025). Optimizing consumer engagement and repurchase intentions: The role of strategic post-purchase communication. *Journal of Retailing and Consumer Services*, *82*, 104095. DOI: 10.1016/j.jretconser.2024.104095

Ozturkcan, S., & Kitapci, O. (2025). A sustainable solution for the hospitality industry: The QR code menus. *Journal of Information Technology Teaching Cases*, *15*(1), 2–7. DOI: 10.1177/20438869231181599

Ozuem, W. (2018). *Digital Marketing Strategies for Fashion and Luxury Brands* (W. Ozuem& Y. Azemi, Eds.). IGI Global. DOI: 10.4018/978-1-5225-2697-1

Palomo-Lovinski, N. (2024). Missed opportunities: Fashion fabric sourcing professionals' use of the MSI in the Higg Index. *Fashion Practice*, *16*(3), 373–390. DOI: 10.1080/17569370.2024.2312925

Pal, R., & Jayarathne, A. (2022). Digitalization in the textiles and clothing sector. In *The digital supply chain* (pp. 255–271). Elsevier. DOI: 10.1016/B978-0-323-91614-1.00015-0

Pandey, M., & Yadav, P. S. (2023). Understanding the role of individual concerns, attitude, and perceived value in green apparel purchase intention; the mediating effect of consumer involvement and moderating role of generation Z&Y. *Cleaner and Responsible Consumption*, *9*, 100120. DOI: 10.1016/j.clrc.2023.100120

Pandey, M., Yadav, P. S., & Pothireddy, R. R. (2024). Role of Gamification in Influencer Marketing. In *Marketing and Gamification* (pp. 157–169). Routledge., DOI: 10.4324/9781032694238-13

Panju, M. (2024). What Goes Around Comes Around?: The Sustainability Paradox of Second-Hand Clothing Marketplaces in a Cross-Cultural Context. *East African Journal of Interdisciplinary Studies*, *7*(1), 1–27. DOI: 10.37284/eajis.7.1.1799

Pant, P., & Kanchi, G. (2024). Sustainability standards for textile processing. In *Sustainable Textile Chemical Processing* (pp. 415–464). CRC Press.

Parthasarathy, V. B., Zafar, A., Khan, A., & Shahid, A. (2024). The ultimate guide to fine-tuning LMS from basics to breakthroughs: An exhaustive review of technologies, research, best practices, applied research challenges, and opportunities. *arXiv preprint arXiv:2408.13296*.

Pecoraro, R., Basile, V., & Bono, V. (2022). Local multi-head channel self-attention for facial expression recognition. *Information (Basel)*, *13*(9), 419. DOI: 10.3390/info13090419

Peng, C., & Mitra, U. (2024). Planning versus learning: Fair space-time scheduling for unwired networks. *IEEE Transactions on Wireless Communications*, *23*(11), 16621–16634. DOI: 10.1109/TWC.2024.3444693

Peng, K., Feng, K., Chen, B., Shan, Y., Zhang, N., Wang, P., Fang, K., Bai, Y., Zou, X., Wei, W., Geng, X., Zhang, Y., & Li, J. (2023). The global power sector's low-carbon transition may enhance sustainable development goal achievement. *Nature Communications*, *14*(1), 3144. DOI: 10.1038/s41467-023-38987-4 PMID: 37253805

Periyasamy, A. P., & Periyasami, S. (2023). Rise of digital fashion and metaverse: Influence on sustainability. *Digital Economy and Sustainable Development*, *1*(1), 16. DOI: 10.1007/s44265-023-00016-z

Perra, N., & Rocha, L. E. C. (2019). Modelling opinion dynamics in the age of algorithmic personalisation. *Scientific Reports*, *9*(1), 7261. Advance online publication. DOI: 10.1038/s41598-019-43830-2 PMID: 31086228

Peters, D., Vold, K., Robinson, D., & Calvo, R. A. (2020). Responsible AI—Two Frameworks for Ethical Design Practice. *IEEE Transactions on Technology and Society*, *1*(1), 34–47. DOI: 10.1109/TTS.2020.2974991

Petro anu, D. M., Pîrjan, A., & Tăbu că, A. (2023). Tracing the influence of large language models across the most impactful scientific works. *Electronics (Basel)*, *12*(24), 4957. DOI: 10.3390/electronics12244957

Pham, D. T. (2024). *Ethos, Identification, and the Environment: Patagonia's Narrative Approach to Sustainability* (Master's thesis, San Diego State University).

Pham, H. (2018). The impact of Blockchain Technology on the improvement of Food Supply Chain Management: Transparency and Traceability: A case study of Walmart and Atria.

Pichert, D., & Katsikopoulos, K. V. (2008). Green defaults: Information presentation and pro-environmental behaviour. *Journal of Environmental Psychology*, *28*(1), 63–73. DOI: 10.1016/j.jenvp.2007.09.004

Pitoura, E., Stefanidis, K., & Koutrika, G. (2022). Fairness in rankings and recommendations: An overview. *The VLDB Journal*, *31*(3), 431–458. DOI: 10.1007/s00778-021-00697-y

Popescu, A. (2024). Enhancing environmental standards in textiles: The role of OEKO-TEX® standard 100. *Bulletin of the Transilvania University of Brasov. Series V, Economic Sciences*, •••, 59–68. DOI: 10.31926/but.es.2024.17.66.1.6

Poursabzi-Sangdeh, F., Goldstein, D. G., Hofman, J. M., Vaughan, J. W., & Wallach, H. (2021). Manipulating and measuring model interpretability. In *Proceedings of the 2021 CHI Conference on Human Factors in Computing Systems* (Article 1). DOI: 10.1145/3411764.3445315

Prashar, A., & Kaushal, L. A. (2025). Nudging sustainable fashion choices: An experimental investigation on generation Z fashion consumers. *Acta Psychologica*, *253*, 104727. DOI: 10.1016/j.actpsy.2025.104727 PMID: 39837072

Prathibhani, H. K. K., & Lakshika, V. G. P. (2023). Sustainable consumer behaviour in clothes disposal in the Sri Lankan context. *Asian Journal of Marketing Management*, *2*(02). Advance online publication. DOI: 10.31357/ajmm.v2i02.6471

Precedence Research. (2025, July 16). Smart labels market accelerates in 2025: Sustainability and e-commerce drive demand globally [Press release]. GlobeNewswire. Retrieved from https://www.globenewswire.com/news-release/2025/07/16/3116563/0/en/Smart-Labels-Market-Accelerates-in-2025-Sustainability-and-E-Commerce-Drive-Demand-Globally.html

Prikshat, V., Patel, P., Varma, A., & Ishizaka, A. (2022). A multi-stakeholder ethical framework for AI-augmented HRM. *International Journal of Manpower*, *43*(1), 226–250. DOI: 10.1108/IJM-03-2021-0118

Prits, E. (2023). From intentions to actions: nudging Generation Z towards sustainable fashion choices through service design.

Priyadarshanie, E. A. A. (2024). Predicting garment quality based on fabric characteristics via machine learning.

Protocol, G. H. G. (2011). *Product life cycle accounting and reporting standard.* World Resources Institute. Retrieved from, https://ghgprotocol.org/product-standard

Provenance Team. (2015, September 21; updated 2023, December 19). Blockchain: the solution for transparency in product supply chains. Provenance. Retrieved from https://www.provenance.org/news-insights/blockchain-the-solution-for-transparency-in-product-supply-chains

Puranik, B., Guldogan, O., Madhow, U., & Pedarsani, R. (2024). Long-term fairness in sequential multi-agent selection with positive reinforcement. *IEEE Journal on Selected Areas in Information Theory, 5*, 424–441. DOI: 10.1109/JSAIT.2024.3416078

Qi, J., Yao, Y., Bai, Y., Xu, B., Li, J., Liu, Z., & Chua, T. S. (2025). An LMM for Efficient Video Understanding via Reinforced Compression of Video Cubes. *arXiv preprint arXiv:2504.15270.*

Qiao, T., Zhang, J., Xu, D., & Tao, D. (2019). Mirrorgan: Learning text-to-image generation by redescription. In *Proceedings of the IEEE/CVF conference on computer vision and pattern recognition* (pp. 1505-1514).

Qin, C., & Rusu, F. (2017, June). Dot-product join: Scalable in-database linear algebra for big model analytics, in *Proceedings of the 29th International Conference on Scientific and Statistical Database Management* (pp. 1–12). DOI: 10.1145/3085504.3085512

Radhakrishnan, S. (2014). The Sustainable Apparel Coalition and the Higg Index. In Muthu, S. S. (Ed.), *Roadmap to sustainable textiles and clothing: Regulatory aspects and sustainability standards of textiles and the clothing supply chain* (pp. 23–57). Springer Science & Business Media., DOI: 10.1007/978-981-287-164-0_2

Rafieian, O., & Yoganarasimhan, H. (2022a). AI and Personalization. SSRN Electronic Journal. DOI: 10.2139/ssrn.4123356

Raiaan, M. A. K., Mukta, M. S. H., Fatema, K., Fahad, N. M., Sakib, S., Mim, M. M. J., Ahmad, J., Ali, M. E., & Azam, S. (2024). A review on large language models: Architectures, applications, taxonomies, open issues, and challenges. *IEEE Access : Practical Innovations, Open Solutions, 12*, 26839–26874. DOI: 10.1109/ACCESS.2024.3365742

Raji, I. D., Smart, A., White, R. N., Mitchell, M., Gebru, T., Hutchinson, B., Smith-Loud, J., Theron, D., & Barnes, P. (2020). Closing the AI accountability gap: Defining an end-to-end framework for internal algorithmic auditing. In *Proceedings of the 2020 Conference on Fairness, Accountability, and Transparency* (pp. 33–44). https://doi.org/DOI: 10.1145/3351095.3372873

Ramasubramanian, V., & Paliwal, K. K. (1992). Fast k-dimensional tree algorithms for nearest neighbor search with application to vector quantization encoding. *IEEE Transactions on Signal Processing*, *40*(3), 518–531. DOI: 10.1109/78.120795

Rana, K., Banerjee, S. P., Agarwal, V., & Chadha, P. (2025). Examining the Role of Artificial Intelligence in Influencing Consumer Preferences and Purchase Intentions toward Green Fashion. *Metallurgical and Materials Engineering*, *31*(4), 982–992. DOI: 10.63278/1542

Rana, N. (2024). Ethical AI Integration in Marketing Strategies for Sustainable E-Commerce Fashion Designing. In *Contemporary Management and Global Leadership for Sustainability* (pp. 218–233). IGI Global Scientific Publishing. DOI: 10.4018/979-8-3693-1273-5.ch013

Rane, N. L., Tawde, A., Choudhary, S. P., & Rane, J. (2023). Contribution and performance of ChatGPT and other Large Language Models (LLM) for scientific and research advancements: A double-edged sword. *International Research Journal of Modernization in Engineering Technology and Science*, *5*(10), 875–899.

Raschka, S. (2024). *Build a large language model (from scratch)*. Simon and Schuster.

Rathore, B. (2019). Fashion sustainability in the AI era: opportunities and challenges in marketing. Eduzone: International Peer Reviewed/Refereed Multidisciplinary Journal, 8(2), 17-24..

Rathore, B. (2023). Beyond Trends: Shaping the Future of Fashion Marketing with AI, Sustainability and Machine Learning. Eduzone : International Peer Reviewed/Refereed Academic Multidisciplinary Journal, 06(02), 16–24. DOI: 10.56614/eiprmj.v6i2y17.341

Ray, S., & Nayak, L. (2023). Marketing Sustainable Fashion: Trends and Future Directions. *Sustainability (Basel)*, *15*(7), 6202. DOI: 10.3390/su15076202

Raza, A., Asif, M., & Akram, M. (2023). Give your hunger a new option: Understanding consumers' continuous intention to use online food delivery apps using trust transfer theory. *International Journal of Consumer Studies*, *47*(2), 474–495. DOI: 10.1111/ijcs.12845

Repenning, A. (2024). Speeding up, slowing down, losing grip: On digital media metronomes and timespace friction in the platformised temporalities of fashion design. *Environment and Planning A. Environment & Planning A, 56*(5), 1503–1520. DOI: 10.1177/0308518X241231691

Reviglio, U., & Agosti, C. (2020). Thinking outside the black box: The case for "algorithmic sovereignty" in social media. *Social Media + Society, 6*(2), 2056305120915613. Advance online publication. DOI: 10.1177/2056305120915613

Rinne, K. J. A. (2025). *AI-Powered Customer Engagement: How Personalization.* Chatbots, and Recommendation Systems Influence E-commerce Customer Satisfaction.

Rizkiatami, A., Masnita, Y., & Kurniawati, K. (2023). Embracing Sustainability in Purchase Behavior Using the Theory of Planned Behavior. *MIX: JURNAL ILMIAH MANAJEMEN, 13*(1), 15. DOI: 10.22441/jurnal_mix.2023.v13i1.002

Roberts, J., Baker, M., & Andrew, J. (2024). Artificial intelligence and qualitative research: The promise and perils of large language model (LLM) 'assistance'. *Critical Perspectives on Accounting, 99*, 102722. DOI: 10.1016/j.cpa.2024.102722

Robinson, P. K. (2009). Responsible retailing: Regulating fair and ethical trade. Journal of International Development. *The Journal of the Development Studies Association, 21*(7), 1015–1026.

Roco, M. C. (2008). Possibilities for global governance of converging technologies. *Journal of Nanoparticle Research, 10*(1), 11–29. DOI: 10.1007/s11051-007-9269-8

Rodrigues Schon, V., & Colombi, C. (2023). Ethical Implications in AI-Powered Trend Research Platforms. *Fashion Highlight, 1*(1), 50–59. DOI: 10.36253/fh-2261

Rohde, F., Wagner, J., Meyer, A., Reinhard, P., Voss, M., Petschow, U., & Mollen, A. (2024). Broadening the perspective for sustainable artificial intelligence: Sustainability criteria and indicators for Artificial Intelligence systems. *Current Opinion in Environmental Sustainability, 66*, 101411. DOI: 10.1016/j.cosust.2023.101411

Roichman, R., Sprecher, B., Blass, V., Meshulam, T., & Makov, T. (2024). The convenience economy: Product flows and GHG emissions of returned apparel in the EU. *Resources, Conservation and Recycling, 210*, e107811. DOI: 10.1016/j.resconrec.2024.107811

Ross, F. (2017). *Co-Creation via Digital Fashion Technology in New Business Models for Premium Product Innovation.*, DOI: 10.4018/978-1-5225-1865-5.ch002

Roumeliotis, K. I., Tselikas, N. D., & Nasiopoulos, D. K. (2023). Llama 2: Early Adopters' Utilization of Meta's New Open-Source Pretrained Model.

Rovira, J., Souza, M. C. O., Nadal, M., & Domingo, J. L. (2025). Human health risks from textile chemicals: A critical review of recent evidence (2019–2025). *Journal of Environmental Science and Health. Part A, Toxic/Hazardous Substances & Environmental Engineering*, *60*(2), 1–13. DOI: 10.1080/10934529.2025.2514406 PMID: 40482050

Roy Choudhury, A. K. (2014). Environmental impacts of the textile industry and its assessment through life cycle assessment. In *Roadmap to sustainable textiles and clothing: environmental and social aspects of textiles and clothing supply chain* (pp. 1–39). Springer Singapore. DOI: 10.1007/978-981-287-110-7_1

Roy, A. (2024). Fashion Innovation Driven by AI: Transforming Design, Manufacturing, and Customer Experience. *Applied IT & Engineering*, *2*(1), 1–8.

Ruan, Y., Maddison, C. J., & Hashimoto, T. B. (2024). Observational scaling laws and the predictability of language model performance. *Advances in Neural Information Processing Systems*, *37*, 15841–15892.

Ruiz-Real, J. L., Uribe-Toril, J., Torres, J. A., & De Pablo, J. (2020). ARTIFICIAL INTELLIGENCE IN BUSINESS AND ECONOMICS RESEARCH: TRENDS AND FUTURE. *Journal of Business Economics and Management*, *22*(1), 98–117. DOI: 10.3846/jbem.2020.13641

Ryan, M. (2023). The social and ethical impacts of artificial intelligence in agriculture: Mapping the agricultural AI literature. *AI & Society*, *38*(6), 2473–2485. DOI: 10.1007/s00146-021-01377-9

Rydenfelt, H., Haapanen, L., Haapoja, J., & Lehtiniemi, T. (2024). Personalisation in Journalism: Ethical insights and blindspots in Finnish legacy media. *Journalism*, *25*(2), 313–333. DOI: 10.1177/14648849221138424

Rzepakowski, P., & Jaroszewicz, S. (2012). Decision trees for uplift modeling with single and multiple treatments. *Knowledge and Information Systems*, *32*(2), 303–327. DOI: 10.1007/s10115-011-0434-0

Safadi, H., & Watson, R. T. (2023). Knowledge monopolies and the innovation divide: A governance perspective. *Information and Organization*, *33*(2), 100466. DOI: 10.1016/j.infoandorg.2023.100466

Sakib, F. A., Khan, S. H., & Karim, A. R. (2024, July). Extending the frontier of ChatGPT: Code generation and debugging. In *2024 International Conference on Electrical, Computer and Energy Technologies (ICECET* (pp. 1–6). IEEE. DOI: 10.1109/ICECET61485.2024.10698405

Sala, S., & Goralczyk, M. (2013). Chemical footprint: A methodological framework for bridging life cycle assessment and planetary boundaries for chemical pollution. *Integrated Environmental Assessment and Management, 9*(4), 623–632. DOI: 10.1002/ieam.1471 PMID: 23907984

Salzano, M., Fung, N., Lin, A., Marchetta, S., Colombo, F., Davis, K., & Zhuang, W. (2024). *AI and Advocacy: Maximizing Potential*. Minimizing Risk.

Samy, T. M., Asham, B. I., Slim, S. O., & Abohany, A. A. (2025). Revolutionizing online shopping with FITMI: A realistic virtual try-on solution. *Neural Computing & Applications, 37*(8), 6125–6144. DOI: 10.1007/s00521-024-10843-6

Sardianou, E., & Briana, M. (2025). Platform-Driven Sustainability in E-Commerce: Consumer Behavior Toward Recycled Fashion. *Recycling, 10*(4), 161. DOI: 10.3390/recycling10040161

Sarkar, M. (2023). Environmental sustainability under E-commerce: A holistic perspective. *European Journal of Development Studies, 3*(3), 1–6. DOI: 10.24018/ejdevelop.2023.3.3.252

Sarna, N. H. (2023). Building Seats at the Table: The Use of Worker-Driven Social Responsibility Agreements to Address Forced Labor in the Global Value Chain. *J. Int'l Bus. & L., 23*, 62.

Scaraboto, D., Shaw, D., & Duffy, K. (2022). Save your wardrobe: Supporting sustainable and mindful clothing consumption. *NIM Marketing Intelligence Review, 14*(1), 54–59. DOI: 10.2478/nimmir-2022-0009

Schmauder, C., Karpus, J., Moll, M., Bahrami, B., & Deroy, O. (2023). Algorithmic Nudging: The Need for an Interdisciplinary Oversight. *Topoi, 42*(3), 799–807. DOI: 10.1007/s11245-023-09907-4

Schmidt Rivera, X. C., Balcombe, P., & Niero, M. (2021). Life cycle assessment as a metric for circular economy.

Schmidt, A. T., & Engelen, B. (2020). The ethics of nudging: An overview. *Philosophy Compass, 15*(4), e12658. DOI: 10.1111/phc3.12658

Schneider, S. (2025). Chatbot Epistemology. *Social Epistemology*, •••, 1–20.

Schultz, P. W., Nolan, J. M., Cialdini, R. B., Goldstein, N., & Griskevicius, V. (2007). The constructive, destructive, and reconstructive power of social norms. *Psychological Science, 18*(5), 429–434. DOI: 10.1111/j.1467-9280.2007.01917.x PMID: 17576283

Schweiger, G., Eckerstorfer, L. V., Hafner, I., Fleischhacker, A., Radl, J., Glock, B., Wastian, M., Rößler, M., Lettner, G., Popper, N., & Corcoran, K. (2020). Active consumer participation in smart energy systems. *Energy and Building, 227*, 110359. DOI: 10.1016/j.enbuild.2020.110359

Sejnowski, T. J. (2018). *The deep learning revolution*. MIT Press. DOI: 10.7551/mitpress/11474.001.0001

Sewell, D., & Hiller, J. S. (2025). Presumptions Of AI Malfunction. *Available at SSRN* 5143853.

Shamsuzzaman, M., Islam, M. M., Hasan, H. R. U., Khan, A. M., & Sayem, A. S. M. (2023). Mapping environmental sustainability of knitted textile production facilities. *Journal of Cleaner Production, 405*, 136900. DOI: 10.1016/j.jclepro.2023.136900

Shao, H., Xu, Y., Ji, Y., Yang, J., & Liu, C. (2019, December). Intra-modality feature interaction using self-attention for visual question answering. In *International Conference on Neural Information Processing* (pp. 215-222). Cham: Springer International Publishing. DOI: 10.1007/978-3-030-36802-9_24

Shao, J., Feng, Y., & Liu, Z. (2024). The impact of big data-driven strategies on sustainable consumer behaviour in E-commerce: A green economy perspective. *Sustainability (Basel), 16*(24), 10960. DOI: 10.3390/su162410960

Sharma, D., Sundravadivelu, K., Khengar, J., Thaker, D. J., Patel, S. N., & Shah, P. (2024). Advancements in Natural Language Processing: Enhancing Machine Understanding of Human Language in Conversational AI Systems. *Journal of Computational Analysis and Applications, 33*(6).

Sharma, M., Shail, H., Painuly, P. K., & Kumar, A. V. S. (2023). *AI-Powered Technologies Used in Online Fashion Retail for Sustainable Business.*, DOI: 10.4018/979-8-3693-0019-0.ch028

Shaw, D., & Duffy, K. (2020). Save Your Wardrobe: Digitalising Sustainable Consumption: Further Insights.

Sheil, B., Anagnostopoulos, C., Buckley, R., Oryem Ciantia, M., Febrianto, E., Fu, J., Gao, Z., Geng, X., Gong, B., Hanley, K., He, P., & Kolomvatsos, K., de C.F.L. Lopes, B., Ninic, J., Previtali, M., Rezania, M., Ruiz-Lopez, A., Sun, J., Suryasentana, S., ... Zhang, P. (. (2026). Artificial intelligence transformations in geotechnics: Progress, challenges and future enablers. *Computers and Geotechnics, 189*, 107604. DOI: 10.1016/j.compgeo.2025.107604

Shen, Z., Hu, Y., & Yin, Y. (2025). Algorithm-generated identity labeling promotes identity-consistent product preferences. *Psychology and Marketing*, *42*(6), 1667–1679. DOI: 10.1002/mar.22195

Shethiya, A. S. (2024). Architecting Intelligent Systems: Opportunities and Challenges of Generative AI and LLM Integration. *Academia Nexus Journal, 3*(2).

Shi, D., Shen, T., Huang, Y., Li, Z., Leng, Y., Jin, R., . . . Xiong, D. (2024). Large language model safety: A holistic survey. *arXiv preprint arXiv:2412.17686.*

Shin, D., & Ahmad, N. B. (2023). Algorithmic nudge: An approach to designing human-centered generative artificial intelligence. *Computer*, *56*(8), 95–99. DOI: 10.1109/MC.2023.3278156

Shin, D., Kee, K. F., & Shin, E. Y. (2023). The nudging effect of accuracy alerts for combating the diffusion of misinformation. *Journal of Broadcasting & Electronic Media*, *67*(2), 141–160. DOI: 10.1080/08838151.2023.2175830

Shin, D., & Zhou, S. (2024). A value- and diversity-aware news recommendation system: Can algorithmic gatekeeping nudge readers to view diverse news? *Journalism & Mass Communication Quarterly*, 10776990241246680. Advance online publication. DOI: 10.1177/10776990241246680

Shyam Sundar, S., & Sampada, S. (2010, July 1). Marathe, Personalization versus Customization: The Importance of Agency, Privacy, and Power Usage. *Human Communication Research*, *36*(3), 298–322. DOI: 10.1111/j.1468-2958.2010.01377.x

Simon, J., Wong, P.-H., & Rieder, G. (2020). Algorithmic bias and the Value Sensitive Design approach. *Internet Policy Review*, *9*(4). Advance online publication. DOI: 10.14763/2020.4.1534

Singh, M., Michael, R. A., Saheb, S. S., Yadav, P. S., Kiran, P. B. N., & Malhi, A. (2025). A Study on Digital Intelligence and Influencer Marketing for Sustainable Diversification of India's Retail Economy. In Advances in Logistics, Operations, and Management Science (pp. 1–22). IGI Global. https://doi.org/DOI: 10.4018/979-8-3693-8492-3.ch001

Singh, M., Syed, S. M., Saheb, S. S., Yadav, P. S., & Kiran, P. B. N. (2025). Role of Influencer Marketing in the Indian Retail Business Sector. In Advances in Marketing, Customer Relationship Management, and E-Services (pp. 105–130). IGI Global. https://doi.org/DOI: 10.4018/979-8-3693-8542-5.ch005

Singh, A., & Joachims, T. (2018). Fairness of exposure in rankings. In *Proceedings of the 24th ACM SIGKDD International Conference on Knowledge Discovery & Data Mining* (pp. 2219–2228). DOI: 10.1145/3219819.3220088

Singh, S. (2024). Artificial intelligence in the fashion and apparel industry. *Tekstilec, 67*(3), 225–240. DOI: 10.14502/tekstilec.67.2024001

Sinha, S., & Lee, Y. M. (2024). Challenges with developing and deploying AI models and applications in industrial systems. *Discover Artificial Intelligence, 4*(1), 55. DOI: 10.1007/s44163-024-00151-2

Sontake, P. (2025). A Review of Artificial Intelligence (AI) Tools in Research Writing. *International Journal of Scientific Research and Technology.*

Spathis, D., & Kawsar, F. (2024). The first step is the hardest: Pitfalls of representing and tokenizing temporal data for large language models. *Journal of the American Medical Informatics Association : JAMIA, 31*(9), 2151–2158. DOI: 10.1093/jamia/ocae090

Sridhar, A., Pesala, B., Radhakrishnan, G., Niezgoda, J., & Gopalakrishnan, S. (2025). Evolution of Artificial Intelligence. In *Artificial Intelligence and Biological Sciences* (pp. 26–37). CRC Press. DOI: 10.1201/9781003492726-2

Steindl, C., Jonas, E., Sittenthaler, S., Traut-Mattausch, E., & Greenberg, J. (2015). Understanding psychological reactance: New developments and findings. *Zeitschrift für Psychologie, 223*(4), 205–214. DOI: 10.1027/2151-2604/a000222 PMID: 27453805

Stern, P. C. (2000). Toward a coherent theory of environmentally significant behavior. *The Journal of Social Issues, 56*(3), 407–424. DOI: 10.1111/0022-4537.00175

Stevenson, T. (2023). Virtual Fashion: Digital Representations of Materiality and Time (Doctoral dissertation, Open Access Te Herenga Waka-Victoria University of Wellington).

Subramaniam, R., Azzuhri, D. S. R., & Wah, D. T. Y. A Review on Combating Counterfeiting by Empowering Consumers Via Nfc Enabled Mobile Computing Leveraging on Blockchain Technology. Available at *SSRN* 5012178. DOI: 10.2139/ssrn.5012178

Subramanian, S., Harrington, P., Keutzer, K., Bhimji, W., Morozov, D., Mahoney, M. W., & Gholami, A. (2023). Towards foundation models for scientific machine learning: Characterizing scaling and transfer behavior. *Advances in Neural Information Processing Systems, 36*, 71242–71262.

Sugadev, M., Niranjana, S., Deepa, N., Dhaarani, T. G., Giri, J., & Samhan, A. A. A. (2024, December). A Novel Development of Virtual Wardrobe Design Based on Artificial Intelligence and Internet of Things Enabled Technologies. In *2024 International Conference on Innovative Computing, Intelligent Communication and Smart Electrical Systems (ICSES)* (pp. 1-6). IEEE. DOI: 10.1109/ICSES63760.2024.10910343

Sultanoğlu, B. (2025) global and local developments in sustainability reporting: key changes and trends. In viii. International symposium on accounting and finance symposuim proceeding book (p. 1).

Sun, Y., He, J., Cui, L., Lei, S., & Lu, C. T. (2024). Exploring the deceptive power of LLM-generated fake news: A study of real-world detection challenges. *arXiv preprint arXiv:2403.18249*.

Sun, C., Fang, Y., Kong, M., Chen, X., & Liu, Y. (2022). Influence of augmented reality product display on consumers' product attitudes: A product uncertainty reduction perspective. *Journal of Retailing and Consumer Services, 64*, 102828. DOI: 10.1016/j.jretconser.2021.102828

Sundermeyer, M., Ney, H., & Schlüter, R. (2015). From feedforward to recurrent LSTM neural networks for language modeling. *IEEE/ACM Transactions on Audio, Speech, and Language Processing, 23*(3), 517–529. DOI: 10.1109/TASLP.2015.2400218

Sundström, M., Hjelm-Lidholm, S., & Radon, A. (2019). Clicking the boredom away – Exploring impulse fashion buying behavior online. *Journal of Retailing and Consumer Services, 47*, 150–156. DOI: 10.1016/j.jretconser.2018.11.006

Sun, J., Zheng, C., Xie, E., Liu, Z., Chu, R., Qiu, J., & Li, Z. (2023). A survey of reasoning with foundation models: Concepts, methodologies, and outlook. *ACM Computing Surveys*.

Sunny, J., Undralla, N., & Madhusudanan Pillai, V. (2020). Supply chain transparency through blockchain-based traceability: An overview with demonstration. *Computers & Industrial Engineering, 150*, 106895. DOI: 10.1016/j.cie.2020.106895

Sunstein, C. R. (2014). Nudging: A very short guide. *Journal of Consumer Policy, 37*(4), 583–588. DOI: 10.1007/s10603-014-9273-1

Sunstein, C. R. (2016). *The ethics of influence: Government in the age of behavioral science*. Cambridge University Press. DOI: 10.1017/CBO9781316493021

Suroto. (2025). Digital nudging strategies, applications, and ethical considerations: A systematic literature review. *International Journal of Innovation in Enterprise System, 9*(1). https://doi.org/DOI: 10.25124/ijies.v9i01.663

Sutton, R. S., & Barto, A. G. (2018). *Reinforcement learning: An introduction* (2nd ed.). MIT Press.

Svensson, V. (2020). The apparel industry's environmental impact, mitigation and adaptation to climate change: A case study of three Swedish companies.

Swanberg, E., & Narmashiri, M. (2025). A Factual Sustainability Chatbot: Leveraging Natural Language Understanding and Embedding Models for Reliable Q&A.

Szatkowski, S., Jaen-Sola, P., & Oterkus, E. (2024). An Efficient Computational Analysis and Modelling of Transferred Aerodynamic Loading on Direct-Drive System of 5 MW Wind Turbine and Results Driven Optimisation for a Sustainable Generator Structure. *Sustainability (Basel)*, *16*(2), 545. DOI: 10.3390/su16020545

Taeihagh, A. (2021). Governance of artificial intelligence. *Policy and Society*, *40*(2), 137–157. DOI: 10.1080/14494035.2021.1928377

Taherdoost, H. (2022). A Critical Review of Blockchain Acceptance Models—Blockchain Technology Adoption Frameworks and Applications. *Computers*, *11*(2), 24. DOI: 10.3390/computers11020024

Tajurahim, N. N. S., Abu Bakar, E., Md Jusoh, Z., Ahmad, S., & Muhammad Arif, A. M. (2020). The effect of intensity of consumer education, self-efficacy, personality traits and social media on consumer empowerment. *International Journal of Consumer Studies*, *44*(6), 511–520. DOI: 10.1111/ijcs.12585

Tamlyn, K. A., Champine, V., Teel, T. L., Abrams, K. M., & Niemiec, R. M. (2025). From self to society: Comparing the social-psychological drivers of personal-sphere, social diffusion, and civic action behaviors in native plant gardening. *Society & Natural Resources*, *38*(9), 1003–1019. DOI: 10.1080/08941920.2025.2494011

Tang, Y., & Yang, Y. (2024). Pooling and attention: What are effective designs for LLM-based embedding models? *arXiv preprint arXiv:2409.02727.*

Tariq, M. U. (2025). AI tools and technologies for management education: Enhancing learning through innovation. In M. R. & S. R. (Eds.), *Integrating AI and machine learning into business and management education* (pp. 105–132). IGI Global Scientific Publishing. https://doi.org/DOI: 10.4018/979-8-3373-2150-9.ch005

Tariq, M. U. (2025). AI-driven digital nomads: Transforming labor markets and industrial growth in the digital economy. In Ordóñez de Pablos, P., Zhang, X., Anshari, M., & Almunawar, M. (Eds.), *AI and digital nomads shaping global industrial technology transitions* (pp. 113–138). IGI Global Scientific Publishing., DOI: 10.4018/979-8-3373-0159-4.ch004

Tariq, M. U. (2025). Green FinTech–Driving sustainable finance and empowering underserved communities. In Masri, M., Sait, M., & Anshari, M. (Eds.), *Promoting inclusivity and accessibility with FinTech* (pp. 279–306). IGI Global Scientific Publishing., DOI: 10.4018/979-8-3373-1112-8.ch010

Tariq, M. U. (2025). Influence of leadership styles on passion-cultivating purpose-driven leadership. In Paradiso-Testa, M. (Ed.), *The purpose of passion in leadership* (pp. 237–262). IGI Global Scientific Publishing., DOI: 10.4018/979-8-3373-2404-3.ch009

Tariq, M. U. (2025). Live streams and community interaction in digital broadcasting. In Erdem, M., & Kuş, Ö. (Eds.), *Advancements in digital broadcasting and content platforms* (pp. 215–240). IGI Global Scientific Publishing., DOI: 10.4018/979-8-3373-1459-4.ch008

Tarnanidis, T. (2024). *Driving Green Marketing in Fashion and Retail* (Tarnanidis, T. K., Papachristou, E., Karypidis, M., & Ismyrlis, V., Eds.). IGI Global., DOI: 10.4018/979-8-3693-3049-4

Textile World. (2024, November 18). KOLAB Collection launches NFC (Near Field Communication)-tagged sustainable clothing line. Textile World. Retrieved from https://www.textileworld.com/textile-world/knitting-apparel/2024/11/kolab-collection-launches-nfc-near-field-communication-tagged-sustainable-clothing-line/

Thaler, R. H., & Sunstein, C. R. (2008). *Nudge: Improving decisions about health, wealth, and happiness.* Yale University Press.

Thiebes, S., Lins, S., & Sunyaev, A. (2021). Trustworthy artificial intelligence. *Electronic Markets, 31*(2), 447–464. DOI: 10.1007/s12525-020-00441-4

Thirumuruganathan, S., Tang, N., Ouzzani, M., & Doan, A. (2020). Data Curation with Deep Learning. In *EDBT* (pp. 277–286).

Thuraisingham, B. M. (2020, March). Can AI be for good amid cyber attacks and privacy violations? A position paper. In *Proceedings of the Tenth ACM Conference on Data and Application Security and Privacy* (pp. 1–4).

Titi, E. S., & Victor, C. (2024). *On the inadequacy of nudging data assimilation algorithms for non-dissipative systems* (arXiv preprint). https://arxiv.org/abs/2411.08273

Tomalin, M., Byrne, B., Concannon, S., Saunders, D., & Ullmann, S. (2021). The practical ethics of bias reduction in machine translation: Why domain adaptation is better than data debiasing. *Ethics and Information Technology*, *23*(3), 419–433. DOI: 10.1007/s10676-021-09583-1

Too, E. C., Yujian, L., Njuki, S., & Yingchun, L. (2019). A comparative study of fine-tuning deep learning models for plant disease identification. *Computers and Electronics in Agriculture*, *161*, 272–279. DOI: 10.1016/j.compag.2018.03.032

Tran, A. (2024). Consumer Culture in the Fashion Industry: Understanding Consumption Patterns and Sustainability Efforts.

Triguero, I., Molina, D., Poyatos, J., Del Ser, J., & Herrera, F. (2023, January). *General-purpose artificial intelligence systems (GPIS): Properties, definition, taxonomy, open challenges, and implications*. arXiv preprint arXiv:2307.14283.

Uluer, M. U., Gök, G., Ünver, H. Ö., & Kılıç, S. E. (2012). Towards a Decision Support Framework for Sustainable Manufacturing. In *Sustainable Manufacturing: Shaping Global Value Creation* (pp. 83–88). Springer Berlin Heidelberg. DOI: 10.1007/978-3-642-27290-5_12

UNFCCC. (2018, September 6). *UN helps fashion industry shift to low carbon*. United Nations Framework Convention on Climate Change. https://unfccc.int/news/un-helps-fashion-industry-shift-to-low-carbon

United Nations. (2019, March 25). UN launches drive to highlight environmental cost of staying fashionable. UN News. Retrieved from https://news.un.org/en/story/2019/03/1035161

Vaidya, C. P., Kulkarni, N., Kulkarni, R., Singh, P., & Singh, A. P. (2023, April). Smart wardrobe: A deep learning model. In 2023 1st International Conference on Cognitive Computing and Engineering Education (ICCCEE) (pp. 1-4). IEEE. DOI: 10.1109/ICCCEE55951.2023.10424541

Vankayalapati, R. K. (2022). AI Clusters and Elastic Capacity Management: Designing Systems for Diverse Computational Demands. *Available at SSRN* 5115889.

Varon, L. M. S. (2025). Longevity extension of textile apparel based on strategies of ecodesign, circular economy and value chain traceability (Doctoral dissertation, Kauno technologijos universitetas.).

Veeramachaneni, V. (2025). Large language models: A comprehensive survey on architectures, applications, and challenges. *Advanced Innovations in Computer Programming Languages*, *7*(1), 20–39.

Viale, R. (2022). *Nudging*. MIT Press. DOI: 10.7551/mitpress/14437.001.0001

Vidakis, K., Mavrogiorgou, A., Kiourtis, A., & Kyriazis, D. (2020, June). A comparative study of short-range wireless communication technologies for health information exchange. In 2020 International conference on electrical, communication, and computer engineering (ICECCE) (pp. 1-6). IEEE. DOI: 10.1109/ICECCE49384.2020.9179478

Vitola, L. S. Digital Innovation for Sustainable Fashion: Virtual Fitting Rooms as a Strategy to Minimize Waste and E-commerce Returns (Doctoral dissertation, Toronto Metropolitan University).

Vladimirova, K., Henninger, C. E., Alosaimi, S. I., Brydges, T., Choopani, H., Hanlon, M., Iran, S., McCormick, H., & Zhou, S. (2024). Exploring the influence of social media on sustainable fashion consumption: A systematic literature review and future research agenda. *Journal of Global Fashion Marketing*, *15*(2), 181–202. DOI: 10.1080/20932685.2023.2237978

Voigt, P., & von dem Bussche, A. (2017). *The EU General Data Protection Regulation (GDPR): A practical guide*. Springer International Publishing., DOI: 10.1007/978-3-319-57959-7

von Zahn, M., Bauer, K., Mihale-Wilson, C., Jagow, J., Speicher, M., & Hinz, O. (2024). Smart green nudging: Reducing product returns through digital footprints and causal machine learning. *Marketing Science*. Advance online publication. DOI: 10.1287/mksc.2022.0393

Vrbančič, G., & Podgorelec, V. (2020). Transfer learning with adaptive fine-tuning. *IEEE Access : Practical Innovations, Open Solutions*, *8*, 196197–196211. DOI: 10.1109/ACCESS.2020.3034343

Vu, N., Ghadge, A., & Bourlakis, M. (2023). Blockchain adoption in food supply chains: A review and implementation framework. *Production Planning and Control*, *34*(6), 506–523. DOI: 10.1080/09537287.2021.1939902

Walsh, T., Levy, N., Bell, G., Elliott, A., Maclaurin, J., Mareels, I. M. Y., & Wood, F. M. (2019). *The effective and ethical development of artificial intelligence: An opportunity to improve our wellbeing*. Australian Council of Learned Academies. https://www.acola.org

Wang, W., Li, Z., Lian, D., Ma, C., Song, L., & Wei, Y. (2024). Mitigating the language mismatch and repetition issues in LLM-based machine translation via model editing. *arXiv preprint arXiv:2410.07054*. DOI: 10.18653/v1/2024.emnlp-main.879

Wang, X., Zhang, X., Luo, Z., Sun, Q., Cui, Y., Wang, J., . . . Wang, Z. (2024). Emu3: Next-token prediction is all you need. *arXiv preprint arXiv:2409.18869.*

Wang, G., Bao, H., Liu, Q., Zhou, T., Wu, S., Huang, T., Yu, Z. F., Lu, C. W., Gong, Y. H., Zhang, Z. X., & He, S. (2024). Brain-inspired artificial intelligence research: A review. *Science China. Technological Sciences*, *67*(8), 2282–2296. DOI: 10.1007/s11431-024-2732-9

Wang, J., & Li, S. (2018). Self-attention mechanism-based system for DCASE2018 Challenge Task 1 and Task 4. *Proc. DCASE Challenge*, 1-5.

Wang, R., Bush-Evans, R., Arden-Close, E., Bolat, E., McAlaney, J., Hodge, S., Thomas, S., & Phalp, K. (2023). Transparency in persuasive technology, immersive technology, and online marketing: Facilitating users' informed decision making and practical implications. *Computers in Human Behavior*, *139*, 107545. DOI: 10.1016/j.chb.2022.107545

Wang, T., Liu, F. F., Xiong, S. S., & Wang, K. (2025). Getting licence or keeping consistent? The role of moral identity in subsequent pro-environmental behaviours. *Asian Journal of Social Psychology*, *28*(1), e12670. DOI: 10.1111/ajsp.12670

Wang, X. M., Li, Q., Yu, D., Li, Q., & Xu, G. D. (2024). Counterfactual explanation for fairness in recommendation. *ACM Transactions on Information Systems*, *42*(4), ART106. Advance online publication. DOI: 10.1145/3643670

Wang, Y., Zhang, J., Shi, T., Deng, D., Tian, Y., & Matsumoto, T. (2024). Recent advances in interactive machine translation with large language models. *IEEE Access : Practical Innovations, Open Solutions*, *12*, 179353–179382. DOI: 10.1109/ACCESS.2024.3487352

Wardani, J., Bos, J. J., Ramirez-Lovering, D., & Capon, A. G. (2022). Enabling transdisciplinary research collaboration for planetary health: Insights from practice at the environment-health-development nexus. *Sustainable Development*, *30*(2), 375–392.

Wasilewski, A., & Zgrzywa-Ziemak, A. (2024). Multi-variant e-commerce user interfaces for business sustainability. *Operations Research and Decisions*, *34*(4), 211–229. DOI: 10.37190/ord240412

Weinmann, M., Schneider, C., & vom Brocke, J. (2016). Digital nudging. *Business & Information Systems Engineering*, *58*(6), 433–436. DOI: 10.1007/s12599-016-0453-1

Werdayani, D., & Widiaty, I. (2021). Virtual fitting room technology in fashion design. *IOP Conference Series. Materials Science and Engineering*, *1098*(2), 022110. DOI: 10.1088/1757-899X/1098/2/022110

Wijewardena, M., & Bhowmik, A. (2025). Green Tags, Real Impact: A study on the impact of Eco-Labeling on Swedish Consumers' Purchase Intentions: A mixed method study in the fashion industry.

Wittenberg, C., Epstein, Z., Berinsky, A. J., & Rand, D. G. (2024). Labeling AI-generated content: promises, perils, and future directions.

World Bank. (2019, September 23). How much do our wardrobes cost to the environment? World Bank. Retrieved from World Bank website World Bank

Wozniak, T., Stieger, M., Schaffner, D., Schu, M., & Lu, G. (2022). Algorithmic nudging for sustainability in e-commerce: Conceptual framework and research agenda. In *Digital Restructuring and Human (Re)action*. DOI: 10.18690/um.fov.4.2022.43

WRAP. (2012). *Valuing our clothes: The evidence base* (35 pp.). Retrieved from, https://www.wrap.ngo/resources/report/valuing-our-clothes-true-cost-how-we-design-use-and-dispose-clothing-uk-2012

WRAP. (2017). *Valuing our clothes: The cost of UK fashion* (54 pp.). Retrieved from, https://www.wrap.ngo/resources/report/valuing-our-clothes-cost-uk-fashion#download-file

Xiong, Y., Chen, X., Ye, X., Chen, H., Lin, Z., Lian, H., . . . Ding, G. (2024). Temporal scaling law for large language models. *arXiv preprint arXiv:2404.17785.*

Xi, Y., Liu, W., Lin, J., Cai, X., Zhu, H., Zhu, J., & Yu, Y. (2024, October). Towards open-world recommendation with knowledge augmentation from large language models. In *Proceedings of the 18th ACM Conference on Recommender Systems* (pp. 12–22). DOI: 10.1145/3640457.3688104

Xu, P., Lee, J., Barth, J. R., & Richey, R. G. (2021). Blockchain as supply chain technology: Considering transparency and security. *International Journal of Physical Distribution & Logistics Management, 51*(3), 305–324. DOI: 10.1108/IJPDLM-08-2019-0234

Xu, Y., Liu, X., Cao, X., Huang, C., Liu, E., Qian, S., Liu, X., Wu, Y., Dong, F., Qiu, C.-W., Qiu, J., Hua, K., Su, W., Wu, J., Xu, H., Han, Y., Fu, C., Yin, Z., Liu, M., & Zhang, J. (2021). Artificial intelligence: A powerful paradigm for scientific research. *Innovation (Cambridge (Mass.)), 2*(4), 100179. DOI: 10.1016/j.xinn.2021.100179

Yadav, P. S., Kiran, P. B. N., Sharma, A., Vemula, R., & Shrama, A. (2025). Customer Acceptance of Sustainable Fintech Innovation. In Financial Innovation for Global Sustainability (pp. 337–357). Wiley. https://doi.org/DOI: 10.1002/9781394311682.ch14

Yadav, P. S., Kiran, P. B. N., Vemula, R., Kumar, V., Kumari, P., & Michael, R. A. (2025). Leveraging AI and Digital Solutions to Enhance Sustainability in Green and Blue Economies. In Advances in Computational Intelligence and Robotics (pp. 53–84). IGI Global Scientific Publishing. https://doi.org/DOI: 10.4018/979-8-3373-0159-4.ch002

Yang, L., Wang, H., Zou, M., Chai, H., & Xia, Z. (2025). Artificial intelligence-driven plant bio-genomics research: a new era. *Tropical Plants, 4*(1).

Yang, J., Jin, H., Tang, R., Han, X., Feng, Q., Jiang, H., & Hu, X. (2024). Harnessing the power of LMS in practice: A survey on ChatGPT and beyond. *ACM Transactions on Knowledge Discovery from Data, 18*(6), 1–32.

Yang, X., Weber, A., & Grimm, A.-K. (2022). The effects of green consumer empowerment in advertising on corporate evaluations and purchase intention: The case of organic food. *Review of Managerial Science, 16*(6), 1877–1909. DOI: 10.1007/s11846-021-00495-4

Yao, Y., Dong, Q., Guan, J., Cao, B., Zhang, Z., Xiao, C., . . . Sun, M. (2021). Cuge: A Chinese language understanding and generation evaluation benchmark. *arXiv preprint arXiv:2112.13610.*

Yeung, K. (2017). 'Hypernudge': Big Data as a mode of regulation by design. *Information Communication and Society, 20*(1), 118–136. DOI: 10.1080/1369118X.2016.1186713

Ye, X. W., & Fu, L. Q. (2024). Joint codebook selection and UE scheduling for unlicensed mmWave NR-U/WiGig coexistence based on deep reinforcement learning. *IEEE Transactions on Mobile Computing, 23*(9), 8919–8934. DOI: 10.1109/TMC.2024.3356442

Yılmaz, K., Aksu, İ. Ö., Göçken, M., & Demirdelen, T. (2024). Sustainable textile manufacturing with revolutionizing textile dyeing: Deep learning-based, for energy efficiency and environmental-impact reduction, pioneering green practices for a sustainable future. *Sustainability (Basel), 16*(18), 8152. DOI: 10.3390/su16188152

Ying, N. S., & Mok, P. Y. (2023). A Review of Blockchain Technology for Sustainable Fashion. Digital Fashion Innovations, 179-204.

Yong, A., Rana, M. E., & Shanmugam, K. (2022, March). Improved shopping experience through RFID based smart shopping system. In *2022 International Conference on Decision Aid Sciences and Applications (DASA)* (pp. 635-644). IEEE. DOI: 10.1109/DASA54658.2022.9765064

Yuan, X., Yuan, S., Cui, Y., Lin, T., Wang, X., Xu, R., . . . Yang, D. (2024). Evaluating character understanding of large language models via character profiling from fictional works. *arXiv preprint arXiv:2404.12726*. DOI: 10.18653/v1/2024.emnlp-main.456

Yu, M. (2021). Design of Remote Fitting Platform Based on Virtual Clothing Sales. *International Journal of Information Systems and Supply Chain Management, 15*(3), 1–12. DOI: 10.4018/IJISSCM.290019

Yu, X., Haroon, M., Menchen-Trevino, E., & Wojcieszak, M. (2024). Nudging recommendation algorithms increases news consumption and diversity on YouTube. *PNAS Nexus, 3*(12), pgae518. Advance online publication. DOI: 10.1093/pnasnexus/pgae518 PMID: 39618512

Zhang, Y., Zheng, Z., & Liu, L. (2024). Design Resource Deployment for Virtual Fitting Applications in the Era of Digital Fashion: An Analysis Based on Kano-QFD. *SAGE Open, 14*(4), 21582440241296627. Advance online publication. DOI: 10.1177/21582440241296627

Zhang, Z., Fort, J. M., & Mateu, L. G. (2023). Exploring the potential of artificial intelligence as a tool for architectural design: A perception study using Gaudí's gaudí'sworks. *Buildings (Basel, Switzerland), 13*(7), 1863. DOI: 10.3390/buildings13071863

Zhong, Y., Liu, J., Zhou, Y. W., Cao, B., & Cheng, T. E. (2022). Robust contract design and coordination under consignment contracts with revenue sharing. *International Journal of Production Economics, 253*, 108543. DOI: 10.1016/j.ijpe.2022.108543

Zingales, N. (2018). Google Shopping: Beware of "self-favouring" in a world of algorithmic nudging. *Competition Policy International – Europe Column*. https://ssrn.com/abstract=3707797

Zingales, N. (2019). Antitrust intent in an age of algorithmic nudging. *Journal of Antitrust Enforcement, 7*(3), 386–418. DOI: 10.1093/jaenfo/jnz010

Zong, M., & Krishnamachari, B. (2022). A survey on GPT-3. *arXiv preprint*

Zubaidah, T. R., Muzdalifah, L., Boyas, J. R., Mustaqim, M., Sholikhah, A., Violita, C. E., & Putrihadiningrum, D. C. (2024, September). Sustainable Business of E-Commerce in the Smart Economy: A Systematic Review of Roles and Challenges for Future Research. In *2024 International Conference on ICT for Smart Society (ICISS)* (pp. 1-7). IEEE. DOI: 10.1109/ICISS62896.2024.10751282

Zhang, [illegible] (2023). [illegible] machine [illegible] [illegible]

Zhou, [illegible] (20[illegible]). [illegible]

About the Contributors

Luzia Arantes (lamorim@ua.pt) holds a PhD in Applied Psychology from the University of Minho, Portugal, and is currently in her final year of a PhD in Marketing and Strategy at the same institution. She is a researcher at Ekonomikas un Kulturas Augstskola (Latvia) and a lecturer at the Polytechnic Institute of Cávado and Ave and the University of Aveiro. She conducts research in the areas of digital marketing, tourism, consumer behavior, sustainability, and artificial intelligence. She is the author and co-author of books and chapters, as well as scientific articles in international journals, including Corporate Social Responsibility and Environmental Management, Journal of Cultural Heritage Management and Sustainable Development, Journal of International Consumer Marketing, Sustainability, and the European Journal of Applied Business Management. Her work has been recognized with several scientific awards, notably the Best Paper Award in Sustainable Marketing & Digital Perspectives, the Best Paper Award in Consumer Behavior, and the Best Doctoral Thesis Award in Vocational Psychology and Career Development of the last decade (2015–2025), awarded by the Portuguese Association for Career Development.

***

Rashmi B H is the Associate Professor & Associate Head in the School of Business and Management working at CHRIST UNIVERSITY. With a Bachelor's degree in Business Management, she has Masters Qualification in Commerce and an M.Phil. She is qualified in the KSET and UGC-NET exams. She completed her doctorate from Tumkur University. Dr Rashmi B H is a marketing researcher and educator at CHRIST University with a strong focus on AI- driven business processes, employee engagement, service quality, and predictive modelling applied to Human Resource contexts and has 21 years of teaching experience. She has contributed to academic discourse through conference proceedings, journal articles, copyright and a patent, and regularly engages in faculty development and invited lectures. She has 4 patents in her credit and has authored several books. Her areas of interest in teaching and research are in Finance, Entrepreneurship, and Marketing.

Deepak Bisht is an academician and researcher with over eight years of teaching experience at undergraduate and postgraduate levels, currently serving as an Assistant Professor at Lovely Professional University, Punjab. He holds a PhD in Commerce with a specialization in services marketing, focusing on the economic viability of tourism in Uttarakhand. His research interests span marketing, tourism studies, and entrepreneurship, and has published extensively in reputed journals and edited volumes.

Meghna Gupta ia a passionate researcher focused on innovation and interdisciplinary approaches, dedicated to advancing knowledge through impactful studies, academic collaborations, and sustainable solutions for future challenges in design and technology.

Ramya H P holds an MBA in finance and is pursuing a Ph.D. in investments from VTU. Currently, she works as an assistant professor at the Department of Management Studies at DSCE, with 16 years of experience. She has conducted workshops and seminars on topics such as financial management using Excel, financial accounting and taxation, and financial statement analysis, and has presented and published research papers in various national and international journals. Additionally, she is trained in personal finance, data processing using Python, taxation, financial modelling, trading strategies, portfolio optimization using the Markowitz model, and investment management. She is also an AICTE-nominated innovation ambassador for the Institute Innovation Council.

Muhammad Ramdani is an information technology professional and researcher with interests in information systems and digital solution development. His work focuses on designing, implementing, and evaluating technology-driven systems that support process efficiency, data-informed decision-making, and digital transformation across organizational and societal contexts. He is currently conducting research at Nanjing University, where his academic activities contribute to the advancement of contemporary digital technologies and interdisciplinary research perspectives.

Sushila Sahani holds a doctorate in Apparel and Textile Science. Her academic and professional journey blends expertise in textiles from material properties to sustainable innovations, with interests in fashion design, intellectual property and ethical consumerism. Her research and educational work explore the connections between textile knowledge and design thinking, highlighting the economic, cultural and sustainable impact of the fashion and textile industry.

Binastya Anggara Sekti has been a lecturer at the Faculty of Computer Science, Esa Unggul University, Jakarta, since 2016. He is actively involved in the Artificial Intelligence and Information Security Study Group. He holds a Bachelor's degree in Informatics Engineering from the Bandung Institute of Technology and a Master's degree in Information Systems Management from Trisakti University, Jakarta. Prior to entering academia, he accumulated over 25 years of professional experience as an IT practitioner in various companies across Jakarta. His work focused on developing data centers for internet service providers and delivering IT solutions for the manufacturing and oil & gas sectors. His research interests include artificial intelligence, cybersecurity, and the development of IT infrastructure.

T. Sureshkumar is a professor at AVS Engineering College, He holds a Ph.D. in Information and Communication Engineering from Anna University, an M.E. in Computer Science Engineering, and an MBA in HR. His research interests include web data mining, document clustering, and intelligent information retrieval, and he has published several papers in reputed journals. He has delivered expert lectures on cryptography and network security at various engineering colleges. Dr. Sureshkumar has actively organized and participated in numerous workshops, seminars, FDPs, and national-level technical symposiums. A life member of ISTE, he has also contributed to departmental development by serving as Placement Coordinator, Graduation Day Coordinator, and Alumni Coordinator. He is known for his leadership in both academic and extracurricular activities and remains committed to fostering innovation and learning among students.

Muhammad Usman Tariq is a strategic higher education leader and scholar with more than 17 years of international experience across academia, research, and industry. He holds dual doctorates, a PhD in Artificial Intelligence and a Doctorate in Business Administration and has published extensively as the author of research articles, case studies, book chapters, and academic texts. His contributions also include several patents, reflecting his applied research in technology, business, and education. He is the Founder and CEO of TheCaseHQ.com, a global hub for professional certification programmes, narrative and video case studies, and digital learning innovation. In addition, he serves as President of the Gulf Higher Education Network (Gulf HE), an initiative dedicated to advancing academic practice, faculty development, and institutional collaboration across the region. He is a Principal Fellow of Advance HE (UK), Chartered Fellow of the CIPD (UK), Senior Fellow of SEDA (UK), and a Senior Member of IEEE, reflecting his standing as both an academic innovator and a global professional leader.

Ahmad Maulana Ulumuddin is an information technology professional with interests in information systems and digital innovation. His work focuses on the development and application of technology-driven solutions to improve operational efficiency, support data-informed decision-making, and enable digital transformation in organizational and societal contexts. He is particularly interested in user-centered system design and the practical adoption of emerging digital technologies.

Kavitha V. is an associate professor in the Department of Computer Science and Engineering at Velalar College of Engineering and Technology. Her research interests include machine learning, AI, and digital image processing.

Pinnika Syam Yadav is a distinguished researcher and academician specializing in business and marketing analytics. He holds a Ph.D. and gained over two years of teaching experience at the Mittal School of Business, Lovely Professional University, where he made significant contributions to academia. Currently, Dr. Yadav serves as an Assistant Professor at Christ University, continuing to excel in research and education. He has notably guided and awarded two Ph.D. scholars, further demonstrating his profound commitment to his field. His innovative approach and extensive knowledge have established him as a leading figure, inspiring young researchers to follow in his footsteps.

Index

A

B

C

D

E

www.ingramcontent.com/pod-product-compliance
Lightning Source LLC
LaVergne TN
LVHW062325300926
849161LV00007B/1576